American-Iranian Dialogues

New Approaches to International History

Series Editor:

Thomas Zeiler, Professor of American Diplomatic History,
University of Colorado Boulder, USA

Series Editorial Board:

Anthony Adamthwaite, University of California at Berkeley (USA)
Kathleen Burk, University College London (UK)
Louis Clerc, University of Turku (Finland)
Petra Goedde, Temple University (USA)
Francine McKenzie, University of Western Ontario (Canada)
Lien-Hang Nguyen, University of Kentucky (USA)
Jason Parker, Texas A&M University (USA)
Glenda Sluga, University of Sydney (Australia)

New Approaches to International History covers international history during the modern period and across the globe. The series incorporates new developments in the field, such as the cultural turn and transnationalism, as well as the classical high politics of state-centric policymaking and diplomatic relations. Written with upper level undergraduate and postgraduate students in mind, texts in the series provide an accessible overview of international diplomatic and transnational issues, events and actors.

Published:

Decolonization and the Cold War, edited by Leslie James and Elisabeth Leake (2015)
Cold War Summits, Chris Tudda (2015)
The United Nations in International History, Amy Sayward (2017)
Latin American Nationalism, James F. Siekmeier (2017)
The History of United States Cultural Diplomacy, Michael L. Krenn (2017)
International Cooperation in the Early 20th Century, Daniel Gorman (2017)
Women and Gender in International History, Karen Garner (2018)
International Development, Corinna Unger (2018)
The Environment and International History, Scott Kaufman (2018)
Canada and the World since 1867, Asa McKercher (2019)
Scandinavia and the Great Powers in the First World War, Michael Jonas (2019)
The First Age of Industrial Globalization: An International History 1815–1918, Maartje Abbenhuis and Gordon Morrell (2019)

Forthcoming:

The International LGBT Rights Movement, Laura Belmonte
Reconstructing the Postwar World, Francine McKenzie
The History of Oil Diplomacy, Christopher R. W. Dietrich
Global War, Global Catastrophe, Maartje Abbenhuis and Ismee Tames

American-Iranian Dialogues

From Constitution to White Revolution, c. 1890s–1960s

Edited by
Matthew K. Shannon

BLOOMSBURY ACADEMIC
LONDON • NEW YORK • OXFORD • NEW DELHI • SYDNEY

BLOOMSBURY ACADEMIC
Bloomsbury Publishing Plc
50 Bedford Square, London, WC1B 3DP, UK
1385 Broadway, New York, NY 10018, USA

BLOOMSBURY, BLOOMSBURY ACADEMIC and the Diana logo are
trademarks of Bloomsbury Publishing Plc

First published in Great Britain 2022
This paperback edition published 2023

Copyright © Matthew K. Shannon, 2022

Matthew K. Shannon has asserted his right under the Copyright, Designs and
Patents Act, 1988, to be identified as Editor of this work.

Cover image: Christine and Michael Westberg pictured in the early 1960s with a group of Iranians
at the Shah Abdol-Azim Shrine in Rey, Iran. Photograph taken by
John A. Westberg and courtesy of Christine Westberg

All rights reserved. No part of this publication may be reproduced or transmitted
in any form or by any means, electronic or mechanical, including photocopying,
recording, or any information storage or retrieval system, without prior
permission in writing from the publishers.

Bloomsbury Publishing Plc does not have any control over, or responsibility for, any
third-party websites referred to or in this book. All internet addresses given in this book were
correct at the time of going to press. The author and publisher regret any inconvenience caused if
addresses have changed or sites have ceased to exist, but
can accept no responsibility for any such changes.

Every effort has been made to trace copyright holders and to obtain their permissions
for the use of copyright material. The publisher apologizes for any errors or
omissions and would be grateful if notified of any corrections that should be
incorporated in future reprints or editions of this book.

A catalogue record for this book is available from the British Library.

Library of Congress Cataloging-in-Publication Data
Names: Shannon, Matthew K., 1983– editor.
Title: American-Iranian dialogues : from constitution to White Revolution,
c. 1890s–1960s / edited by Matthew K. Shannon.
Other titles: From constitution to White Revolution, c. 1890s–1960s
Description: London ; New York : Bloomsbury Academic, 2021. |
Series: New approaches to international history |
Includes bibliographical references and index.|
Identifiers: LCCN 2020055552 (print) | LCCN 2020055553 (ebook) |
ISBN 9781350118720 (hb) | ISBN 9781350118737 (ePDF) |
ISBN 9781350118744 (eBook)
Subjects: LCSH: United States–Relations–Iran. | Iran–Relations–United States. |
Iran–History–20th century.
Classification: LCC E183.8.I55 A624 2021 (print) |
LCC E183.8.I55 (ebook) | DDC 327.73055–dc23
LC record available at https://lccn.loc.gov/2020055552
LC ebook record available at https://lccn.loc.gov/2020055553

ISBN: HB: 978-1-3501-1872-0
PB: 978-1-3502-2813-9
ePDF: 978-1-3501-1873-7
eBook: 978-1-3501-1874-4

Series: New Approaches to International History

Typeset by Newgen KnowledgeWorks Pvt. Ltd., Chennai, India

To find out more about our authors and books visit www.bloomsbury.com
and sign up for our newsletters.

Contents

List of Illustrations	vii
Series Editor Preface	viii
Acknowledgments	ix
Note on Transliteration	x

Introduction: Toward Connected History   1
Matthew K. Shannon

1. Flags of Inconvenience: State Failure, Nationhood, and Contested Sovereignty in the Late Qajar Encounter with the United States   17
   John Ghazvinian
2. The Shuster Mission of 1911 and American Perceptions of Iran's First Revolution   33
   Kelly J. Shannon
3. Heritage Diplomacy and US-Iran Relations: The Case of the Iranian Antiquities Law of 1930   57
   Kyle Olson
4. Pandering in the Persian Gulf: Arabia, Iran, and Anglo-American Relations, 1900–71   73
   Firoozeh Kashani-Sabet
5. De-Nationalized: Mohammad Reza Pahlavi, the Consortium, and Global Oil, 1954–64   95
   Gregory Brew
6. Alborz, Bethel, and Community: Missionary Institutions in Postwar Tehran   113
   Matthew K. Shannon
7. American Academics and US Technical Aid for Iranian Modernization   131
   Richard Garlitz
8. "We Learned How to Be Friends": What Oral History Tells Us about the American Peace Corps in Iran   149
   Jasamin Rostam-Kolayi
9. "Support the 41": Iranian Student Activism in Northern California, 1970–3   167
   Ida Yalzadeh

10 Professional Transnationalism and Iranian-American Im/mobility in Michigan 183
Camron Michael Amin

Conclusion: Third Parties, Non/State Actors, and the Ambiguities of US Imperial Power 203
Cyrus Schayegh

Bibliography 221
Notes on Contributors 225
Index 229

Illustrations

Figures

5.1	Middle East oil production, 1951–61	104
5.2	Revenues from oil (millions of US$), 1948–60	104
5.3	Consortium nominations (thousands bpd), 1957–66	105
C.1	"Netayej-e siasi-ye mah-e masnuʿi"	208
C.2	"Har do bi-raqib-and. Eshkoda dar zamin va qamar-e masnuʿi dar āsemān"	209

Table

3.1	Periodization of the Early History of Iranian Archaeology	58

Series Editor Preface

New Approaches to International History takes the entire world as its stage for exploring the history of diplomacy, broadly conceived theoretically and thematically, and writ large across the span of the globe, during the modern period. This series goes beyond the single goal of explaining encounters in the world. Our aspiration is that these books provide both an introduction for researchers new to a topic and supplemental and essential reading in classrooms. Thus, *New Approaches* serves a dual purpose that is unique from other large-scale treatments of international history; it applies to scholarly agendas and pedagogy. In addition, it does so against the backdrop of a century of enormous change, conflict, and progress that informed global history but also continues to reflect on our own times.

The series offers the old and new diplomatic history to address a range of topics that shaped the twentieth century. Engaging in international history (including but not especially focusing on global or world history), these books will appeal to a range of scholars and teachers situated in the humanities and social sciences, including those in history, international relations, cultural studies, politics, and economics. We have in mind scholars, both novice and veteran, who require an entrée into a topic, trend, or technique that can benefit their own research or education into a new field of study by crossing boundaries in a variety of ways.

By its broad and inclusive coverage, *New Approaches to International History* is also unique because it makes accessible to students current research, methodology, and themes. Incorporating cutting-edge scholarship that reflects trends in international history, as well as addressing the classical high politics of state-centric policymaking and diplomatic relations, these books are designed to bring alive the myriad of approaches for digestion by advanced undergraduate and graduate students. In preparation for the *New Approaches* series, Bloomsbury surveyed courses and faculty around the world to gauge interest and reveal core themes of relevance for their classroom use. The polling yielded a host of topics, from war and peace to the environment; from empire to economic integration; and from migration to nuclear arms. The effort proved that there is a much-needed place for studies that connect scholars and students alike to international history, and books that are especially relevant to the teaching missions of faculty around the world.

We hope readers find this series to be appealing, challenging, and thought-provoking. Whether the history is viewed through older or newer lenses, *New Approaches to International History* allows students to peer into the modern period's complex relations among nations, people, and events to draw their own conclusions about the tumultuous, interconnected past.

Thomas Zeiler, University of Colorado, Boulder, USA

Acknowledgments

There are, quite naturally, many people to thank for getting an edited volume to press. First and foremost, I am thankful for my fellow contributors. After signing on to the project in 2018, they sustained their personal health and professional commitments through a global pandemic to write chapters that are intellectually stimulating, methodologically rigorous, and, quite simply, fascinating.

Beyond those names that grace the table of contents, Bloomsbury provided opportunity, advice, and support. I thank Thomas Zeiler for the invitation to contribute to *New Approaches to International History*, an important series for scholars wishing to explore new research lines and areas of inquiry. Abigail Lane was a magnificent editor who, along with Maddie Holder and the copy-editing and production teams, ensured that deadlines were met. The peer reviewers helped sharpen the framing, as did James Goode, who connected authors and provided early advice on the concept. I owe a special debt of gratitude to Kyle Olson for doing transliteration work for the entire volume and for explaining the scheme on the adjacent page. Finally, I am grateful to the universities, centers, and organizations that, between 2018 and 2021, provided forums where various combinations of contributors discussed the research featured in this book.

Matthew K. Shannon
Abingdon, VA
Spring 2021

Transliteration

This volume uses a transliteration system that is adapted from the style guide of the journal *Iranian Studies*, which itself is a modified form of the transliteration system of the *International Journal of Middle East Studies*. No diacritics are used, with the exception of the macron over the long "ā," and half circles are used to designate the *ayn* and *hamzeh*. Otherwise, we have, wherever possible, followed these guides and sought internal consistency within the volume.

Inspired by Reza Zia-Ebrahimi's note in *The Emergence of Iranian Nationalism: Race and the Politics of Dislocation*, we privileged oral recognizability in transliteration, making the following modifications to the IS/IJMES system: the short vowel *dammeh* (often rendered "u") as "o," the long vowel *vāv* (often rendered "ou" or "oo") as "u." The diphthong often rendered as "ow," as in "Khosrow," is rendered as "o," except in cases where there is a standard English spelling, for example, *Nowruz*. The diphthongs that are orthographically rendered in Persian as a *yeh* in combination with either a *kasreh* (i.e., "e") or a *fatheh* (i.e., "a") are commonly encountered as either "ei"/"ey" or "ai"/"ay" in English. Here, there is perhaps the greatest possibility for inconsistency, but we have deferred to convention in determining the transliteration in these cases, that is, *Hossein* rather than *Hosseyn*, but *Keyhān* rather than *Keihān*. In cases where a *yeh* is followed by a vowel (e.g., *siasi*), except in cases where the *yeh* is followed by another *yeh*, the *yeh* has been dropped.

We followed these grammar and style rules: The half-space has been rendered as a hyphen when appropriate. This includes the separation of grammatical particles, such as the present progressive prefix *mi-* that appears before verb stems, as well as the postfix *hā*, and both forms of *ezāfeh* (*-e* and *-ye*). This includes word-final stressed *yeh* constructions, such as in the case of *nā-gofteh-hā-i*. It also includes compound nouns such as *nezām-nāmeh*. Transliterations of titles containing proper nouns have retained the capitalization scheme appropriate for English. Only the noun-stem is capitalized, however. With respect to the many forms that *al-* or *-l-* can take in Persian names and titles derived from Arabic, for example, *ed-, ad-, od-, as-, os-*, and so forth, we have rendered all instances as *al-* for consistency's sake (e.g., *Mozaffar al-Din Shah Qajar* rather than *Mozaffar ad-Din Shah Qajar* or *Mozaffaraddin Shah Qajar*).

The careful reader will note that proper names that have conventional English spellings have not been modified according to this system; these include toponyms such as Tehran and Isfahan, the names of Iranians who are regularly mentioned in Western sources, such as Ayatollah Khomeini, as well as diasporic Iranians whose names are spelled according to national convention where they reside and their own personal renderings. There is also slight variation in the transliteration of Persian words and proper names when compared to those in other languages, such as Armenian or Arabic.

Introduction: Toward Connected History

Matthew K. Shannon

American-Iranian Dialogues examines the individual and collective experiences that gave meaning to the encounter between the United States and Iran from the 1890s through the 1960s. In doing so, the book extends the cultural and transnational turns into the study of US-Iran relations.[1] These "turns" have redirected the research agendas of scholars throughout the humanities, including those involved with professional organizations such as the Society for Historians of American Foreign Relations and the Association for Iranian Studies, to name just a few. The concept for this volume arose from conversations with colleagues at the 2018 Iranian Studies conference at the University of California Irvine's Samuel Jordan Center for Persian Studies.

Scholars have not shied away from writing about Dr. Jordan, the most well-known and oft-studied American educationalist in Iran. Compared with the "amateurs" of the nineteenth century, Jordan was among the modern "professionals" who, either informally or formally, represented the United States in Iran and around the world during the twentieth century.[2] But his tenure in Iran, which spanned the late 1890s to the early 1940s, is typically understood in isolation from the broader historical forces of the modern period. As a consequence, missionaries such as Samuel Martin Jordan are removed from conversations about the many "unofficial" Americans who resided in late Qajar and Pahlavi Iran. The legacy of the cultural encounter that Jordan embodied is overwhelmed in the historiography by studies of Cold War crises—especially the 1953 coup that overthrew Prime Minister Mohammad Mosaddeq, the 1979 Iranian Revolution that overthrew Mohammad Reza Shah Pahlavi, and the spate of conflicts and controversies since the severance of diplomatic relations between the United States and Iran in 1980.[3] Moreover,

---

[1] Frank Ninkovich and Liping Bu, eds., *The Cultural Turn: Essays in the History of U.S. Foreign Relations* (Chicago, IL: Imprint, 2001); Robert Gross, "The Transnational Turn: Rediscovering American Studies in a Wider World," *Journal of American Studies* 34, no. 3 (2000): 373–93; Thomas Zeiler, "The Diplomatic History Bandwagon: A State of the Field," *Journal of American History* 95, no. 4 (2009): 1053–73.

[2] Arthur Boyce, "Alborz College of Teheran and Dr. Samuel Martin Jordan," in *Cultural Ties between Iran and the United States*, ed. Ali Pasha Saleh (Tehran: Her Imperial Majesty's National Committee for the American Revolution Bicentennial, 1976), 155–234; John Ghazvinian, *America and Iran: A History, 1720 to the Present* (New York: Knopf, 2021), chapters 3–4 on "amateurs" and "professionals."

[3] Osamah Khalil, ed., *United States Relations with China and Iran: Toward the Asian Century* (New York: Bloomsbury, 2020).

the history of Americans in Iran is disconnected from the scholarship on Iranians and Iranian-Americans in the United States, a situation that this volume attempts to rectify.[4] The United States was as much a site of negotiation as was Iran, whether one considers the networks and ideologies of Iranian students in the United States or the meaning of "Iran" in the American imagination. By bringing together different scholarly communities, *American-Iranian Dialogues* moves the conversation toward a "connected history" of the United States and Iran.[5]

It is an exciting time to study the history of "Iran facing others" and "Iran without borders," and this book is part of a long-running conversation that is gaining new historiographic traction.[6] While the United States is not prominent in the literature on Iran's transnational and cultural ties with the world, scholars have applied the binational framework to Iran's relations with other countries. There are histories of "the English amongst the Persians" and Iranians in "Jane Austen's London."[7] Scholars have also unpacked Iran's intellectual encounters with Ireland, Russia, Syria, and countries "both Eastern and Western."[8] Many, though not all, of these texts are edited collections because of the temporal, spatial, methodological, theoretical, and linguistic diversity required to undertake such studies. Ali Ansari's volume on global perceptions of Iran is exemplary.[9] Other edited volumes revolve less around a category of analysis than a particular period.[10] The most pertinent is Roham Alvandi's international history of the "Age of Aryamehr." It includes an array of analytically rich chapters on Mohammad Reza Shah Pahlavi's Iran during the 1960s and 1970s. While that book presents slices of Iran's "global entanglements" from the period, it tilts toward Pahlavi elites, includes no chapters on the United States, and, in most cases, the Iranian nation-state remains the sole vantage point.[11]

---

[4] Neda Maghbouleh, *The Limits of Whiteness: Iranian Americans and the Everyday Politics of Race* (Stanford, CA: Stanford University Press, 2017).

[5] Paul Kramer, "Power and Connection: Imperial Histories of the United States in the World," *American Historical Review* 116, no. 5 (2011): 1348–91.

[6] Abbas Amanat and Farzin Vejdani, eds., *Iran Facing Others: Identity Boundaries in a Historical Perspective* (New York: Palgrave Macmillan, 2012); Hamid Dabashi, *Iran without Borders: Towards a Critique of the Postcolonial Nation* (New York: Verso, 2016); Nikki Keddie and Rudi Matthee, eds., *Iran and the Surrounding World: Interactions in Culture and Cultural Politics* (Seattle: University of Washington Press, 2002).

[7] Denis Wright, *The Persians amongst the English* (New York: I.B. Tauris, 1985); Wright, *The English amongst the Persians* (New York: I.B. Tauris, 2001); Nile Green, *The Love of Strangers: What Six Muslim Students Learned in Jane Austen's London* (Princeton, NJ: Princeton University Press, 2016).

[8] Houchang Chehabi and Grace Neville, eds., *Erin and Iran: Cultural Encounters between the Irish and the Iranians* (Boston, MA: Ilex, 2015); Stephanie Cronin, ed., *Iranian-Russian Encounters: Empires and Revolutions since 1800* (New York: Routledge, 2013); Nadia von Maltzahn, *The Syria-Iran Axis: Cultural Diplomacy and International Relations in the Middle East* (New York: I.B. Tauris, 2013); Afshin Matin-Asgari, *Both Eastern and Western: An Intellectual History of Iranian Modernity* (New York: Cambridge University Press, 2018).

[9] Ali Ansari, ed., *Perceptions of Iran: History, Myths and Nationalism from Medieval Persia to the Islamic Republic* (New York: I.B. Tauris, 2014). See also David Bagot and Margaux Whiskin, eds., *Iran and the West: Cultural Perceptions from the Sasanian Empire to the Islamic Republic* (New York: I.B. Tauris, 2018); Hamid Dabashi, *Persophilia: Persian Culture on the Global Scene* (Cambridge, MA: Harvard University Press, 2015).

[10] Edmund Herzig and Willem Floor, eds., *Iran and the World in the Safavid Age* (New York: I.B. Tauris, 2011).

[11] Roham Alvandi, ed., *The Age of Aryamehr: Late Pahlavi Iran and its Global Entanglements* (London: Gingko, 2018). Scholars now study the many arenas of Iran's global affairs. Examples

American-Iranian Dialogues, by contrast, offers a framework for rethinking the history of "the eagle and the lion."[12] It eschews national leaders and government officials in Washington and Tehran, and is attentive to the multidirectional flow of people and ideas between the United States and Iran. The contributors find that the United States was significant to Iran—and Iran to the United States—during the late nineteenth and early twentieth centuries, a time otherwise associated with European preponderance in Persia and US preoccupation with the Western Hemisphere. When examining the Cold War era, the authors stress the continuance of older forms of cultural influence and new types of transnational ties despite the transformation of American power on the world stage. The chapters are situated "between two revolutions," with reference to Mohammad Reza Shah Pahlavi's White Revolution of the 1960s instead of Ayatollah Khomeini's Islamic Revolution of 1979.[13] From the 1890s to the 1960s, Americans and Iranians engaged in dialogues with the "other" to negotiate new identities and material realities in an imperial and globalizing world.

The opening bookend is the Constitutional Revolution and "the broader constitutional period."[14] The period began in the 1890s when a confluence of events, including but not limited to the Tobacco Revolt and the assassination of Naser al-Din Shah, reoriented Iran's domestic affairs and position in the world. The Constitutional Revolution crested in 1906 with the creation of a parliament (Majles) and, of course, a constitution. Iran's first revolution, and its place among the democracies of the world, ended abruptly when Britain and Russia settled the so-called Great Game at its expense. The constitutional period eroded more gradually as the Qajars, having ruled Iran since the late eighteenth century, retained power through the Great War.[15] The

---

include but are not limited to: William Figueroa, "China and the Iranian Left: Transnational Networks of Social, Cultural, and Ideological Exchange, 1905-1979" (PhD diss., University of Pennsylvania, 2020); Arang Keshavarzian and Ali Mirsepassi, eds., *Global 1979: Geographies and Histories of the Iranian Revolution* (New York: Cambridge University Press, 2021); Chelsi Mueller, *The Origins of the Arab-Iranian Conflict: Nationalism and Sovereignty in the Gulf between the World Wars* (New York: Cambridge University Press, 2020); Negar Mottahedeh, *Whisper Tapes: Kate Millett in Iran* (Stanford, CA: Stanford University Press, 2019); Robert Steele, *The Shah's Imperial Celebrations of 1971: Nationalism, Culture and Politics in Late Pahlavi Iran* (New York: I.B. Tauris, 2021).

[12] James Bill, *The Eagle and the Lion: The Tragedy of American-Iranian Relations* (New Haven, CT: Yale University Press, 1988). The scholarship of James F. Goode is most notable. Goode, *The United States and Iran, 1946-1951: The Diplomacy of Neglect* (New York: St. Martin's Press, 1989); Goode, *The United States and Iran: In the Shadow of Musaddiq* (New York: St. Martin's Press, 1997).

[13] Ervand Abrahamian, *Iran between Two Revolutions* (Princeton, NJ: Princeton University Press, 1982). Another modification of Abrahamian's framework is Liora Hendelman-Baavur, *Creating the Modern Iranian Woman: Popular Culture between Two Revolutions* (New York: Cambridge University Press, 2019).

[14] Kamyar Ghaneabassiri, "U.S. Foreign Policy and Persia, 1856-1921," *Iranian Studies* 35, nos. 1-3 (2002): 147. Nikki Keddie was an early proponent of extending the constitutional period into the late nineteenth century. Nikki Keddie, *Religion and Rebellion in Iran: The Tobacco Protest of 1891-92* (London: Frank Cass, 1966).

[15] Houri Berberian, *Roving Revolutionaries: Armenians and the Connected Revolutions in the Russian, Iranian, and Ottoman Worlds* (Berkeley: University of California Press, 2019); Mansour Bonakdarian, *Britain and the Iranian Constitutional Revolution of 1906-1911: Foreign Policy, Imperialism, and Dissent* (Syracuse, NY: Syracuse University Press, 2006); Houchang Chehabi and Vanessa Martin, eds., *Iran's Constitutional Revolution: Popular Politics, Cultural Transformations and Transnational Connections* (New York: I.B. Tauris in Association with Iran Heritage Foundation, 2010).

broader constitutional period ended in the early 1920s when Reza Shah Pahlavi started a new dynasty and a national program of "authoritarian modernization."[16] Despite dynastic turnover, many global trends of the late Qajar era continued to influence Pahlavi Iran's relationship with the world. During the early Pahlavi period, the United States appeared to some Iranians as an attractive alternative to the European powers and, therefore, "exceptionalist" discourses about the United States held sway longer in Iran than in other parts of the world.[17]

The constitutional period coincided with, and at pivotal moments was influenced by, America's "global dawn" and the birth of the US imperium across Asia.[18] Historians have long examined the causes, consequences, and contexts of the US wars with Spain, Cuba, and the Philippines. In addition to histories of 1898—the year of Samuel Martin Jordan's departure for Iran—scholars from Emily Rosenberg to Ian Tyrrell have foregrounded the significance of non-state actors in forging the earliest ties between the United States and the world.[19] Prior to the First World War, imperial networks shaped the lives of missionaries such as Jordan, informed who represented Iran in the United States, and created the conduits through which American archaeologists and economic advisers arrived in "the land of sophy."[20] If the development of "Iranianness" was an imagined process that involved the United States during the constitutional period, Americans also looked toward Iran to understand their place among the nations and networks of the modern world.[21]

Perceptions of *Āmrikā* and interactions with actual Americans informed aspects of Iran's global engagement through the reign of Mohammad Reza Shah.[22] The last shah ruled from 1941 to 1979, and he steered Iran toward the United States in the realms of diplomacy, military and economic cooperation, and cultural exchange. Through the mid-twentieth century, many on both sides of the aisle believed that the United States offered a model of development that could inform Iranian reform efforts. Within the context of the Cold War, a plethora of state and non-state actors descended on Iran as the United States attempted to use "soft power" and "public diplomacy" to win hearts

---

[16] Touraj Atabaki and Erik Zurcher, eds., *Men of Order: Authoritarian Modernization under Ataturk and Reza Shah* (London: I.B. Tauris, 2004).

[17] Greg Grandin, "Your Americanism and Mine: Americanism and Anti-Americanism in the Americas," *American Historical Review* 111, no. 4 (2006): 1042–66; Ussama Makdisi, *Faith Misplaced: The Broken Promise of U.S.-Arab Relations: 1820–2001* (New York: PublicAffairs, 2010).

[18] Frank Ninkovich, *Global Dawn: The Cultural Foundation of American Internationalism, 1865–1890* (Cambridge, MA: Harvard University Press, 2009).

[19] Kristin Hoganson, *Fighting for American Manhood: How Gender Politics Provoked the Spanish-American and Philippine-American Wars* (New Haven, CT: Yale University Press, 1998); Ernest May, *Imperial Democracy: The Emergence of America as a Great Power* (New York: Harcourt, Brace and World, 1961); Emily S. Rosenberg, *Spreading the American Dream: American Economic and Cultural Expansion, 1890–1945* (New York: Hill and Wang, 1982); Ian Tyrrell, *Transnational Nation: United States History in Global Perspective since 1789* (New York: Palgrave, 2015).

[20] Roger Stevens, *The Land of the Great Sophy* (London: Methuen, 1962).

[21] Firoozeh Kashani-Sabet, "Cultures of Iranianness: The Evolving Polemic of Iranian Nationalism," in *Iran and the Surrounding World*, ed. Keddie and Matthee, 162–81. For context see John Torpey, *The Invention of the Passport: Surveillance, Citizenship and the State* (New York: Cambridge University Press, 2018).

[22] Sattareh Farmanfarmaian with Dona Munker, *Daughter of Persia: A Woman's Journey from Her Father's Harem through the Islamic Revolution* (New York: Three Rivers Press, 1992), 73, 106.

and minds around the world.²³ The Washington-Tehran alliance made available new forms of mobility and exchange, but individuals had considerable room to maneuver as they mediated the encounter between superpower America and late Pahlavi Iran.

The Cold War partnership culminated with the shah's White Revolution during the closing bookend to the volume: the "long sixties." Spanning the mid-1950s to the mid-1970s, this period gave birth to new forms of global exchange, youth culture, technological feats, and the expectation that states could revise the social contract by improving the material well-being of their citizens.²⁴ In Iran the developmentalist push was oil driven, internationally mediated, and hailed as the White Revolution. Launched in 1963, this royal reform initiative gave women suffrage, began land reform, and started a literacy initiative, among other moves. While historians have long debated the degree to which the impetus for "modernization" came from Washington, the attention here turns to the educationalists, technical advisers, oil men, cultural figures, and Peace Corps volunteers who connected the United States and Iran during the long sixties.²⁵ This same period also saw multitiered circuits of migration bring increasing numbers of Iranian students to the United States, some of whom formed the first Iranian-American communities. They made American friends, engaged in local and national debates, and transformed communities in states such as California and Michigan. There was, indeed, a robust and contested binational dialogue prior to the popularization of discourses about *Gharb-zadegi* (Westoxication) in the 1960s.²⁶

Soon thereafter, the "shocks of the global" revolutionized Iran and its relationship with the United States and the world.²⁷ In the mid-1970s the international agenda shifted toward the politics of oil, human rights, and revolution. And with the aid years over, the White Revolution was eclipsed by the shah's "Great Civilization." As Cyrus Schayegh has written elsewhere, this was a non-territorial "imperial project" based

---

[23] Matthew K. Shannon, *Losing Hearts and Minds: American-Iranian Relations and International Education during the Cold War* (Ithaca, NY: Cornell University Press, 2017).

[24] Arthur Marwick, *The Sixties: Cultural Revolution in Britain, France, Italy, and the United States, c.1958-c.1974* (New York: Oxford University Press, 1998), 15–18. On US-Iran relations, see Ben Offiler, *US Foreign Policy and the Modernization of Iran: Kennedy, Johnson, Nixon, and the Shah* (New York: Palgrave Macmillan, 2015).

[25] James F. Goode, "Reforming Iran during the Kennedy Years," *Diplomatic History* 15, no. 1 (1991): 13–29; Roland Popp, "An Application of Modernization Theory during the Cold War? The Case of Pahlavi Iran," *International History Review* 30, no. 1 (2008): 76–98; April Summitt, "For a White Revolution: John F. Kennedy and the Shah of Iran," *Middle East Journal* 58, no. 4 (2004): 560–75. More broadly, see Sara Lorenzini, *Global Development: A Cold War History* (Princeton, NJ: Princeton University Press, 2019); Odd Arne Westad, *The Global Cold War: Third World Interventions and the Making of Our Times* (New York: Cambridge University Press, 2005).

[26] Ali Mirsepassi, *Transnationalism in Iranian Political Thought: The Life and Times of Ahmad Fardid* (New York: Cambridge University Press, 2017), 149–50; Jalal Al-e Ahmad, *Occidentosis: A Plague from the West*, trans. R. Campbell (Berkeley, CA: Mizan Press, 1984).

[27] Niall Ferguson, Charles Maier, Erez Manela, and Daniel Sargent, eds., *The Shock of the Global: The 1970s in Perspective* (Cambridge, MA: Harvard University Press, 2010). See also Daniel Sargent, *A Superpower Transformed: The Remaking of American Foreign Relations in the 1970s* (New York: Oxford University Press, 2017).

on "a vision of Iran as a civilisational-developmental beacon for the world."[28] In the last decade of Pahlavi power, the shah embraced the very language that had, in the first place, guided American influence into Iran. At the same time, the "American Century" closed amid the fallout from the Vietnam War, the economic restructuring of the international system, and a brief unraveling of the globalist consensus that had propelled US foreign policy since the Second World War. The *American moment* in Iran, therefore, ended conterminously with the move to an interdependent world.[29] To borrow from Brian Edwards, the 1970s brought about new ends of American influence in Iran.[30] The decade that ended with the 1979 revolution resembled our contemporary world more than the one Samuel Martin Jordan inhabited.

***

The first two chapters examine the *origin stories* of the modern American-Iranian encounter. John Ghazvinian's chapter is based on documents from Iran's Foreign Ministry Archives in Tehran. He reinterprets the "open door," finding that it was, in fact, Iranians who pursued economic and cultural opportunities in the United States.[31] Shortly after diplomatic relations were established in 1883, Iran sent envoys to Washington and posts around the United States. Hossein-Qoli Khān Nuri, or "Haji Washington," arrived in 1888 and spent a year in the United States before returning to Iran.[32] In 1893, at the same world's exhibition where Frederick Jackson Turner declared the American frontier closed, Iranian diplomats staged a "Persian Palace" to introduce their country to the American heartland and high society. While many readers will be familiar with Pahlavi-era diplomats such as Ardeshir Zahedi, the diplomatic corps of the late Qajar era is less known. Often of Armenian, Assyrian, and Bahā'i backgrounds, these international men of industry conducted diplomatic and consular work in Gilded Age cities and reported back to the Bureau of American Affairs, which Iranian state-builders created during the reign of Mozaffar al-Din Shah Qajar to professionalize the

---

[28] Cyrus Schayegh, "Iran's Global Long 1970s: An Empire Project, Civilisational Developmentalism, and the Crisis of the Global North," in *The Age of Aryamehr*, ed. Alvandi, 265–6.

[29] For a special issue on what Henry Luce called the "American Century," see *Diplomatic History* 23, no. 2 (1999). See also Andrew Bacevich, ed., *The Short American Century: A Postmortem* (Cambridge, MA: Harvard University Press, 2012); Robert Herzstein, *Henry R. Luce, Time, and the American Crusade in Asia* (New York: Cambridge University Press, 2005); Walter LaFeber, Richard Polenberg, and Nancy Woloch, *The American Century: A History of the United States since the 1890s*, 7th ed. (New York: Routledge, 2015).

[30] Brian Edwards, *After the American Century: The Ends of U.S. Culture in the Middle East* (New York: Columbia University Press, 2016).

[31] The original articulation is William Appleman Williams, *The Tragedy of American Diplomacy* (New York: W.W. Norton, 1959). Michael Hunt reframed the open door to refer to international travelers in the United States rather than the expansion of US markets abroad. Hunt, *The Making of a Special Relationship: The United States and China to 1914* (New York: Columbia University Press, 1983). See also Qingjia Edward Wang, "Guests from the Open Door: The Receptions of Chinese Students into the United States, 1900s-1920s," *Journal of American-East Asian Relations* 3, no. 1 (1994): 55–75.

[32] *Hajji Washington*, directed by Ali Hatami (1982), streaming; James F. Goode, "A Good Start: The First American Mission to Iran, 1883–1885," *Muslim World* 74, no. 2 (1984): 100–18; Goode, "Samuel Benjamin: Unorthodox Observer of the Middle East," *Islam and Christian-Muslim Relations* 9, no. 1 (1998): 23–9.

Foreign Ministry and balance their country's relationship with the foreign powers.[33] At the same time, Armenian and Assyrian Christians began to settle in American cities such as Chicago. Ghazvinian thus offers a reading of the early Iranian foreign service *and* the early Iranian-American diaspora.[34] Some Iranians received a US passport, but this "flag of convenience," to borrow from Ghazvinian, could quickly turn into a "flag of inconvenience" when conscripted into the US military during the First World War. Many were more concerned about the fate of their families along the Persian-Ottoman-Russian borderlands than the survival of strangers in Western Europe.

Kelly Shannon turns to the Shuster Mission and American perceptions of Iran during the Constitutional Revolution. W. Morgan Shuster's economic mission in 1911 was among the first significant non-missionary American endeavors in Iran. In some ways part of William Howard Taft's "dollar diplomacy," Shannon argues that Shuster—a former colonial official in Cuba and the Philippines—developed anti-imperial sentiments as a private citizen while serving as treasurer-general of the constitutionalist government in Tehran.[35] The title of his memoir indicates as much, but this chapter is the first analytic history based on Shuster's papers at the Library of Congress and documents at the US National Archives.[36] While Russian and British intrigue led to Shuster's expulsion from Iran in December 1911 after just six months on the job, newspapers such as the *New York Times* translated the episode for American readers. When covering Shuster's Iranian counterparts, US print media complicated "American Orientalism" with story lines on national self-determination and "progressive" reform.[37] The reporting exhibited a "good Iranian, bad Iranian" dynamic, however. Americans saw the Qajars as despotic and, in an updated version of "Herodotus' Cyrus," they compared the constitutionalists to their own middle-class progressive reformers.[38] In Shuster a precedent was set whereby the United States would rely on non-state actors as "chosen instruments" in Iran.[39] When considered

---

[33] On the late Pahlavi period, see Abbas Milani, ed., *A Window into Modern Iran: The Ardeshir Zahedi Papers at the Hoover Institution Library and Archives* (Stanford, CA: Hoover Institution Press, 2019).

[34] Vasili Shoumanov, *Assyrian American Association of Chicago: 100 Years* (Charleston, SC: Arcadia, 2018).

[35] Emily S. Rosenberg, *Financial Missionaries to the World: The Politics and Culture of Dollar Diplomacy, 1900–1930* (Durham, NC: Duke University Press, 2003); Mangol Bayat, *Iran's Experiment with Parliamentary Governance: The Second Majles, 1909–1911* (Syracuse, NY: Syracuse University Press, 2020). See also E. Berkeley Tompkins, *Anti-Imperialism in the United States: The Great Debate, 1890–1920* (Philadelphia: University of Pennsylvania Press, 1970); Ian Tyrrell and Jay Sexton, *Empire's Twin: U.S. Anti-Imperialism from the Founding Era to the Age of Terrorism* (Ithaca, NY: Cornell University Press, 2015).

[36] W. Morgan Shuster, *The Strangling of Persia: Story of the European Diplomacy and Oriental Intrigue That Resulted in the Denationalization of Twelve Million Mohammedans: A Personal Narrative* (New York: Century, 1912).

[37] Douglas Little, *American Orientalism: The United States and the Middle East since 1945* (Chapel Hill: University of North Carolina Press, 2004); Alan Dawley, *Changing the World: American Progressives in War and Revolution* (Princeton, NJ: Princeton University Press, 2003).

[38] Sam Fayyaz and Roozbeh Shirazi, "Good Iranian, Bad Iranian: Representations of Iran and Iranians in *Time* and *Newsweek* (1998–2009)," *Iranian Studies* 46, no. 1 (2013): 53–72; Lynette Mitchell, "Herodotus' Cyrus and Political Freedom," in *Perceptions of Iran*, ed. Ansari, 101–18.

[39] Rosenberg, *Spreading the American Dream*. See also Kelly J. Shannon, "Bernath Lecture: 'Approaching the Islamic World,'" *Diplomatic History* 44, no. 3 (2020): 387–408.

together, the first two chapters underscore the two-way impact of the opening salvos of the modern US-Iran relationship. If the professionalization of Iran's diplomatic corps was fastened to the birth of the Iranian-American community, the Constitutional Revolution and Shuster Mission were linked to American notions about good governance and progressive reform.

After the collapse of the Qajar Dynasty in 1925, the cultural internationalism of the interwar years sat uneasily alongside the nationalist and nationalizing measures of Reza Shah Pahlavi, who at once aimed to develop Iran and roll back the capitulations that his predecessors granted to foreign powers.[40] Scholars have written about the "Fordist connections" between and "the automotive integration" of Iran and the United States during this period, along with the construction of the Trans-Iranian Railway.[41] Kyle Olson builds on foundational works of archaeological diplomacy to explain how, after Reza Shah's ascension to power, Iranian nationalist reformers drew on the work of Americans such as Arthur Upham Pope to annul the French archaeological monopoly in 1927. That cleared the way in 1930 for the passage of Iran's Law for the Protection of National Vestiges. Olson analyzes drafts of the Antiquities Law and historicizes it through a close reading of the correspondence between Horace Jayne, the director of the University of Pennsylvania Museum, and Frederick Wulsin, Penn's man in Tehran. By the 1930s, Iran was open to American archaeologists; Penn had teams in Iran's northeast and the University of Chicago's Oriental Institute excavated Persepolis.[42] While new opportunities abounded, controversies brewed over *partage*, or the division of finds between international teams and Iranians. Especially irritating to Iranian officials was the occasional intervention by the US State Department on behalf of American archaeologists. Notwithstanding these problems, the archaeological regime brought about by the Antiquities Law of 1930 survived until 1962 and ushered in what Olson calls a "golden age" in heritage diplomacy between the United States and Iran. By underscoring the point that archaeologists were among America's earliest interlocutors in Pahlavi Iran, Olson demonstrates that, despite the reliance on non-state actors, the United States was far from isolationist during the interwar years. To borrow from an earlier generation of scholarship on the era, Iran was at once an "awkward dominion" and an "elusive quest" for American archaeologists in the 1920s and 1930s.[43]

---

[40] Akira Iriye, *Cultural Internationalism and World Order* (Baltimore, MD: Johns Hopkins University Press, 1997). See Ali Ansari, *The Politics of Nationalism in Modern Iran* (New York: Cambridge University Press, 2012); Stephanie Cronin, ed., *The Making of Modern Iran: State and Society under Riza Shah, 1921–1941* (New York: Routledge Curzon, 2003); Bianca Devos and Christoph Werner, eds., *Culture and Cultural Politics under Reza Shah: The Pahlavi State, New Bourgeoise and the Creation of a Modern Society in Iran* (New York: Routledge, 2014).

[41] Nile Green, "Fordist Connections: The Automotive Integration of the United States and Iran," *Comparative Studies in Society and History* 58, no. 2 (2016): 290–321; Mikiya Koyagi, *Iran in Motion: Mobility, Space, and the Trans-Iranian Railway* (Stanford, CA: Stanford University Press, 2021).

[42] James F. Goode, *Negotiating for the Past: Archaeology, Nationalism, and Diplomacy in the Middle East, 1919–1941* (Austin: University of Texas Press, 2007); Kishwar Rizvi, "Art History and the Nation: Arthur Upham Pope and the Discourse on 'Persian Art' in the Early Twentieth Century," *Muqarnas* 24 (2007): 45–65.

[43] Frank Costigliola, *Awkward Dominion: American Political, Economic, and Cultural Relations with Europe, 1919–1933* (Ithaca, NY: Cornell University Press, 1984); Melvyn Leffler, *Elusive Quest: America's Pursuit of European Stability and French Security, 1919–1933* (Chapel Hill: University of North Carolina Press, 1979).

The next two chapters bring novel approaches to subjects that have long occupied scholars: Anglo-American strategy in the Persian Gulf and oil in modern Iranian history. Firoozeh Kashani-Sabet argues that the United States inherited the British colonial policy of cultivating identity politics in the Gulf to construct an ethnolinguistic nation-state system that protected metropolitan security and economic interests.[44] With sources ranging from the National Library and Archives of Iran to the Qatar Digital Library, along with British and American diplomatic records, this chapter extends "frontier fictions" southward in space and forward in time to demonstrate how the sectarian politics of the imperial powers impacted the subaltern lives of Persianate communities across the Gulf.[45] The chapter begins in the aftermath of the First World War and finds that the "Wilsonian Moment" failed to help Iran pursue its regional claims, or acquire economic sovereignty over the Anglo-Iranian Oil Company. Rather than "American ascendance and British retreat," the narrative arc after the Second World War was one of Arab ascendance and Persian retreat.[46] The chapter concludes that the British withdrawal in 1971 from posts "east of Suez" did not lead the United States to pursue a "twin pillars" or "Iranian primacy" policy. Rather, Anglo-American policy built a regional order that contained Iran to the plateau and tilted the balance of power in the Persian Gulf toward the Sunni Arab states that have enjoyed less fleeting alliances with the United States.[47]

Gregory Brew analyzes what he calls the "global integration" of Iranian oil during the period of relatively stable energy markets from the mid-1950s through the mid-1960s. Brew employs sources from the National Archives of the United States and the United Kingdom, the British Petroleum collection at the University of Warwick, and material from the Foundation for Iranian Studies to put a new twist on the place of oil in international history. His analysis has more in common with "corporatist" studies of public-private cooperation and research on "political economy" than with Cold War "revisionists" who saw the acquisition of markets and material as the primary driver of US global expansion.[48] Prime Minister Mohammad Mosaddeq nationalized Iran's

---

[44] Ussama Makdisi, *Age of Coexistence: The Ecumenical Frame and the Making of the Modern Arab World* (Berkeley: University of California Press, 2019); Lawrence Potter, ed., *Sectarian Politics in the Persian Gulf* (New York: Oxford University Press, 2014).
[45] Firoozeh Kashani-Sabet, *Frontier Fictions: Shaping the Iranian Nation, 1804–1946* (Princeton, NJ: Princeton University Press, 1999).
[46] Erez Manela, *The Wilsonian Moment: Self-Determination and the International Origins of Anticolonial Nationalism* (New York: Oxford University Press, 2007); W. Taylor Fain, *American Ascendance and British Retreat in the Persian Gulf Region* (New York: Palgrave Macmillan, 2008).
[47] Roham Alvandi, *Nixon, Kissinger, and the Shah: The United States and Iran in the Cold War* (New York: Oxford University Press, 2014); Jeffrey Kimball, "The Nixon Doctrine: A Saga of Misunderstanding," *Presidential Studies Quarterly* 36, no. 1 (2006): 59–74; Robert Litwak, *Détente and the Nixon Doctrine: American Foreign Policy and the Pursuit of Stability, 1969–1976* (New York: Cambridge University Press, 1984).
[48] Frank Costigliola and Michael Hogan, eds., *Explaining the History of American Foreign Relations*, 3rd ed. (New York: Cambridge University Press, 2016), chapters 3–4; David Painter, "Oil, Resources, and the Cold War, 1945–1962," in *The Cambridge History of the Cold War, Vol. 1: Origins*, ed. Melvyn Leffler and Odd Arne Westad (New York: Cambridge University Press, 2010), 486–507. See also Justus Doenecke, "Revisionists, Oil and Cold War Diplomacy," *Iranian Studies* 3, no. 1 (1970): 23–33; Doenecke, "Iran's Role in Cold War Revisionism," *Iranian Studies* 5, nos. 2–3 (1972): 96–111.

oil industry in 1951, and his ouster in the CIA-sponsored coup of 1953 paved the way in 1954 for the establishment of an international consortium that, in Brew's analysis, "denationalized" the country's most valuable resource.[49] The shah's priority was to increase revenues from oil production to fund the military and support socioeconomic development. The US government equated security with development and, for that reason, urged reluctant American majors to take a 40 percent share in the consortium alongside European companies. The shah was chafed under the postcoup oil agreement, and by 1957 he began independent production and broke the fifty-fifty precedent. The monarch's multiple points of leverage empowered him to occupy a middle position among the oil-producing states of the Middle East and still accrue the financial benefits of doing business with the consortium. While it was possible for international firms to denationalize Iranian oil in 1953–4, the chapter ends with a conflict in 1963–4 that, while settled amicably, hinted that an "oil revolution" and a recalibration of alliance politics was in the offing.[50]

To complement these regional and international frameworks, Matthew Shannon zooms in on the urban landscape of postwar Tehran to examine the American Presbyterian institutions of the late Pahlavi period. Most historians construct an artificial divide in the narrative that separates the work of missionaries from the US government interventions of the Second World War and Cold War. For that reason, the monographic literature on American missionaries in Iran remains cloistered in the nineteenth century.[51] Scholars who move the analysis into the twentieth century focus on Reza Shah's reign and, especially, the Alborz College of Tehran, which operated during the 1920s and 1930s under Samuel Martin Jordan's direction.[52] The school closed in 1940, but despite the nationalization of Iran's education system and the transformation of American power during the Cold War, Presbyterians staffed and administered multiple institutions in Tehran during the postwar decades. Shannon uses records from the Presbyterian

[49] Interestingly, the subtitle to Shuster, *The Strangling of Persia*, refers to how British and Russian interventions "resulted in the denationalization" of Iran during the Constitutional Revolution. On the 1953 coup and the subsequent consortium, see Mary Ann Heiss, *Empire and Nationhood: The United States, Great Britain, and Iranian Oil, 1950–1954* (New York: Columbia University Press, 1997); Malcolm Byrne and Mark Gasiorowski, eds., *Mohammad Mosaddeq and the 1953 Coup in Iran* (Syracuse, NY: Syracuse University Press, 2004); Ervand Abrahamian, *The Coup: 1953, the CIA, and the Roots of Modern U.S.-Iranian Relations* (New York: New Press, 2013).
[50] Christopher Dietrich, *Oil Revolution: Anticolonial Elites, Sovereign Rights, and the Economic Culture of Decolonization* (New York: Cambridge University Press, 2017). See also Andrew Scott Cooper, *The Oil Kings: How the U.S., Iran, and Saudi Arabia Changed the Balance of Power in the Middle East* (New York: Simon and Schuster, 2011); Victor McFarland, *Oil Powers: A History of the U.S.-Saudi Alliance* (New York: Columbia University Press, 2020).
[51] Adam Becker, *Revival and Awakening: American Evangelical Missionaries in Iran and the Origins of Assyrian Nationalism* (Chicago: University of Chicago Press, 2015); Thomas S. R. O. Flynn, *The Western Christian Presence in the Russias and Qajar Persia, c. 1760–1870* (Leiden: Brill, 2017).
[52] Thomas M. Ricks, "Alborz College of Tehran, Dr. Samuel Martin Jordan and the American Faculty: Twentieth-Century Presbyterian Mission Education and Modernism in Iran (Persia)," *Iranian Studies* 44, no. 5 (2011): 627–46; Michael Zirinsky, "A Panacea for the Ills of the Country: American Presbyterian Education in Inter-War Iran," *Iranian Studies* 26, nos. 1–2 (1993): 119–37; Zirinsky, "Render Therefore unto Caesar the Things Which Are Caesar's: American Presbyterian Educators and Reza Shah," *Iranian Studies* 26, nos. 3–4 (1993): 337–56; Zirinsky, "Inculcate Tehran: Opening a Dialogue of Civilizations in the Shadow of God and the Alborz," *Iranian Studies* 44, no. 5 (2011): 657–69.

Historical Society to examine three of them: the Alborz Foundation for student advising and language training; the Community School for English-speaking students; and the Iran Bethel School for young Iranian women. American missionary institutions were important nodes of connection and sites of binational negotiation that had implications for individuals, communities, and the "pedagogic state" of Pahlavi Iran.[53]

The next two chapters turn to American technical assistance to Iran during the "age of speed."[54] During the 1950s and 1960s, new technologies and modes of transportation collided with the demands of state-sponsored development initiatives to expand the means of and reasons for migration between the United States and Iran. Richard Garlitz studies technical assistance to Iranian universities from Harry Truman's "Point Four" program in the 1950s through the creation of the US Agency for International Development in the 1960s.[55] Based on repositories in Utah and related university records, Garlitz explains how US aid dollars sent Utahns and other educationalists to Iran on contract to support the colleges and schools of the University of Tehran.[56] Established by Reza Shah in the mid-1930s, the nation's leading center of learning assumed strategic significance for Washington during the Cold War. During the late 1950s and early 1960s, Utah State University ran an extension program at Karaj Agricultural College, and Brigham Young University sent advisers to the Teacher Training College. While the Utah schools targeted preexisting colleges within the University of Tehran, the University of Southern California helped to found the Institute (later College) of Business and Public Administration. Garlitz is critical of the advisers for parroting the modernization theorists of the day and for attempting to transplant an allegedly universal model of development to other parts of the world. America's "mandarins of the future" had a mixed record, and while their Iranian partners welcomed material assistance, they often rejected American ideas or adapted them to the needs of Iran's higher education system.[57]

If Garlitz gauges aid initiatives based on their stated goals of transforming institutions and practices in Iran, Jasamin Rostam-Kolayi captures meaning-making and the impact of aid-era programs on individuals from both countries.[58] The chapter is as much an international history of John F. Kennedy's signature program as it is an interpersonal one, in large part because of the interviews that its author conducted

[53] Afshin Marashi, *Nationalizing Iran: Culture, Power, and the State, 1870–1940* (Seattle: University of Washington Press, 2008), chapter 3.
[54] Nathan Citino, *Envisioning the Arab Future: Modernization in U.S.-Arab Relations, 1945–1967* (New York: Cambridge University Press, 2017).
[55] Richard Garlitz, *A Mission for Development: Utah Universities and the Point Four Program in Iran* (Logan: Utah State University Press, 2018).
[56] David Menashri, *Education and the Making of Modern Iran* (Ithaca, NY: Cornell University Press, 1992). On the broader context, see Ethan Schrum, *The Instrumental University: Education in the Service of the National Agenda after World War II* (Ithaca, NY: Cornell University Press, 2019).
[57] Nils Gilman, *Mandarins of the Future: Modernization Theory in Cold War America* (Baltimore, MD: Johns Hopkins University Press, 2003); Michael Latham, *Modernization as Ideology: American Social Science and "Nation Building" in the Kennedy Era* (Chapel Hill: University of North Carolina Press, 2000); Latham, *The Right Kind of Revolution: Modernization, Development, and U.S. Foreign Policy from the Cold War to the Present* (Ithaca, NY: Cornell University Press, 2011).
[58] Other examples include Christopher T. Fisher, "'Moral Purpose is the Important Thing': David Lilienthal, Iran, and the Meaning of Development in the US, 1956–63," *International History Review* 33, no. 3 (2011): 431–51; Andrew Warne, "Psychoanalyzing Iran: Kennedy's Iran Task Force and the Modernization of Orientalism, 1961–3," *International History Review* 35, no. 2 (2013): 396–422.

with American Peace Corps (*Sepāh-e Solh-e Āmrikā*) volunteers who served in Iran.[59] While frameworks abound for historicizing the program, Rostam-Kolayi draws on interviews to explain how Peace Corps Iran was, in her phrasing, a Cold War innovation and deviation.[60] Young Americans unwittingly entered Pahlavi-era Iran at the height of the White Revolution, and they transformed the government initiative into a vehicle for experiencing internationalist growth, acquiring cultural empathy, and establishing lifelong friendships. As a result, the American volunteers and their Iranian students and friends forged alternative understandings about each other and the world they inhabited. In this history of cultural transfer and transmission, the impact was as much on the future politics, emotions, and cookbooks of returned American volunteers as it was on the languages and landscapes of Iran.[61] By 1976, Iran's independence on the world stage and rising tensions with the United States compelled the volunteers to terminate the program. Postrevolutionary problems notwithstanding, the returned volunteers remain connected with Iran and organized through the Peace Corps Iran Association.[62] Rostam-Kolayi's chapter is the first of three to employ oral history and, in the case of the next chapter, a personal collection of papers, to shed light on the more recent episodes in American-Iranian and Iranian-American histories.

Migration defined new realities for young Iranians, too, and the final two chapters offer different perspectives on the history of Iranian students in the United States. Ida Yalzadeh explores the political activism of the Iranian Student Association in Northern California by examining a demonstration that took place at the Iranian consulate in San Francisco in 1970. Meant to be a peaceful sit-in, local authorities arrested and tried "the forty-one."[63] Based on the private papers of Bay-area activist and scholar Parviz Shokat, the chapter is testimony to the multiple registers on which the Iranian Student Association and its regional branches engaged with American and global audiences. While previous research emphasizes their impact on global discourses of socialism, third worldism, and human rights, Iranian students also informed debates in the United States about justice, race, and immigration.[64] Rather than focus on the

---

[59] Jasamin Rostam-Kolayi, "The New Frontier Meets the White Revolution: The Peace Corps in Iran, 1962–76," *Iranian Studies* 51, no. 4 (2018): 587–612; Rostam-Kolayi, "'Beautiful Americans': Peace Corps Iran in the Global Sixties," in *The Routledge Handbook of the Global Sixties: Between Protest and Nation-Building*, ed. Chen Jian, Martin Klimke, Masha Kirasirova, Mary Nolan, Marylin Young, Joanna Waley-Cohen (New York: Routledge, 2018), 303–14.

[60] Elizabeth Cobbs Hoffman, *All You Need Is Love: The Peace Corps and the Spirit of the 1960s* (Cambridge, MA: Harvard University Press, 1998). Regional case studies include Larry Grubbs, *Secular Missionaries: Americans and African Development in the 1960s* (Amherst: University of Massachusetts Press, 2009); Fernando Purcell, *The Peace Corps in South America: Volunteers and the Global War on Poverty in the 1960s* (New York: Palgrave Macmillan, 2019). See also Jonathan Zimmerman, *Innocents Abroad: American Teachers in the American Century* (Cambridge, MA: Harvard University Press, 2006).

[61] Jessica C. E. Gienow-Hecht, "Cultural Transfer," in *Explaining the History of American Foreign Relations*, 2nd ed., ed. Michael Hogan and Thomas Paterson (New York: Cambridge University Press, 2004), chapter 16. A similar experience is described in David Pollack, Ruth E. Van Reken, and Michael Pollack, *Third Culture Kids: Growing Up among Worlds* (Boston, MA: Nicholas Brealey, 2017).

[62] Peace Corps Iran Association. Available online: https://peacecorpsiran.org/ (accessed March 23, 2021).

[63] *Defend the 41* (Berkeley, CA: Iranian Student Association in the United States, Defense Section, January 1973).

[64] Afshin Matin-Asgari, *Iranian Student Opposition to the Shah* (Costa Mesa, CA: Mazda, 2002); Golnar Nikpour, "Claiming Human Rights: Iranian Political Prisoners and the Making of a Transnational

repressive capacities of Iranian security organizations, this chapter underscores the disciplinary powers of the US state with regard to minority groups and international students, and it delineates a link between foreign policy and the racialization of Iranians in the United States. "Asia" informed a racialized definition of "America" in the late nineteenth century, and Yalzadeh shows that it continued to do so in the late twentieth century.[65] Race and region emerge as important frames for understanding the experiences of Iranians and Iranian-Americans around the United States.[66]

Camron Michael Amin unearths the educational networks that attracted young Iranians to southeastern Michigan. Amin directs the Michigan Iranian-American Oral History Project and offers readers a glimpse into some of his early interviews.[67] A central finding is that, during the late Pahlavi period, education was a "push" and a "pull" factor in determining Iranian mobility.[68] In Iran, the US embassy and organizations such as the American Friends of the Middle East facilitated educational migration, and Iranian government policies encouraged study abroad. Most interestingly, contingent factors such as one's training, the encouragement of a friend, or support of a mentor influenced individual decisions to go abroad and, in many cases, remain there. Meanwhile, the University of Michigan-Ann Arbor, Michigan State University, and Wayne State University attracted Iranian students and postgraduates to Detroit instead of other metropolitan areas.[69] In contrast to historians who foreground the politicization of the Iranian student *movement*, the focus here is on the hybridity of the broader Iranian student *community*.[70] Some of Amin's interviewees discuss how, after the 1979 revolution, they remained connected with Iran through institutions such as the Persia House of Michigan (*Khāneh-ye Irān-e Mishigān*), while others sustained physical mobility and could travel to Iran. Whatever the case, the pre-1979 student diaspora was the foundation of the post-1979 Iranian-American community.

***

Movement, 1963-1979," *Humanity* 9, no. 3 (2018): 363–88; Eskandar Sadeghi-Boroujerdi, "The Origins of Communist Unity: Anti-Colonialism and Revolution in Iran's Tri-Continental Moment," *British Journal of Middle Eastern Studies* 45, no. 5 (2018): 796–822; Shannon, *Losing Hearts and Minds*.

[65] See also Susannah Aquilina, "Common Ground: Iranian Student Opposition to the Shah on the US/Mexico Border," *Journal of Intercultural Studies* 32, no. 4 (2011): 321–34; Manijeh Nasrabadi and Afshin Matin-Asgari, "The Iranian Student Movement and the Making of Global 1968," in *The Routledge Handbook of the Global Sixties*, 443–56.

[66] Mohammad Chaichian, "First Generation Iranian Immigrants and the Question of Cultural Identity: The Case of Iowa," *International Migration Review* 31, no. 3 (1997): 612–27; Mohsen Mobasher, *Iranians in Texas: Migration, Politics, and Ethnic Identity* (Austin: University of Texas Press, 2012); Saba Soomekh, *From the Shahs to Los Angeles: Three Generations of Iranian Jewish Women between Religion and Culture* (Albany: State University of New York Press, 2012).

[67] Michigan Iranian-American Oral History Project. Available online: https://library.umd.umich.edu/miaohp/index.php (accessed March 23, 2021).

[68] Ronald Takaki, *A Different Mirror: A History of Multicultural America* (New York: Back Bay, 2008).

[69] State universities have typically been framed within external projection narratives rather than ones that focus on the internationalization of American education. A relevant example is John Ernst, *Forging a Fateful Alliance: Michigan State University and the Vietnam War* (East Lansing: Michigan State University Press, 1998).

[70] Matin-Asgari, *Iranian Student Opposition to the Shah*.

American-Iranian Dialogues maps the binational relationship from debates about modernity at the fin de siècle through the advent of the postmodern age. Rather than understand the exchanges between the United States and Iran in terms of a singular, static, and self-contained "dialogue of civilizations," the chapters explore how individuals, networks, and ideas intersected at different points on a transnational plane to produce multiple contested dialogues.[71] By examining these linkages, the authors reframe the conversation about the binational relationship in terms of a "connected" or "crossed history." To borrow from the seminal writing on the concept, "the relational, interactive, and process-oriented dimensions of *histoire croisée* lead to a multiplicity of possible intercrossings."[72] This was true for US-Iran relations from the 1890s to the 1960s, and beyond.

The connections of that era flowed along a veritable superhighway with many entrances and exits; its own tollbooths, weigh stations, and rest stops; and diverse travelers that had blind spots, moved at different speed limits, and, yes, got in accidents. This cultural infrastructure was a collective project that was envisioned, constructed, and experienced by a host of actors and organizations from the United States and Iran. They were, in most instances, unaffiliated with states, but each chapter discusses cases that differ considerably from the others. Some historical actors were members of nongovernmental organizations (NGOs). NGOs are best understood as "institutionalized groupings of people and resources … operating outside the direct authority of any particular government or collection of governments." The twentieth century was, according to the historian Akira Iriye, "a century of NGOs," with voluntary, nonprofit organizations proliferating around the world. International NGOs like the Ford Foundation and the American Friends of the Middle East greased the gears of mobility between the United States and Iran, as did intergovernmental organizations such as the United Nations. Other types of "intermediary institutions" were significant. American institutions of higher education, for example, sent faculty members and recent graduates to Iran and hosted international students on their campuses. While aid programs drew on university expertise, they were sponsored by the US and Iranian governments. Moreover, many of the most significant cultural programs—first among them the Fulbright program—were state sponsored. There was, therefore, a permeability to state and non-state endeavors that created uneasy relationships to power. Other non-state entities—ranging from for-profit oil companies and multinational corporations to underground political parties, advocacy networks, and student organizations—shared lanes with NGOs, universities, and other transnational travelers. There were layers of difference between them, but most were, in the most basic sense, "non-state actors" engaged in worldly pursuits. If humans are

---

[71] *Dialogue among Civilizations: The Round Table on the Eve of the United Nations Millennium Summit* (Paris: UNESCO, 2001), 23–30. Available online: https://unesdoc.unesco.org/ark:/48223/pf0000123890 (accessed April 14, 2021).

[72] Michael Werner and Bénédicte Zimmermann, "Beyond Comparison: *Histoire Croisée* and the Challenge of Reflexivity," *History and Theory* 45, no. 1 (2006): 30–50, quote on p. 39. For a related discussion, see "AHR Conversation: On Transnational History," *American Historical Review* 111, no. 5 (2006): 1441–64.

capable of harnessing the powers of destruction, production, and integration, the actors discussed on the following pages were integrative agents in "international society."[73]

By drawing on the expertise of scholars from across fields and with a range of perspectives, methodologies, and linguistic abilities, the following chapters aim to avoid asymmetrical renderings of shared histories, offering instead a relatively symmetrical reading of what was, and is, a "multisited" and "multidirectional" relationship between Americans and Iranians. The points of connection—along with the individuals and networks involved, and the contexts and discourses that surrounded them—tended to "mutate in motion" and generate dialogues across space and time.[74] While some of these connections were part and parcel of larger global processes, their "historical actuality is more precisely rooted."[75] In the pages that follow, the authors position those processes within the contested connected history of American-Iranian relations.

---

[73] Jeremi Suri, "Non-Governmental Organizations and Non-State Actors," in *Palgrave Advances in International History*, ed. Patrick Finney (New York: Palgrave Macmillan, 2005), 223–46, quotes on pp. 223 and 226; Akira Iriye, "A Century of NGOs," *Diplomatic History* 23, no. 3 (1999): 421–35, especially p. 428; Erez Manela, "International Society as a Historical Subject," *Diplomatic History* 44, no. 2 (2020): 184–209. See also Margaret Keck and Kathryn Sikkink, *Activists beyond Borders: Advocacy Networks in International Politics* (Ithaca, NY: Cornell University Press, 1998), chapter 1; Barbara Keys, "Nonstate Actors," in *Explaining the History of American Foreign Relations*, 3rd ed., eds. Costigliola and Hogan, chapter 7; Lyman Cromwell White, *International Non-Governmental Organizations: Their Purposes, Methods, and Accomplishments* (New Brunswick, NJ: Rutgers University Press, 1951).

[74] Kramer, "Power and Connection," 1365.

[75] Frederick Cooper, *Colonialism in Question: Theory, Knowledge, History* (Berkeley: University of California Press, 2005), 100. See also pp. 197–200.

1

Flags of Inconvenience: State Failure, Nationhood, and Contested Sovereignty in the Late Qajar Encounter with the United States

John Ghazvinian

Iranian history from 1896 to 1926 has traditionally been treated by historians as a period that witnessed the near complete disintegration of royal control and effective state sovereignty in the face of growing encroachments from European imperial powers. It is also, typically, presented as a period that witnessed a concomitant growth in domestic reform movements espousing constitutionalism and modern nationalism as a response to these structural weaknesses.[1] The international histories of the late nineteenth and early twentieth centuries, though they touch on these subjects, are lopsided in their focus on Iran's relations with Great Britain and Russia. Certainly, there is truth to much of this narrative about the Qajar state's institutional weakness and the impact of the so-called Great Game. However, this chapter argues that a much richer appreciation of late Qajar "decline" can be gained from examining Iran's early state and non-state relations with the United States.

This is not, it should be stated, a traditional "diplomatic history" of US-Iran relations.[2] Rather, it seeks to instrumentalize the mechanisms of diplomatic protocol and representation in the service of a multifaceted narrative about Iranian sovereignty and belonging in a globalizing world. Too often, there is an artificial division of labor between diplomatic historians and those interested in questions of the subaltern,

---

[1] Virtually every standard account of modern Iranian history recounts some version of this narrative. Some examples include Ervand Abrahamian, *A History of Modern Iran* (Cambridge: Cambridge University Press, 2008); Ali Ansari, *Modern Iran: Reform and Revolution* (London: Routledge, 2007); Michael Axworthy, *A History of Iran: Empire of the Mind* (New York: Basic Books, 2008); Nikki Keddie, *Modern Iran: Roots and Results of Revolution* (New Haven, CT: Yale University Press, 2006).

[2] Examples of traditional diplomatic histories include James Bill, *The Eagle and the Lion: The Tragedy of American-Iranian Relations* (New Haven, CT: Yale University Press, 1988); James F. Goode, *The United States and Iran, 1946-1951: The Diplomacy of Neglect* (New York: St. Martin's Press, 1989); Abraham Yeselson, *United States-Persian Diplomatic Relations* (New Brunswick, NJ: Rutgers University Press, 1956).

the constructed, the neglected, and the interstitial.³ Eschewing such divisions, this chapter repositions the mechanisms of diplomacy within a broader story of contested sovereignty, nationhood, and belonging. Specifically, it does so by looking at Iran's consular and diplomatic representatives in the United States—a community of officials in which ethno-religious minorities, many of whom were not "Iranian," were heavily represented. This argument is based on Iranian primary sources, including those held at the Foreign Ministry Archives in Tehran. These documents offer a more textured understanding of this moment in US-Iran relations than has traditionally been available to historians working only with American sources.

Following the assassination of Naser al-Din Shah in 1896, the Qajar state renewed its emphasis on bureaucratic professionalism, especially in foreign policy. In the process, the state became increasingly reliant on an informal sector of traders and cultural emissaries in the conduct of that policy. From the early 1900s, especially, a growing network of Armenian, Assyrian, and Bahā'i notables, most of whom had never set foot in Iran and did not speak Persian, took up appointments as Iranian consuls in large US cities. Initially, this transnational network of émigrés, antique dealers, and industry magnates represented Iran competently. But in the years following the Constitutional Revolution (1905–11), they descended into squabbling and chaos, much like Iran's own political elite. Most interestingly, some Assyrians and Armenians began to settle in Chicago and New York in the 1890s, and they sometimes used their US citizenship as a flag of convenience to engage in anti-government activity in Iran with US diplomatic protection. When the First World War broke out, however, many were keen to renew their Iranian passports to avoid the US military draft. This precipitated a complex scandal in which various Iranian consuls accused one another of profiteering from passport fees. The Iranian minister in Washington himself disappeared completely in 1910. For some time thereafter, it was not clear who represented the Iranian government in Washington, as the consuls bickered and presented rival claims to the US State Department.

All of these episodes, individually, are rich in colorful detail and revealing of multiple underexplored facets of early US-Iran relations. But taken together, they represent a historical moment—one in which sovereignty, nationhood, and Iranian identity were open to considerable negotiation and interpretation. This moment, in other words, intersects in important ways with our existing understanding of the constitutional period in Iran, as well as the ultimate collapse of the Qajar state.

Building the Bureau of American Affairs

The tumultuous reign of Mozaffar al-Din Shah Qajar (1896–1907) is almost always described as a merry-go-round of incompetence, corruption, foreign exploitation, and

---

[3] Examples of the latter include Matthew K. Shannon, *Losing Hearts and Minds: American-Iranian Relations and International Education during the Cold War* (Ithaca, NY: Cornell University Press, 2017); Ussama Makdisi, *Artillery of Heaven: American Missionaries and the Failed Conversion of the Middle East* (Ithaca, NY: Cornell University Press, 2009); Nile Green, *The Love of Strangers: What Six Muslim Students Learned in Jane Austen's London* (Princeton, NJ: Princeton University Press, 2016).

careering debts, all of which left the Iranian state in a position of devastating weakness and servility. It is true that Iran's spending, and the corresponding orgy of borrowing from European banks, reached dizzying heights in this period and set up a series of structural challenges from which the Qajar state was never able to recover. However, one of the most underappreciated aspects of Mozaffar al-Din Shah's reign is the progress Iran was able to make toward the creation of a serious, professional foreign service corps. For much of his time in power, the shah was served by competent, reform-minded ministers who ushered in a series of important bureaucratic and administrative advances that introduced a measure of efficiency and professionalism to the Iranian civil service. It was an atmosphere that extended to the Foreign Ministry, run by the highly skilled Moshir al-Dowleh. With changes in the ministry, Iran could, for the first time in years, devote sustained attention to its relationship with the United States. For much of the 1890s, as the last years of Naser al-Din Shah descended into volatility and public protest, relations with the United States had drifted into a state of benign neglect. Now, under Mozaffar al-Din Shah, they were renewed with an unexpected degree of energy and vigor.

The new era was marked by the arrival, in December 1900, of a new Iranian minister in Washington—General Ishāq Khān Mofakhkham al-Dowleh. It was the first time Tehran had sent an envoy to head the Washington legation in more than eleven years, since the departure of Hossein-Qoli Khān Nuri. And it was immediately apparent that Ishāq's arrival was long overdue. Within the first few weeks, he was inundated with more than two hundred expressions of interest from American businesses eager to trade with Iran, indicating a certain level of pent-up demand.[4] He was under specific orders from Tehran to promote and regulate US-Iranian trade, beginning with the establishment of consulates in every American city where there was a demand for Iranian merchandise or an interest in Iranian markets.[5] As a diligent and energetic career diplomat with many years of experience, Ishāq took this task seriously. He believed that establishing a stable American market for Persian carpets could do wonders for his country's economy, and he even argued for a certification scheme to protect consumers against fraudulent products.[6] Ishāq also felt it was important for Iran's new commercial consulates to be staffed by men with business experience and international contacts.[7]

Of course, all of this was easier said than done. In 1901 the Iranian community in the United States was virtually nonexistent, and Tehran was not likely to send people to the country just to act as commercial attachés. It took him nearly a year, but eventually, in New York City, Ishāq found interest in a man by the name of Dikran Kelekian. He was an Armenian antiques trader from Turkey who had been living in New York for the

---

[4] Archives of the Ministry of Foreign Affairs of the Islamic Republic of Iran (hereafter "FM") 1318-29-12, fol. 12. Although there is no date on this dispatch, it is in a file of documents from 1318 and is mixed in with dispatches from Shavvāl and Zi al-Qaʿdeh of that year. These months of the Hijri calendar correspond to January/February 1901. The tone of the dispatch also corresponds with those written during Ishāq's first few weeks in Washington.
[5] "Shah Is Seeking American Trade," *New York Herald*, December 9, 1900.
[6] Ishāq to Foreign Ministry, 16 Moharram 1320 (April 25, 1902), FM 1320-10-3, fol. 43.
[7] Foreign Ministry to Ishāq, 27 Rabiʿ al-Sani 1320 (August 2, 1902), FM 1320-10-3, fol. 128.

previous nine years, and he had supplied many of the wares on display at the Persian pavilion during the Chicago World's Fair of 1893.[8] It was a curious choice, perhaps, given the long history of Iranian-Ottoman enmity, but as an Armenian living abroad, Kelekian was not likely loyal to the Sultan. More importantly, he was a respected authority on Persian antiquities with a clear stake in raising their profile in America. To Tehran, he seemed like a safe pair of hands. In 1902, therefore, Dikran Kelekian's Fifth Avenue art gallery became the Imperial Consulate of Persia in New York.[9]

The selection of Kelekian established a precedent. The following year, another Armenian Ottoman, Haig Herant Pakraduni, was made Iranian consul in Philadelphia.[10] Like Kelekian, Pakraduni was a businessman based in the United States, and like Kelekian, he must have thought that the ceremonial title of "Consul to His Imperial Majesty the Shah of Persia" would provide a boost to his printing business. Pakraduni happily retained the title until his death in 1937, even though, by 1911, it appears he had lost all contact with the Iranian government.[11] The year after that, yet another Armenian rug trader from Istanbul, Milton Seropian, was made Iranian consul in St. Louis.[12] None of these men had ever set foot in Iran, and it is unlikely that they spoke a word of Persian. But they all had clear commercial interests in improving US-Iranian ties. Before long, it seemed that anyone with a stake in promoting the Persian rug trade, or any other trade with Iran, was eligible to wear the imperial sash. In some cases, they did not even need to be Middle Eastern. In 1903, Ishāq appointed Alfonso Rutis, a Brazilian rug trader based in New Jersey, to the post of consul-general for New Jersey and Pennsylvania. Rutis quickly used the position to his advantage as he attempted to sell torpedo boats to the Iranian government in 1904.[13]

Under Ishāq, Iran's diplomatic corps in the United States began to resemble an international business network of rug traders, art dealers, and sundry industrialists with big ideas. It was all part of a larger vision Ishāq had for professionalizing and expanding Iran's presence in America. In this vision he was supported by his cousin, Morteza Khān, director of the newly established "Bureau of American Affairs" at the Foreign Ministry back in Tehran. Together, Ishāq and Morteza presided over a sweeping expansion of diplomatic activity in the Western Hemisphere, including the initiation

---

[8] Marilyn Jenkins-Madina, "Collecting the 'Orient' at the Met: Early Tastemakers in America," *Ars Orientalis* 30 (2000): 73. My thanks to Nanette Kelekian for alerting me to this reference. See also "The American Artists," *New York Times*, April 5, 1903, 7.

[9] Jenkins-Madina, "Collecting the 'Orient,'" 75. It was not, however, "the first Persian consulate in the United States," as Jenkins-Madina and others have claimed. In October 1888, when Hossein-Qoli Khān Nuri arrived as Persia's first minister to Washington, he immediately appointed Henry Ruthven Pratt to be consul-general in New York. *Register of the Department of State* (Washington, DC: US Government Printing Office, 1907), 121. There is some evidence Alfonso Rutis had been consul in Philadelphia since the early 1890s. *Public Ledger Almanac* (Philadelphia, PA: George Childs, 1894), 89.

[10] Foreign Ministry, Tehran, Office of Protocol, copy of credential letter, Moharram 1321 (roughly April 1903), FM 1321-11-6, fol. 11; Certificate from President Theodore Roosevelt, December 11, 1903, FM 1322-4-10, fol. 70. Confusingly, there are also documents from Moharram 1320 (roughly April 1902) describing his appointment as vice consul. FM 1320-25-5, ff. 1–3.

[11] Six-month report on Pakraduni by ʿAli-Qoli Khān, December 1, 1911 to May 1912, FM 1321-11-6, fol. 17.

[12] *Register of the Department of State*, 121. Death certificate No. 45562, Missouri State Archives, describes him as an "oriental rug merchant."

[13] Rutis to Ishāq Khān, 2 Shaʿbān 1322 (October 12, 1904), FM 1322-9-5, ff. 57–8, 80–2.

of Iranian relations with Argentina, Colombia, Haiti, and Uruguay. Isḥāq even took a five-month trip to Latin America. With Pakraduni in charge during his absence, Isḥāq presented his credentials to the Mexican president and otherwise learned all that he could about the geopolitics of the Western Hemisphere.[14] To assist Isḥāq in his work, Morteza sent Nivdun Khān—a civil servant who had been educated in Switzerland and the United States and was fluent in four languages—to Washington as the legation's permanent secretary.[15] At the end of 1904, when Isḥāq returned to Tehran, Morteza replaced him as minister to Washington.

Between them, Isḥāq and Morteza achieved great success in their efforts to increase Iran's profile in America. But this was not just due to their professionalism or their activities in the commercial and political arenas. They were also suave and sophisticated characters who managed to charm and seduce much of official Washington—and the American public—with their cosmopolitan manners. Isḥāq, a career diplomat who had lived in several European capitals and enjoyed such genteel pastimes as polo and hunting, was described by American newspapers as "a man of imposing presence, tall, athletic and of rather handsome features. He is unmarried and travels alone."[16] Morteza, meanwhile, was portrayed as an exotic, wealthy Persian playboy—"A Multi-Millionaire from the Land of Omar Khayyam," in the words of the *New York Times*.[17] Within three days of his arrival in the United States, he was pulled over for speeding through the streets of Manhattan, and the newspapers breathlessly reported that in the passenger seat was a "young woman of no mean pretensions to beauty."[18]

All of this was part of a larger pattern that was emerging in the image of "Iran" in the United States at the turn of the century. In the fantastical imagination of many Americans, Iran's urbane, exotic diplomats and consuls looked like they had walked out of the pages of an oriental fairy tale.

And if there was one man who embodied this new type of Persian-American sophisticate, it was ʿAli-Qoli Khān. He was an ambitious young aristocrat who married one of America's wealthiest women and quickly found himself the toast of high society in the early years of the twentieth century.[19] The fairy tale romance began around 1899, when ʿAli-Qoli was only 22 years old.[20] A secret devotee of the Bahāʾi faith, ʿAli-Qoli traveled around the world and ended up in Boston, where he quickly charmed his way in with a well-heeled set of Brahmins and cold roast New England blue bloods. The story goes that, during a visit to a wealthy family's home one day, he admired a painting of a beautiful young lady hanging over the piano, only to turn around and

---

[14] Isḥāq to Foreign Ministry, 6 Zi al-Qaʿdeh 1320 (February 4, 1903), FM 1320-10-3, fol. 70; ephemera, FM 1321-11-5, fol. 91, 1321-11-6, ff. 10–11; *Iran*, November 17, 1903, 6.
[15] FM 1321-11-6-18.
[16] "Shah Is Seeking American Trade."
[17] "A Multi-Millionaire from the Land of Omar Khayyam," *New York Times*, February 26, 1905.
[18] "The Benzine Blizzard of Gen. Morteza Khan," *New York Times*, February 19, 1905, 7.
[19] His full name was Mirzā ʿAli-Qoli Khān Zarrābi Kalāntar, Nabil al-Dowleh, b. 1878. Karim Suleimāni, *Olqāb-e Rijāl, Dowreh-ye Qājāriyyeh* (Tehran, 2000), 195.
[20] "Appointed Consul General," *New York Times*, September 22, 1915, 22.

find the living specimen standing nearby.²¹ She was Florence Breed, daughter of New England's largest manufacturer of ladies' shoes and heiress to a considerable fortune.²² Within a few months, the pair was married, and ʿAli-Qoli Khān settled into a new life in the United States.

The society pages enjoyed every moment of the couple's matrimony. Florence Breed was now "Madame Kuli Khan," the newly minted "Persian princess," whose mere presence at soirées and club luncheons brought with it an instant air of oriental sophistication and gaggles of cooing social sketch writers.²³ For his part, ʿAli-Qoli Khān found that his marriage gave him access to an entire world of American wealth and power that he never imagined existed. Before long, ʿAli-Qoli Khān was living the quintessential life of American privilege. He owned a house in the Hamptons, and occasionally rented a palatial summer estate in the Catskills north of New York City where he housed and entertained Iranian students when they came to the United States for their university studies.²⁴ He developed a friendship with the millionaire philanthropist and convert to the Bahāʿi faith, Phoebe Hearst, who funded his West Coast speaking tour in 1909.²⁵ Later in his career, ʿAli-Qoli established a "Persian Arts Center," with branches in New York, San Francisco, and Pasadena, California.²⁶ Well into the 1950s, he was still giving lectures on rugs and antiquities to eager groups of American millionaires.²⁷

In August 1910, after more than a decade in the United States, ʿAli-Qoli Khān was named Iran's *chargé d'affaires* in Washington. His appointment represented a remarkable achievement for someone whose Bahāʿi faith had become something of an open secret.²⁸ The Bahāʿi—a messianic offshoot of Shia Islam—were deeply mistrusted in Iran, where they were seen as cultlike and heretical. Many in Iran viewed them as politically troublesome after 1852 when a group of Bahāʿis tried to assassinate Naser al-Din Shah. In Iranian political circles, ʿAli-Qoli Khān's appointment as *chargé* would almost certainly have raised eyebrows. But to Americans, largely unaware of such old-world nuance, ʿAli-Qoli Khān and his "Persian princess" continued to serve as an iconic embodiment of Persian chic in the years before the First World War.

Equally as wealthy—and far more flamboyant—was the antiques dealer Haigazoun Hohannes Topakian. He became famous for the extravagant parties at his "Persian Court"—the white marble mansion that he built according to "oriental design" on his

---

[21] My thanks to Gity Etemad, grand-niece of ʿAli-Qoli Khān, for sharing this bit of family history with me.

[22] Florence was the daughter of Francis W. Breed, of Lynn, Massachusetts. Clarence W. Hobbs, *Lynn and Surroundings* (Lynn, MA: Lewis and Winship, 1886), 143.

[23] See, e.g., "An American Beauty Decorated for Learning," *Los Angeles Times*, December 6, 1912, 11; "Moving Tableaux of Girls of Orient," *New York Times*, November 19, 1913, 9; "Society in Brilliant Assemblies in Season's Second Week," *New York Times*, November 23, 1913, X2.

[24] Many of ʿAli-Qoli Khān's official correspondence with the Iranian Foreign Ministry was addressed to and from his home in East Hampton. FM 1336-21-1 *passim*. For his accommodations in the Catskills, see Seyyed Hassan Tāqizādeh, *Zendegi-ye Tufāni* (Tehran: Enteshār-eʿElmi, 1993), 174–80.

[25] Marzieh Gail, *Arches of the Years* (Oxford: Ronald, 1991), 56–8.

[26] New York Public Library, Arthur Upham Pope papers, Box 1.

[27] "Newport Colony Attends Festival," *New York Times*, July 12, 1939, 26; "Maxim Karoliks Hosts in Newport," *New York Times*, July 25, 1939, 24.

[28] "Persia in America," *New York Observer and Chronicle*, July 27, 1911, 111.

40-acre estate in Morris Plains, New Jersey. Fourth of July at the Persian Court was a staple in the social calendar of the early 1900s, with the great and the good of New York society flocking to Topakian's parties dressed like Arabian shaykhs or Persian princes. Caravans bearing roast lambs, stuffed with rice and spices, were wheeled up the hill to the sprawling gardens and dumped onto gold and bronze tables. This extravagance was made available to guests as they admired the nearly two hundred autographed portraits of celebrities that adorned the walls of the mansion.[29] The irony of it all, which seemed lost on most of the visitors to the Persian Court, was that Topakian was not actually Persian. He had never been to Iran in his life and probably did not speak Persian. Topakian was an Armenian citizen of the Ottoman Empire who emigrated to New York in 1887, and he quickly amassed a fortune selling Persian and Turkish rugs to eager American buyers intoxicated with the aura of oriental mystique that his association with Persia conferred.[30] Ever the savvy businessman, Topakian must have known that "Armenian Court" would not have had quite the same ring to it.

Topakian first made a name for himself at the 1893 Chicago World's Fair. There he played a pivotal role as commissioner of the Iranian exhibition. While he hoped to turn a profit, he put up the entirety of the money needed to build a "Persian Palace" and stuff it with carpets and ornamental objects from his own collection.[31] He claimed to have spent $75,000 of his own money on the enterprise, and subsequently spent two years lobbying the Iranian government to reward him with some sort of formal title in recognition of his efforts.[32] Letter after letter was forwarded to Tehran from various Chicago bigwigs, all attesting to Topakian's "zeal" and "energy" in adding to Iran's prestige in America. His supporters knew enough to carefully omit any mention of the scandal caused by the presence of gyrating belly dancers at the pavilion.[33] The Foreign Ministry eventually pacified him with a third-class Order of the Lion and Sun, but it took another fifteen years before Topakian earned the recognition that he clawed after so unceremoniously.[34] In 1909, he was appointed to be Iranian consul-general in New York.

Topakian replaced Dikran Kelekian, who had been consul since 1902. Both men were Armenian antique dealers from the town of Kayseri (Caesarea), in eastern Turkey, who had been deeply involved in the Chicago World's Fair of 1893. Given these similarities, one might expect that Topakian "inherited" the consulship from Kelekian. But the men were likely bitter rivals, and the position was one that Topakian must have relished taking from Kelekian. In 1904 it was Kelekian, and not Topakian, who was chosen to be Iran's commissioner at the St. Louis World's Fair. The decision must have

---

[29] "Oriental Frills to One Celebration," *New York Times*, July 5, 1907; "Consul Topakyan Takes a Burglar," *New York Times*, April 12, 1911, 1; "Persian Ex-Consul Killed in Long Fall from the Yale Club," *New York Times*, October 14, 1926, 1.

[30] Henry C. Pitney Jr., ed., *History of Morris County New Jersey* (New York: Lewis Historical, 1914), 2: 49–51.

[31] Clarence Andrews and George Stewart, "Foreign Nations at the World's Fair," *North American Review* 156, no. 438 (1893): 611–13.

[32] FM 1329-20-5-4.

[33] FM 1311-23-6-1 and 2 and 5. For the belly dancing scandal, see John Ghazvinian, *America and Iran: A History, 1720 to the Present* (New York: Knopf, 2021), 48–9.

[34] FM 1329-20-5-2.

infuriated the latter, who considered himself the genius behind Iran's successful earlier exhibition in Chicago. Possibly Tehran saw it differently. After the embarrassment caused by the belly dancer scandal in Chicago, the Iranian government might have been displeased with Topakian, and it is possible that, for this reason, he spent several years in the political wilderness. Whatever the case, by 1909, with a new regency government in place in Tehran, he was back in favor and Kelekian was out.[35]

By the time of his appointment as New York consul, Topakian was being described as "the world's largest importer of costly rugs"—a reputation he was happy to nourish at the highest echelons of American power.[36] In 1909 he presented Theodore Roosevelt with a Persian carpet valued at $50,000. It was an extraordinary piece of work, handcrafted over several years by a team of master weavers and covered in pearls, rubies, and turquoise.[37] It was believed to be the most expensive gift ever presented to a US president by a private citizen, and it reportedly excited Roosevelt so much that he bounded up the stairs to show it to his wife.[38] The following year, Topakian presented another carpet to William Taft, but there is no record of this president's reaction. Topakian, whose collection of Persian art would be valued in the hundreds of millions today, could well afford to be generous.[39] But he was not indiscriminate in his generosity. Always more comfortable in the company of Republicans, his idea of a gift for Taft's successor, the Democrat Woodrow Wilson, was a cheap painting of the Statue of Liberty.[40]

In the years from 1905 to 1911, Iran was enveloped in the chaos of the Constitutional Revolution. This was a period of great upheaval that initially succeeded in imposing constitutional limits on the powers of the shah, but subsequently unleashed a bloody civil war between constitutionalists and royalists. However, it is notable that during these tumultuous years, the Foreign Ministry established, for the first time, a competent cadre of consuls to represent Iran in the United States. The country's two most senior diplomats in the United States during this time were an unlikely duo—an Armenian Turk who spoke no Persian and a mysterious Bahāʻi who was married to an American. Both were fabulously wealthy and neither was ever far from the headlines. Together, ʻAli-Qoli Khān and H. H. Topakian created an image of Iran that was magical, mysterious, and often ostentatious, as well as flawlessly urbane—a cross between a Parisian salon and the *Thousand and One Nights*. But they also established, along with figures such as Pakraduni, Seropian, Rutis, and others, a professional network of consular offices dedicated to advancing US-Iran commercial relations. Iran, for the first time, had an address and a calling card in the United States.

---

[35] It takes a certain amount of self-restraint not to dream up scenarios about the remarkably similar circumstances of their deaths. In 1926, Topakian fell out of a 17-story window on Vanderbilt Ave. In 1951, Kelekian fell out of a 21-story window on Central Park South.

[36] *Men and Women of America* (New York: L.R. Hamersly, 1910), 1546.

[37] "$50,000 Rug in White House," *New York Times*, February 18, 1909, 1; "Persian Ex-Consul Killed in Long Fall from the Yale Club," 1.

[38] Topakian's rug hung with pride in the Oval Office for years, but it is unclear what ultimately became of it.

[39] When the Persian Court burned down in 1908, the house alone was valued at $20,000. But the contents would have been far more valuable. "Fine Country House Burns," *New York Times*, September 16, 1908, 1.

[40] "Persian Ex-Consul Killed in Long Fall from the Yale Club," 1.

It was not to last long. At the turn of the century, Ishāq and Mortezā put in place a network of consulates, run by ambitious non-Iranians, ethno-religious minorities, and commercially minded internationalists, which functioned well for a time. But the network that grew out of their careful stewardship soon degenerated into a slumgullion of petty squabbling and unraveling chaos. Given the fallout from the constitutional period, these personal and commercial rivalries in the United States unfolded amid a lack of serious oversight from the government in Iran. It was a situation that mirrored the growing dysfunction at the heart of the Qajar state.

Diplomats, Assyrians, and the Citizenship Question

With all the glamor and panache that surrounded the name "Persia" at the turn of the century, Americans could be forgiven, perhaps, for succumbing so easily to the storybook image of perfumed princes running their fingers through piles of gold and diamonds. But the Iranian experience in America was about much more than the "Persian Court" in Morris Plains or ʿAli-Qoli Khān's house in East Hampton. Outside of the spotlight and away from the headlines, a very different kind of Iranian was beginning to call the United States home. These Iranians were more likely to be a carpenter, a bricklayer, or a factory worker than an antiquities dealer. In the early years of the twentieth century, the streets of Chicago's Near North Side were beginning to fill with Assyrian Christians from the mountains of northwest Iran. And they, too, played a noticeable role in the unfolding paralysis of Qajar diplomacy in the United States.

In the 1880s and 1890s, a small trickle of Assyrian Iranians, probably inspired by the American missionaries who had lived in their midst for half of a century, began to arrive in the United States. Initially, most arrivals were young men pursuing theological studies in American seminaries. But by 1905, there were thirty Assyrian families living in the area around the intersection of Clark and Huron Streets.[41] By 1910, Chicago's Assyrian Iranian population numbered over one thousand and included an active and close-knit Christian community of construction workers, tailors, and shopkeepers, all served by a Persian church and a Persian Sunday school.[42] During the First World War, Assyrian massacres in Iran forced more families to flee, and by the 1920s the Assyrian community of Chicago stood around three thousand.[43] In 1912, as the community rapidly expanded, an Iranian consulate was established in Chicago, and the man named to the post of Iranian consul-general was the manufacturing mogul Richard Crane (great-grandfather of the actor Chevy Chase). His honorary vice consul was Sarkis Baba. He was a prominent Assyrian building contractor and naturalized US citizen who had lived in Chicago since the late 1890s. Soon after taking the post, Baba found himself in the middle of a convoluted scandal that, like the disintegration of Iran's first cadre

---

[41] John Michael and Sheren Jasim, "Assyrians of Chicago," Assyrian International News Agency. Available online: www.aina.org/aol/ethnic.htm (accessed August 12, 2019).

[42] Vasili Shoumanov, *Assyrians in Chicago* (Chicago, IL: Arcadia Press, 2001), 11–12; Michael and Jasim, "Assyrians of Chicago."

[43] Michael and Jasim, "Assyrians of Chicago."

of diplomats in the United States, spoke volumes about the decaying machinery of the Qajar state.[44]

Most Assyrian Christians came to the United States out of destitution and desperation. They were keen to flee the endless acts of intercommunal violence that characterized life in places like Urmia, which was their original home and, not coincidentally, the location of the first American missionary post in Iran. For some, however, US citizenship was also seen as a personal flag of convenience, allowing them to return to Iran and engage in anti-government activities with the full protection and privileges that an American passport conferred. In the 1890s and early 1900s, American diplomats in Iran struggled repeatedly with Iranian subjects they regarded as "troublemakers," or political subversives who turned to the US consulate every time they wanted protection against their own government. This was true, not just of Assyrian Iranians but also for the Armenian Iranians who, for the most part, hailed from the northwest region of the country. These two groups of Iranian Christians lived around Urmia and Tabriz, and they frequently had an uneasy relationship with each other.

Archival sources are laconic, but they clearly reveal that the use of US citizenship as a flag of convenience by Iranian Christians became a significant issue for US diplomats around the turn of the century. In the spring and summer of 1898, the US legation in Tehran became so frustrated by the phenomenon that it engaged in a lengthy back-and-forth with Washington about how to address the issue. At immediate stake was the fate of Mihran Bagdasarian, a Turkish Armenian who moved to the United States nine years earlier, became a naturalized citizen, and then arrived in Iran claiming to be a missionary for an American denomination called the "Disciples of Christ." In Iran, Bagdasarian was accused of sheltering and abetting radical Armenian nationalists. When he was arrested by authorities, the US legation scrambled to intervene on his behalf. Though committed to his duty to protect Americans, the US minister in Tehran, Arthur Hardy, fumed to his superiors in Washington about "pseudo citizens" like Bagdasarian, who "belong to that troublesome class of naturalized subjects whose chief object in changing their nationality is to return and live abroad under the protection of the United States." Hardy complained that in far too many cases "naturalization has been secured solely for the purpose of evading local laws," and he begged for some kind of general guidance from the State Department in these cases.[45] Iranian law, he noted, did not view such people as anything other than Iranians. The British legation in Tehran tended to agree. Both saw a material difference between an Iranian

---

[44] *Chicago Blue Book of Selected Names*; State Department report; *Khabarnāmeh-ye dākheli-ye nedā-ye haqiqat*. Richard T. Crane Jr. was the younger son of Richard Teller Crane, the founder of R. T. Crane & Bro., a famous Chicago-based manufacturer of pipes and plumbing. About two years after his father died in 1912, Richard Jr. inherited most of the company's holdings. His older brother Charles was a philanthropist and world traveler who took a particular interest in Arabia, Persia, and Central Asia.

[45] Arthur Hardy to William Day, August 8, 1898, and Hardy to John Hay, December 21, 1898, *Papers Relating to the Foreign Relations of the United States, with the Annual Message to the President Transmitted to Congress December 5, 1898* (Washington, DC: US Government Printing Office, 1901), pp. 525, 528, documents 452 and 453. Available online: https://history.state.gov/historicaldocuments/frus1898/d452, and https://history.state.gov/historicaldocuments/frus1898/d453 (accessed March 30, 2021).

claiming dual citizenship and a native-born American who had come to Iran to engage in missionary work, trade, or some other activity. The US *chargé d'affaires* in Tehran, John Tyler, who had far more experience in the country than Hardy, backed up his boss and echoed his concerns. "When it can be proved," Tyler said, "as is the case with some of these men, that their only object in going to the United States and staying just long enough to become entitled to citizenship, with out [sic] fulfilling any of the duties appertaining thereto, is simply to obtain protection in a foreign state, some different treatment should be extended to them."[46]

At the turn of the century, the main question was to whom, exactly, did these Iranian-American Christians "belong"? Were they naturalized Americans, entitled to all the same privileges and rights as native-born citizens? Or were they transnational troublemakers, using their US passports as a flag of convenience to avoid justice in their native land?

In Iran, the Constitutional Revolution and civil war of the early 1900s called into question all previous understandings of Iranianness and the rights of religious minorities. And the peculiar situation of Iranian-American Christians, some of them flitting back and forth with impunity, and many of them deeply invested in the events of their "home country," was highly illustrative of the contested nature of central government control and national belonging in Iran. The case of Iranian-American Christians demonstrates how readily these contestations were mapped along with Iran's diplomatic relationship with the United States.

The most visible manifestation of this phenomenon occurred at the Iranian legation in Washington. In April 1909, at the height of Iran's civil war, the Iranian minister in Washington, Morteżā Khān, disappeared. In his absence, ʿAli-Qoli Khān got himself appointed to the position of *chargé* and, in 1911, informed the State Department that he took the post because Morteżā had been recalled. The following year, however, Morteżā reappeared in Washington, together with a lawyer, insisting that he was still the Iranian minister and, therefore, ʿAli-Qoli's boss.[47] Two years of bewildering confusion ensued, with the State Department baffled about whom to believe. Eventually, in 1914, a new minister, Mehdi Khān Qarāgozlu, was sent to Washington from Tehran.[48] But this was only the beginning of the trouble.

---

[46] John Tyler to Sherman, April 21, 1898, *Papers Relating to the Foreign Relations of the United States 1898*, p. 518, document 439. Available online: https://history.state.gov/historicaldocuments/frus1898/d439 (accessed March 30, 2021). Interestingly, Iranian archives reveal a similar level of concern about the phenomenon. In September 1904, Isḥāq Khān wrote to Tehran, concerned that a number of Assyrians from Urmia who had come to the United States to study were returning, expecting to be recognized as US citizens. The office of foreign affairs in Tabriz said it could not see them as Americans, adding: "They're born and raised here and everyone recognizes them around here, like the rays of the sun." He noted, just as Hardy and Tyler had done a few years earlier, that the British consul in Iran did not recognize as British those who had returned from Britain with British passports. Mufakhar-al-dawlih [sic] to Foreign Ministry, 27 Jomādā al-Sāni 1322 (September 8, 1904), FM 1322-4-10, fol. 33.

[47] Record Group (RG) 59, Records of the Department of State, Central Decimal File, 701.9111/29, Henry Finkel to Secretary of State, January 5, 1912, US National Archives and Records Administration II (hereafter NARA), College Park, MD.

[48] In September 1912, the State Department cabled to Minister Charles Russell in Tehran: "Ascertain in strict confidence ... standing of Mirza Ali Kuli Khan ... with present Persian Government." RG 59, 701.9111/31a, NARA.

Since the early years of the century, most of Iran's consular positions had fallen to ethnic and religious minorities with family roots or business ties in the United States. Whatever their background, all were naturalized Americans. As long as Ishāq and Morteza were in charge, things had been fine. From 1909 to 1914, however, there was no effective oversight from the Foreign Ministry in Tehran and, therefore, no Iranian minister in Washington. In the meantime, the Armenian, Assyrian, and Bahā'i representatives of Iran in the United States squabbled endlessly among one another as each believed himself somehow uniquely more qualified than the others. By the time Mehdi Khān turned up in 1914, he found himself distinctly unwelcome. The consuls resented Mehdi and considered him a novice who knew nothing about the United States or its way of life. Mehdi, for his part, resented being pushed around by the consuls. To his mind, the consuls were merely self-interested businessmen with no real connection to Iran. The conflict was particularly acute with 'Ali-Qoli Khān, who was quickly moved out of the Washington legation and given the job of New York consul.[49] But to some extent, Mehdi's difficulties were not isolated to his experiences with 'Ali-Qoli. They were replicated with nearly every consul, each of whom resented the oversight of their own personal fiefdoms.

One of the most intractable problems Mehdi faced was with Chicago's Assyrian community and Iran's vice consul in the city, Sarkis Baba. When the First World War broke out—and especially after the United States entered the war in April 1917 and passed the Selective Service Act one month later—many Assyrians put aside their hatred for Iran and sought to renew their expired Iranian passports to avoid being drafted into the US military. Some also wanted passports so they could travel to Iran and fight against the Kurds, whose irregular militias, backed in some cases by the Ottoman Empire, were mired in a bloody exchange of massacres with Assyrian and Armenian militias in Urmia. But most Chicago Assyrians hated the Iranian government so much that they refused to pay the fees required for renewal of their Iranian passports. As a result, Sarkis Baba, possibly with the help of 'Ali-Qoli Khān, looked for creative ways around the regulations. He was even suspected by Mehdi, Iran's official minister in Washington and thus his boss, of profiteering. To make matters worse, it appears that some Chicago Assyrians took matters into their own hands and began counterfeiting passports and denouncing the Iranian government for "extortion."

This was an interesting reversal of the situation from just a few years earlier. Around the turn of the century, Iranian-American Christians sought US passports as a form of protection for when they went to Iran and engaged in anti-government activity. Now, it seemed, the same passport was a liability that came with the expectation to serve in the US military. By 1917, it was an *Iranian* passport that was coveted because it allowed easy entry into Iran and a world of radical militancy. Dreams of ethno-religious heroism in northwest Iran must have been more appealing to a young Assyrian man in Chicago in 1917 than the thought of fighting and dying in the trenches of Western Europe. Once

---

[49] Topakian lost this position following a feud with 'Ali-Qoli Khān over which of them was going to represent Iran at the Panama-Pacific Exposition in San Francisco in 1915. 'Ali-Qoli prevailed, but in San Francisco he found himself scrambling to substantiate his authority after he was accused of "slandering" a doorman.

again, nationality was a fungible asset, instrumentalized as a form of protection by a vulnerable religious minority.

A closer look at the Chicago passport dispute provides a window into the mechanisms and infrastructure of Iranian diplomacy. More specifically, it confirms how badly those mechanisms had deteriorated by the middle of the 1910s. The problem began in the spring of 1916 when the Iranian minister in Washington, Mehdi Khān, discovered that Sarkis Baba had issued several passports to Chicago residents without the authority of the Washington legation, and without demanding that applicants produce expired passports as proof of their Iranian nationality. Mehdi responded by instructing the Chicago vice consul to refer all future applicants to Washington. In addition to the usual $2 fee for the new passport, applicants would have to pay a fine of either $3 or $5, depending on how many years their passport was in arrears.[50] Baba dutifully transmitted these instructions to the Assyrian community via announcements in local newspapers. It was at this point that matters escalated dramatically.

Incensed by what they believed was an act of extortion by the Iranian government, some two hundred Assyrian Iranians gathered at a raucous meeting called by Paul Newey, editor of the *Assyrian American Herald*. He was already involved in the controversy, having taken it upon himself to issue Iranian passports to local residents for a flat fee of $5.50. It was not clear where these "passports" came from, but Baba believed the source was "an Armenian in Philadelphia," perhaps Pakraduni.[51] Whatever the case, Newey spent much of the meeting denouncing the Washington legation and the Chicago consulate as "robbers and cut-throats and thieves." Rather than work through Iran's diplomatic corps, he told the crowd to go to the Russian consulate in Chicago to obtain free passports and travel documents for getting to Iran. The assembled locals met everything Newey said with "fierce" whistling and applause, and they shouted curses at the Iranian government. Baba responded by suing Newey in court for slander.[52]

For a time, the escalating dispute was resolved by a one-time amnesty issued by the Foreign Ministry in Tehran that allowed Chicago Assyrians to renew expired passports for a flat fee of $4.[53] But this was not the end of the matter. Mehdi accused Baba of failing to forward him money already collected for previously issued handwritten passports.[54] And so it continued. Endless letters and accusations now bounced between the two men, until eventually, Baba traveled to Washington to personally clear his name with his superior. This, too, went nowhere. By the summer of 1917, ʿAli-Qoli Khān, who on Mehdi's arrival had been demoted from *chargé* in Washington to consul-general of New York, waded into the dispute. He sided overtly with his protégé, Baba, and engaged in a vicious personal spat with Mehdi. Once again, the *casus belli* was the issue of passports. In August, Mehdi claimed that he had made three unsuccessful attempts to deliver passport stamps to ʿAli-Qoli at his residences in New York, Washington, and East Hampton, Long Island, but that in all three instances the post office was unable

[50] Baba to Mehdi Khān, 28 Rajab 1334 (May 31, 1916), FM 1366-21-3, fol. 14.
[51] Ibid.
[52] Baba to Mehdi, 9 Shaʿbān 1334 (June 11, 1916), FM 1336-21-3, ff. 4–5.
[53] Mehdi to Baba, 29 Zi al-Hejjeh 1334 (October 27, 1916), FM 1336-21-3, fol. 24.
[54] Mehdi to Baba, 14 Rabiʿ al-Avval 1335 (January 8, 1917), FM 1336-21-3, fol. 21.

to locate him. The implication was that he had no fixed abode. ʻAli-Qoli, for whom personal prestige was everything, took particular offense to this implication and sent copies of the US Diplomatic List to Tehran so the Foreign Ministry could verify his published postal addresses.[55] He also claimed that Mehdi had intentionally left his name off the packages to make them more difficult to deliver. "I don't know if the minister thinks I'm a child, or thinks he is trying to trick a child," ʻAli-Qoli fumed. "I am sending the delivery receipt, signed by my valet Reza, to you. I want you to see the unusual and unorthodox things he's been doing. I want to alert you to his behavior so he doesn't think I'm his vassal. I am a diplomat and special servant of the state, and after years of work, have earned this title."[56]

From Mehdi's perspective, ʻAli-Qoli spent far too much time cultivating his personal prestige among New York society and not enough time attending to consular work. "We need a consul in New York, and he's never there," Mehdi complained to Tehran. The postal address he claimed in New York was that of his handicapped father-in-law. "The Consul-General needs a permanent, fixed location, whether there is work there or not," Mehdi wrote. "He should be in the office one or two hours. I've asked him many times to find a fixed place for himself and attend to people's needs."[57]

Ultimately, the dispute boiled down to a matter of personal style and understandings of how Iranian society should be projected in an increasingly globalized world. ʻAli-Qoli, the suave cosmopolitan sophisticate, was most at ease in the company of American socialites and felt that he was being attacked for his worldliness. Mehdi, the pious Iranian traditionalist, felt that ʻAli-Qoli put on too many airs and graces. There was, no doubt, an element of Muslim-Bahāʻi tension, laced with its nationalist-internationalist fault lines, running through the dispute. Mehdi suggested that "if ʻAli-Qoli is really ready to be consul, it would be better for him to come and host his dinners and parties in New York City" rather than the Hamptons. "He only wanted this job for his own prestige; not because he wanted to be of service to the country."[58]

Lost was the actual issue of the passports and the fate of the young Iranian men attempting to avoid being drafted into the US military. The Foreign Ministry in Tehran, when it was not busy adjudicating the personal squabbles of its American consuls, took a dim view of Assyrian Iranian draft dodging, arguing that it was good for young Iranians to serve in a Western military force to learn important skills that would be of use both to them and to Iran.[59] It is easy to see why Tehran might have adopted this attitude, given the threat that would have been posed by large numbers of disloyal Iranian exiles returning to fight against the Kurds and their Ottoman allies in the increasingly lawless northwest frontier of Iran. There was also the question of wartime strategy. Though officially neutral in the war, Qajar Iran was generally sympathetic to the Ottomans and the Central Powers. Whatever the case, the consuls in the United States seemed far less interested in these matters of national security than they were in settling the insults against their personal dignity. In September 1917, as Sarkis Baba stood accused by

[55] ʻAli-Qoli Khān to Foreign Ministry, 21 Shavvāl 1335 (August 10, 1917), FM 1336-21-1, fol. 5.
[56] ʻAli-Qoli Khān to Foreign Ministry, 14 Zi al-Qaʻdeh 1335 (September 1, 1917), FM 1336-21-1, ff. 23–4.
[57] Mehdi to Foreign Ministry, 12 Zi al-Qaʻdeh 1335 (August 30, 1917), FM 1336-21-1, ff. 44–6.
[58] Ibid.
[59] ʻAli-Qoli Khān to Foreign Ministry, 7 Jomādā al-Avval 1336 (February 18, 1918), FM 1336-21-1, fol. 31.

Mehdi of profiteering and embezzlement, the Foreign Ministry suggested stripping the Chicago vice consul of his post. In response to these attacks, ʿAli-Qoli Khān attempted to defend his Assyrian friend by noting that "he is a man of wealth, and doesn't disgrace himself for four dollars like certain Armenians."[60]

This was a pointed remark. ʿAli-Qoli held a deep personal animus for Topakian, whom he had replaced in New York and with whom he had tussled for the position of Iranian commissioner to the Panama-Pacific Exposition in California in 1915. By contrast, ʿAli-Qoli was close to Sarkis Baba, whom he had recommended for the position of Chicago vice consul. Mehdi, meanwhile, seemed more at ease with Topakian than any of the other consuls for whom he nursed a thoroughgoing disdain. One would never have known that, somewhere in the world, there was an actual war going on.

The Foreign Ministry in Tehran came to be utterly exhausted by these tedious disputes and repeatedly urged all parties to set aside their disagreements and focus on serving the national interest.[61] But it was of little use. By the end of 1917, the disagreement between Mehdi and ʿAli-Qoli descended into unrestrained bickering. ʿAli-Qoli felt Mehdi's simple and unpretentious lifestyle to be something of an embarrassment to his country. "I drive a $4000 car and am the toast of Washington," snorted ʿAli-Qoli in one of his dispatches. "Mehdi lives in a small rented flat with only one servant."[62] Mehdi retorted that ʿAli-Qoli wines and dines "all and sundry" and insisted that diplomacy was about more than just "fancy outfits."[63] ʿAli-Qoli, he said, was an attention-seeking *bon vivant* who spent too much time in the Hamptons to be able to take his job seriously. ʿAli-Qoli, in turn, claimed that Mehdi had amassed piles of unpaid vehicular registration fines and that the newspapers were reporting on this embarrassment to Iran.[64] Mehdi, he claimed, was attacking him "because he sees that I have prestige and property and reputation in the US. Maybe he should spend the 8000 tomans he gets, and the 20 or 30 thousand he has, on a proper home. And if he doesn't want to do even this much, why does he keep pestering me?"[65] Eventually, the Foreign Ministry in Tehran removed both men from their positions.

Conclusion

It is easy to get lost in the myriad of personal and professional disputes that characterized the late Qajar diplomatic corps in the United States. In fact, the drama far exceeded the examples presented in this chapter. However, it is important to identify the overarching phenomena that these examples reveal. Three are important: the many arenas of Qajar dysfunction, the position of ethno-religious minorities in Iran, and the emergence of the US-Iran relationship.

---

[60] ʿAli-Qoli Khān to Foreign Ministry, 14 Zi al-Qaʿdeh 1335 (September 1, 1917), FM 1336-21-1, ff. 23–4.
[61] Instructions, 6 Safar 1336 (November 21, 1917), FM 1336-21-1, fol. 5.1; telegram from Foreign Ministry, Office of US Affairs, to ʿAli-Qoli Khān, 25 Safar 1336 (December 10, 1917), FM 1336-21-1, fol. 7.
[62] ʿAli-Qoli Khān to Foreign Ministry, 14 Zi al-Qaʿdeh 1335 (September 1, 1917), FM 1336-21-1, ff. 23–4.
[63] Mehdi to Foreign Ministry, 12 Zi al-Qaʿdeh 1335 (August 30, 1917), FM 1336-21-1, ff. 44–6.
[64] ʿAli-Qoli Khān to Foreign Ministry, 14 Zi al-Qaʿdeh 1335 (September 1, 1917), FM 1336-21-1, ff. 23–4.
[65] Ibid.

Collectively, the cases presented here underscore the fundamental dysfunction of the Qajar state, as well as the remarkably fluid notion of Iranian national belonging that often accompanied that dysfunction. For virtually every character in this story, with the possible exception of Mehdi, the notion of "being Iranian" was, in one way or another, a fungible commodity—instrumentalized when convenient, jettisoned when superfluous. In a clearer manner than the traditional narratives about Mozaffar al-Din Shah and European concessions, this chapter demonstrates the growing inability of the Qajar state to exert centralized control or exercise meaningful sovereignty during its final years.

This is also a story of ethno-religious minorities in Iran and their transnational networks of kinship, survival, and competition. What does it mean, for example, that every Armenian involved in Iranian consular work in the United States during this period seemed to hail from Kayseri, in Turkey, and that nearly all were highly competitive antiques dealers or rug traders? What does it mean that Iran's most senior diplomatic representative in the United States for a time was a Bahā'i—a situation that was unlikely to have been officially tolerated by, and may well have been kept secret from, Tehran? What does it mean that this well-connected Bahā'i seemed to nurse a hatred of Armenians but a closeness to the Assyrian community of Chicago? Why did Iran's minister in Washington seem more comfortable in the company of Armenians than anyone else? And finally, to whom exactly did the Assyrian young men of Chicago's Near North Side "belong"? Were they Iranians or Americans? Both or neither? And who had the power to determine the answer to such questions? While the focus of this chapter has been on the United States, these are precisely the kinds of questions that consumed Iran in the early 1900s, as constitutionalists and others attempted to forge a modern state from the ashes of a decaying absolutist kingdom in a way that incorporated "citizenship" rights and some notion of national belonging for all native-born Iranians. And they are precisely the kinds of questions that should interest historians of Iran who seek to color between the lines of the received narrative about political decline, constitutionalism, and revolution in the early twentieth century.

The answers to these questions reframe the history of Iran's bilateral diplomacy with the United States in a way that diverges from the narratives and methods of traditional diplomatic historians. Unable to rely on a truly professional, paid cadre of career diplomats and consuls sent from Tehran, Iran during these years conferred the title of honorary consul on a number of wealthy émigrés—most from the Ottoman Empire but at least one from Brazil—and asked them to represent Iranian commercial interests in major US cities. For a time, this was done with considerable professionalism. But when the Iranian state began to disintegrate in the 1910s, that same infrastructure of outsourced consular representation became an Achilles heel in Iran's ability to manage its interests in the United States. In the process, the evolution and devolution of the late Qajar diplomatic corps in the United States turned up some fascinating questions about what it meant to be "Iranian" in these years—as well as what it meant to be "American."

2

The Shuster Mission of 1911 and American Perceptions of Iran's First Revolution

Kelly J. Shannon

Iran's first revolution, the Constitutional Revolution (1905–11), was the first mass democratic movement in the Islamic world.[1] During the revolution, Iranian nationalists successfully advocated for a constitutional monarchy; fought to defend their recently adopted constitution from Mohammad Ali Shah Qajar, who sought to quash the country's fledgling parliament after he took the throne in 1907; and battled to maintain their nation's sovereignty in the face of Russian and British imperial manipulation. While the United States was not a central player in Iranian affairs during this period, a handful of Americans, mostly missionaries and financial experts, nevertheless became involved in the revolution and consequently shaped American and Iranian views of one another. The most influential of these Americans was 34-year-old financial expert W. Morgan Shuster, who led a small group of Americans to advise constitutionalist Iran in its attempts to reform its financial system during the final year of the revolution.

The democratic impulse of Iranian constitutionalists—as well as Shuster's powerful position as Iran's treasurer-general, his sensational ouster by imperial Russia in December 1911, and his public relations campaign to promote sympathy for Iran's constitutionalists—influenced the attentive American public's perceptions of and support for Iran. It was during the Constitutional Revolution that large numbers of Americans and Iranians formed enduring perceptions of one another that contextualized future American-Iranian interactions. The roles played by non-state actors, public opinion, and cultural perceptions are therefore important to understanding the broader history of US-Iran relations, alongside official state-to-state relations. While Iran historically did not feature much in the American imagination, Shuster's story and outspoken support for Iran's constitutionalists stirred support for their cause in the US public sphere at the time. The constitutionalists' attempts to reform their country and defend its sovereignty from British and Russian

---

[1] Americans typically referred to Iran as "Persia" until the early 1930s. I use the terms "Persia" and "Iran" interchangeably in this chapter to refer to the nation of Iran.

imperialism appealed to Progressive Era Americans' notions of justice, democracy, and fair play. Consequently, Iranians became more sympathetic and legible to the "attentive public"—that is, those Americans who regularly followed the news and global affairs.[2]

The Constitutional Revolution and US-Iran Relations

At the dawn of the twentieth century, Iran was a nation in turmoil. The Qajar Dynasty and its monarchs had failed to meet the needs of its people. Various shahs attempted uneven and ultimately failed reform programs over the course of the nineteenth century, leaving the country with an "arbitrary and unsystematic" government, in the words of historian Vanessa Martin.[3] Moreover, while Europeans never formally colonized Iran, the country was caught in the middle of the "Great Game" between Russia and Great Britain. The two empires forced a series of economic concessions from the Qajar government that gave them monopolies over key industries, including the infamous D'Arcy oil concession to Britain in 1901. The Russians set up the Cossack Brigade in 1879, a modern, disciplined army supposedly loyal to the shah but led by Russian officers.[4] It became clear that the Qajars were unable to resist foreign manipulation, and each new concession sparked popular protests. The turn of the twentieth century also brought a wave of revolutionary upheaval across the globe. Much like Russia, China, Portugal, Mexico, and the Ottoman Empire, Iran was ripe for revolution in the early years of the new century.[5]

Mass grassroots protests broke out in the summer of 1905 and continued through 1906, as tens of thousands of Iranians called for the creation of new laws, the fairer enforcement of existing laws, the removal of foreign influence, and the creation of a representative national assembly. Mozaffar al-Din Shah Qajar (r. 1896–1907) finally acceded to the protesters' demands and signed an order in August 1906 to convene a national assembly, which drafted a constitution that October. The shah died in January 1907, just five days after he ratified the new constitution. Iran had become a constitutional monarchy with limited royal power and an elected parliament, or Majles.

[2] For a discussion of the "attentive public" and the role of public opinion in US foreign relations, see Melvin Small, "Public Opinion," in *Explaining the History of American Foreign Relations*, 1st ed., ed. Michael J. Hogan and Thomas G. Paterson (Cambridge: Cambridge University Press, 1991), 166–7.
[3] Vanessa Martin, *Islam and Modernism: The Iranian Revolution of 1906* (Syracuse, NY: Syracuse University Press, 1989), 10.
[4] Michael Axworthy, *Empire of the Mind: A History of Iran* (New York: Basic Books, 2008), 192–200; and M. Reza Ghods, *Iran in the Twentieth Century: A Political History* (Boulder, CO: Lynne Rienner, 1989), 13–30.
[5] Egas Moniz Bandeira, "China and the Political Upheavals in Russia, the Ottoman Empire, and Persia: Non-Western Influences on Constitutional Thinking in Late Imperial China, 1893–1911," *Journal of Transcultural Studies* 8, no. 2 (2017): 40–78; Charles Kurzman,"*Mashrutiyat, Mesrutiyet*, and Beyond: Intellectuals and the Constitutional Revolutions of 1905–12," in *Iran's Constitutional Revolution: Popular Politics, Cultural Transformations and Transnational Connections*, ed. Houchang Chehabi and Vanessa Martin (London: I.B. Tauris in Association with Iran Heritage Foundation, 2010); Nader Sohrabi, "Historicizing Revolutions: Constitutional Revolutions in the Ottoman Empire, Iran, and Russia, 1905–1908," *American Journal of Sociology* 100, no. 6 (1995): 1383–447; and Erik Jan Zürcher, "The Young Turk Revolution: Comparisons and Connections," *Middle Eastern Studies* 55, no. 4 (2019): 481–98.

The new shah, Mohammad Ali Shah Qajar (r. 1907–9), was determined to roll back the revolution. He bided his time until June 1908, when he ordered the Cossack Brigade to bombard the Majles. After the delegates surrendered, the shah closed the assembly, arrested and executed some of its leaders, and returned the country to absolute rule. Unwilling to abandon their fledgling democracy, constitutionalists resisted the shah fiercely in the provinces. They eventually won the day in July 1909 when they seized the capital city of Tehran, deposed Mohammad Ali Shah and replaced him with his young son, and reinstated the Majles. For the next two years, the Majles governed without royal interference. During this period, constitutionalist Iran struggled to extricate itself from debt to European banks, end British and Russian imperial meddling in Iran's affairs, and build a modern nation-state. In the end, the constitutionalist movement failed largely because of foreign intervention; Russia invaded Iran in December 1911 and brought the revolution to an end.[6]

Unlike Russia and Great Britain, the United States had little to do with Iran's revolution. After establishing diplomatic contact in the 1850s, the US government's relationship with Iran through the first decade of the twentieth century was generally friendly but distant.[7] Direct diplomatic dealings between the two nations before the First World War were minimal, and the United States maintained a strict policy of noninvolvement in Iran's affairs during the Constitutional Revolution, even when American citizens were directly involved in the revolutionary upheaval.[8] This meant

---

[6] Axworthy, *Empire of the Mind*, 202–7; Hamid Dabashi, *Iran: A People Interrupted* (New York: New Press, 2007), 67–104; Fakhreddin Azimi, *The Quest for Democracy in Iran: A Century of Struggle Against Authoritarian Rule* (Cambridge, MA: Harvard University Press, 2008), 19–43; and Ghods, *Iran in the Twentieth Century*, 30–44. For more on the Constitutional Revolution, see Janet Afary, *The Iranian Constitutional Revolution, 1906–1911: Grassroots Democracy, Social Democracy, and the Origins of Feminism* (New York: Columbia University Press, 1996); Ali M. Ansari, ed., *Iran's Constitutional Revolution of 1906 and Narratives of Enlightenment* (London: Gingko Library, 2016); Mangol Bayat, *Iran's First Revolution: Shi'ism and the Constitutional Revolution of 1905–1909* (New York: Oxford University Press, 1991); Chehabi and Martin, eds., *Iran's Constitutional Revolution*; Ahmad Kasravi, *History of the Iranian Constitutional Revolution, Volume One*, trans. Evan Siegel (Costa Mesa, CA: Mazda, 2006); Ahmad Kasravi, *History of the Iranian Constitutional Revolution, Volumes Two and Three*, trans. Evan Siegel (Costa Mesa, CA: Mazda, 2015); Vanessa Martin, *Iran Between Islamic Nationalism and Secularism: The Constitutional Revolution of 1906* (London: I.B. Taurus, 2013); and Martin, *Islam and Modernism*.

[7] American-Persian Treaty of Friendship and Commerce, December 13, 1856, ratified and entered into force June 13, 1857, in *The United States and Iran: A Documentary History*, ed. Yonah Alexander and Allan Nanes (Frederick, MD: Aletheia Books, 1980), 2–5; James Bill, *The Eagle and the Lion: The Tragedy of American-Iranian Relations* (New Haven, CT: Yale University Press, 1988), 16; and Firoozeh Kashani-Sabet, "The Portals of Persepolis: The Role of Nationalism in Early U.S.-Iranian Relations," in *Rethinking Iranian Nationalism and Modernity*, ed. Kamran Scot Aghaie and Afshin Marashi (Austin: University of Texas Press, 2014), 139.

[8] For examples, see: Letter from John N. Wright to Robert E. Speer, April 22, 1909, Presbyterian Church of the USA Board of Foreign Missions Correspondence and Reports, 1833–1911, microfilm, reel 274, volume 204, Presbyterian Historical Society, Philadelphia, PA; Document No. 51, letter from Acting Secretary of State Huntington Wilson to Charles F. Russell, American Minister to Tehran, September 6, 1911, Record Group (RG) 59, Records of the Department of State, Central Decimal File, 891.00 Political Affairs [891.00 General] 891.00/500–737, Records of the Department of State Relating to Internal Affairs of Persia, 1910–1929, microfilm no. 715, roll 3, US National Archives and Records Administration II (hereafter NARA), College Park, MD; and File No. 761.91/12, Telegram from the Secretary of State [Philander Knox] to the American Minister at Teheran [Charles F. Russell], December 1, 1911, *Papers Relating to the Foreign Relations of the United States, with the Annual Message to the President Transmitted to Congress December 7, 1911* (Washington, DC: US Government Printing Office, 1918), document 993. Available online: https://history.state.gov/historicaldocuments/frus1911/d993 (accessed August 8, 2018).

that people acting in a private capacity, not US diplomats or policymakers, were the Americans who exercised the most power in shaping the American-Iranian relationship during the early twentieth century. These non-state actors included American missionaries, financial experts, journalists, and authors of travelogues and other cultural products that reflected and shaped American perceptions of Iran.

The Constitutional Revolution is primarily a story about the collision of Iran's aspirations for sovereignty, justice, and democracy with British and Russian imperialism. Americans contributed little to the drama that unfolded in Iran. Despite the constitutionalists' hopes that the United States would support their cause, and despite the attentive American public's support for the revolution, the US government remained strictly neutral regarding Iran's political situation. This was in keeping with long-standing American foreign policy tradition. Americans in Iran at the time also generally attempted to remain above the fray, although some missionaries—whose presence in Iran dated to the 1830s—expressed support for and provided medical care and supplies to constitutionalist rebels as they battled royalist forces in 1908–9.[9] In the sole instance of an American taking up arms, the 24-year-old missionary Howard Baskerville died while fighting alongside the constitutionalists in Tabriz in April 1909.[10] Yet Baskerville was more useful to the revolutionaries as a martyr and symbol of American friendship than he had been as a fighter.

There was one American who played an outsized role in the final phase of the Constitutional Revolution: W. Morgan Shuster. From May through December 1911, Shuster and his small team of fellow Americans worked to reorganize the Iranian government's finances. Shuster and the three other American financial experts—Frank S. Cairns, Charles I. McCaskey, and Bruce G. Dickey—who accompanied him to Tehran in 1911 were state actors prior to their sojourn in Iran. All had served in the US colonial administration of the Philippines and/or Cuba.[11] However, in keeping with

---

[9] Letter from Wright to Speer; and Abraham Yeselson, *United States-Persian Diplomatic Relations, 1883–1921* (New Brunswick, NJ: Rutgers University Press, 1956), 94–8.

[10] Letter from Wright to Speer; Yeselson, *United States-Persian Diplomatic Relations*, 94–8; Letter from Annie R. Wilson to Mr. and Mrs. Baskerville, Tabriz, Persia, April 20–30, 1909, PCUSA BFM Corresp., reel 274, vol. 204, Presbyterian Historical Society; S. Rezazadeh Shafaq, *Howard Baskerville: The Story of an American Who Died in the Cause of Iranian Freedom and Independence* (Cambridge, MA: Ty Aur Press, 2008 [1959]); Firoozeh Kashani-Sabet, "American Crosses, Persian Crescents: Religion and the Diplomacy of US-Iranian Relations, 1834–1911," *Iranian Studies* 44, no. 5 (2011): 623; and Address by Shafaq at memorial and plaque-unveiling ceremony at the grave of Howard C. Baskerville, Tabriz, Iran, September 1950, Alumni Records Collection, Howard C. Baskerville, 1907, File #AC104, Seeley G. Mudd Manuscript Library, Princeton University, Princeton, NJ.

[11] E. J. Edwards, "Five Young Yankees Will Reform Persia's Finances: Will Make an Entire Reorganization of the Ancient Financial System of the Newly Awakened Monarchy," *New York Times*, April 16, 1911, Sunday Magazine, SM9. Ralph W. Hills, who had not served in Cuba or the Philippines, also traveled with Shuster as far as Constantinople in the spring of 1911, but he never made it to Iran because his children became ill and he had to return home. Shuster, Cairns, McCaskey, Dickey, and Hills all brought their families with them, which was unusual for foreign advisers to the Iranian government. An additional eleven American men came to Tehran to join Shuster's team months later, but they did not arrive until November–December 1911. These new arrivals had little impact because of the Russian invasion and Shuster's dismissal. W. Morgan Shuster, *The Strangling of Persia: Story of the European Diplomacy and Oriental Intrigue That Resulted in the Denationalization of Twelve Million Mohammedans: A Personal Narrative* (New York: Century, 1912; Washington, DC: Mage, 1987), 216.

policy at the time, these men severed all official ties with the US government in order to contract their services to Iran as private citizens; in the view of the United States, these Americans were non-state actors. Once in Iran, however, in an arrangement that was unusual for American advisers to foreign governments, the men held Iranian government positions. Shuster himself occupied the powerful post of treasurer-general. From the Iranian perspective, the men of the Shuster Mission were Iranian state actors, although they remained foreigners and conceivably informal representatives of the United States.

The Historiography of Early US-Iran Relations

Many historians have acknowledged the auspicious beginnings of the US-Iran relationship, but few have examined the period before the Second World War in depth. The body of English-language scholarship on the early period of US-Iran relations is small, and the subset that examines American-Iranian relations during the Constitutional Revolution is smaller still—although there is a robust literature on the revolution itself. With the exception of articles and book chapters by Firoozeh Kashani-Sabet, publications on US-Iran relations during the Constitutional Revolution consist primarily of orthodox studies of state-to-state diplomacy, as well as of the Shuster Mission.[12] But these studies leave out questions of culture, public opinion, and the impact of non-state actors.

The activities of American Protestant missionaries in Iran have garnered relatively more scholarly attention, and existing scholarship provides a sense of their impact on Iranians in the nineteenth and early twentieth centuries. While the missionaries won few converts to American-style Protestantism, the schools and hospitals they founded and ran provided welcome services for the Iranian people. The scholarship on American missionaries in Iran primarily consists of excellent journal articles by scholars such as Jasamin Rostam-Kolayi and Michael Zirinsky. They illustrate how American missionaries influenced Iranian nationalism and modernism, and they detail how missionary activities often fostered a positive image of the United States among

---

[12] Bill, *The Eagle and the Lion*; Kashani-Sabet, "American Crosses, Persian Crescents"; Kashani-Sabet, "Portals of Persepolis"; Kamyar Ghaneabassiri, "U.S. Foreign Policy and Persia, 1856–1921," *Iranian Studies* 35, nos. 1–3 (2002): 155–61; Yeselson, *United States-Persian Diplomatic Relations*; John A. DeNovo, *American Interests and Policies in the Near East, 1900–1939* (Minneapolis: University of Minnesota Press, 1963); James F. Goode, "A Good Start: The First American Mission to Iran, 1883–1885," *Muslim World* 74, no. 2 (1984): 100–18; Goode, "Samuel Benjamin: Unorthodox Observer of the Middle East," *Islam and Christian-Muslim Relations* 9, no. 1 (1998): 23–9; Mehdi Heravi, *Iranian-American Diplomacy* (Bethesda, MD: Ibex, 1999 [1969]); Badi Badiozamani and Ghazal Badiozamani, *Iran and America: Rekindling a Love Lost* (Manhattan Beach, CA: East-West Understanding Press, 2005); and Mansour Bonakdarian, "U.S.-Iranian Relations, 1911–1951," Iran Chamber Society, n.d. Available online: http://www.iranchamber.com/history/articles/pdfs/us_ir_1911_1951.pdf (accessed July 24, 2015).

Iranians.¹³ However, most of these studies are not in conversation with diplomatic history and do not center on the Constitutional Revolution specifically.

Shuster is well known to historians of US-Iran relations, yet he remains curiously understudied. Studies of the early binational relationship or of the Constitutional Revolution that discuss the Shuster Mission mostly mention it in passing; historians generally characterize the mission as marking the beginning of the period of friendly American-Iranian relations.¹⁴ There exists only one book-length study of the Shuster Mission, published in 1974, but it is primarily a narrative history with little analysis and a limited source base.¹⁵ Shuster's own book, *The Strangling of Persia*, published in 1912, remains the most substantive account of his time in Iran.¹⁶ To date, scholars have not gone beyond recounting and sometimes evaluating Shuster's actions, and they suggest that he created a positive impression of Americans *in* Iran at the time. None have really analyzed his views or his impact on American public perceptions *of* Iran.

---

[13] Md. Abul Kalam Azad, "Legacy of the American Presbyterian Mission in Iran," *Journal of the Asiatic Society of Bangladesh* (Hum.) 58, no. 1 (2013): 191–205; Adam Becker, *Revival and Awakening: American Evangelical Missionaries in Iran and the Origins of Assyrian Nationalism* (Chicago: University of Chicago Press, 2015); Houchang Chehabi, "Diversity at Alborz," *Iranian Studies* 44, no. 5 (2011): 715–29; Joseph L. Grabill, *Protestant Diplomacy and the Near East: Missionary Influence on American Policy, 1810-1927* (Minneapolis: University of Minnesota Press, 1971); Linda Colleen Karimi, "Implications of American Missionary Presence in 19th and 20th Century Iran" (MA thesis, Portland State University, 1975), Dissertations and Theses. Available online: https://pdxscholar.library.pdx.edu/open_access_etds/1827/ (accessed September 3, 2017); Jasamin Rostam-Kolayi, "From Evangelizing to Modernizing Iranians: The American Presbyterian Mission and its Iranian Students," *Iranian Studies* 41, no. 2 (2008): 213–40; Michael P. Zirinsky, "Harbingers of Change: Presbyterian Women in Iran, 1883–1949," *American Presbyterians* 70, no. 3 (1992): 173–86; and Michael Zirinsky, "A Panacea for the Ills of the Country: American Presbyterian Education in Interwar Iran," *American Presbyterians* 72, no. 3 (1994): 187–201. Firoozeh Kashani-Sabet published an article that placed missionary activity in a broader perspective, mostly in the context of American and Iranian views of one another's religions, but diplomacy and other forms of engagement between the two nations did not appear in her analysis. See Kashani-Sabet, "American Crosses, Persian Crescents," 607–25.

[14] Afary, *Iranian Constitutional Revolution*, 7, 177, 184, 186, 204, 308–10, 314, 323, 332–3, 336, 339–40; Azimi, *Quest for Democracy in Iran*, 42–3; Badiozamani and Badiozamani, *Iran and America*, 23–5; Amin Banani, *The Modernization of Iran, 1921-1941* (Stanford, CA: Stanford University Press, 1961), 37–8; David Collier, *Democracy and the Nature of American Influence in Iran, 1941-1979* (Syracuse, NY: Syracuse University Press, 2017), 7–8, 300; Dabashi, *Iran*, 83–5, 102; Ghaneabassiri, "U.S. Foreign Policy and Persia," 155–61; Ghods, *Iran in the Twentieth Century*, 43–4; Nathan Gonzalez, *Engaging Iran: The Rise of a Middle East Powerhouse and America's Strategic Choice* (Westport, CT: Praeger Security International, 2007), 32, 34–5; Grabill, *Protestant Diplomacy and the Near East*, 147, 149–50; Heravi, *Iranian-American Diplomacy*, 20, 23, 25, 30–3, 53–7, 114; Kashani-Sabet, "Portals of Persepolis," 152–3; Stephen Kinzer, *All the Shah's Men: An American Coup and the Roots of Middle East Terror* (Hoboken, NJ: John Wiley and Sons, 2008), 37; Akan Malici and Stephen G. Walker, *Role Theory and Role Conflict in U.S.-Iran Relations: Enemies of Our Own Making* (New York: Routledge, 2017), 27–30, 36; Martin, *Islam and Modernism*, 190; Michael Kahl Sheehan, *Iran: The Impact of United States Interests and Policies, 1941-1954* (Brooklyn, NY: Theo. Gaus' Sons, 1968), 2–3; and Yeselson, *United States-Persian Diplomatic Relations*, 112, 105–28, 153, 181–93, 228, 230. Remarkably, James Bill's now-classic study, which discusses other Americans who had an impact on US-Iran relations prior to the Second World War, contains no mention of Shuster. Bill, *The Eagle and the Lion*. See also the apparently unpublished manuscript: Elisha P. Douglass, "Anglo-Russian Friction, 1907–1911, and the Morgan Shuster Affair," 1947, Box 1, W. Morgan Shuster Papers, MMC323, Manuscript Division, Library of Congress, Washington, DC.

[15] Robert A. McDaniel, *The Shuster Mission and the Persian Constitutional Revolution* (Minneapolis, MN: Bibliotheca Islamica, 1974), 124–210.

[16] Shuster, *Strangling of Persia*.

Though the existing literature on early US-Iran relations offers valuable insight into the foundations of American-Iranian engagement, the current literature offers only episodic and fragmentary glimpses of this important period.[17] This chapter seeks to enhance scholarly knowledge of this early period by analyzing the perceptions of constitutionalist Iran in the US public sphere and Shuster's influence on these perceptions. Moreover, this is the first study to explain Shuster and his mission on their own terms. As Iran's treasurer-general, Shuster attempted to institute financial reforms and to shield Iran from British and Russian imperialism. Previous financial advisers from Europe had either used their positions in Iran to enrich themselves or had done the bidding of Russia and Great Britain. In contrast, Shuster and his team befriended the constitutionalists and nationalists in the Majles, snubbed the European legations, declared British and Russian interests in Iran illegitimate, and worked seriously to provide Iran with an efficient and modernized treasury. Russia eventually intervened to oust Shuster, suspend the Majles, and end the revolution. Consequently, other scholars have concluded that Shuster's actions caused many Iranians to see Americans positively.[18]

I argue that Shuster pushed the attentive American public to see Iranians—at least the constitutionalists—positively, as well. Public opinion and cultural perceptions remain underexplored aspects of the early binational relationship, yet American views of Iran and Iranians are important components of a more complete understanding of US-Iran relations. The meaning that Americans and Iranians derived from their early interactions, and the perceptions of one another during the revolution, formed an important basis for later binational engagements as the United States became increasingly entangled in Iran's affairs over the course of the twentieth century. The Shuster Mission, in particular, played a critical role in influencing how many Americans at the time understood Iran and its first revolution.

The Shuster Mission

Morgan Shuster is an intriguing figure. Born in Washington, DC in 1877, he was a graduate of Colombian University and Law School, which is today George Washington University. In 1899, while still in his early twenties, Shuster went to Cuba to work in customs collection; he left Cuba in 1901 to become the US customs collector in Manila. Starting in 1906, Shuster was the Secretary of Public Instruction in the Philippines and a member of the Second Philippine Commission, headed by future president William

---

[17] John Ghazvinian's book on the entire history of US-Iran relations fills in many topical and methodological gaps in the historiography. John Ghazvinian, *America and Iran: A History, 1720 to the Present* (New York: Knopf, 2021).

[18] Ghaneabassiri, "U.S. Foreign Policy and Persia," 155; Kashani-Sabet, "Portals of Persepolis," 152; McDaniel, *Shuster Mission and the Persian Constitutional Revolution*; and Homa Katouzian, "Prologue: The Poetry of the Constitutional Revolution," in *Iran's Constitutional Revolution*, ed. Chehabi and Martin, 1, 9.

Howard Taft.[19] Shuster resigned in early 1909 and returned home to Washington, DC, where he practiced law until going to Iran in 1911 at the age of 34. Thus, his early career followed the streams of empire. He was first an agent of US imperialism in Cuba and the Philippines, and he then became an outspoken critic of European imperialism in Iran.

Unfortunately, the historical record on Shuster prior to 1911 is spotty. Shuster's personal papers focus in great detail on his time in Iran and the months immediately following his return home, but they omit his decade in Cuba and the Philippines almost entirely.[20] Based on the available US government documents relating to Shuster's work in the Philippines, it appears as though Shuster wholeheartedly embraced the American "civilizing mission" during that period.[21] He was also the epitome of white, middle-class Progressivism; he believed in honesty, expertise, fair play, and efficient management. Progressivism was diverse and encompassed a multitude of movements, but Shuster belonged to a generation of Progressives who—despite their differences—sought to "wield state power on behalf of the common good."[22] Along with their quest for social justice at home, many American Progressives also looked abroad. Although Progressives disagreed sharply over the colonization of new territories like the Philippines, Progressive internationalists hoped "their reformist efforts at home might become part of a wider, global transformation in which popular needs would surpass the dictates of laissez-faire, and participatory democracy would replace imperial and dictatorial tyranny."[23] Such beliefs drove Shuster's work as a tool of US empire-building in Cuba and the Philippines, as well as his later efforts on behalf of Iranian constitutionalism. As customs collector in Manila, Shuster sought to eliminate corruption and enforced the letter of the law, even when he disagreed with it.[24] His

---

[19] Certificate of appointment of W. Morgan Shuster to Collector of Customs for the Philippine Islands by the Civil Governor of the Philippine Islands, September 15, 1901, Box 1, Shuster Papers; Certificate of appointment of W. Morgan Shuster to Insular Collector of Customs by the Governor-General of the Philippine Islands, November 1, 1905, Box 1, Shuster Papers; and Certificate of appointment of W. Morgan Shuster to the Philippine Commission by President Theodore Roosevelt, December 10, 1906, Box 1, Shuster Papers.

[20] Shuster Papers.

[21] The collections at NARA College Park containing information on Shuster's time in the Philippines are as follows: RG 350, Records of the Bureau of Insular Affairs, Philippine Commission, Library Materials; RG 350, Records of the Bureau of Insular Affairs, General Classified Files, 1898–1914 [Declassified NND 760024]; and RG 350, Records of the Bureau of Insular Affairs, General Records Relating to More Than One Island Possession, Classified Files Relating to Custom Matters in the Island Possessions, 1898–1914. These records are frustratingly incomplete and only contain a few scattered letters relating to or authored by Shuster during his time as customs collector in Manila, as well as his annual reports as customs collector and Secretary of Public Instruction and the annual reports of the Philippine Commission. Much of the records on Shuster from 1901 to 1909 appear not to have been retained by NARA.

[22] Glen Gendzel, "What the Progressives Had in Common," *Journal of the Gilded Age and Progressive Era* 10, no. 3 (2011): 333.

[23] Michael E. Latham, "Progressive Internationalism and the Road Not Taken," *Reviews in American History* 31, no. 4 (2003): 288. See also Alan Dawley, *Changing the World: American Progressives in War and Revolution* (Princeton, NJ: Princeton University Press, 2003).

[24] C-60-84: Letter from W. Morgan Shuster to Col. Clarence Edwards, April 7, 1902, Entry 8, Box 7 (C-38 to C-60-95), RG 350, Records of the Bureau of Insular Affairs, General Records Relating to More Than One Island Possession, Classified Files Relating to Custom Matters in the Island Possessions, 1898–1914, NARA; and C-60-88: "Exhibit D," W. Morgan Shuster's recommendations for revising Chinese Exclusion, March 24, 1902 (enclosed with C-60-84), Entry 8, Box 7, RG 350.

punctiliousness often made him unpopular, although it impressed his superiors.[25] While only his official reports as Secretary of Public Instruction appear to have survived, he seems to have been just as diligent and reform-minded in this post.[26]

The Shuster who went to Iran in 1911 still embodied the Progressive spirit, but he was quite different in one respect: Shuster became an anti-imperialist. In 1911 through 1912, Shuster was an outspoken critic of Russian and British imperial attempts to subjugate Iran. After his return home, he publicly denounced imperialism in general—including the version practiced by the United States.[27] It is possible that Shuster was changed by his years in the Philippines, and that his experiences there pushed him down an anti-colonial path that became more pronounced in Iran. Shuster had resigned his position as Secretary of Public Instruction in the Philippines for reasons unknown.[28] He may simply have wanted to return home after nearly a decade away, but it is also possible that his front-row view of American empire in action planted seeds of doubt about the "civilizing mission." While Shuster did not criticize American imperialism before going to Iran, he never again worked for the US government after leaving the Philippines, despite opportunities to do so. President Taft invited Shuster to head an American commission to Liberia in the spring of 1909, but he declined the position and chose to practice law instead.[29]

---

[25] C-60-79: Letter from W. Morgan Shuster to Col. Clarence Edwards, December 13, 1901, Entry 8, Box 7, RG 350; C-60-84: Letter from Shuster to Edwards, April 7, 1902; C-60-85: "Exhibit A," description of smuggling and other customs violations and how Shuster responded, March 11, 1902 (enclosed with C-60-84), Entry 8, Box 7, RG 350; C-60-90: Letter from Mr. D. Samson complaining about W. Morgan Shuster, March 7, 1902 (enclosed with C-60-84), Entry 8, Box 7, RG 350; C-567-after 11: Telegram from Col. Clarence Edwards to William Howard Taft, June 5, 1901, Entry 8, Box 27 (C-531-53 to C-572-25), RG 350; C-567-15: Letter from Charles. A. Conant to Col. Clarence Edwards, enclosing newspaper clipping praising W. Morgan Shuster, September 15, 1901, Entry 8, Box 27, RG 350. See also G. S. Weigall, plaintiff-appellee, vs. W. Morgan Shuster, Collector of Customs of the Philippine Islands, defendant-appellant, G.R. No. 1435, Tracey, J., 28 September 1908, Republic of the Philippines, Supreme Court, Manila, The Corpus Juris, 1908 Jurisprudence, available online: https://thecorpusjuris.com/judiciary/jurisprudence/1908/09/gr-no-1435.php (accessed May 14, 2019); and Excerpt of Minutes of Philippine Commission, September 1906, Box 1, Shuster Papers.

[26] Report of the Philippine Commission, 1907, Part 1, Entry 59, Vol. 159, RG 350, Records of the Bureau of Insular Affairs, Philippine Commission, Library Materials, Philippines—Miscellaneous, NARA; Report of the Philippine Commission, 1907, Part 3, Entry 59, Vol. 161, RG 350; Report of the Philippine Commission, 1908, Part 1, Entry 59, Vol. 166, RG 350; Report of the Philippine Commission, 1908, Part 2, Entry 59, Vol. 164, RG 350; and Report of the Philippine Commission, 1909, Entry 59, Vol. 167, RG 350.

[27] "Denies that Japan Wants Philippines," *New York Times*, January 9, 1915, 15; and "Filipino Self-Rule in '48, Shuster Plan," *New York Times*, December 5, 1926, front page.

[28] "Shuster Resigns," *The Evening Star* (Washington, DC), February 11, 1909, 2, Library of Congress, Chronicling America: Historic American Newspapers. Available online: https://chroniclingamerica.loc.gov (accessed May 31, 2019).

[29] There was a lot of controversy over the Liberia Commission in general, and when Shuster turned down Taft's invitation to head the commission, it led to a lot of speculation in the press about why Shuster declined. The State Department blamed Shuster's health, while some newspapers speculated that Shuster did not want to serve on a commission that had a black member, Emmett J. Scott of the Tuskegee Institute, because Shuster was from Washington, DC, a Jim Crow city. Shuster himself explained that he had just returned home from nearly a decade abroad in tropical countries and had no desire to travel abroad again so soon. "Liberian Commission Completed," *New-York Daily Tribune*, April 7, 1909, 3, Chronicling America; "Chairman Shuster Resigns," *New York Times*, April 17, 1909, 2; "Shuster Declines Mission," *Evening Star* (Washington, DC), April 17, 1909, front page, Chronicling America; "W. M. Shuster Resigns," *New-York Daily Tribune*, April 17, 1909, 2, Chronicling America; and "Difficulty Being Experienced by President Taft," *The Advocate* (Charleston, WV), April 22, 1909, front page, Chronicling America.

As a dutiful representative of the United States, Shuster publicly supported the US imperial project while in the Philippines. Yet he was explicitly not a representative of the United States when he went to Iran in 1911; he kept his own counsel. While a US official in Cuba and the Philippines in his twenties, Shuster the attorney and rules-oriented Progressive had followed the law in performing his duties. In Iran, however, he was one of the people fashioning the law, and he was now a 34-year-old with mature convictions and a powerful position. In Iran, Shuster conceivably was freer to criticize imperialism than he had been before. Shuster also aligned himself with Iranian nationalists and constitutionalists from day one. Clearly, he was already inclined to support the constitutionalists' anti-imperial position. He did not arrive in Tehran an impartial party, and this may have been the result of his prior experiences with American empire. Of course, it is also quite possible that Shuster's years in the Philippines did not affect his views of empire. That would mean that it was only his experiences in Iran that caused his anti-imperial transformation. What *is* certain is that Shuster left Iran in January 1912 an avowed opponent of Western imperialism.

Shuster's immediate and increasingly vocal opposition to British and Russian meddling in Iran's affairs proved irritating to Great Britain and ultimately intolerable to Russia. When Russia invaded Iran in late 1911, ousting Shuster was a primary motivation. Although many of the treasurer-general's actions antagonized both Russia and Britain, Russia viewed him as a particular threat. Shuster's success would have damaged Russian economic interests in Iran, as did his blatant disregard for what Russia viewed as its sphere of influence in northern Iran.[30] Shuster proposed to appoint two British citizens to treasury posts in northern Iran; he confiscated the estates of Shoʻāʻ al-Saltaneh, Mohammad Ali Shah's brother and a Russian client; and he authored a scathing open letter in the London *Times* criticizing British and Russian behavior in Iran. These actions, among others, prompted Russia to issue ultimatums to the Iranian government demanding Shuster's dismissal. When the Majles refused to yield, Russian troops invaded and marched on the capital, ultimately forcing the Iranian cabinet to suspend the Majles and fire Shuster in December 1911.[31]

Morgan Shuster departed Tehran in early January 1912. His Iranian adventure made him a minor celebrity back in the United States, and he used the spotlight to rally American public support for Iranian constitutionalism and to condemn European imperialism in Iran. While the US news media already expressed support for Iranian constitutionalists, there is evidence that Shuster's message resonated with Americans and helped to cement a positive view of Iranians in the US public sphere.

---

[30] Without consulting the Iranians, Great Britain and Russia signed the Anglo-Russian Convention of 1907, which divided Iran into spheres of influence and indicated that the two powers would cooperate in Iran. "Anglo-Russian Entente, 1907—Part 1: Agreement Concerning Persia," The Avalon Project, Yale Law School Lillian Goldman Law Library. Available online: http://avalon.law.yale.edu/20th_century/angrusen.asp#art1 (accessed June 7, 2019).

[31] Shuster, *Strangling of Persia*, 69–79, 136–230; and "Appendix C: Mr. Shuster's Open Letter to the London 'Times,'" October 21, 1911, in Shuster, *Strangling of Persia*, 358–71.

Perceptions of Iran in the American Public Sphere before the Shuster Mission

Prior to the start of the Constitutional Revolution, Americans had little understanding of Iran, or "Persia" as they called it at the time. The US government remained studiously aloof from Iranian affairs. In keeping with the principles of the Monroe Doctrine, American diplomats saw the Middle East as belonging in the European sphere of influence and therefore sought minimal political entanglement in the region. The United States pursued trade, monitored the safety of American citizens there, and offered vague statements of friendship to the Iranian government. This official neglect of Iran occurred despite Iranian attempts since the nineteenth century to secure concrete aid from the United States to resist the pressures that Britain and Russia exerted on their country. American disinterestedness contrasted favorably with European imperial designs in the Middle East and Central Asia. This made the United States appealing to Iranians, but this very disinterestedness also made the US government a poor ally for revolutionary Iran. So long as American citizens in Iran were safe and secure, the US government saw no reason to concern itself with Iranian politics.

Prior to the revolution, Iran mattered neither to US foreign policymakers nor to the American public. American Orientalists, artists, and writers were interested in Persian culture, as Hamid Dabashi demonstrated in his book *Persophilia*, but most Americans had only a vague notion that Persia was somewhere in the "Near East."[32] American tourists and religious pilgrims to Islamic countries in the nineteenth and early twentieth centuries traveled primarily to the biblical Holy Land, bypassing Iran on their routes through Egypt, the Levant, and what is now Turkey. Aside from missionaries and a handful of diplomats, few Americans had direct experience with Iran or Iranians prior to the twentieth century. For the public, then, Persia was bound up in the broader American Orientalist imagination about the supposedly exotic and inferior East. The US public sphere contained little sense of Persia as a distinct place.

This situation began to change as a result of the Constitutional Revolution. While Iran did not at this time became a primary topic of public discourse, American journalistic reporting on the Constitutional Revolution brought Iran into sharper relief for the attentive public. An analysis of mainstream periodicals in the United States illustrates American perceptions of Iran during the revolution. Print media was the primary source of information about the wider world for Americans in the early twentieth century. Print media both reflected and helped to shape American public opinion, especially when the average American had limited real-world experience with Iran and Iranians. A survey of news articles on Iran from the *New York Times*, a national paper of record, indicates that there was a predictable spike in reporting on the country during the revolution. The greatest number of articles appeared in 1911

---

[32] Hamid Dabashi, *Persophilia: Persian Culture on the Global Scene* (Cambridge, MA: Harvard University Press, 2015).

and early 1912 during the Shuster Mission and its immediate aftermath.[33] This survey also reveals that, because of the revolution and the Shuster Mission, American views of Iranians became more ambiguous and less consistently negative and Orientalist than American views of other Muslim-majority peoples, like Arabs, Turks, or Filipino Moros, during the same period.[34]

Certain topics captured the attention of American journalists more than others and, hence, likely had more influence on the attentive public's perceptions of Iran. While missionary accounts and campaigns for support did influence their coreligionists' views of Persia, missionaries in Iran appeared in American reporting very seldom during the Constitutional Revolution. Even Howard Baskerville's dramatic death made little impact. Most US newspapers included a few brief, matter-of-fact statements that he was killed in Iran in 1909, and there was no apparent public reaction to that news.[35] The Constitutional Revolution itself, however, combined with Morgan Shuster's sensational story and subsequent public relations campaign, drew significant attention in the US public sphere that led to widespread sympathy for the Iranian constitutionalist cause among the attentive American public.

There was fairly regular US newspaper reporting on Iran throughout the revolution, especially in the *New York Times*, although it is unlikely that any American reporters were actually on the ground in the country. The paper's articles about Iran and Iranians published between 1905 and 1911 fall into three general categories. The most numerous were short, descriptive articles that relayed news of important events that occurred in Iran. There were also several public interest pieces on Bahāʿism and on Iranians in the United States, such as ʿAli-Qoli Khān, the Persian *chargé d'affaires* in Washington, DC. These were feature articles with photographs and ornate decoration. Despite sometimes employing Orientalist stereotypes—particularly when criticizing Muslim persecution of Bahāʿis—these articles advanced fairly positive portraits of their Iranian subjects for readers.[36] In addition to the straightforward news reports and

[33] See ProQuest Historical Newspapers database, which provides a graph depicting the number of articles published that contain the keyword "Persia" between 1880 and 1920. According to this database, over three hundred more articles were published about "Persia" from 1900 to 1909 than the average number of articles published from 1880 to 1889 and 1890 to 1899.

[34] Edward Said, *Orientalism* (New York: Vintage Books, 1978); and Karine Walther, *Sacred Interests: The United States and the Islamic World, 1821–1921* (Chapel Hill: University of North Carolina Press, 2015).

[35] "American Leader of Persians Slain: H. C. Baskerville Made a Sortie," *New York Times*, April 21, 1909, 2; Article 7 [no title], *New York Times*, April 21, 1909, 2; Article 9 [no title], *New York Times*, April 22, 1909, 6; "Russia to Hurry Army into Persia," *New York Times*, April 22, 1909, 6; "United States Warns Shah; Will Be Held to Strict Responsibility for American Interest," *New York Times*, April 22, 1909, 6; Article 10 [no title], *New York Times*, April 30, 1909, 4; and "Impetuous Youth: American Killed Leading Persians," *Los Angeles Times*, April 21, 1909, 17.

[36] "Devoting Life to Bahaism: Sydney Sprague Lives in Persia and Has Wedded a Niece of the Bahai," *New York Times*, June 25, 1911, Cable News, Wireless and Sporting Sections, C1; Article 12 [No Title], *New York Times*, September 24, 1911, Wireless and Sporting Sections, C2; "Bahaism, Founded in Martyrdom, Taking Root Here: Though This Persian Religion Was Established Only 70 Years Ago, Its Followers Have Suffered Persecutions Rivaling Those of the Early Christians—Now Numbers 10,000,000 Adherents," *New York Times*, July 2, 1911, Sunday Magazine, SM8; "Every Continent Contributes to the Student Roll of Columbia University," *New York Times*, April 15, 1906, Sunday Magazine, SM5; "Left Wife in Persia to Study Bible Here," *New York Times*, December 8, 1910, 10; "The Lure of America for the Far East Is Growing," *New York Times*, October 2, 1910, Sunday Magazine, SM13; and "Consul Topakyan Takes a Burglar: Nabs Him and Ropes Him and Sends Him by Vehicle to Police Who Wouldn't Respond," *New York Times*, April 12, 1911, 1.

public interest pieces, American news media also printed several pro-constitutionalist articles and editorials. These were typically longer pieces, including feature articles in the *New York Times* Sunday magazine.[37]

The nature of the Constitutional Revolution appealed to Progressive Era Americans. While Progressivism encompassed many different groups and forms of social and political activism, in general the kinds of Americans who read newspapers like the *New York Times* during the first decade of the twentieth century were influenced by white, middle-class Progressive culture and values. These Americans tended to be reformers who believed that social problems could be solved through the application of education, expertise, and efficiency. They saw government as a positive tool for social change and, among other things, emphasized democracy, merit, and fair play. In the United States, these middle-class Progressives fought political corruption and expanded democracy by introducing the ballot initiative, referendum, and recall. That large numbers of Iranians fought for and then defended a democratically elected Majles and other seemingly progressive reforms—in a part of the world most Americans had been conditioned to see as inherently corrupt and despotic—captured US public attention and spoke to the Progressive imagination. Iran's cause likely later appealed to Shuster for the same reasons.

In December 1907, at the end of Mohammad Ali Shah's first year on the throne, the *New York Times* reported on the power struggle between the shah and Majles and on Russian and British involvement in Iran's growing political crisis. The report informed its readers that "there is no question that the National Council of Persia really represents all that there is in Persia of progressive spirit and that all hope of advancement depends on the strength the Council can acquire."[38] Later, in September 1909, after Mohammad Ali Shah's unsuccessful 1908 coup attempt against the Majles and his resulting deposition, the *New York Times* ran a feature article in its Sunday magazine, complete with photographs and decorative headline fonts, entitled "How Persia Passed through Revolution to Her Liberty." The title alone implied that the revolution resulted in Iran's liberty, an American core value since the United States' own revolution. Although the article relied upon well-established Orientalist tropes to describe the history of Qajar rule in Iran as despotic, it praised the revolution itself. The piece explained that the Constitutional Revolution was the result of "the determined effort of a long-oppressed people to secure freedom and representation in their government." These were presented as noble goals that the article asserted would justify the blood spilled in Iran, that is, should the constitutional government succeed and endure.[39]

Other articles were more effusive in their praise of Iranian constitutionalists. A July 1909 article reported—albeit incorrectly—that Russia planned to withdraw its troops from northern Iran, which it had invaded that spring in the aftermath of Mohammad Ali Shah's deposition and on the pretext of protecting foreigners in the region. The

---

[37] See stories cited in the text below.
[38] "The Appeal of Persia," *New York Times*, December 19, 1907, 8.
[39] "How Persia Passed through Revolution to Her Liberty," *New York Times*, September 12, 1909, Sunday Magazine, SM12.

article included unambiguous praise for Iran's revolutionaries, which constituted fully half of the article's text:

> They [the Iranians] have effected a brilliant coup [in overthrowing Mohammad Ali Shah], they have behaved with wisdom and moderation at an intoxicating moment, and they have a clear run to the goal of their ambition. The reactionary power is broken, and must remain in the dust while the Nationalists are firm and careful. Everybody in Persia who takes any interest in politics is with them … Tact and magnanimity have distinguished their actions since their moment of triumph, and there is nothing left to the foreigner but to congratulate and wish success to the new venture … The direction of events has been taken out of foreign hands, and it rests once more where it ought to rest—with the Persians themselves.[40]

Wisdom, moderation, self-control, tact, and magnanimity were all characteristics prized by middle-class American Progressives. To describe Iran's constitutionalists in these terms was to cast them as sympathetic and admirable figures for the article's readers.

There is evidence that support for Iranian constitutionalists went beyond American journalists. In April 1909 the *New York Times* reported on an address to the Women's Republican Club in New York City by Nivdun Khān, a member of the Persian legation in the United States. He described Iranian women's critical contributions to the revolution, which included arms smuggling, public demonstrations, and secretly printing revolutionary literature. As a result of his account, the paper reported: "The Republican women voted to send their good wishes to the organized women of the East working in the interest of good government."[41] The women of the New York City Republican Club clearly saw progressive-minded Iranian and American women as working toward the same goal: "good," or representative and honest, government. Shuster's book later reinforced these ideals.

Taken as a whole, American reporting on Iran before the Shuster Mission contained clear pro-constitutionalist themes. Despite the violence and periodic reports of chaotic conditions in Iran, there was a sense that the revolution was motivated by noble principles that Americans shared, namely, the desire for representative government and democracy. The reports also indicated that revolution was a last resort in the face of Mohammad Ali Shah's despotism. These historical dynamics implicitly contradicted long-standing Orientalist stereotypes of Muslim peoples as both inherently violent and passively accepting of despotic rule. The portrayal of the constitutionalists as principled, honest, wise, and in control of their passions would have appealed to middle-class Americans living in the Progressive Era. In all, the *New York Times*—when it strayed from putatively factual reporting—generally cast the shah as a corrupt, anti-democratic leader who deserved to be overthrown. By contrast, the newspaper positioned the

---

[40] "New Persian Situation: People to Be Allowed to Work Out Their Own Salvation," *New York Times*, July 29, 1909, Special Cable News Section, C4.
[41] "Oriental Women Deep in Politics: Always Foremost in Revolutions," *New York Times*, April 14, 1909, 8.

Iranian constitutionalists as protagonists who, like Progressives at home, endeavored to make their government more representative, honest, and efficient. Therefore, they were worthy of American sympathy and admiration.

Perceptions of Iran in the American Public Sphere during the Shuster Mission

American news articles about Iran only increased in number and partiality during and immediately following the Shuster Mission of 1911. Unsurprisingly, American newspapers were more interested in Iranian affairs once Americans became directly involved in the political drama unfolding overseas. That direct involvement came about because the Taft administration (1909-13) emphasized dollar diplomacy in its foreign policy. Under this policy, the US government facilitated private American loans to foreign governments, provided that those governments employed US financial experts as advisers to reorganize their financial systems in line with American directives. Of course, such reorganization typically benefited American banks and corporations.[42]

The Shuster Mission was in keeping with dollar diplomacy in many respects. The United States readily agreed to Iran's request for advisers, and Taft himself recommended Shuster. But the situation was also unique. Most American advisers went to countries in the US sphere of influence, usually in Latin America. Iran was decidedly not a country within the American orbit. In fact, the 1907 Anglo-Russian Convention declared Iran firmly within the European sphere of influence, and without consulting Iran. President Taft conceivably saw Iran's request for American financial advisers as an opportunity to spread informal US influence to a new region.

Yet Shuster and his team apparently worked in the interests of Iran, not US financial and business interests. The Americans could have steered Iran toward US banks or companies had they so desired, but they appear not to have attempted this. The Iranian government received no American loans (although it wanted them), and the treasurer-general demurred when Iranian officials suggested that they seek closer formal ties to the United States.[43] The Majles appointed Shuster and his team, and the Americans ultimately served at their pleasure. Otherwise, Shuster explained, as treasurer-general he had "entire control of the financial operations and fiscal affairs of that country."[44] The financial decisions of all government branches—including cabinet ministries—had to go through Shuster. He certainly had the power to push Iran in a direction beneficial to American financial or trade interests, but Shuster and his team

---

[42] For an explanation of dollar diplomacy, see Emily S. Rosenberg, *Financial Missionaries to the World: The Politics and Culture of Dollar Diplomacy, 1900-1930* (Durham, NC: Duke University Press, 2003).

[43] Diary of W. Morgan Shuster, May–December 1911, Box 1, Shuster Papers; and *Strangling of Persia*, 122, 153, 188–9. Shuster attempted to negotiate for a loan with the London branch of Seligman Brothers, rather than a US bank, but the negotiations failed due to the political situation with Russia and Great Britain.

[44] Shuster, *Strangling of Persia*, 6.

chose not to do so. In this way, the Shuster Mission departed from dollar diplomacy. Moreover, as treasurer-general, Shuster's powerful position in Iran's government was unprecedented. In contrast to the typical dollar diplomacy arrangement, Shuster and his team were not simply advisers; they exercised direct power as high-ranking Iranian government officials. Although the Shuster Mission ultimately did not conform to the Taft administration's typical approach to extending US economic influence abroad, it did shape how the attentive American public saw Iran.

Given the unusual nature of the Shuster Mission, it was a sensational topic that drew significant attention in the US public sphere. While most news reports relating to Iran in 1911 and early 1912 focused primarily on Shuster, they did draw more attention to the situation of Iranians. Shuster used the intense public interest in his story to criticize British and Russian policy toward Iran and to campaign for Iran's Majles and constitutionalists. According to the available evidence, this all translated into the attentive American public's increased sympathy for Iranian constitutionalists and a reduction in Orientalist depictions of Iranians at the time.

From Shuster's appointment in late spring 1911 through the early months of his mission that summer, US newspapers typically expressed curiosity and pride that Iran chose Americans as advisers. Those same newspapers also praised Shuster and the Iranians for meeting the many challenges they faced.[45] An April 1911 *New York Times* Sunday magazine feature article by E. J. Edwards—respected author of the famous "Holland" column, which was one of the most widely read syndicated columns in the United States at the turn of the century—reported on the appointment of American advisers to Persia and provided short biographical sketches of Shuster and his team. It also included an extended celebration of Persian "progress" under the constitutionalist government. Edwards contrasted this view of a progressive Iran with an Orientalist depiction of the ousted Mohammad Ali Shah, whose Turkish ancestry the journalist emphasized. This was perhaps a way to differentiate the shah's alleged Oriental despotism from Iran's constitutionalists, whom the same article praised unambiguously in non-Orientalist terms.[46]

With clear approval, Edwards noted: "The desire for and determination to have a sound and effective fiscal system manifested by the Persians is only one indication of the new spirit by which they are ruled. Severe tests have shown that they are firmly set on carrying out a modern, progressive, and enlightened policy in all directions." These policies included, according to Edwards, administrative reforms based upon "Western ideas of government and progress," an emphasis on education (including for girls), freedom of the press, and the founding of new civic institutions, all accompanied by the people's spirit of independence and democracy. And "in all these activities the

---

[45] "American to Direct Finances of Persia: W. Morgan Shuster Made Treasurer General of Asiatic Nation on Knox's Recommendation," *New York Times*, February 11, 1911, 3; "Commission Off for Persia: Americans Engaged to Reorganize Finances of Shah's Government," *New York Times*, April 9, 1911, Cable News Wireless and Sporting Section, CM11; "Intrigues in Persia Met by Shuster: American Overcomes Belgian and Russian Diplomatic Obstacles to His Handling Shah's Finances," *New York Times*, July 31, 1911, 4; and "Ex-Shah of Persia Seeks the Throne He Gave Away: Mohammed Ali, on Those Head a Reward Is Placed by Parliament, Is the Leader In Plots Involving Other Nations," *New York Times*, August 6, 1911, Sunday Magazine, SM7.

[46] Edwards, "Five Young Yankees."

Persians are giving special attention to the example of the people of the United States."[47] The message was clear: Shuster and his men were engaged in a noble mission to assist Iran in achieving "progressive" goals that would make Iran more like the United States and therefore worthy of support.

Such articles quickly gave way to even more forceful pro-Shuster and pro-Iran pieces that fall and winter due to Russian opposition to Shuster's agenda. What began with Russian calls for his dismissal ended with an intervention in late December that forced Shuster's ouster and the dissolution of the Majles. By November and December 1911, *New York Times* reporting took on the tone of a melodrama. The paper cast Russia and sometimes Britain as greedy, treacherous villains bent on "swallowing Persia," while Shuster was the "plucky" hero defending Persia, the damsel in distress.[48]

A November 1911 Sunday magazine article is illustrative of this type of editorializing. Its headline blazed dramatically from the page, "How Russia Came to Make War on W. Morgan Shuster: The Thirty-Four-Year-Old American Who Defied the Czar—He Went to Persia to Save Her From Financial Ruin and Is Upsetting the International Plot for Her Partition." It began by asking, "Was it possible that she [Iran] was to escape the jaws of the two sharks by such an unheard-of device as getting a handful of Americans to make a nation of her?" The piece's author argued that the Shuster Mission would have been Persia's salvation but for Russian and British interference. Describing how Shuster and his team, "five thoroughly American Americans," approached their task like good Progressives, "without fear or favor, without axes to grind, and with no interest on earth except that of rendering business-like service to their employers," the article explained that Russia sought Shuster's dismissal precisely because he and his team were upright men. The Americans refused to bow to foreign pressure, so the Russian bear "growled" when it "broke off diplomatic negotiations [with the Persian government] and landed troops." Shuster was unintimidated, and "he will not back down," for "all his life long he had been accustomed to facing difficult propositions, and a Czar or two was nothing to him."[49]

Shuster, the exemplar of middle-class, white, Progressive manhood, was clearly the main protagonist in the *New York Times*' coverage of the unfolding crisis in Iran. Articles like this one also feminized Iran and cast it in need of American rescue. In these ways, the articles echoed both Orientalist stereotypes that feminized Muslim men and broader American racist depictions that characterized non-Europeans at the turn of the twentieth century as effeminate, weak, and often in need of American tutelage. Yet American reporting was not consistently Orientalist or stereotypical in its depiction of Iranians.[50] The *New York Times* praised the manly bravery of the constitutionalists and nationalists

---

[47] Ibid.
[48] "Britain and Russia Swallowing Persia," *New York Times*, November 14, 1911, 6; "Mr. Shuster to Go," *New York Times*, December 23, 1911, 8; and "Russia Calming Down," *New York Times*, December 12, 1911, 10.
[49] Charles Willis Thompson, "How Russia Came to Make War on W. Morgan Shuster: The Thirty-Four-Year-Old American Who Defied the Czar—He Went to Persia to Save Her from Financial Ruin and Is Upsetting the International Plot for Her Partition," *New York Times*, November 26, 1911, Sunday Magazine, SM3.
[50] In an interesting parallel, Iranian identities were also fluid and evolving during this period. See Neda Maghbouleh, *The Limits of Whiteness: Iranian Americans and the Everyday Politics of Race* (Stanford, CA: Stanford University Press, 2017); and Reza Zia-Ebrahimi, *The Emergence of Iranian Nationalism: Race and the Politics of Dislocation* (New York: Columbia University Press, 2018).

in the Majles who stood up to Russia and refused to accede to its demand that they fire Shuster.[51] When the Iranian cabinet—not the elected Majles members who had appointed Shuster—finally gave in and dismissed the treasurer-general at the end of December, the paper was quick to note that Iran had no other choice and blamed Russia for Shuster's ouster. What followed was the melodrama's inexorable, tragic conclusion: forced to send Shuster away and disband the Majles, Persia was now unprotected. The Russian villain let his troops rampage throughout the countryside to punish Persia for her defiance, and Persia's budding democracy was brutally murdered by foreign intrigue.[52]

Shuster Rallies the American Public

Upon his return, Shuster used his media spotlight to reinforce the narrative of tragedy and to campaign for the American public's support for Iran. Henceforth, his version of events dominated American perceptions of what had happened to Iran's revolution. While it is possible that Shuster enjoyed the limelight, his outrage at Russia and Britain and his admiration for Iran's reformers appear to have been genuine. His outspokenness, and the sensational nature of his experiences, kept Iran in the public eye for months after his return, well into 1912. Shuster's personal scrapbooks contain dozens of newspaper articles about his public relations campaign upon his return home, and newspapers across the United States—and abroad—broadcast his account with alacrity.[53] According to Shuster, Iranian constitutionalists and nationalists were self-sacrificing, honorable men and women who loved their country and sought to reform it so that it might become a modernized, prosperous, democratic nation-state not unlike the United States. But imperial Britain and Russia had strangled Iran's infant democracy in its cradle—as the title of Shuster's highly cited 1912 memoir, *The Strangling of Persia*, asserted.[54] All liberty-loving, progressive Americans should be outraged about Britain's and Russia's "selfish" and "bullying" actions in Iran.[55]

In making his case, Shuster advanced an anti-imperialist and remarkably anti-Orientalist argument to his audience. Yet in late 1909, Shuster had publicly expressed Orientalist and Islamophobic views when describing the Muslim Moro population of the Philippines, whom he characterized as "untamed fanatics" that were "by nature

---

[51] "Sweeping Majority for Rejection: Czar's Troops for Teheran," *New York Times*, December 2, 1911, 1; "Czar's Troops for Teheran: Order Follows Persia's Point-Blank Refusal to Dismiss Mr. Shuster," *New York Times*, December 2, 1911; and "Persians Stick to Shuster," *New York Times*, December 19, 1911, 1.

[52] For examples, see "Punitive Force Sent into Persia," *New York Times*, December 25, 1911, 1; and "Persia's Fault, Says Sazonoff: Czar's Foreign Minister Defends the Repressive Measures to Times Correspondent," *New York Times*, January 3, 1912, 1.

[53] Scrapbooks, 1900–1912, microfilm, reel 1, Shuster Papers.

[54] Shuster, *Strangling of Persia*.

[55] Appendix C: "Mr. Shuster's Open Letter to the London 'Times,'" October 21, 1911, in Shuster, *Strangling of Persia*, 370, 371.

turbulent, lawless and bloodthirsty."[56] At that point he clearly held to the prevailing assumptions, described by historian Karine Walther, about the Moros—and all Muslims, by extension—held by US policymakers at the time. Americans used these prejudicial views to justify the colonization of the Philippines and the genocidal tactics that the United States deployed against the Moros from 1899 through 1913.[57] Yet Shuster did not apply these same assumptions to Iranians in 1911–12.

Because of his experiences in Iran and his close contact with Iranians—as opposed to his lack of contact with Moros while in the Philippines—Shuster became a zealous convert to Iran's cause and wholly committed himself to work in the interest of the constitutionalists and the Iranian people. Shuster was moved by the constitutionalists' battle for justice, sovereignty, and democracy, and he believed they could have succeeded if not for European obstructionism. Based on the manner in which he spoke about Iran and Iranians, it is conceivable that Shuster had not fully absorbed the prevailing racist and Orientalist notions that, in the United States, characterized Islam and democracy as incompatible and cast Muslims as incurably backward and inferior to white, Protestant Americans.[58]

The difference is striking between Shuster's statements about Iranians and most other contemporary American discussions about Islam and Muslims.[59] Many scholars have demonstrated that Americans primarily understood and represented Muslim-majority countries within the Orientalist framework of religion in the late nineteenth and early twentieth centuries.[60] Shuster was an outlier because he did not use the lens of religion to explain Iran to the American public. In his book, private diary, and interviews with journalists, Shuster barely mentioned Shia Islam, the dominant religion in Iran. When he did bring it up, it was always in passing and rarely carried explicit or implied judgment about Islam.[61] *The Strangling of Persia* mentions Islam or

---

[56] W. Morgan Shuster, "Our Philippine Policies and Their Results: An Address Delivered at Clark University, September 14, 1909, during the Conference Upon the Far East," *Journal of Race Development* 1, no. 1 (1910): 59, 73.

[57] Walther, *Sacred Interests*, 157–237.

[58] Early-twentieth-century Iran, though a Muslim-majority nation, was also home to many religious minorities, from Christians and Bahāʾis to Jews and Zoroastrians.

[59] I should also note that, while Shuster used Orientalist and Islamophobic stereotypes to discuss Filipino Moros, he also took pains to defend Catholic Filipinos—with whom he did have direct experience while in the Philippines—from dominant US characterizations of them at the time as racially inferior and inherently backward. Based on this track record, Shuster appears generally to have questioned racial and other stereotypes of foreign peoples once he had direct personal experiences with those peoples. See Shuster, "Our Philippine Policies," 68–71.

[60] There is extensive literature on this, inspired by Edward Said's *Orientalism*. Some representative examples include Jacob Rama Berman, *American Arabesque: Arabs, Islam, and the 19th-Century Imaginary* (New York: New York University Press, 2012); Holly Edwards, ed., *Noble Dreams, Wicked Pleasures: Orientalism in America, 1870–1930* (Princeton, NJ: Princeton University Press, 2000); Amira Jarmakani, *Imagining Arab Womanhood: The Cultural Mythology of Veils, Harems, and Belly Dancers in the U.S.* (New York: Palgrave Macmillan, 2008); Timothy Marr, *The Cultural Roots of American Islamicism* (New York: Cambridge University Press, 2006); Malini Johar Schueller, *U.S. Orientalisms: Race, Nation, and Gender in Literature, 1790–1890* (Ann Arbor: University of Michigan Press, 1998); and Walther, *Sacred Interests*. See also Firoozeh Kashani-Sabet, "Before ISIS: What Early America Thought of Islam," *Sociology of Islam* 8, no. 1 (2020): 17–52.

[61] Shuster diary; Shuster, *Strangling of Persia*; and Scrapbooks, 1900–1912, Boxes 2–11, microfilm, reel 1, Shuster Papers. Shuster's scrapbooks contain hundreds of newspaper articles published in the United States and Europe about his time in Iran in 1911 and his views on Iran throughout 1912 after he left Tehran.

Muslims (whom Shuster called "Mohammadans") only a handful of times in its four hundred pages of text. When Shuster does mention Islam, it is usually only to note Iran's demographics or the sympathy that other Muslims had for Iran's plight, with no additional commentary.[62] Yet Shuster repeatedly noted how Britain's and Russia's status as Christian nations did nothing to prevent their bad behavior. Instead, he stated bluntly that "two powerful and presumably enlightened Christian countries played fast and loose with truth, honor, decency and law, one, at least, hesitating not even at the most barbarous cruelties to accomplish its political designs."[63]

Shuster often seemed to provide a subtle rebuke to American Orientalist assumptions. He made it a point several times in his book to describe how large numbers of Iran's "Islamic priests," as he called them, supported the revolution, even though the clerical class "stood to lose much of its traditional influence and privilege."[64] If, as Orientalist thinking went, Islam was inimical to democracy and modernity, why would the mullahs support constitutionalism? Shuster's arguments implied that superficial American assumptions were wrong.

Shuster also turned Orientalist stereotypes of Muslim women on their head when he praised Iranian women's participation in the revolution.[65] Although he noted women's subordinate status in Iran, he conspicuously did not blame this on Islam, as Americans traditionally had done. Leading with a wry reference to Orientalist stereotypes, he instead explained:

> It is not too much to say that without the powerful moral force of those so-called chattels of the oriental lords of creation the ill-starred and short-lived revolutionary movement, however well conducted by the Persian men, would have early paled into a mere disorganized protest. The women did much to keep the spirit of liberty alive. Having themselves suffered from a double form of oppression, political and social, they were the more eager to foment the great Nationalist movement for the adoption of constitutional forms of government.[66]

In contradiction to dominant American stereotypes, Shuster did not characterize Iranian women as silent, helpless victims of Islamic despotism.

When Shuster did criticize Iranians—primarily members of the prerevolution elite who occupied various cabinet positions—he judged them by the same criteria he applied to Americans and Europeans. Shuster was unsparing in his criticism of those who sought only their own gain, were corrupt, or were lackeys of Russia or Britain. Unlike American Orientalist criticisms of Muslims, however, Shuster did not blame these men's greed, corruption, or lack of patriotism on their religion. Theirs were purely personal failings.[67]

---

[62] Shuster, *Strangling of Persia*, 87, 188, 226, 262, 305n. 1, 332, 333.
[63] Ibid., xiii–xiv.
[64] Ibid., 192. See also xviii, 182–4, 240; and Shuster Scrapbooks.
[65] Shuster Scrapbooks; Shuster, *Strangling of Persia*, 191–7; and Afary, *Iranian Constitutional Revolution*, 177, 184, 186, 204.
[66] Shuster, *Strangling of Persia*, 191–2.
[67] Shuster criticized cabinet ministers and other members of the royalist elite throughout his book. Ibid., 239–40.

In contrast, Iranians who were patriotic, honest, and worked hard to build a better country earned Shuster's praise, whether Muslim or non-Muslim. Shuster expressed admiration for a number of Iranians, and he was often effusive in his compliments. Ephraim Khān, chief of police in Tehran and an Armenian Christian with whom Shuster worked closely, drew Shuster's acclaim for his trustworthiness and courageous defense of the capital. The American declared Ephraim Khān "a man of great resource, undoubted military genius and unflinching courage."[68] Shuster also commended Hossein-Qoli Khān Navāb, the former minister of foreign affairs, whom Shuster described as "honest," "a high-minded gentleman and a patriot of unfailing devotion to the interests of his country," and "a man whose character and attainments would win for him a high place in any land and under any conditions."[69]

Based on his assessment of the constitutionalists' characters and abilities, Shuster unequivocally dismissed the notion that Iranians were incapable of building a modern nation-state or running their own affairs. No new government could be expected to operate perfectly from the start, he explained, and Iran's Majles certainly faced a host of domestic challenges. Yet Shuster was confident that constitutionalism's failure in Iran was not the fault of the Iranians. After praising the Majles members for their patriotism and "remarkable talent, character and courage," Shuster declared: "No Parliament can be rightly deemed incompetent when it has the support of an entire people, when it recognizes its own limitations [by hiring advisers like himself], and when its members are willing to undergo great sacrifices for their nation's dignity and sovereign rights ... The Medjlis [sic] stood for an honest and progressive administration of Persia's affairs."[70] As for the Iranian people:

> They changed despotism into democracy in the face of untold obstacles. Opportunities were equalized to such a degree that any man of ability could occupy the highest official posts. As a race they showed during the past five years an unparalleled eagerness for education ... A remarkable free press sprang up over night, and fearless writers came forward to denounce injustice and tyranny whether from within their country or without. The Persians were anxious to adopt wholesale the political, ethical and business codes of the most modern and progressive nations.[71]

Despite the unquestioned faith in "modern and progressive nations" that this statement indicates, Shuster's characterization of the Iranian people nevertheless flew in the face of the common wisdom in the United States that Muslims were incapable of modernizing unless they converted to Christianity or were ruled by the West. Shuster asserted that Iranians possessed the capacity to build a successful parliamentary democracy, and he charged that European greed and intrigue were to blame for the death of that incipient democracy.

---

[68] Ibid., 86–7. A national hero, Ephraim Khān was born Ephraim Davidian, and his name is often also spelled Yeprem, Epʻrem, or Efrem. Aram Arkun, "Epʻrem Khan," *Encyclopaedia Iranica*. Available online: http://www.iranicaonline.org/articles/eprem-khan (accessed April 30, 2020).
[69] Shuster, *Strangling of Persia*, 97, 94.
[70] Ibid., 241, 242.
[71] Ibid., 245.

As Shuster's earlier statements about the Moros indicated, he obviously was not immune from Orientalist thinking, but he apparently rejected Orientalism as applied to Iranians. He made his case vigorously to the attentive American public that they should see the constitutionalist cause positively and understand Iranians as not unlike Americans. There is some anecdotal evidence that Shuster's arguments resonated. As journalists reported on the Russian attacks on Shuster and broadcast Shuster's outspoken and defiant support for Iran in November and December 1911, the *New York Times* alluded to public pressure on the Taft administration to intervene.[72] Members of the House of Representatives even proposed resolutions that December calling for US action to support Shuster and Iran, which potentially included military intervention.[73] The resolutions never made it to a vote, and the Taft administration announced that it held firm to its policy of neutrality.

Large crowds gathered to hear Shuster speak about Iran in multiple venues upon his return to the United States in early 1912, and those in attendance celebrated Shuster and his vigorous defense of Iran.[74] These crowds, the proposed congressional resolution, the Taft administration's need to defend its Iran policy, and the popularity of Shuster's *The Strangling of Persia*—which has been reprinted many times in the century since its publication—suggest that there was significant public opinion in favor of Shuster and constitutionalist Iran. While Orientalism did not disappear from American characterizations of Iranians, Shuster's anti-imperialist, anti-Orientalist, and pro-constitutionalist arguments did influence how Americans saw Iran at the time. They also translated into increased sympathy for Iranians among the attentive American public and contributed to the less consistently Orientalist depictions of Iranians that emerged in the US public sphere in the early twentieth century.

Conclusion

Shuster's stance in favor of Iranian constitutionalism and against Western imperialism—which by 1915 included American imperialism—was radical. Most Americans did not go as far as he did, but the evidence is suggestive that American perceptions of Iran shifted in a positive direction during the Constitutional Revolution. This shift was largely the result of the Shuster Mission, and it is important for various reasons.

---

[72] "Russia Calming Down"; "No Move by US to Save Shuster," *New York Times*, November 29, 1911, 3; "Persia Begs Our Congress for Aid," *New York Times*, December 5, 1911, 6; Article 3 [No Title], *New York Times*, December 7, 1911, 5; "No Action on Persia: Decision Reached by Democratic Leaders in Washington," *New York Times*, December 7, 1911, 5; "Safeguarding Shuster: State Department Says It Is Doing Its Best to Protect Him," *New York Times*, December 16, 1911, 1; Article 5 [No Title], *New York Times*, December 23, 1911, 3; and Front Page 4 [No Title], *New York Times*, December 21, 1911, 1.

[73] "No Action on Persia"; and "Directing the Secretary of State to report to the House the status of W. Morgan Shuster," Mr. Levy, Committee on Foreign Affairs, Bill No. 62 H.Res. 336, House Proceedings, *Congressional Record*, 62nd Cong., 2nd sess., December 12, 1911, p. 286, Record ID CR-1911–1912. ProQuest Congressional.

[74] "Crowd Storms Hall to Hear Shuster: Police Called to Restrain Stampede," *New York Times*, February 25, 1912, 9.

First, the news media's attention to Iran's revolution and the Shuster Mission made Iran appear as a less distant place for Americans than before. This, in turn, helped distinguish Iran from other Muslim-majority countries and perhaps accounts for the more ambiguous, less consistently Orientalist American characterizations of Iran that emerged in the years following the revolution. Newspaper articles during the revolution and Shuster's public relations campaign on Iran's behalf made the American attentive public understand that Iranians wanted representative government, true national sovereignty, and "progress." Moreover, they deserved sympathy because the British and Russian empires had retarded that progress.

Second, the controversy over the Shuster Mission made a lasting impression in the American public sphere that translated into greater American attention to Iran thereafter. Shuster's story cast Iranians as sympathetic, and it instilled a sense that American "know-how" was welcome in Iran. Thus, despite the official US policy of noninvolvement at the time, American non-state actors increasingly traveled to Iran and forged ties with Iranians in the decades to come. American citizens provided humanitarian aid to Iran during the First World War, even though most US attention was on Europe during the war and Iran was not an official combatant. The attentive American public, and the Woodrow Wilson administration, then vocally opposed the Anglo-Iranian Agreement in 1919, which would have made Iran a virtual British colony. In an attempt to offset the British oil monopoly, American companies, notably Standard Oil and Sinclair, sought to enter the Iranian market in the 1920s. In the 1920s and again in the 1940s, the Iranian government followed the Shuster precedent and hired American financial advisory teams headed by Arthur Chester Millspaugh.[75] By the 1940s, the US government followed the lead of these non-state actors and became increasingly involved in Iran's affairs.

The Constitutional Revolution and the Shuster Mission laid the foundation for increased American interest in, perceptions of, and contacts with Iran and Iranians. While the events of these early years had their own historical dynamics, the trends that began during the constitutional era continued in the years to come. This early period is therefore important to understanding the longer history of the American-Iranian relationship.

---

[75] Iran initially requested that Shuster reprise his role as a financial adviser in the 1920s, and Shuster was willing, but the State Department blocked Shuster's return to Tehran and steered the Iranians toward Millspaugh.

3

Heritage Diplomacy and US-Iran Relations: The Case of the Iranian Antiquities Law of 1930

Kyle Olson

In the 1920s, the appearance of the Lorestān Bronzes on the Western art market and Persian expositions at World's Fairs, particularly the 1926 Sesquicentennial in Philadelphia, stimulated American interest in Iranian antiquity.[1] This interest transformed into an active pursuit following the 1927 termination of the French archaeological monopoly in Iran, unlocking but not opening the door to American involvement in the field of Iranian archaeology.[2] American expeditions could only begin after November 3, 1930, with the passage of the Law for the Protection of National Vestiges, otherwise known as the Iranian Antiquities Law.[3] In this chapter, I analyze the diplomatic struggles over the passage and initial implementation of this law. I not only demonstrate how the American archaeological enterprise in Iran began but also reveal the general character of US-Iran bilateral relations during this time.

While this sequence of events is recognized as a pivotal moment in Iranian archaeology, the historical development of the field is typically divided into eras based on different landmarks (see Table 3.1). I contend, however, that the passage of the Iranian Antiquities Law marks a more salient turning point than the First World War or the cancellation of the French monopoly for two principal reasons. First, it created a new legal and diplomatic framework for the conduct of archaeology in Iran. Second,

---

[1] Kishwar Rizvi, "Art History and the Nation: Arthur Upham Pope and the Discourse on 'Persian Art' in the Early Twentieth Century," *Muqarnas* 24 (2007): 45–65.
[2] Kamyar Abdi, "Nationalism, Politics, and the Development of Archaeology in Iran," *American Journal of Archaeology* 105, no. 1 (2001): 51–76; James F. Goode, *Negotiating for the Past: Archaeology, Nationalism, and Diplomacy in the Middle East, 1919–1941* (Austin: University of Texas Press, 2007); Mohammad Qoli Majd, *The Great American Plunder of Persia's Antiquities, 1925–1941* (Lanham, MD: University Press of America, 2003).
[3] Abdi, "Nationalism, Politics, and the Development of Archaeology in Iran," 59; Ali Mousavi, "The History of Archaeological Research in Iran," in *The Oxford Handbook of Ancient Iran*, ed. Daniel T. Potts (Oxford: Oxford University Press, 2013), 7–9; Nader Nasiri-Moghaddam, "Archaeology and the Iranian National Museum: Qajar and Early Pahlavi Cultural Policies," in *Culture and Cultural Politics under Reza Shah: The Pahlavi State, New Bourgeoisie and the Creation of a Modern Society in Iran*, ed. Bianca Devos and Christopher Werner (New York: Routledge, 2014), 121–48 (133); Shapur M. Shahmirzadi, "A Review of the Development of Archaeology in Iran," *Asar* 12–14 (1986): 140.

the points of contention that emerged surrounding the law continue to resonate to the present day, principally but not exclusively in the form of divided collections.[4]

My account of this episode of archaeological diplomacy[5]—that is, the negotiation of official policies and local practices of archaeological, preservation, and heritage work in a range of foreign countries by Western archaeologists—reexamines the sources used in Mohammad Qoli Majd's chronicle of archaeology in 1920s-1930s Iran.[6] These sources are from the University of Pennsylvania, an early sponsor of American archaeological expeditions to Iran. The sources include a dense network of correspondence between the Penn Museum director, Horace Jayne, and his agents Arthur Upham Pope and Frederick Wulsin; the chief of the Division of Near Eastern Affairs at the US State Department, Wallace Murray; and the various American diplomats who served in Tehran between 1927 and 1931, principally Hugh Millard, David Williamson, Charles Hart, and William Hornibrook.[7] I supplement Majd's narrative with additional correspondence and various annotated drafts of the Antiquities Law, all of which are stored at the Penn Museum, to focus on a lesser-known character in the story, Frederick R. Wulsin.

While Wulsin ultimately played only a minor role in shaping events, he is a significant figure because he was the first archaeologist to apply for and receive an excavation permit after the law's ratification. Furthermore, his letters provide much needed context on the stakes of and contestation over the passage of the law, and they show the greater-than-expected degree to which the US State Department was actively involved in Iranian politics during the 1920s and 1930s.[8] The contours of these events and the shifting power relations they reveal explain a lot about Reza Shah's reign during the interwar period, and they foreshadow the conflicts between the United States and Iran over Iran's natural resources in later decades.

Table 3.1 Periodization of the Early History of Iranian Archaeology

Goode 2007		Mousavi 2013		Young 1986	
–1914	Great Age of Collection	1884–1927	French Era	–1939	Pre-Second World War
1919–39	Years of Negotiation	1931–79	International Era	1945–68	Post-Second World War

---

[4] Abdi, "Nationalism, Politics, and the Development of Archaeology in Iran"; Kamyar Abdi, "Reviewed Work(s): The Great American Plunder of Persia's Antiquities 1925–1941 by Mohammad Gholi Majd," *Iranian Studies* 37, no. 4 (2004).
[5] Christina Luke and Morag Kersel, *US Cultural Diplomacy and Archaeology: Soft Power, Hard Heritage* (New York: Routledge, 2013), 46.
[6] Majd, *The Great American Plunder*.
[7] Abdi, "Reviewed Work(s): The Great American Plunder."
[8] James Bill, *The Eagle and the Lion: The Tragedy of American-Iranian Relations* (New Haven, CT: Yale University Press, 1988), 16; cf. Mansour Bonakdarian, "Great Expectations: U.S.-Iranian Relations, 1911–1951," in *U.S.-Middle East Historical Encounters*, ed. Abbas Amanat and Magnus Thorkell Bernhardsson (Gainesville: University Press of Florida, 2007), 126–9; Guive Mirfendereski, *The Privileged American: The U.S. Capitulations in Iran, 1856-1979* (Costa Mesa, CA: Mazda, 2014), 35–65.

Breaking the French Monopoly

Prior to the passage of the Iranian Antiquities Law, the French *Délégation scientifique en Perse* held a monopoly—conceded in 1900 by Mozaffar al-Din Shah Qajar—on all archaeological activity in Iran. This concession granted the French exclusive rights to excavate in Iran, special privileges regarding Susa, generous *partage* terms, and exemptions from customs duties.[9] Over the next two decades, reform-minded nationalist politicians who opposed the shah's capitulations in oil, tobacco, railroads, and banking also targeted this concession.[10] Opposition to the French archaeological monopoly should thus be seen in the context of reforms in commercial, criminal, and civil codes, along with attempts to more strictly regulate and even curtail foreign interventions in Iranian affairs during early Pahlavi rule.[11]

Revolutionary associations,[12] such as the Society for National Heritage (SNH),[13] played an important role in this opposition to foreign intervention. From its establishment in 1921 onward, the SNH worked to create a National Antiquities Service.[14] But its members knew, from a previous failed attempt, that no institution or legal code for the protection and promotion of Iranian antiquities could be established as long as the French monopoly remained in place.[15] Thus, the SNH began work toward the annulment of the concession. Among other efforts toward this end, the SNH invited and funded Western Orientalists to deliver private and public lectures and to publish on the arts and culture of ancient Iran. Two scholars played an outsized role in this period: Arthur Upham Pope and Ernst Emil Herzfeld.[16]

By the SNH's request, in 1925, Herzfeld compiled a list of archaeological, architectural, and cultural works that formed the basis for Iran's first register of national heritage sites. Pope, for his part, delivered a series of "powerful and profound orations"[17] on the greatness of Persian culture and its roots in the innate and natural genius of the Persian people, while also praising the patronage of Iran's rulers.[18] Pope's audiences consisted primarily of cultural and political elites, including Reza Khān and

---

[9] Goode, *Negotiating for the Past*, 127; Nasiri-Moghaddam, "Archaeology and the Iranian National Museum."

[10] Michael Zirinsky, "Riza Shah's Abrogation of Capitulations, 1927–1928," in *The Making of Modern Iran: State and Society under Riza Shah, 1921–1941*, ed. Stephanie Cronin (London: Routledge 2003), 89–94; see also Abdi, "Nationalism, Politics, and the Development of Archaeology in Iran," 55.

[11] Stephanie Cronin, "Introduction," in *The Making of Modern Iran*, ed. Cronin, 1.

[12] Nikki R. Keddie, *Qajar Iran and The Rise of Reza Khan 1796–1925* (Costa Mesa, CA: Mazda, 1999).

[13] Talinn Grigor, "Recultivating 'Good Taste': The Early Pahlavi Modernists and Their Society for National Heritage," *Iranian Studies* 37, no. 1 (2004): 17n. 1.

[14] Rizvi, "Art History and the Nation," 45; see also Abdi, "Nationalism, Politics, and the Development of Archaeology in Iran," 56; Grigor, "Recultivating 'Good Taste'," 25–6; Mousavi, "The History of Archaeological Research in Iran," 7.

[15] Nasiri-Moghaddam, "Archaeology and the Iranian National Museum," 124–7.

[16] Goode, *Negotiating for the Past*, 133; Grigor, "Recultivating 'Good Taste'," 27–33; Ali Mousavi, "Ernst Herzfeld, Politics, and Antiquities Legislation in Iran," in *Ernst Herzfeld and the Development of Near Eastern Studies, 1900–1950*, ed. Ann C. Gunter and Stefan R. Hauser (Leiden: Brill, 2005), 449–50; Rizvi, "Art History and the Nation," 47.

[17] Grigor, "Recultivating 'Good Taste'," 31.

[18] Rizvi, "Art History and the Nation," 47.

the Council of Ministers; his words were particularly inspiring to those who sought to redefine Iranian statehood during the transition from Qajar to Pahlavi dynasties.[19]

With the increasing intensity of the nationalist struggles against Qajar-era capitulations and the accession of Reza Shah to the throne in April 1926, the SNH used Herzfeld's monuments register and Pope's lectures to launch a parliamentary attack on the legality of the French monopoly.[20] This action was vehemently opposed by the British, who feared the precedent it might set for other concessions, particularly the one held by the Anglo-Persian Oil Company.[21] At this point, Horace Jayne, director of the Penn Museum, saw an opportunity and requested that the American legation intervene to pressure the French to relinquish their monopoly voluntarily.[22] By October 1927, with American mediation, the French and Persian governments agreed to annul the concession. The resulting compromise obliged the Persian government to appoint French architect and art historian André Godard as director-general of a newly formed Persian Antiquities Service.[23]

Following this, Herzfeld resumed negotiations with the Iranian government for permission to conduct systematic archaeological research at Persepolis and Pasargadae.[24] He could not, however, conduct excavations without special permission from the Council of Ministers. Herzfeld consequently strove to persuade the Persian government to adopt an antiquities law. In October 1929, he drafted a bill for consideration by the Council of Ministers.[25] Around the same time, the Minister of Education, Mirzā Yahyā Khān Qarāgozlu, presented his own bill to the ministers.[26] The next two years were a period of intense negotiation and struggle between Iranian politicians, foreign diplomats, archaeological institutions, and their agents.[27] This period concluded in November 1930 with the final ratification of the law and its *nezām-nāmeh*, the *Reglement d'Application*, which would govern archaeological research in Iran until 1962.[28]

---

[19] Ibid.; Abdi, "Nationalism, Politics, and the Development of Archaeology in Iran," 110; see also Reza Zia-Ebrahimi, *The Emergence of Iranian Nationalism: Race and the Politics of Dislocation* (New York: Columbia University Press, 2016).

[20] Nasiri-Moghaddam, "Archaeology and the Iranian National Museum," 130; see also Grigor, "Recultivating 'Good Taste,'" 30–3.

[21] Majd, *The Great American Plunder*, 60–1; see also Gregory Brew, "In Search of 'Equitability': Sir John Cadman, Rezā Shah and the Cancellation of the D'Arcy Concession, 1928-33," *Iranian Studies* 50, no. 1 (2017): 125–48.

[22] Majd, *The Great American Plunder*, 63–9.

[23] Ibid., 70; Mousavi, "The History of Archaeological Research in Iran," 7.

[24] Ali Mousavi, *Persepolis: Discovery and Afterlife of a World Wonder* (Boston, MA: De Gruyter, 2012), 160.

[25] Goode, *Negotiating for the Past*, 140; Nasiri-Moghaddam, "Archaeology and the Iranian National Museum," 131–2.

[26] Majd, *The Great American Plunder*, 76; Nasiri-Moghaddam, "Archaeology and the Iranian National Museum," 131–2.

[27] Majd, *The Great American Plunder*.

[28] Nasiri-Moghaddam, "Archaeology and the Iranian National Museum," 132, 139–43; Ezzatollah Negahban, *Fifty Years of Iranian Archaeology: A Memoir* (Tehran: Iranian Cultural Heritage Organization, 1997), 62; cf. Goode, *Negotiating for the Past*; Majd, *The Great American Plunder*.

Competing Visions: The Negotiation of the Antiquities Law

The negotiations of 1929–30 revolved around the two bills authored by Herzfeld and Qarāgozlu.[29] Herzfeld's proposal drew upon precedents set by Greek, Iraqi, and Egyptian antiquities regulations, which were highly favorable to foreign enterprises.[30] The model for Qarāgozlu's proposal is less clear, but its articles strongly reflected his position as a member of an influential faction of landowners in the Court and Majles. Qarāgozlu's main concern was to secure the rights of landowners to excavate on their own properties and to control their finds with minimal governmental oversight.[31]

A letter from Arthur Upham Pope to Horace Jayne in late January 1930 illustrates the uncertain climate created by the negotiations over the Antiquities Law. Pope drew special attention to several points that included the regulation of ongoing excavations and the renewability of permits; Pope's fear that the Persian government might abuse its right to exclude certain items of "exceptional importance" from *partage*; questions about the rights of landowners to finds on their properties; high export duties (an area where he had a substantial and notorious conflict of interest); and the "disposal of surplus objects," which Pope saw as an area of great potential with respect to exchanges with foreign museums and recognized collectors.[32]

By May 1930, two important events had occurred. First, Herzfeld and Qarāgozlu presented revised versions of their bills to the Council of Ministers. According to Pope, at this juncture, passage of the law seemed imminent. He told Jayne that he found the Herzfeld bill as "satisfactory as any law governing antiquities anywhere." In particular, Pope noted that it permitted foreign institutions to undertake excavations under a reasonable regulatory framework. He was especially pleased that it included the crucial provision of giving foreign expeditions half of excavated material, excluding the Persian government's prior selection of a few objects of exceptional importance.[33]

Second, on the advice of the American *chargé d'affaires*, David Williamson, Jayne dispatched Frederick Wulsin to Tehran to replace Pope as a more direct representative of the Penn Museum's interests in the negotiations.[34] By his account, Wulsin's objective was to "work out a compromise text acceptable to everyone, and to prevent misunderstandings between those interested."[35] Upon arrival in Tehran in April

---

[29] Goode, *Negotiating for the Past*, 147–8.
[30] Abdi, "Nationalism, Politics, and the Development of Archaeology in Iran"; see also Magnus T. Bernhardsson, *Reclaiming a Plundered Past: Archaeology and Nation Building in Modern Iraq* (Austin: University of Texas Press, 2005), 3; Elliott Colla, *Conflicted Antiquities: Egyptology, Egyptomania, Egyptian Modernity* (Durham, NC: Duke University Press, 2007); Goode, *Negotiating for the Past*.
[31] E. E. Herzfeld to H. F. Jayne, October 10, 1929, University of Pennsylvania Museum of Archaeology and Anthropology Administrative Records, Horace H.F. Jayne Director's Office Records 1929–1940 (hereafter UPMAR Jayne): Container 7, Folders 8–9; see also Goode, *Negotiating for the Past*, 148; Majd, *The Great American Plunder*, 76.
[32] A. U. Pope to H. H. F. Jayne, January 21, 1930, UPMAR Jayne: Container 14, Folders 11–12.
[33] A. U. Pope to H. H. F. Jayne, March 7, 1930, UPMAR Jayne: Container 14, Folders 11–12.
[34] D. Williamson to H. H. F Jayne, December 14, 1929, UPMAR Jayne: Container 19, Folder 2.
[35] Majd, *The Great American Plunder*, 77.

1930, he immediately consulted with members of the American legation, while Pope and his ally J. B. Mirzāyāntz in the Majles, Herzfeld, Godard, and Minister of Court Abdolhossein Teymourtash hashed out a palatable agreement.[36] At this juncture, the points of contention remained the questions of restrictions on commercial excavations, indemnification of landowners, ownership of excavated finds, and export regulations.

The negotiations during May 1930 were less than satisfactory, in part because Herzfeld's bill had fallen out of favor with the Council of Ministers. Wulsin relayed two different translations of Qarāgozlu's draft to Horace Jayne, highlighting three concerning articles. In this proposal, Article 7 stipulated that, prior to excavation, archaeologists would be required to purchase the land for an inflated price and, after excavation, sell it back to the original owner at a considerable loss. Article 8 imposed a flat five-year limit to excavation by any foreign society, and it stipulated that, in the case of places "declared national monuments," the Persian government would have the right to retain "everything which bears on Persian history or art—in other words everything worth having—and divide the rest with the excavator."[37] According to Article 14 of the draft law, everything excavated on private land would belong to the Persian landowner.[38]

By mid-June, in consultation with Teymourtash, Wulsin and Pope reworked Qarāgozlu's proposal. They focused their efforts on protecting the interests of foreign excavators without raising the ire of landowners.[39] Specifically, Wulsin proposed that expeditions be able to rent private land rather than buy it, divide finds excavated on private land with landowners, and be exempt from export duties.[40] Wulsin sent Jayne another copy of the draft, this time highlighting three points. He emphasized that he deliberately followed Qarāgozlu's language wherever possible so that he could still claim that it was an Iranian law. But several "objectionable" articles related to excavation were changed "very fundamentally and much improved." Finally, Wulsin noted that the law still provided insufficient administrative procedures, but he knew that other matters were more pressing and that "our only chance of getting anything is not to ask too much."[41]

In any case, Wulsin's verdict at this juncture was that his and Pope's proposal represented progress over Qarāgozlu's original bill. It was far from ideal, but they knew that the proposal would yet be subjected to daily deliberation and a long process of ratification in the Majles.[42] Wulsin pointed to two external factors influencing the negotiations. The first was the prestigious Burlington House exhibition slated to be held in London the following year. The second was the anti-American sentiment stemming from complications with American involvement in the Trans-Iranian Railway syndicate. Wulsin's opinion was, regarding the former, that if Pope's gambit of "no law, no show" failed, because of the latter factor, "we may be a long time in getting

---

[36] Ibid.
[37] F. R. Wulsin to H. H. F. Jayne, June 3, 1930, UPMAR Jayne: Container 20, Folder 1.
[38] Ibid.
[39] Majd, *The Great American Plunder*, 77.
[40] F. R. Wulsin to H. H. F. Jayne, June 29, 1930, UPMAR Jayne: Container 20, Folder 1.
[41] F. R. Wulsin to H. H. F. Jayne, June 13, 1930, UPMAR Jayne: Container 20, Folder 1.
[42] F. R. Wulsin to H. H. F. Jayne, June 17, 1930, UPMAR Jayne: Container 20, Folder 1.

any law at all."[43] In the end, the Wulsin-Pope draft was rejected by the Council of Ministers on June 21, opening the door to a reconsideration of the Herzfeld proposal.

At this point, most of the involved parties left the capital for the summer. Nevertheless, discussion and maneuvering continued, both in Tehran and abroad. Pope went to work on the Burlington House show in London, and Wulsin went to Paris, where he met with an influential statesman and member of the SNH, Hossein Alā'. Alā' confirmed Wulsin's and Pope's suspicions that the fundamental issue holding up the negotiation was a broader question over the disposition of below-ground wealth. Alā''s position was that archaeology was a test case in a broader policy struggle between different nationalist factions over the future of oil, timber, and mineral rights. Evidently, as part of the backdrop to the renegotiation of the D'Arcy concession and the eventual signing of the Anglo-Persian Oil Company concession in 1932–3,[44] archaeology became a trial balloon in the legal struggle to define "government property," especially as it related to oil exploration.[45]

During his seasonal absence from Tehran, Qarāgozlu left Mohammad Ali Foroughi in charge of his affairs as minister of education. Sensing an opportunity, Godard revised Herzfeld's bill and convinced Foroughi to present a translation of it to the Council of Ministers. To everyone's surprise, the Council of Ministers quickly passed the bill to the Majles on October 12, before Qarāgozlu had returned.[46] Wulsin reasoned to Jayne that "[Qarāgozlu] had known what was coming but could not bear to stay in town and face it."[47] The translated Herzfeld-Godard bill initially met stiff opposition in the Majles before it was passed. Evidently, the Council of Ministers was motivated by Pope and wanted to secure suitable antiquities regulation before the Burlington House exhibition.[48] For that reason, the Majles resubmitted a hastily revised version before adjourning until spring. The Council of Ministers, led by Foroughi, reintroduced the bill as an "urgent measure." This forced an immediate vote with a minimum of deliberation and resulted in the ratification of the bill into law on November 3, 1930.[49]

In the next two sections, I examine two of the five articles of the Law for the Protection of National Vestiges that regulated foreign expeditions. Three of the five concern land (Article 13), exportation (Article 18), and the drafting of a *Reglement d'Application* (Article 19), which, while important, warrant their own separate studies.[50] I focus on the articles governing excavation permits (Article 11) and *partage* (Article 14), and the first cases of their implementation.[51] The broader point that

---

[43] F. R. Wulsin to H. H. F. Jayne, June 13, 1930, UPMAR Jayne: Container 20, Folder 1.
[44] Brew, "In Search of 'Equitability,'" 2–3.
[45] F. R. Wulsin to H. H. F. Jayne, June 29, 1930, UPMAR Jayne: Container 20, Folder 1. This view was restated in a subsequent letter from Wulsin to Jayne dated November 28, 1930:

> [The Law] will serve as a precedent for a law on the nationalization of mines and forests which is soon to be presented and which is anathema to the landholders; hence, the opposition. We shall have trouble with the same landholders in the future, I am afraid, as they would like to discredit the antiquities law now that it is passed.

[46] Majd, *The Great American Plunder*, 79.
[47] F. R. Wulsin, Untitled Final Report on Tureng Tepe Accession, November 10, 1937, UPMAR Jayne: Container 20, Folder 2.
[48] F. R. Wulsin to H. H. F. Jayne, August 12, 1930, UPMAR Jayne: Container 20, Folder 1.
[49] Majd, *The Great American Plunder*, 78–9.
[50] Nasiri-Moghaddam, "Archaeology and the Iranian National Museum," 140–2.
[51] Majd, *The Great American Plunder*, 106–10, 127–93.

these examples highlight is stated clearly in a letter from Frederick Wulsin to Horace Jayne dated November 28, 1930. In it, Wulsin explained that the Iranian regulatory environment of the time was extraordinarily inchoate, especially when compared to the situations in Iraq, Egypt, and Palestine. He wrote: "The law itself is a novelty. Every precedent for its administration has to be created, and the official hierarchy in general has to learn what its clauses mean and how they are to be applied. The first excavators will serve as laboratory animals for this course of education, and they will need plenty of tact, patience and diplomacy."[52] Wulsin's prediction was correct.

Article 11: Permits

Article 11 deals with the issuance of permits. It gives exclusive rights to the Iranian state to conduct excavations, which the state may dispose of "directly, or delegate it by special authorization to academic institutions, societies, or individuals." This article specifies that the authorization must "indicate the site of the excavations, their extent and estimated duration." The first "excavation permits" demonstrate that, at this juncture, the process was only partially formalized; all issuances of permission and authorization were handled in private letters between the petitioner and the regulating authority. Moreover, authorization and permission were distinct legal categories. In all cases, permission was granted before authorization could be negotiated, and the two were handled by separate authorities. Complicating matters, these offices changed after the final ratification of the *Reglement d'Application*.[53] Nevertheless, certain aspects of the authorizations, in terms of the length of the contract and its renewability, appear in all examples, though the degree of explicitness with which the law and additional stipulations were invoked varied.

The first case draws out the distinction between authorization and permission. Following the ratification of the Antiquities Law, Frederick Wulsin swiftly submitted a petition for two excavations to Prime Minister Mehdi Qoli Hedayat on November 6, 1930. The first was for rights to excavate at Istakhr. The second was for a five-year, renewable authorization for Hecatompylos (i.e., Sad Darvāzeh), the yet-to-be-located capital of the Parthians, and for exploration of the surrounding Damghan plain.[54] On December 27, 1930, Wulsin informed Jayne that permission had been denied for Istakhr but granted for Damghan, as determined by the prime minister on December 21, 1930. It states, "as translated by Mirzayantz": "Refer to the Ministry of Public Education and it will sign the official contract with you."[55] On this basis, I argue for a distinction between permission and authorization. While the former required a letter from the prime minister, the latter was an "official contract," or an "excavation permit," negotiated with the Ministry of Education. This pattern is mirrored in Herzfeld's

---

[52] F. R. Wulsin to H. H. F. Jayne, November 28, 1930, UPMAR Jayne: Container 20, Folder 1.
[53] The *Reglement* was published serially in newspapers and not translated. Wulsin claimed that he sent Jayne a copy, but no such document is retained in the Penn Museum archives.
[54] F. R. Wulsin to M. Q. Hedayat, November 6, 1930, UPMAR, Tureng Tepe, Iran Expedition Records: Container 1.
[55] F. R. Wulsin to H. H. F. Jayne, December 27, 1930, UPMAR Jayne: Container 20, Folder 1.

November 1930 application process for clearance to begin a highly circumscribed program of activity at Persepolis.[56]

Concerning the channels of authority, the documents themselves show that, after the implementation of the *Reglement d'Application* in February 1931, permission was granted by the Council of Ministers collectively rather than by the prime minister alone. Erich Schmidt's receipt of authorization for excavations at Rey in 1933 shows that Godard became the primary, but not sole, regulatory authority within the Ministry of Education in his capacity as the director of the Antiquities Service. The director-general of the Ministry of Education was a cosignatory, but Godard appears to have been the primary arbiter.[57] This was also the case for Herzfeld's 1933 authorization to work at Istakhr, which was issued by Godard and the director-general of the Ministry of Education, Valiollah Khān Nasr.[58]

To illustrate the point, Wulsin's November 1930 application for permission to excavate Hecatompylos was submitted to, and permission was issued by, Prime Minister Hedayat on behalf of the "Persian Government." At this stage, authorization was under the jurisdiction of the Ministry of Education, but the specific arbitrating official is unclear. Following the passage of the *Reglement d'Application*, this two-step process remained in place, but permission was granted by the Council of Ministers rather than by the prime minister, and authorization was the remit of Godard under the aegis of the Ministry of Education.

Regarding the content of these documents, Wulsin's "official contract" for excavation authorization at Damghan is instructive. It states: "The Persian Government grants the permission of excavation within the limits of Damghan for the discovery of the old city of Hecatompylos for five years to Pennsylvania Museum and [the University of Pennsylvania], according to the law of November 3, 1930. This permission is renewable every five years."[59] After receiving permission, Wulsin counseled Jayne to delay signing an official contract for authorization on account of three factors: (1) the impending passage of the *Reglement d'Application*, whose terms were not yet finalized; (2) the need to visit Damghan and determine the precise limits of the area of investigation; and (3) the need to consult with Godard. Wulsin was particularly concerned that the Ministry of Education would require advance specification of the number and location of test pits.[60]

In early January 1931, Wulsin consulted with Mirzāyāntz regarding the precise wording of the contract in the aforementioned three areas. He asked that all related operations be carried out in accordance with the Antiquities Law and its *Reglement d'Application*. Wulsin also asked that the Penn Museum be authorized to conduct surveys and dig test pits, or trial trenches, in the location of their choosing within a radius of 10 *farsakhs* (*c.* 62 km) centered on the town at Damghan. He hoped that this

---

[56] Majd, *The Great American Plunder*, 128.
[57] Ibid., 106.
[58] Ibid., 141–2.
[59] F. R. Wulsin to H. H. F. Jayne, December 27, 1930, UPMAR Jayne: Container 20, Folder 1.
[60] F. R. Wulsin to H. H. F. Jayne, January 9, 1930, December 27, 1930, UPMAR Jayne: Container 20, Folder 1; F. R. Wulsin to H. H. F. Jayne, February 6, 1930, December 27, 1930, UPMAR Jayne: Container 20, Folder 1.

radius would determine the outer boundary of objects to be considered for *partage*. Finally, Wulsin expected that, once the location of Hecatompylos had been sufficiently fixed, the Antiquities Service of the Ministry of Education would be notified of "the right to conduct definitive excavations over a circle with a radius of two *farsakhs* with its center at the actual ruins."[61] It appears that these terms were accepted by the Ministry of Education in their issuance of formal authorization. Schmidt's permit for Rey in 1933 followed much the same template, stipulating the location, duration, and renewability of the formal authorization.[62]

Herzfeld's permit to begin work at Persepolis differed from both the Damghan and Rey documents. Here, permission and authorization were one and the same. Herzfeld received a letter from Prime Minister Mehdi Qoli Hedayat, dated December 16, 1930, that acknowledged the application for authorization from November 28 of the same year and stipulated the precise parameters of the work. These stipulations provided for the clearance of the main ceremonial platform, preparation for the preservation, repair, and reconstruction of small buildings, and work on water channels; they did not grant permission for scientific excavation or *partage*.[63]

James Breasted and Herzfeld were not satisfied with this limited scope. In November– December 1931, Herzfeld applied for and received an additional authorization to work in the "environs of Persepolis." It granted the authority "to dig in the area known as [the plain of Persepolis] within a radius of 10 kilometers on the same conditions as formerly prescribed for Persepolis, provided the work on non-Governmental lands is done with the consent of the proprietors of such lands and the plan of the dig is submitted to the Government."[64] In addition, in the summer of 1933, Herzfeld applied for authorization to excavate at a small prehistoric mound three kilometers south of Persepolis, as well as in small mounds remaining from the ruins of Istakhr. The permission letter in this case appears somewhat differently than the others. Not only is it directly addressed to Herzfeld, but the authorization explicitly invoked Article 22 of the *Reglement d'Application*, stipulating the obligatory "presence of the technical member of the staff of the Division of Antiquities." Furthermore, the authorization was for a non-renewable term of only two years.[65]

Authorizations primarily aimed to delimit the geographic zone of activity fix the duration of the authorization and, in some cases, determine the potential for future contracts. The authorizations offer no specific reasons for the varying radii, durations of excavation, and terms of renewability. In any case, the amount of time that elapsed between petition for permission and receipt of authorization was between two and three months. Thus, administrative procedures in the application of Article 11 of the Law for the Protection of National Vestiges operated smoothly. This contrasts starkly with the application of Article 14 concerning the division of finds.

---

[61] F. R. Wulsin to J. B. Mirzāyāntz, January 9, 1930, UPMAR, Tureng Tepe, Iran Expedition Records: Container 1.
[62] Majd, *The Great American Plunder*, 106.
[63] Ibid., 128.
[64] Ibid., 141.
[65] Ibid., 141–2.

Article 14: *Partage*

Article 14 encompasses *partage*, or the division of finds. It stipulates that "if the excavations have been undertaken by a third party, the state may select and appropriate up to ten items of historical or artistic value and donate half of the remainder to the finder, keeping the other half itself."[66] The language of Article 14 created two issues regarding its implementation. First, Article 14 delimited certain roles with domain-specific authority, namely, "The [Persian] Government" and "The Discoverer," understood to mean "scientific institutions, individuals, or firms." But it left unspecified the office responsible for selecting which of the lots would belong to whom. Second, Article 14 left wide latitude for the practical interpretation of its stipulated protocols. With respect to *partage*, the article says that divisions of finds apply to "whatever is found in one place and in one season," but it is entirely silent on procedure. This silence quickly became a point of contestation within the domain of *partage*. I illustrate this through three examples: Tureng Tepe 1931 (excavated by Frederick R. and Susanne E. Wulsin), Tepe Hissar 1931–2 (excavated by Erich F. Schmidt), and Takht-e Jamshid 1934–5 (excavated by Ernst E. Herzfeld). I draw attention to three key features of each event: (1) the setting, timing, and individuals involved; (2) the estimation of commensurate value between the divided collections; and (3) the subsequent positive and/or negative disposition of different individuals and groups toward the outcome of events.

The first division of finds under the new law occurred on September 18, 1931, between Wulsin and Godard, with "Wulsin as representative of the University Museum in Philadelphia and [the] Kansas City Museum, and Godard, as representing the Persian Government."[67] The first salient feature of the Tureng Tepe division is the setting(s) in which it occurred and the parties involved. It is important to understand that *partage* occurred in two stages with the division and selection of lots. The initial division of the finds into two groups occurred in Wulsin's Tehran "workshop" and involved only Wulsin and Godard. This was followed by the selection of the lots at the Ministry of Education, involving a much wider range of parties. In this case, Godard represented the government and decided to cede its right to the prior selection of ten pieces. Moreover, Godard and Wulsin took care to ensure the division was fair, and the minister of education concurred on the commensurability of the lots at the final selection. In the end, they decided by drawing straws. Finally, it seems that all parties were positively disposed to this relatively low-stakes *partage* event because it required no further negotiation or diplomatic intervention.

The second division of finds under the new law concerned Tepe Hissar, the Penn Museum's second excavation in Iran. After the first season of excavation closed, and in contrast to Wulsin's experience just a few months prior, Schmidt's finds were shipped directly to the Ministry of Education, rather than to Schmidt's house in Tehran. The March 1932 *partage* of Hissar was much more extravagant than that of Tureng. Schmidt and Godard took three months to present the lots as an "attractively

---

[66] Nasiri-Moghaddam, "Archaeology and the Iranian National Museum," 141–2; F. R. Wulsin to H. H. F. Jayne, November 26, 1930, UPMAR Jayne: Container 20, Folder 1.
[67] Majd, *The Great American Plunder*, 97.

arranged" museum exhibit at the Ministry of Education. The exhibit was presented with a line down the center of the room dividing the equal and commensurate lots. Again, Godard elected not to retain ten unique pieces for the Persian government. By all accounts, this event was quite the scene. There were many visitors and witnesses to the government's decision, which was, this time, made personally by the prime minister. According to American Minister Charles Hart's testimony of the event, this *partage* seemed to have pleased all involved and resulted in no conflicts over value commensuration.[68] What changed from the first to the second *partage* event relates to location, how the settings were arranged, and who occupied the role of selector of the lots. What is most interesting, however, is that *partage* was paid more attention at this event. This is evidenced by a vitriolic and condemnatory editorial in the newspaper *Shafaq-e Sorkh*,[69] and also by the extravagant display of the Hissar division of finds. Moreover, the official selector of the lots was the prime minister himself. Indeed, there were rising stakes surrounding *partage*.

The third case study concerns the *partage* of Takht-e Jamshid, or Persepolis, in December 1934, which was far more contested than either of the first two.[70] The struggle in this event concerned, first, whether there would be a division of finds at all and, second, the terms and conditions of the division. The tensions stemmed from the Persian government's contention that Herzfeld's permit for Persepolis was a special case to which the Antiquities Law did not apply, and, for that reason, there would be no division of finds. As the artifacts produced by Herzfeld's contracted activities started to pile up, the expedition's sponsor, the Oriental Institute of the University of Chicago, sought to renegotiate the terms of the permit. After nearly a year of heated negotiations that involved numerous ultimatums and threats of negative publicity, the Oriental Institute ultimately strong-armed the Persian government into agreeing to a *partage* through the application of diplomatic pressure via the State Department's legation in Tehran. The Oriental Institute's position was that it sought to bring the authorization in line with the letter of the law, but the new permit was conspicuously favorable to their interests.[71] The Oriental Institute ended up with more than a standard fifty-fifty *partage* share; it received an unprecedented cut of the unique objects, including thirty thousand Elamite administrative tablets, many of which remained on long-term loan in Chicago until recently.[72] In contrast to the two previous *partage* events, the division of finds took place at Persepolis on the palace terrace itself between Godard and Herzfeld's assistant, Friedrich Krefter, with no other Iranian government officials present.

This event differs from the previous two in terms of setting, role inhabitation, commensuration, and disposition. First of all, the order of division and selection of

---

[68] Ibid., 105.
[69] As in ibid., 99–100:

> It is His Majesty whom we beseech to stop the division of these treasures by [cup and pound] like beets and carrots. It is our belief and that any of sensitive patriotic Persian that it is a thousand times better for these objects to remain buried as they were for several thousand years than their being dug and divided [...] only to afford decorations for foreign museums.

[70] Ibid., 159–91.
[71] Ibid., 215–19.
[72] Jebraʿel Nokandeh and Christopher Woods, eds., *Persepolis, Chicago, Tehran: The World of the Persepolis Fortification Tablets* (Tehran: Oriental Institute and National Museum of Iran, 2019).

the lots had been reversed. The Oriental Institute demanded a set of objects that the Persian government would never agree to give up, and then used State Department pressure to extort its share. This effectively meant that the lots were selected before being divided, leaving the apportionment of the small finds to occur later. The selection itself, which previously occurred at the Ministry of Education, instead took place via letters between Breasted, Murray, and Hornibrook, under pressure from the American minister in Tehran, and during audiences with the new prime minister, Mohammad Ali Foroughi. This process moved the locus of decision-making out of Godard's hands. The location of the division of the lots changed as well, taking place *at* Persepolis, rather than in Tehran.

This sequence of events produced very different conceptions of commensuration and, consequently, different evaluations than had been the case with Tureng and Hissar. In the Persepolis case, the issue of the value of heritage featured much more prominently than in the previous two examples. Both the Persian government and the Oriental Institute placed a great deal of value on Persepolis, though in this instance, the Oriental Institute got the upper hand by securing the better of the two lots through diplomatic pressure, Herzfeld's skullduggery, and Godard's collusion. The Persian government viewed the entire event negatively, insofar as it originally did not desire a *partage* related to Persepolis at all, despite the non-*partage* of Persepolis actually being in contravention of the law. One of the key points that emerges out of Majd's account and the Penn Museum archive is that, more than anything else, Persian government officials objected to the application of American diplomatic pressure during the affair. This is evidenced by their continued requests for the American legation to stay out of the matter. By this point, the Persian government's stated preference was to negotiate directly with the Oriental Institute.[73] Finally, it should be noted that the Near Eastern Affairs desk chief at the US Department of State, Wallace Murray, was enthusiastic about the resolution of this conflict. At the same time, Breasted was almost as negatively disposed toward it as the Persian government, primarily because he wanted an even larger share of the *partage* than he ultimately received.[74]

Conclusion: Implications and Future Directions

What does this account of archaeological diplomacy reveal about the general conditions of US-Iran relations during the interwar period and the early years of Pahlavi rule? In this chapter, I have shown how American individuals, institutions, and diplomats navigated and negotiated the business of statecraft and policymaking in Iran during the late interwar period, that is, the interval just before the United States emerged as the preeminent imperial hegemon in Iranian and global affairs. One illustrative point, highlighted by the historian James Goode, is how the US diplomatic corps reacted to Herzfeld's initial permit for Persepolis. Because Breasted had understood this permit as an option for a future concession rather than an outright and immediate authorization,

---

[73] Majd, *The Great American Plunder*, 215.
[74] Ibid., 186–8.

he almost did not accept the agreement. Reflecting on this, US *chargé d'affaires* Hugh Millard wrote to David Williamson to express his dismay that American efforts in Iran represented one "flub after another."[75] These "flubs" included a number of diplomatic imbroglios that occurred during the 1920s, including the murder of Robert Imbrie, the failure of the Millspaugh mission, and the withdrawal of the Ulen group from the national railroad syndicate. In this context, Millard argued that archaeology was the most effective means by which the United States could increase its prestige in Iran. Indeed, the US State Department, through Wallace Murray, urged the diplomatic corps to support American archaeologists in Iran at all costs. As in 1930, archaeology seemed to represent the nation's brightest hope to burnish its reputation in Tehran.[76]

These views should be understood in the context of what James Bill described as a "reservoir of goodwill" between Iran and the United States before the Second World War. Prior to the war, the United States was seen as a geopolitical counterweight to the machinations of the British and Russian empires. In this context, goodwill accumulated largely from the activities of individual Americans who lived and worked in Iran. Bill emphasizes personalities such as Howard Baskerville, Samuel Jordan, and Louis and Grace Dreyfus.[77] We may add to this list archaeologists and art historians such as Frederick and Susanne Wulsin, Arthur Upham Pope, Myron Bement Smith, Joseph Upton, and Charles K. Wilkinson. The events narrated above show that, in contrast to the failed efforts of American companies to involve themselves in Iranian oilfields,[78] American archaeologists were extraordinarily successful in negotiating access to "the field" in Iran during the 1920s and 1930s.

Heritage diplomacy was not conducted by the archaeologists alone, however. In fact, contrary to arguments that the United States pursued a non-interventionist policy in Iran until after the Second World War,[79] there is ample attestation of US State Department involvement in the field of Iranian archaeology. In particular, the Persepolis affair of 1934–5 was seen by the US diplomatic corps as a high-stakes event, requiring the personal intervention of the American minister to resolve the dispute over the terms of the concession between Herzfeld, Breasted, Foroughi, and Reza Shah.[80] Wallace Murray was a key figure, directing the revolving door of American diplomats in Tehran to monitor and support the American archaeological enterprise during this period. As Murray stated in a letter to the assistant secretary of state: "The Department has taken a close interest in the activities in Iran of the Oriental Institute of the University of Chicago. We have felt we were fully warranted in assisting this institution in its difficulties in Iran because of the unusual cultural value of the scientific work which was being done in that country."[81] At times, the

---

[75] Goode, *Negotiating for the Past*, 146–7.
[76] Ibid.
[77] Bill, *The Eagle and the Lion*, 16–17.
[78] Ibid., 27; Brew, "In Search of 'Equitability,'" 14–16; Mirfendereski, *The Privileged American*; Zirinsky, "Riza Shah's Abrogation," 87–8.
[79] E.g., Zirinsky, "Riza Shah's Abrogation," 87.
[80] Majd, *The Great American Plunder*, 178, 215.
[81] Ibid., 233.

difficulties experienced by the American archaeological enterprise in Iran resulted from political externalities. The most important external factor during the drafting of the Antiquities Law related to the precedent that it was seen to set for oil and mineral exploration. In another example, Erich Schmidt experienced difficulties in 1936 with his aerial survey and directorship of excavations at Rey and Persepolis because of the breakdown of US-Iran relations over the Jalāl incident.[82] In the 1920s and 1930s, as today, foreign archaeological enterprise and geopolitics were inextricably linked, and it remains difficult to understand the historical contours of the former without some consideration of the latter.

The questions raised in this chapter are part of a broader trend in the study of American foreign relations, as scholars focus less on the narrow realms of political, diplomatic, and military leadership and more on the role of non-state actors in international affairs.[83] At the same time, however, the history of foreign expeditions conducted by American archaeologists, especially to the Middle East, should be understood in the context of the United States' emergence as a superpower in the years after the First World War.[84] During the interwar years, the United States extended its cultural, political, and economic reach, which afforded a greater degree of access for American archaeologists to countries such as Iran.[85] While there were initially hopes that the United States and its representatives abroad would conduct themselves differently than the preceding empires, early encounters convinced some Iranians that American missions were little better than those of the traditional European powers, which had sought to dominate the Middle East and extract its natural and cultural resources.[86]

The events discussed in this chapter also relate to the history of American cultural diplomacy. This aspect of US foreign policy was composed largely of individual and institutional initiatives that did not technically operate under official directives from the US State Department until later.[87] Indeed, American cultural diplomacy during the years prior to the establishment of organizations such as Voice of America and the United States Information Agency suffered from poor coordination between the State Department and the many moving parts and pieces involved in international cultural work.[88] In future research, the relationship between the American diplomatic corps and field scientists such as archaeologists, as well as the interactions between both groups and their Iranian counterparts, should be further studied and contextualized within the shifting conditions of US-Iran relations.

---

[82] Ibid., 225–6.
[83] Kelly J. Shannon, "Foreign Relations and U.S. in the World—A Historiographical Survey," in *The Routledge History of the Twentieth-Century United States*, ed. Jerald Podair and Darren Dochuck (New York: Routledge, 2018), 166–8.
[84] Bernhardsson, *Reclaiming a Plundered Past*, 3.
[85] Christina Luke, *A Pearl in Peril: Heritage and Diplomacy in Turkey* (Oxford: Oxford University Press, 2018).
[86] Bernhardsson, *Reclaiming a Plundered Past*, 4; Lynn Meskell, *A Future in Ruins: UNESCO, World Heritage, and the Dream of Peace* (Oxford: Oxford University Press, 2018).
[87] Michael L. Krenn, *The History of United States Cultural Diplomacy: 1770 to the Present Day* (London: Bloomsbury Academic, 2017).
[88] Ibid., 55.

US-Iran relations have been riddled with contradictions, even at times of relative and assumed harmony.[89] Even as American archaeologists established a relatively positive track record in the field of Iranian archaeology,[90] the early period of this history was characterized by gross power imbalances. This chapter has foregrounded the circumstances under which an Iran novice and relatively underqualified junior museum curator—Frederick Wulsin—arrived in Tehran and was immediately able to meet with cabinet members and other high-ranking government officials. Moreover, as the Persepolis affair demonstrates, American institutions, through their prestige, financial clout, and personal connections to State Department officials, were able to extract concessions from the Persian government in the form of renegotiated permits and generous *partage* agreements. These power imbalances and their shifting configuration over time constitute the subject of ongoing research into the history of American archaeological expeditions to Iran.

The 1960s and 1970s, in particular, have been considered a "golden age," not only in the history of archaeology in Iran but specifically of *American* archaeology in Iran. During this period, at least two generations of Near Eastern archaeologists were trained in Iran, and many of them took Iranian archaeology to the theoretical and methodological forefront of the field worldwide.[91] The history of archaeology during the 1960s and 1970s is still largely a chronicle of who excavated what, where, and when, but it can be approached from the analytic perspective employed in this chapter. Indeed, this "golden age" is another key inflection point in the history of US-Iran archaeological diplomacy. In 1962 a new law, drafted by the Iranian Antiquities Service, superseded the 1930 Law for the Protection of National Vestiges.[92] While the 1962 law imposed new restrictions on foreign enterprises, it coincided with two decades of intensive collaboration between American and Iranian archaeologists. By studying the correspondence between the historical actors, along with the legal frameworks that regulated the conduct of archaeological expeditions, we can develop a more comprehensive understanding of US-Iran relations and the relationship between archaeology and geopolitics more broadly.[93] In the present-day context of severely curtailed relations between American and Iranian heritage professionals, one of the only ways forward is to delve into our shared past as inspiration for more connected and equitable futures.

---

[89] Matthew K. Shannon, "American–Iranian Alliances: International Education, Modernization, and Human Rights during the Pahlavi Era," *Diplomatic History* 39, no. 4 (2015): 661–88.
[90] Abdi, "Reviewed Work(s): The Great American Plunder."
[91] Kamal Aldin Niknami, *Methodological Aspects of Iranian Archaeology: Past and Present* (Oxford: BAR International Series, 2000).
[92] F. Rainey to Mr. Darakshesh, Minister of Education, January 3, 1962, UPMAR, Unaccessioned Hasanlu Archive Correspondence Files. I thank Penn Museum archivist Alessandro Pezzati for graciously allowing me to access these files, which originally belonged to Professor Robert Dyson.
[93] Nadia Abu El Haj, *Facts on the Ground: Archaeological Practice and Territorial Self-Fashioning in Israeli Society* (Chicago: University of Chicago Press, 2001).

4

Pandering in the Persian Gulf: Arabia, Iran, and Anglo-American Relations, 1900–71

Firoozeh Kashani-Sabet

The Persian Gulf, a strategic waterway connecting South Asia (and by extension Africa) to the Middle East, emerged as a battleground between Arabians and Iranians during the twentieth century. The unequal settlements of the world wars, in particular, spawned a modern version of the ethnic rivalry that has historically divided these communities. Tensions over the economic and cultural dominance of the Persian Gulf, fueled by Anglo-American diplomacy, gradually favored Arabian prerogatives over Iranian ones in contested territorial domains. This privileging had its roots in British imperial policies in the Middle East and the Persian Gulf, as I have argued elsewhere.[1]

The interwar years heralded many changes for the Middle East and left a spate of unresolved boundary and territorial issues that have plagued the region to this day. Iran's relationship with what became the "Arab world" grew complicated and was not always oppositional. In fact, the notion of a monolithic and all-encompassing "Arab world," which came to define much of the contemporary Middle East, did not enjoy broad usage before the mid-twentieth century when it gained currency with Arabists defending the rights of Palestinians and with the creation of the Arab League in 1945.[2] This concept, however, was deeply problematic for Iran and other states because it gave the false impression that, after the First World War, it was only Sunni and Christian Arabs that gained uncontested control of territories claimed

---

[1] Firoozeh Kashani-Sabet, "Colorblind or Blinded by Color: Race, Ethnicity and Identity in Iran," in *Sites of Pluralism: Community Politics in the Middle East*, ed. Firat Oruç (Oxford: Oxford University Press, 2019), 153–80. Also, Mehmet Darakcıoğlu and Firoozeh Kashani-Sabet, "Vagabond Routes: Sailing the Persian Gulf and the Red Sea," in *Twin Seas: The Persian Gulf and the Red Sea, Compared*, ed. Eric Tagliacozzo, forthcoming.

[2] Albert Habib Hourani, *Great Britain and the Arab World* (London: J. Murray, 1945), 8–9; Margaret Pope, *ABC of the Arab World* (London: The Socialist Book Centre, 1946). Aide memoire, the Arab Ministers to the Secretary of State, annex to Memorandum of Conversation of same date, October 12, 1945, *Foreign Relations of the United States, 1945: Volume VIII, the Near East and Africa* (Washington, DC: US Government Printing Office, 1969), p. 768, document 746. Available online: https://history.state.gov/historicaldocuments/frus1945v08/d746 (accessed March 30, 2021).

by Arab nationalists.[3] That other claimants—Assyrians, Armenians, Kurds, Turks, and Iranians, to name a few—to the same territories were assessing the impact of these significant shifts in the political, ethnic, and religious maps of the Middle East seemed to matter little to Arab nationalists, and such nuances infrequently became talking points in the leading Arabic publications of the era.[4]

This inattention was especially true of the Persian Gulf. Given the relative poverty, as well as the dearth of urban infrastructure of its communities, the region did not inspire Arab nationalist attention or zeal in the early twentieth century, though Iraq was a separate matter. Although oil was not yet found in Arabian territories, general interest in oil had garnered journalistic attention in the Arabic press.[5] However, in both of these locales—Iraq and south of the Persian Gulf—Persianate communities appeared largely (and conveniently) invisible in British and Arabic sources. At times, their numbers, as recorded by some British administrators, were too miniscule to have any real political or historical significance—especially in Kuwait, Bahrain, Qatar, and Oman.[6] Persian sources, however, told a different story. Already in 1911, the Persian newspaper *Habl al-Matin*, published in Calcutta (Kolkata) and Tehran, sounded an alarm. The newspaper warned Iranians to register protests against any treaties concluded by its competitors in the region: "Never [should Iranians] satisfy themselves with anything but having singular priority in the Persian Gulf, for they will not be able to undo the ensuing harms."[7] This prescient piece anticipated that any competition in these waters would result in disadvantages for Iran.

As the Ottomans watched their territories shrink, they paid renewed attention to Iraq and the southern regions of the Gulf.[8] The Ottomans even created maps that referred to these disputed waters as the "Gulf of Basrah" (*basra körfezi*).[9] Prior to the war, the Ottoman Empire attempted to lay claims to Bahrain, Kuwait, and other nearby regions. The Ottomans renounced their ambitions in the unratified Anglo-Turkish Agreement of 1913, but the British perspective on the positions of either the Ottoman Empire or Iran was remarkably consistent: a denial of legitimacy and the assertion that Britain "had dealt with Bahrein as an independent State."[10] The British

---

[3] For Ba'athist writings, see Michel Aflaq, *Choice of Texts from the Ba'ath Party Founder's Thought* (Firenze: Cooperativa Lavoratori, 1977).

[4] For example, *Al-Ahram* contained very few articles on Iranians, Kurds, and Turks from 1920 to 1929, especially concerning rival territorial claims.

[5] *Al-Hilal*, 1922/23, vol. 31, "al-Bitrul," p. 512, which includes a brief history of its use—also, p. 392. For an interesting chronology of the Arab revival, see *Al-Hilal*, Jabr Dumit, "Nihzat al-sharq al-'Arabi," vol. 31, pp. 1057–64.

[6] John Gordon Lorimer, *Gazetteer of the Persian Gulf, Oman, and Central Arabia* (1908), 538, 769, however, documented scattered communities of Persians.

[7] *Habl al-Matin*, no. 36, 11 Rabi' al-Avval 1329 (March 13, 1911), p. 2, also pp. 1–4. For more on Iranian concerns in Larestān, Bandar-e Langeh, Bushehr, and other regions around the Persian Gulf, see *Habl al-Matin*, no. 3, 3 Rajab 1328 (July 11, 1910), pp. 17–20; and *Habl al-Matin*, no. 40, 17 Rabi' al-Sani 1329 (April 17, 1911), p. 17.

[8] Frederick F. Anscombe, *The Ottoman Gulf: The Creation of Kuwait, Saudi Arabia, and Qatar, 1870–1914* (New York: Columbia University Press, 1997).

[9] Map of Basrah and Gulf of "Basrah," Başbakanlik Osmanli Arşivi.

[10] British Library, IOR/R/15/2/1744, "File 29/3 (1 A/36) Institution of Bahrain and Kuwait Nationality" [4r] (7/14), p. 2. "File 29/3 (1 A/36) Institution of Bahrain and Kuwait Nationality" [5r] (9/14). Also, IOR/L/PS/12/3818, Coll 30/99 "Koweit & Bahrain Nationality. Date of institution of" [74r] (154/202). Accessed via Qatar Digital Library (hereafter QDL). Available online: https://www.qdl.qa/en. QDL is a partnership between the Qatar Foundation, the Qatar National Library, and the British

also became wary of possible American claims to "capitulatory rights" in Kuwait.[11] Subsequently, British authorities had to contend with Iraq's requests for clarity and documentation regarding its nationality laws as pertaining to Kuwaiti and Bahraini residents.[12]

Competition over control of the Persian Gulf intensified before the outbreak of the First World War, in part because of German expansionism and support for the Baghdad Railway, which had intended to reach Kuwait. Iran, too, became a battleground for the great powers—a point most egregiously demonstrated in the Anglo-Russian Convention of 1907 that attempted to partition Iran.[13] This competition played a role in defining the diplomatic ethos of post-First World War Middle East states, many of which with British support acquired a dominant veneer of Arabness through top-down programs of Arabization. The state Arabization programs of the interwar era contained little discussion of the ethno-linguistic diversity of the minorities in their midst.

Iran's enduring objections to its territorial contraction partly explained why the country focused so much attention on resolving outstanding border disputes after the First World War. Historical claims of dominance over extensive stretches of land and cultures caused hostilities with other ethnic groups, especially Iran's Arab neighbors. During the interwar era, sometimes virulent anti-Persian rhetoric infused the pronouncements of Arab policymakers such as Sati al-Husri, yet his Western biographer and renowned Arabist, William Cleveland, made little mention of his subject's anti-Persian prejudices.[14] Persian anti-Arab sentiment similarly gained steam during these years as Pahlavi Iran tried its hand at Persianization.[15]

Library. The QDL website has many digitized documents from the British Library, including the India Office Records (IOR) used in this chapter.

[11] IOR/L/PS/12/3818, Coll 30/99 "Koweit & Bahrain Nationality. Date of institution of." [24r] (54/202). For a fascinating memorandum prepared by the US State Department's Division of Near Eastern Affairs years later detailing American interests in Bahrain and its environs, see History Vault: File 003100-012-0335, Division of Near Eastern Affairs, "Memorandum on the Bahrein Oil Concession," submitted to the chargé d'affaires in Iraq, [October 5], 1931. Unless otherwise noted, all ProQuest History Vault citations refer to the "US Diplomatic Post Records" on various countries in the Middle East.

[12] IOR/L/PS/12/3818, Coll 30/99 "Koweit & Bahrain Nationality. Date of institution of." [7r] (20/202).

[13] Habl al-Matin, no. 35, 4 Rabi' al-Avval 1329 (March 6, 1911), pp. 10–12. For discussions of constitutional politics, Mohammad Ali Shah, and E. G. Browne, see same issue, pp. 11–13.

[14] William Cleveland, The Making of an Arab Nationalist: Ottomanism and Arabism in the Life and Thought of Sati Al-Husri (Princeton, NJ: Princeton University Press, 1972). By contrast, see Fanar Haddad, who discusses the anti-Iranian bias in post-First World War Iraq largely within the context of Shia/Sunni sectarianism: Fanar Haddad, Sectarianism in Iraq: Antagonistic Visions of Unity (Oxford: Oxford University Press, 2011), especially p. 50. Also, Reeva Simon informatively discusses al-Husri's biases: Reeva S. Simon, "The Imposition of Nationalism on a Non-Nation State: The Case of Iraq During the Interwar Period, 1921–1941," in Rethinking Nationalism in the Arab Middle East, ed. James P. Jankowski and Israel Gershoni (New York: Columbia University Press, 1997), 87–104.

[15] Firoozeh Kashani-Sabet, Frontier Fictions: Shaping the Iranian Nation, 1804–1946 (Princeton, NJ: Princeton University Press, 1999). Also Kashani-Sabet, "Colorblind or Blinded by Color." For another analysis, see Chelsi Mueller, "The Persian Gulf, 1919–39: Changes, Challenges, and Transitions," Journal of Arabian Studies 8, no. 2 (2018): 259–74.

Outside of Iran—especially in Iraq, Kuwait, and Bahrain—Persians frequently lost their identities or rights as citizens of newly emerging states.[16] Whereas within Iran itself some non-Persian minorities could be recognized as citizens comprising the Iranian nation with *de jure*, if not always *de facto*, rights for political participation. For example, the Iranian citizenship and nationality law of 1925 provided certain provisos for such recognition.[17] Around the same time in Iraq, US sources noted that "more Persians left the country than entered it," and approximately "5,000 more subject[s] of Irak entered than left." This same report observed that, apart "from temporary visitors, such as pilgrims and transport workers, most visitors were classed as workers and merchants."[18] Iran subsequently issued new passport (*tazkireh*) and visa regulations that clarified categories of entry and temporary residence for visitors.[19] It also renewed efforts to police "frontier villages" and manage the use of passports there. In localities that lacked the ability to distribute passports and regulate their use, the customs offices managed and supervised the movement of people between and across borders.[20]

While Iran could not assert unequivocal military dominance in any of these contested domains (Basrah, Bahrain, Kuwait, and Dubai as a few examples) after the First World War, neither could other indigenous ethnic groups. To make this statement is not to argue for Iran's right to expansionism in Iraq, or elsewhere in the Middle East. It is, rather, to point out the lopsided dynamics of British colonial policies, which made concerted efforts to circumscribe the presence and influence of Iran—the only oil-exporting nation at that time—to the Iranian plateau and deny Iran the opportunity to claim additional territory in the lower-lying Persian Gulf basin. This was done to protect British and later Anglo-American imperial security interests.[21] This bias in British and American policymaking was also tied to what Priya Satia has called "the idea of Arabia." As Satia explains: "Rather than abandon the effort to grasp Arabia's political and geographical realities, they [the Western powers] invented a new intelligence strategy that prioritized knowledge acquired through intuition over sense data and stipulated lengthy immersion as the only effective preparation for this work. By intuition, the agents meant the *acquired* ability to *think like an Arab*, an empathetic mimicry of the 'Arab mind.'"[22] By contrast, Lord Curzon, the viceroy of India and self-anointed imperial expert on Persia, labeled Iran "the Persian problem"—a description that aptly summed up British perspectives.[23]

---

[16] Miriam Cooke, *Tribal Modern: Branding New Nations in the Arab Gulf* (Berkeley: University of California Press, 2014), 60–2.

[17] History Vault: File 003099-001-0282, January 1, 1925–December 31, 1925, No. 1106, May 22, 1925, W. Smith Murray to the Department of State and Enclosure.

[18] History Vault: File 003099-001-0046, "Annual Report of Commerce and Industry, 1924," May 23, 1925, from Vice Consul George Gregg Fuller, Tehran, Iran, p. 60.

[19] National Library and Archives of Iran (hereafter NLAI) File 240/73526. The records in this entire batch of correspondence, which include specific cases and legislation, are extremely relevant to these subjects.

[20] NLAI File 240/73526: Tehran, Regulations of 28 Shahrivar 1312. Hereafter, all dates from the Persian calendar are in the following format: 28/6/1312 (September 19, 1933).

[21] Analyzing this history may also help to explain aspects of the Islamic Republic's current decision-making in the Middle East and the Persian Gulf.

[22] Priya Satia, "The Defense of Inhumanity: Air Control and the British Idea of Arabia," *American Historical Review* 111, no. 1 (2006): 23.

[23] George Nathaniel Curzon, *Persia and the Persian Question* (1892), 1: 2. Also, Henry James Whigham, *The Persian Problem: An Examination of the Rival Positions of Russia and Great Britain in Persia with Some Account of the Persian Gulf and the Bagdad Railway* (London: Isbister, 1903). Lorimer also discusses Curzon's analysis of the "Persian problem" in *Gazetteer*, 1: 321. For more on this issue, see

A degree of territorial stability gradually returned to Iran with the rise of Reza Khān, later Reza Shah Pahlavi, and his often vicious disarmament of tribal groups. After the coup of 1921, Reza Khān pursued military campaigns intended to unify Iran's provinces. He succeeded in suppressing the various tribes and battling Shaykh Khaz'al, who was intent on carving out an autonomous territorial sphere in the south. The campaign against Khaz'al was hard fought, with the region suffering from "crop failures" and hunger. Khaz'al had been traveling between Basrah and southern Iran, where Iranian military forces eventually apprehended him.[24] Over time, the identity of Khuzestan (also known as "Arabistan" in various sources) fueled Arabian expansionism and challenged Iran's long-standing claims to a region that Iranians viewed as a center of their country's pre-Islamic Elamite civilization.[25] British sources increasingly regarded Arabistan as predominantly occupied by Arabian tribes, though it was acknowledged, for example, that "Persian is spoken in Mahommerah [sic] concurrently with Arabic." However, "outside the towns, Arabic is almost universally spoken."[26] Unlike British accounts, which tended to minimize the influence of Persianate culture in these areas, Persian sources showed sensitivity to the fact that these domains had formed an integral part of a perceived historical Iran (despite the vague and ahistorical nature of the concept) and remained an area in which contemporary Iran had a vested interest.[27]

While the Qajars had to navigate pro-Arab imperial policies, Pahlavi Iran had to accustom itself to a disadvantageous world order. The international system that was established after the First World War and fortified after the Second World War appropriately insisted that Iran accommodate minorities (ethnic, religious, and linguistic) within and beyond its borders, but without always giving Iranian citizens reciprocal political recognition and inclusion elsewhere. These unbalanced developments undermined Iran's influence in the Middle East and marginalized Persianate culture outside of Iran. The culture wars played out starkly in Iraq and the Persian Gulf after the First World War—an era that simultaneously witnessed the expansion of Arabian (and Arab) positions and Arabization policies, from Egypt to Iraq. Colonial knowledge inherited from British officials shaped regional policies in, as well as Anglo-American diplomatic approaches to, the Persian Gulf during and after the Second World War. Thereafter, the conflicts of the Cold War, especially Mohammad Mosaddeq's battle for economic independence and oil

---

Darakcıoğlu and Kashani-Sabet, "Vagabond Routes." Colonel Douglas Craven Phillott's *Colloquial English-Persian Dictionary in the Roman Character* (1914) received an interesting review by linguist and army officer, Lieutenant Colonel David Lockhart Robertson Lorimer, who made the following observation: "In the present state of Persian lexicography there is much to be said for recording words for which there is only local warrant. Many may prove to be of more general extension than was at first suspected. This, however, does not apply to words used in Baghdad, Basrah, Kuwait, and Bahrain." "Notice of Books," *Journal of the Royal Asiatic Society of Great Britain and Ireland* (1919): 440.

[24] History Vault: File 003099-001-0592, January 1, 1925–December 31, 1925, Confidential US Diplomatic Post Records, Middle East 1925–1941 Iran.

[25] Elizabeth Carter and Matthew W. Stolper, *Elam: Surveys of Political History and Archaeology* (Berkeley: University of California Press, 1984), 103.

[26] Arnold T. Wilson, "Report on the Trade and Commerce of the Province of Arabistan for the Year ended March 22, 1910," in Great Britain, Foreign Office, *Diplomatic and Consular Reports: Annual Series*, no. 4594 (London, 1910): 7.

[27] See Darakcıoğlu and Kashani-Sabet, "Vagabond Routes." Also, Kashani-Sabet, *Frontier Fictions*, chapters 1, 4, and 7.

nationalization, further marginalized Iran in the Persian Gulf and hardened the rivalry between Persians and Arabs in the region.

This chapter chronicles the impact of Iran's waning influence in the Persian Gulf during the Pahlavi years. The regional containment of Pahlavi Iran began as a British policy enacted by colonial administrators to monopolize Iran's oil and simultaneously protect Great Britain's territorial holdings throughout the Gulf. In these endeavors, and later for the United States during the Cold War, Iran was often deemed recalcitrant. Despite Mohammad Reza Shah Pahlavi's relationship with the United States, Iran failed to reverse long-standing trends or permanently improve its position in the Middle East prior to Great Britain's withdrawal from the Persian Gulf in 1971. The Islamic Republic's efforts after 1979 to expand beyond its current territorial borders—and the related tendency in the United States to position Iran as a foil for Saudi Arabia and other Arab states—must be evaluated against this historical backdrop.

Power, Oil, and Imperial Legacy

In 1908, Iran arose as the first oil state in the Middle East. Petroleum gushed forth from a well in Masjed-e Soleimān, and within a year, on April 14, 1909, Great Britain sealed its control over Iran's oil production by creating the Anglo-Persian Oil Company (APOC) "with an authorised capital of £2,000,000 sterling."[28] America had no share in Iran's oil at that time; nonetheless, APOC acquired twenty thousand tons of piping from the United States for the construction of its refinery in Khuzestan.[29] By the 1920s, APOC showed interest in searching for oil in other parts of the Persian Gulf. John Randolph, the American consul in Iraq, reported that, in 1925, APOC "sent geologists to Muscat who went into the interior and made more or less of an oil survey of the country, but nothing is known as yet as to what they discovered, if anything."[30] Muscat's population at that time was estimated to be around two thousand.

Britain solidified its Middle East dominance in the interwar years through a series of international agreements and bilateral treaties. As a result, the League of Nations granted London authority over Palestine and Iraq, and Britain's so-called residency in the Persian Gulf reached its historic height. However, Iran did not easily relinquish control of its oil. In 1919, and again in 1933, when Iran insisted on renegotiating the terms of its oil agreement, it defied the status quo. The country quickly became a key source of revenue and energy for Great Britain, which remained keen on upholding its dominance. That control could only be sustained through economic means and dependency relationships that did not always interest Iranian political leaders. At the same time, Britain attained supremacy in Iraq after the First World War and reluctantly acknowledged, but did not easily accommodate, long-standing Iranian interests there.

---

[28] *The Petroleum Review*, July 31, 1909, 76.
[29] US Congress, *US Congressional Serial Set*, 61st Cong., vol. 91, no. 5794 (Washington, DC: US Government Printing Office, 1910), 196.
[30] History Vault: File 003104-007-0001, Report from John Randolph, American Consul, Baghdad, Iraq, December 29, 1927.

In determining the boundaries of southern Iraq, investigative journalist Sir Percival Phillips, who was sent to the spot in the early 1920s to determine British objectives, contended that Britain "should retain" portions of Basrah "to safeguard the oil fields in Western Persia."[31] Iraq was, after all, crucial for British postwar supremacy in the oil industry. As Phillips observed: "The Anglo-Persian Company, the most powerful syndicate in the Middle East, is now drilling along the Iraq-Persian frontier, and several wells are already producing."[32] The pervasive influence of APOC connected the regions of Basrah and southwestern Iran as the company's agents "are scattered throughout the country." Phillips, whose charge included assessing the legitimacy of Britain's investment in Iraq, sardonically acknowledged the points in its favor: "You will hear many arguments from the oil interests—and other private corporations tied financially to Iraq—why Great Britain should continue to sink money in Mesopotamia. ... Yet oil is more expensive in Mesopotamia than in India."[33] The burden on the British taxpayer for maintaining League of Nations mandates such as Iraq was controversial and a subject of heated debate.

Beyond control of Iraq, identity politics shaped many conversations concerning the interwar states of the Middle East. In the Persian Gulf and Iraq, the British laid out a neat, but unrealistic, linear division between Arab(ian)s and Persians. American traveler and famed New York lawyer Paul Drennan Cravath, who visited these regions and wrote about them in 1925, perhaps summed it up best:

> To the traveler the chief interest of Baghdad is its people. Being the center of caravan routes extending eastward into Persia and beyond and on the north into Turkey and Turkestan, and to the west and south into Syria and Arabia, its population is perhaps the most cosmopolitan and varied of any Asiatic city. Its bazaars swarm with Syrians, Turks from all parts of Turkey, Armenians, Arabians, Persians, Turkomans, Africans, Kurds, Jews, Afghans and Indians, to say nothing of the country who are of composite race.[34]

Cravath served as one of the founding members of the Council on Foreign Relations in 1919, and his impressive client list included corporate giants such as Westinghouse, Royal Dutch/Shell, and General Motors.[35]

Cravath aptly highlighted the remoteness of Baghdad and the obstacles to reaching that city from Europe, which required an "ocean streamer to Bombay, by coasting steamer from Bombay to Basra, and from there by river streamer—a journey that took the better part of a month."[36] The British had built a railroad during the war to connect Baghdad

---

[31] Sir Percival Phillips, *Mesopotamia: The "Daily Mail" Inquiry at Baghdad* (London: Associated Newspapers, 1922), 16.
[32] Ibid., 21–2.
[33] Ibid., 22.
[34] Paul D. Cravath, *Letters Home from India and Irak* (New York: J. J. Little and Ives, 1925), 137.
[35] Kermit L. Hall, ed., *The Oxford Companion to American Law* (New York: Oxford University Press, 2002), 185.
[36] Cravath, *Letters Home from India and Irak*, 137.

to Basrah and "another to the Persian border on which occasional trains run."[37] During his travels, Cravath met with Gertrude Bell, the British colonial administrator in Iraq who "speaks Arabic fluently," and who was interested in archaeological research led by the British Museum and the University of Pennsylvania at Ur. Bell also served as his interpreter in an interview with King Faysal of Iraq, who did not speak English.[38] Cravath remarked that the King "was rather darker in color than the average inhabitant of Irak," whom he described as "almost white" in Baghdad.[39] Their conversation focused mostly on "petroleum," which was causing the monarch distress as he strove to reach an equitable deal with the British.[40] Cravath rightly detected the difficulties Faysal faced in leading Iraq as a Sunni Arab, considering that "most of the inhabitants of Irak belong to the Shiah sect."[41] Just years earlier, the revolt of 1920, which elicited a harsh response from the Royal Air Force, in turn drew a stern rebuke from Colonel Thomas Edward Lawrence.[42] The revolt signified the need for a substantial British force to keep order in Iraq.

The complicated ethnic map of the Persian Gulf contributed to regional competition. During the interwar years, Arabia and Iran pursued competing interests in Bahrain and maintained boundary disputes with Iraq. As a result, Iran took its time to recognize Iraq and similarly did not immediately recognize Hijaz.[43] In 1929, Iran sent Persian envoy ʿAin al-Molk, formerly its consul-general in Damascus, on a mission to Ibn Saʿud in the hopes of resolving the outstanding obstacles that had prevented Iran's "formal recognition of the Hedjaz."[44] Competition only escalated given the anticipated economic value of oil believed to exist in these areas. The discovery of oil in commercial quantities in Iraq (1927), Bahrain (1931), Kuwait (1938), Saudi Arabia (1938), Qatar (1939), Abu Dhabi (1958), Oman (1964), and Dubai (1966) not only consumed Anglo-American diplomacy but also fueled a resurgent Iranian nationalism that strove to restore territorial and economic gains.[45]

The expression "Anglo-American" in the context of Persian Gulf international diplomacy is both pertinent and problematic. Such terminology justifiably suggests partnership, cooperation, and unity of cause between British and American objectives in the Persian Gulf and its neighboring states. However, it also glosses over differences in British and American approaches to the region. Some historians have analyzed Anglo-American diplomacy through the prism of Middle East politics since the Second World War.[46] By

---

[37] Ibid., 137–8.
[38] Ibid., 140.
[39] Ibid., 141 and 138.
[40] Ibid., 141.
[41] Ibid., 139.
[42] T. E. Lawrence, "Mesopotamia," *Sunday Times*, August 22, 1920. Available online: http://www.telstudies.org/writings/works/articles_essays/1920_mesopotamia.shtml (accessed April 21, 2021). Also, Lawrence to the editor of *The Times*, July 22, 1920. Available online: http://www.telstudies.org/writings/letters/1919-20/200722_the_times.shtml (accessed April 21, 2021). Lawrence, an Arabist, proposed that Arabic become the "Government" language in Iraq.
[43] Kashani-Sabet, *Frontier Fictions*, 222–3.
[44] History Vault: File 003104-003-0493, File No. 800, Richard R. Willey, "Political Notes," July 17, 1929. For an Iranian perspective on Bahrain, see Said Nafisi, *Bahrain: Hoquq-e hezār-o-haft-sad sāleh-ye Irān* (Tehran: Ketābforushi-ye Tahuri, 1955).
[45] Roger Owen and Sevket Pamuk, *A History of Middle East Economies in the Twentieth Century* (Cambridge, MA: Harvard University Press, 1998), 84–5.
[46] Simon Davis, "The Persian Gulf in the 1940s and the Question of an Anglo-American Middle East," *History* 95, no. 1 (2010): 64–88.

contrast, I look more closely at regional politics through the shifting balance of power in the Persian Gulf to demonstrate that Arab nationalism fit British aims and defined Anglo-American understandings of the Gulf's territories, resources, and inhabitants.

To Britain and the United States, the neat division of two coasts along the Persian Gulf—an Arabian and a Persian one—became a convenient paradigm, but one that did not accurately represent the ethnic diversity of these borderlands. This paradigm specifically sought to minimize Iran's presence and historical claims south of the Persian Gulf by giving pride of place instead to Arabian historical narratives. As a result, by the time the United States enacted its "twin pillar" policy, which sought to balance Iran and Saudi Arabia as the guarantors of regional security during the 1970s, the deck was stacked against Iran. The United States could not give equal weight to Persians and Arabs in the Gulf because Iran had already lost the culture wars and economic struggles in the region. In studying diplomacy in the Persian Gulf, I write against scholars who have relied exclusively on English-language (principally Anglo-American) sources and those who have adopted an unnuanced paradigm of the two coasts to document what was, in fact, a shared past.

Territorial Counterclaims

As Ibn Saʿud strove to subdue tribal unrest in the Arabian Peninsula and at the same time relieve tensions with Imam Yahya of Yemen, Iran confronted anew the impact of its territorial contraction. In 1932, Iran presented its case to the League of Nations for its claim to Bahrain. The American view of these tensions did not immediately show support for either side, and it appeared that US Consul Augustin Ferrin had become quite familiar with the arguments of both players. He noted that Britain and the al-Khalifah family based their territorial claims on key bilateral treaties, while Iran contended that "the inhabitants of Bahrein are largely of Persian blood and almost entirely of the Shiah religion."[47] Disputes over the sovereignty of Bahrain escalated as Britain and Iran both hardened their positions over questions relating to travel documents, visas, and citizenship.[48] Ferrin noted, moreover, that British "contentions in regard to Bahrein are given in detail" in Arnold Wilson's account of the Persian Gulf, published in 1928.[49]

It is beyond the purview of this chapter to discuss the intricacies of the Bahrain controversy in detail, but tenacious British efforts to delegitimate Iranian claims and grievances in Bahrain, Kuwait, and Iraq pointed to a persistent pattern of minimizing Persianate presence and influence outside the plateau.[50] At the same time, British and

---

[47] History Vault: File 003099-006-0410, Augustin W. Ferrin, "Bahrein," February 20, 1929, Report No. 39.
[48] Kashani-Sabet, *Frontier Fictions*, 221.
[49] History Vault: File 003099-006-0410, Ferrin, Report No. 39. Also, Arnold T. Wilson, *The Persian Gulf* (Oxford: Oxford University Press, 1928).
[50] Kashani-Sabet, "Colorblind or Blinded by Color"; and Darakcıoğlu and Kashani-Sabet, "Vagabond Routes."

subsequently American foreign officers regarded Khuzestan as principally inhabited by Arabs, and not Persians, often very justifiably criticizing Iran for its unequal treatment of its Arab denizens in an era of heightened Persian nationalism. In 1935, for example, Iran tried to bolster its educational efforts in Khuzestan. An internal Iranian memorandum stated that prompt attention to cultural matters became necessary because "a significant cross-section" of the region's population were members of Arabic-speaking tribes "disinclined" to converse in Persian. Although Persian-language elementary schools existed, Arab tribal children were "deprived" of the opportunity of attending such schools.[51]

Outside of Iran, the rights of Persian residents, however, were not addressed by Britain—the mandatory authority in Iraq and the imperial overseer of Bahrain, Kuwait, and the Trucial shaykhdoms. In Iraq this double standard became the norm in dealing with Iranian or Persianate communities. Persians, when mentioned in British administrative records, were often counted as paltry and insignificant or as "alien" communities.[52] This issue became especially problematic when Bahrain passed a nationality and immovable property law on May 8, 1937. This legislation was directed in part against Persians, given that a significant portion of the behind-the-scenes deliberations and caveats concerned those of Persian nationality in Bahrain.[53] The Iranian community struggled to navigate around this legislation, and in 1938 a group of merchants and the headmaster of the Iranian school there met "to discuss the question of immovable property owned by Persians in Bahrain." To skirt around the restrictions, the group decided "not to send lists of their property to the Agency but to transfer their property to their children who have been born in Bahrain and treated as Bahrain subjects."[54] Ultimately, the legislation "restricted ownership by Iranians to their residences and places of work." Other nationals who had purchased land in Bahrain included "Saudi Arabians and, to a lesser extent, Iraqis, the latter are mostly Jews."[55] The issue of nationality became similarly fraught with legal and political implications

---

[51] NLAI File 297/10177: Edareh-ye Iyalat-e Moʿāref-va-Owqāf-e Khuzestan, dated 18/11/14 (February 8, 1936). Also, for a relevant article on Khuzestan published during this interval, see Qāʿem Maqāmi, "Ashāyer-e Khuzestan," *Yādgār,* no. 7 (Esfand 1323/February–March 1945): 18–24.

[52] Historical Section, Foreign Office, Great Britain, and George Walter Prothero, *Peace Handbooks* (London: H. M. Stationery Office, 1920), 28–9 and 33. Also, Kashani-Sabet, "Colorblind or Blinded by Color."

[53] IOR/L/PS/12/3795, Coll 30/78 "Bahrein Nationality Law. Bahrein Property Law: Registration of certain foreigners in Bahrein by the Agency. Ownership of property by foreigners in Bahrein (King's Reg. No. 1 of 1937)" [48r] (96/896); Coll 30/78 [85r] (170/896); Coll 30/78 "[104r] (208/896). Please note that some of this history, pursued simultaneously but independently of my research on the subject, is covered in Chelsi Mueller's excellent recently published book, *The Arab-Iranian Conflict: Nationalism and Sovereignty in the Gulf Between the World Wars* (Cambridge: Cambridge University Press, 2020), 208–10. Although our analytical frameworks differ markedly, Mueller adds important dimensions to the history, including Reza Shah's views of and policies toward the Persian Gulf.

[54] IOR/L/PS/12/3795, Coll 30/78 "Bahrein Nationality Law. Bahrein Property Law: Registration of certain foreigners in Bahrein by the Agency. Ownership of property by foreigners in Bahrein (King's Reg. No. 1 of 1937)" [66r] (132/896). Extract from Intelligence Summary No. 19 of the Political Agent, Bahrain, October 16–31, 1938.

[55] IOR/L/PS/12/3795, Coll 30/78 "Bahrein Nationality Law. Bahrein Property Law: Registration of certain foreigners in Bahrein by the Agency. Ownership of property by foreigners in Bahrein (King's Reg. No. 1 of 1937)" [51r] (102/896).

regarding claims of Iranians and dual nationals (Bahraini/Iranian). In these claims, some British authorities argued that "the 'master nationality' rule prevents Persian nationality being invoked in Bahrein by a person who possesses dual Bahrein and Persian nationality."[56] While British officials bickered over wording, the impact of the legislation on immovable property owned by Persians in Bahrain was precisely to hamper Iranian integration as Persians living in Bahrain.

As Bahrainis and Iranians tightened their borders and tested the durability of their cultural ties, Iran's Interior Ministry and one of its provincial offices in Larestān requested that Iranian migrants who had traveled to Bahrain in previous years, mainly due to a drought and bad harvest, be welcomed home and treated well upon their return.[57] Although these particular Iranian communiqués did not directly mention the nationality and property legislation as a cause for return, the timing remains significant. However, other correspondence pointedly addressed the concerns of Iranians returning from Bahrain. Because Iran considered Bahrain a part of its territory, it tried to transfer the property of migrants by establishing comparable value through Iran's silver-based currency.[58] Iranian government correspondence proceeded with the belief that Bahrain "is counted as a part of Iran," but converting currency was complicated because Iran had not established a branch of the *Bānk-e Melli* there, and most transactions used either the rupee or the lira as currency, not the Persian rial.[59]

These regulations affected the Persian residents of Bahrain in different ways. One active and notable employee of the Iranian Justice Department, Ahmad Farāmarzi, submitted a communication to the prime ministry office concerning nationality laws in Bahrain and their implications for resident Persians. An interesting figure, Farāmarzi traced his lineage to the Farāmarzān families of Larestān. Early in life he ran afoul of the law for his political activism, and he eventually went to Bahrain, where he faced British ire for his opposition there. Upon his return to Tehran, Farāmarzi launched a journalistic and media career, and eventually served as representative in the Iranian parliament. He also authored an important book on the Persian Gulf during the political rule of Karim Khān Zand.[60] In his memorandum of May 25, 1939, he assessed the nationality and property laws, which "compelled Iranians to accept Bahraini nationality or to sell their property. And, if they did not sell their property in time, the Bahrain government would assess and register their property." Farāmarzi observed that "some who did not have unshakeable patriotic faith" (*'imān-e rāsekh-e vatan parasti*) had accepted Bahraini nationality and protected their property.[61] However, those who

---

[56] IOR/L/PS/12/3795, Coll 30/78 "Bahrein Nationality Law. Bahrein Property Law: Registration of certain foreigners in Bahrein by the Agency. Ownership of property by foreigners in Bahrein (King's Reg. No. 1 of 1937)" [95r] (190/896). E/1069/14/91, Foreign Office, March 21, 1938.

[57] NLAI File 98/293/14501: Memorandum No. 41519/2779, dated 31/5/1317 (August 22, 1938).

[58] NLAI File 240/641: Treasury Department, dated 27/4/1318 (July 19, 1939).

[59] NLAI File 240/641: Treasury Department, dated 17/4/1318 (July 9, 1939).

[60] Sahim al-Din Khazāʿi and Esmāʿil Sepāhvand, "Barresi-ye Vizhegi-hā va Ahammiyat-e Ketāb-e Karim Khān-e Zand va Khalij-e Fars," *Rāhyāft-e Tārikhi*, no. 14 (Spring 1395 (2016)): 81–94. Also, Ahmad Farāmarzi, *Karim Khān-e Zand va Khalij-e Fars* (Tehran: Dāvarpanāh, 1346/1967).

[61] NLAI File 240/641: Ahmad Farāmarzi's Letter to Prime Ministry Office, dated 3/3/1318 (May 25, 1939).

did not take on Bahraini citizenship had their properties in Manama assessed at one-third or one-fourth of their actual value. In particular, Farāmarzi complained that his father's property, which consisted of fertile land with economic potential both within and outside the city, had been grossly undervalued. The legislation forced individuals like Farāmarzi's father to migrate to Dashtestān, Iran, even though his wife and close relatives remained in Bahrain.[62]

The interwar nationality clashes in Bahrain and Iran displayed in sharp relief the impact that the post-First World War order had on individuals in the Persian Gulf. The British were determined to sustain their overt or *de facto* administrative control of certain coastal areas and, as a result, Arab, Persian, and at times Indian identities became the subject of official dispatches. In 1936 the British consulate in Bushehr requested information and clarity regarding an individual, Abdol Rahim, who, according to British law, legally held a British passport since his father, Mirzā Mehdi, was born in India. Abdol Rahim had routinely received permission for short-term residency but was told in 1936 that he was considered an "Iranian subject." Britain requested additional information to understand on what basis this determination had been made.[63] Iran made the determination based on its understanding that Abdol Rahim was born in Bushehr to an Iranian mother. His father was known as "Ahmad Mirzā Mehdi" and resided in Bushehr.[64]

These issues arose in the context of Persian concerns that "authorities in Dubai, similar to those in Bahrein and Kuwait decided lately to reduce the influence of resident Iranians of those regions to the extent possible."[65] Earlier, in 1930, Shaykh Saʿid Bin Maktum sent out a notice prohibiting Iranians from wearing Pahlavi hats. Maktum addressed this "notice" to "Persian subjects who reside in our territory and those who frequent it." The warning stated that "the wearing of Persian head wear, is prohibited in our town and whoever wears it shall not escape punishment." In addition, any Iranian "unwilling to obey" this regulation "should return to his home in Persia where he can wear what he likes."[66] Shaykh Maktum had apparently grown concerned that Iranians who had been "domiciled" in Dubai from between "20 and 60 years" donned the attire. Moreover, "their children born in Dibai [sic] were regarded by him as his own subjects," and they, too, "had put on the costume."[67] Dress—a marker of identity and site of cultural contestation in Iran itself—had become a source of contention in the broader Persian Gulf region as well.

---

[62] Ibid.
[63] NLAI File 355/541: Inquiry from British Consulate General (Bushehr) to Governor of Southern Ports and Appanages (Bushehr), dated 4/3/1315 (May 25, 1936).
[64] NLAI File 355/541: Confidential Memorandum, Interior Ministry, Office of Police, Bushehr and Ports (shahrbāni-ye Bushehr va Banādar), dated 27/4/1315 (July 18, 1936).
[65] NLAI File 355/541: Memorandum 109M, dated 11/10/1317 (December 31, 1938).
[66] Saʿid Bin Maktum, "Notice," 21 Shavvāl 1348 (March 22, 1930). Viewed in person at the British Library and available via QDL: IOR/L/PS/12/3442, Coll 28/39 "Persia: Printed Correspondence 1929–1936" [562r] (1134/1174). Also: IOR/L/PS/12/3442, Coll 28/39 "Persia: Printed Correspondence 1929–1936" [561v] (1133/1174).
[67] IOR/L/PS/12/3442, Coll 28/39 "Persia: Printed Correspondence 1929–1936." Letter from Political Resident in the Persian Gulf to His Majesty's Minister, Tehran, No. 14/T, May 13, 1930.

British sources routinely underreported Iranian grievances and at the same time scrupulously recorded Arab complaints against Iran. Charles Belgrave, the British adviser to the al-Khalifah family, among others, discussed Iran's regrettable mistreatment of Shaykh Khaz'al, though the shaykh's ambitions undoubtedly played a role in his removal.[68] In 1931 the British legation in Tehran also considered the ill-treatment of Haji Hamid Bin Haji Abud Bahraini, "twice deported from Persia." It asserted unequivocally that "this unfortunate man has been very harshly treated by the Persian Government," even as it conceded that "the Persian Government are not altogether without justification" about questioning his whereabouts.[69]

Around the same time, Belgrave received a letter from the Baladiyah of Manama stating that "all Persian beggars, especially those infected with contagious deseases [sic], should be prohibited from entering Bahrain, and that, such of them as are already in Bahrain, should be repatriated to Persia in the interests of public health."[70] In his diary, Belgrave also wrote in 1927: "Looked at a lot of Persian beggars who arrived here & settled to send them back to where they came from."[71] British authorities discussed the legality of such an ordinance and determined that "[i]t is within the powers of the Bahrein Government to prohibit the Persian beggars, infected with contagious disceases [sic], from entering into Bahrein but those that are already in Bahrein can only be repatriated to Persia if they commit some offence."[72] It appeared that Iranians of various classes, from landowners to indigents, found it progressively difficult to settle in Bahrain.

Similar social policies extended to prostitutes who attracted the attention of American and Iranian authorities. A Persian woman in Bahrain named Robābeh Seyāreh had apparently placed her daughter in an American mission school. American correspondence indicated that Robābeh visited the American mission hospital to receive treatment for venereal disease and "openly admitted that she was a prostitute."[73] However, the Iranian foreign minister, Ghaffār Khān Jalāl, had not made that determination, either out of discretion or naiveté. Seyāreh acceded to having her daughter, described as "a bright little girl," attend the mission school for a time. Shortly thereafter, the Bahrain police "rounded up all the foreign prostitutes and deported them. Robada [sic] was with them."[74] Bahraini authorities then determined that the girl was not Robābeh's daughter at all. While the fate of these individuals remains unknown, such episodes speak to

---

[68] Charles Belgrave, *Belgrave Diaries*, 64. Available online: https://14f2011.com/files/rc_library/Belgrave%20Diaries_0.pdf (accessed April 21, 2021).
[69] IOR/R/15/1/323, "File 19/109 VI (C 45) Bahrain Relations with Foreign Powers." Also, IOR/L/PS/18/B485, "Memorandum on Bahrein."
[70] IOR/R/15/2/1218, "File 6/11 Resolutions passed by the Baladiyahs (Municipalities of Manama and Muharraq) and correspondence regarding deputations of officials in the Baladiyah."
[71] Belgrave, *Belgrave Diaries*, 328.
[72] IOR/R/15/2/1218, "File 6/11 Resolutions passed by the Baladiyahs (Municipalities of Manama and Muharraq) and correspondence regarding deputations of officials in the Baladiyah." No. 733 of 1928. Political Agency, Bahrain, November 3, 1928.
[73] History Vault: File 003099-014-0703, Encl. No. 1 to Dispatch 1240 of October 4, 1932, from Legation Tehran to Arabian Mission, Bahrain, August 6, 1932.
[74] History Vault: File 003099-014-0703, Encl. No. 1 to Dispatch 1240.

the chaos, as well as the silent and overt disenfranchisement, of indigent Iranians in neighboring communities overseen by Britain and its Arabian allies.

To be fair, Iran fielded similar complaints. Some two years later, a Bahraini proprietor, Haji Abd al-Rezā, protested his arrest by Iranian police and charged that he had been detained inappropriately.[75] These episodes spoke to the ways in which new nationality laws and passport regulations discouraged casual border passages and made residency increasingly difficult for ethnic minorities in states that were enshrining monolithic identities either in support of or in resistance to British interventions. Arabian sensitivity to, and at times suspicion of, Iranians prompted discriminatory policies rooted in patriotic sentiment, indicating that ethnically motivated regulations cut both ways. In other words, Iran was not the sole player in the Persian Gulf to enact such a policy. These policies were the by-product of the post-First World War settlements and a legacy of European ethno-linguistic nationalism foisted upon the Middle East.

America and the Politics of Nationalization from World Wars to the Cold War

Britain's skewed policies in the Persian Gulf favored Arabian interests over Iranian ones. This was primarily due to its desire to maintain a tight grip over Iranian oil and to remain the dominant economic power in these waters. The introduction of US interests to the Persian Gulf and subsequent Anglo-American competition challenged British preponderance. British "hostility" toward American interests, as previously toward Ottoman and Persian ones, could not be easily brushed aside in places such as Bahrain. Moreover, British intransigence toward Iran complicated America's relationship with that country. America had tried on multiple occasions, going back to the unratified Anglo-Persian Treaty of 1919, to find a middle ground between Britain and Iran when dealing with regional affairs.[76] Although American-Iranian relations sizzled with small conflagrations from time to time, the United States did not initially script a policy that depended upon limiting Iranian interests south of the Persian Gulf. That changed, however, during the years of the early Cold War.

Oil was a major reason why the US view of the Gulf changed. Prior to the First World War, American petroleum companies expressed an interest in Middle Eastern oil by negotiating with the Turkish Petroleum Company—dealings that after years of wrangling concluded with an agreement in 1928 that granted America a share in the enterprise. A year earlier, oil had been discovered in Kirkuk, Iraq, and in 1929 the

---

[75] NLAI File: Iyalat-e Khuzestan, Ahvaz, dated 22/11/1311 (February 11, 1933).
[76] John A. DeNovo, *American Interests and Policies in the Middle East, 1900–1939* (Minneapolis: University of Minnesota Press, 1963), 168; and Daniel Yergin, *The Prize: The Epic Quest for Oil, Money, and Power* (New York: Simon and Shuster, 1991). My citations refer to the 2008 edition (New York: Free Press, 2008), 170–2. For other related subjects, see Karl Twitchell, *Saudi Arabia, with an Account of the Development of Its Natural Resources*, 3rd ed. (Princeton, NJ: Princeton University Press, 1958); Anthony Sampson, *The Seven Sisters: The Great Oil Companies and the World They Shaped* (New York: Hodder and Stoughton, 1975).

controlling business changed its name to the Iraq Petroleum Company (IPC).[77] The arrangement with IPC laid out leasing areas and recognized the interests of key oil firms, including APOC, Royal Dutch/Shell, the American Near East Development Corporation, and the Compagnie Française des Pétroles.[78] During the interwar years, America developed oil interests in Bahrain and described the political status and identity of the island in this way: "Bahrein is in theory an independent Arab state under British protection but is not a British protectorate; in practice, the administrative powers of the Sheikh are restricted by the terms of the various conventions signed with Great Britain."[79] This seemingly straightforward observation encapsulated the entrenched understanding that had come to signify the ethnicity of communities south of the Persian Gulf. This was the same perspective that fueled Iran's stubborn efforts to dispute this apparent truism and assert itself in Bahrain.

Iran's reluctance to renounce its claims became an unnecessary and inconvenient nuisance in the Anglo-American scramble for oil in Bahrain and the Persian Gulf. In 1925 Eastern and General Syndicate, Limited, a British enterprise, received a concession from the Shaykh of Bahrain. New Zealander Major Frank Holmes facilitated this transaction and also pursued opportunities in Kuwait.[80] In 1929 Standard Oil of California formed the Bahrain Petroleum Company (BAPCO). Regarding Britain's rebuttal to Iran's claims of sovereignty over Bahrain and other "historical precedents," US Consul Charles C. Hart was intrigued that "our own similar action of 1822 with respect to the revolted Spanish colonies in South America was cited."[81] Britain considered a "modification of the Nationality clause," though America found it frustrating that Britain did not abide by an "open door" policy in the dominions it oversaw.[82] On June 1, 1932, BAPCO struck oil, with tons of oil spewing from one well alone.[83]

The landscape of the Persian Gulf changed immeasurably in the 1930s. A major change came when oil was discovered in Kuwait and the Arabian Peninsula. Ibn Saʿud's finance minister, ʿAbdullah ibn Sulayman, concluded a deal with Standard Oil of California (SOCAL)—the parent company of BAPCO—to search for oil.[84] Oil

---

[77] DeNovo, *American Interests*, 198.
[78] History Vault: File 003100-012-0335, Division of Near Eastern Affairs to Jefferson Patterson, May 8, 1930.
[79] History Vault: File 003100-012-0335, Division of Near Eastern Affairs to the *chargé d'affaires*, Iraq, [October 5], 1931.
[80] Archibald H. T. Chisholm, *The First Kuwait Oil Concession Agreement: A Record of the Negotiations 1911–1934* (London: Frank Cass, 1975), 81–2. Also, Clive Leatherdale, *Britain and Saudi Arabia, 1925–1939: The Imperial Oasis* (London: Frank Cass, 1983), 191–2. For related US correspondence, see History Vault: File 003100-012-0335, January 1, 1931–December 31, 1931, Confidential US Diplomatic Post Records, Middle East 1925-1941 Iraq.
[81] History Vault: File 003099-014-0703, No. 1269, Charles C. Hart, "British Rebuttal of Persian Claim to Sovereignty over Bahrain Islands," October 28, 1932, p. 3.
[82] History Vault: File 003100-012-0528, Telegram, Department of State to American Embassy in London, March 26, 1932.
[83] "RICH OIL STRIKE IN BAHREIN," *Times of India*, June 11, 1932. Also, Gennaro Errichiello, "Foreign Workforce in the Arab Gulf States (1930–1950): Migration Patterns and Nationality Clause," *International Migration Review* 46, no. 2 (2012): 389–413; and Charles Walter Hamilton, *Americans and Oil in the Middle East* (Houston, TX: Gulf, 1962), 129.
[84] Madawi al-Rasheed, *A History of Saudi Arabia* (Cambridge: Cambridge University Press, 2002), 91.

gushed forth in 1938, and the stage was set for the emergence of Saudi Arabia and, by extension, the United States, as a major player in the Persian Gulf. It is telling that the solidification of Saudi-American relations, and the rise of both states in the Persian Gulf, appeared at a time when Iran's fortunes waned. Iran tried unsuccessfully to achieve an equitable agreement with Britain and the Anglo-Persian Oil Company. By this point, another well at Haft Kel had begun producing oil, but revenues accrued to the Iranian government from oil profits fluctuated from year to year. Other factors transformed the oil landscape of the Persian Gulf. The global depression of the 1930s left a negative impact on oil markets, and in 1931 the Iraq Petroleum Company concluded terms that guaranteed a minimum royalty to the Iraqi government. For these and other reasons, Reza Shah was impelled to renegotiate Iran's deal with APOC.[85]

In 1932, recognizing the diplomatic impasse, Iran canceled the D'Arcy concession of 1901, which had initiated Britain's oil exploration in the country. Iranian deputies discussed this matter intensely in the 117th session of the 8th Majles (or parliament). Prior to this decision, Iranian deputies requested that a representative from APOC be sent to the country for negotiations, but the company refrained from doing so. Given the stalemate, Iran's representatives reasoned that, since the agreement had been reached before the creation and sanction of the Majles, the agreement did not represent the best interests of the nation. They therefore endorsed the decision to cancel the concession.[86] Several months earlier, in the 96th session of the 8th Majles, Representative Ruhi called the oil wells "the definite property and the inalienable right of Iran."[87] The League of Nations also became involved in the dispute and published the text of the cancellation.[88]

After rancorous negotiations, in 1933 APOC finally agreed to give the Iranian government a new agreement that still left many unhappy. The area under the concession was significantly reduced, but the original concession, which was to end in 1961, was extended another 32 years to 1993. APOC, which was soon renamed the Anglo-Iranian Oil Company, paid £1 million to settle past dues, and instead of receiving 16 percent of oil profits, the revenue to Iran would be calculated in a different manner, with 20 percent of profits given to shareholders.[89] This arrangement remained far less equitable than the fifty-fifty deal that Saudi Arabia would strike with the Arabian American Oil Company (ARAMCO)—founded in 1938 with the discovery of oil in commercial quantities just a few short years later.[90]

---

[85] Peter J. Beck, "The Anglo-Persian Oil Dispute 1932–33," *Journal of Contemporary History* 9, no. 4 (1974): 125.
[86] Mozākerāt-e majles-e shurā-ye melli, mashruh-e majles-e hashtom (8th Majles), 117th Session, dated 10/9/1311 (December 1, 1932).
[87] Mozākerāt-e majles-e shurā-ye melli, mashruh-e majles-e hashtom (8th Majles), 96th Session, dated 28/4/1311 (July 19, 1932).
[88] Parviz Minā, "Oil Agreements in Iran," *Encyclopaedia Iranica*. Available online: https://iranicaonline.org/articles/oil-agreements-in-iran (accessed March 17, 2021).
[89] Beck, "Anglo-Persian Oil Dispute," 142–3.
[90] Irvine H. Anderson, *Aramco, the United States, and Saudi Arabia: A Study of the Dynamics of Foreign Oil Policy, 1933–1950* (Princeton, NJ: Princeton University Press, 1981), 179–97, on the background to the fifty-fifty agreement.

The rise of Germany fanned British suspicions that members of Iran's elite harbored sympathies for the Nazis. These tensions played out in the late 1930s in the British protectorates of the Persian Gulf, including Bahrain. In one instance, "two Persians were arrested by the Police on the allegation that they had declared openly that the Germans would soon defeat England as they had defeated France." However, since "[w]itnesses were afraid to depose in open court," the issue was "settled" by having the suspects declare openly in a mosque that they had made no such utterances.[91] The status of the Baharna and the Hawala in Bahrain grew complicated as well since the British did not always know how to classify them.[92]

The Second World War left another trail of destruction in the Middle East and ushered in a decade of regional violence and turmoil. In Iran, domestic politics entered a radical phase that culminated in the rise of Prime Minister Mohammad Mosaddeq and the oil nationalization movement. In neighboring states, the creation of the Arab League in 1945, followed by the birth of the State of Israel, fueled strident Arab nationalism.[93] In 1950 Saudi Arabia achieved the fifty-fifty deal that had eluded Iran.[94] As US officials in President Harry Truman's administration observed: "the oil row now in Iran between that country and England, and in which the United States is vitally interested, is a powder keg which could well explode and spread its destruction throughout the entire restless Middle East."[95] In 1951, two years after the shah's first trip to the United States, Dr. Mosaddeq and his National Front took over the movement to nationalize Iran's oil industry from the British. With the resounding support of the Majles, this occasion marked the creation of the National Iranian Oil Company.[96]

American policy toward Iran during the Cold War aimed "to prevent the country from coming under communist control," and the US government reasoned that an "equitable liquidation of the oil controversy" could facilitate this cause.[97] Behind the

---

[91] IOR/L/PS/12/3813 Coll 30/93 "Position of Bahrein subjects in Persia and of Persian subjects in Bahrein." Honorable Lieutenant-Colonel C. G. Prior, June 22, 1940.
[92] Ahmed al-Dailami, "'Purity and Confusion': The Hawala between Persians and Arabs in the Contemporary Gulf," in *The Persian Gulf in Modern Times: People, Ports, and History*, ed. Lawrence G. Potter (New York: Palgrave Macmillan, 2014), 299–326. For discussions of the Baharna, see Kashani-Sabet, "Colorblind or Blinded by Color." Also, Nelida Fuccaro, *Histories of City and State in the Persian Gulf: Manama since 1800* (Cambridge: Cambridge University Press, 2009), 165–6, for especially interesting discussions. James Onley also discusses this history: James Onley, *The Arabian Frontier of the British Raj: Merchants, Rulers, and the British in the Nineteenth-Century Gulf* (Oxford: Oxford University Press, 2007).
[93] This narrative will be developed in more detail in my future work. On the US and Arab nationalism, see Salim Yaqub, *Containing Arab Nationalism: The Eisenhower Doctrine and the Middle East* (Chapel Hill: University of North Carolina Press, 2004).
[94] Katayoun Shafiee, *Machineries of Oil: An Infrastructural History of BP in Iran* (Cambridge, MA: MIT Press, 2018), 165–6.
[95] History Vault: File 002195-019-0001, January 1, 1950–December 31, 1953, President Harry S. Truman's Office Files, 1945–53, Part 2: Correspondence Files, "Memorandum Re Oil Cartel Investigation."
[96] Mozākerāt-e majles-e shurā-ye melli, mashruh-e majles-e shānzdahom (16th Majles), 143rd Session, dated 15/2/1330 (May 6, 1951).
[97] History Vault: File 002196-031-0764, President Harry S. Truman's Office Files, 1945–53, Part 3: Subject Files, 1945–1953, Part 3: Subject Files, "The Position of the United States with Respect to Iran."

scenes, however, the United States also recognized the dire economic realities that faced Great Britain, mainly a weak pound and fears of "bankruptcy."[98] Iran's move to nationalize the oil industry came at a terrible time for Britain economically, which hardened its position toward Iran.

In the end, the 1953 coup removed Mohammad Mosaddeq and restored the shah as Iran's ruler. The coup remains a matter of ongoing debate, revision, and controversy, with scholars stressing a range of factors that compelled Dwight Eisenhower, who assumed the US presidency just months prior to the coup, to collude with the British and topple the Mosaddeq government. What is clear is that, after the coup, the Iranian oil industry moved under an international consortium. Moreover, the Anglo-Iranian Oil Company was renamed British Petroleum in 1954 and was forced to relinquish its monopoly over Iranian oil. Yet Iran still had to contend with large conglomerates to manage its petroleum industry.[99] Iranian nationalism, in other words, did not achieve some of its most essential objectives during the Mosaddeq period.

Iran's Retreat and Arabian Dominance

Britain's long-standing reluctance to acknowledge the rights and sizable presence of Persianate communities south of the Persian Gulf became an entrenched, if unwritten, policy that significantly diminished the power, influence, and financial potential of Iran and Iranians outside of the plateau. This dominant perspective also informed America's approaches to the Persian Gulf after the Second World War when it emerged as the preponderant Western power in the region and strengthened allies such as Saudi Arabia.

Developments throughout the Middle East also reduced Iran's capacity to project regional influence and sustain ethno-linguistic pluralism in the Gulf. Nearby, a resurgent Egypt under Gamal Abdel Nasser moved toward a nationalization project of a similar nature. In November 1951 Mosaddeq traveled to Egypt on his return from the United States, and in an emotional encounter with journalists there he declared that "a united Iran and Egypt will together demolish British imperialism."[100] The fall of Mosaddeq tested the ties between Egypt and Iran, which had just years earlier been united in marriage between the royal families. Despite fissures in the Arab coalition, from Iraq to Saudi Arabia the ideology of Arab nationalism, though far from monolithic, gained steam in multiple, if competing, contexts. At the same time, Nasser's successful campaign in 1956 to nationalize the Suez Canal further eroded Britain's influence in the Middle East and the Persian Gulf, or anywhere Arab nationalism had taken root.

---

[98] History Vault: File 002196-031-0764, President Harry S. Truman's Office Files, 1945–53, Part 3: Subject Files, Telegram, Department of State, No. 2808, November 10, 1951.

[99] Shafiee, *Machineries of Oil*, 227–31. On the coup, see Malcolm Byrne and Mark Gasiorowski, eds., *Mohammad Mosaddeq and the 1953 Coup in Iran* (Syracuse, NY: Syracuse University Press, 2004); Ervand Abrahamian, *The Coup: 1953, the CIA, and the Roots of Modern U.S.-Iranian Relations* (New York: New Press, 2013); Mary Ann Heiss, *Empire and Nationhood: The United States, Great Britain, and Iranian Oil, 1950–1954* (New York: Columbia University Press, 1997).

[100] "Mossadegh Asks Egypt-Iran Bond," *Los Angeles Times*, November 23, 1951. Also, "Iran Premier Pledges Ties with Egypt: Mossadegh Declares Two Will Demolish British Imperialism," *Washington Post*, November 23, 1951. Both available via ProQuest Historical Newspapers.

As Arab nationalism crested in the 1950s and 1960s, Britain retrenched to what was, in the imperial parlance, "east of Suez," while also pursuing a policy of "interdependence" with its stronger and wealthier American ally.[101]

In the late 1960s and early 1970s, British imperial retreat became an evacuation. The British resolution in 1968 to depart from the southern littoral of the Persian Gulf in 1971 had far-reaching consequences for Saudi Arabia, Iran, and the former Trucial States. Britain's withdrawal formalized a new balance of power in the region that had been in the making for decades. America stepped in, not always in tandem with Britain, and sometimes in disagreement. But the United States nonetheless inherited Britain's conception of the Persian Gulf as being neatly divided along two coasts: one Arabian and another Persian. While the United States began the twentieth century with a relatively balanced view of intra-regional rivalries, its Cold War experiences with nationalist leaders from Mosaddeq to Nasser hardened American views.

External patronage and the discovery of oil bequeathed a disproportionate amount of wealth and power to a handful of dynasts and dynasties. This occurred without an equitable distribution of influence and representation to other groups (South Asians, Africans, Baluchis, and Persians, to name a few) that long resided in these countries. Given this reality, our understanding of the Persian Gulf region requires a fundamental historical reorientation.[102] Much has been said about America's enactment of a Twin Pillar policy, which pledged US support to Pahlavi Iran and Saudi Arabia in their efforts to police the Persian Gulf.[103] However, Iran had already lost in the regional rivalry to Saudi Arabia by the time the Richard Nixon and Gerald Ford administrations adopted the Twin Pillar policy in the 1970s.

After 1971, when Iran accepted Bahrain's independence, Iran lost the ability to restore any semblance of balance in the region. Oil money bolstered Arab(ian) nationalism in unprecedented ways through the educational and political infrastructure of multiple states in the Persian Gulf. In particular, Saudi Arabia, with American acquiescence, achieved an unprecedented "preponderance of power," which Iran could not challenge

---

[101] Christopher M. Davidson, "Arab Nationalism and British Opposition in Dubai, 1920–66," *Middle Eastern Studies* 43, no. 6 (2007): 879–92. Also, Simon C. Smith, *Britain's Revival and Fall in the Gulf: Kuwait, Bahrain, Qatar, and the Trucial States, 1950–71* (London: Routledge Curzon, 2004); and Jill Crystal, *Oil and Politics in the Gulf: Rulers and Merchants in Kuwait and Qatar* (Cambridge: Cambridge University Press, 1990), 40 and 113 for the community of Persians and Shia in Kuwait and Qatar, but relying on British statistics. Crystal also discusses the development of Arab nationalism in various settings. On post-Suez Anglo-American relations, see W. Taylor Fain, *American Ascendance and British Retreat in the Persian Gulf Region* (New York: Palgrave Macmillan, 2008), chapters 3–4.

[102] For classic and key works, see the following: Fereydoun Adamiyat, *Bahrein Islands: A Legal and Diplomatic Study of the British-Iranian Controversy* (New York: Frederick A. Praeger, 1955); Edmund C. Bosworth, "The Nomenclature of the Persian Gulf," *Iranian Studies* 30, nos. 1–2 (1997): 77–94; Miriam Cooke, *Tribal Modern: Branding New Nations in the Arab Gulf* (Berkeley: University of California Press, 2014); J. B. Kelly, *Britain and the Persian Gulf, 1795–1880* (Oxford: Oxford University Press, 1968); Majid Khadduri, "Iran's Claim to the Sovereignty of Bahrayn," *American Journal of International Law* 45, no. 4 (1951): 631–47; Lawrence G. Potter, ed., *The Persian Gulf in History* (New York: Palgrave Macmillan, 2009).

[103] Rouhollah K. Ramazani, *The Persian Gulf and the Strait of Hormuz* (Alphen aan den Rijn: Sijthoff and Noordhoff, 1979), 120. Also, Stephen Brannon, "Pillars, Petroleum and Power: The United States in the Gulf," *Arab Studies Journal* 2, no. 1 (1994): 4–10.

effectively.[104] Elsewhere, Arab (and Arabian) nationalism in Kuwait, Bahrain, and Iraq overrode the identity of Persians, many of whom accepted Kuwaiti, Bahraini, or Iraqi citizenship for expediency and, with it, a superficial Arab or Arabian identity. This nationalist phenomenon is not unique to Iran, Saudi Arabia, or other countries of the Persian Gulf or Middle East. What remains unique is the relative inattention that Persian minority groups have received in Anglo-American and Arab scholarship. This silence reflects the marginalization of Iran and America's embrace of British policies that facilitated the erasure, silencing, and disempowerment of Persianate communities south of the Persian Gulf.

Missteps in Anglo-American policymaking have added to the tragedy of Arab-Persian misunderstanding by encouraging an artificial divide that has erased a long history of coexistence and community, not only in the premodern era but thereafter, too. Even in the heyday of Persian nationalism in the 1960s, when the shah took on the grandiose title, "Aryamehr," and when Arab nationalism swept the Levant and the Persian Gulf, Saudi Arabia and Iran actually pursued cultural and educational exchanges. In one case, Iran tried to accommodate Saudi Arabia's request for two instructors in the field of carpet weaving. Still, as a result of Anglo-American policies in the Persian Gulf during the first two-thirds of the twentieth century, such instances of cooperation proved to be the exception rather than the rule.[105]

Conclusion

Writing in 1974, Archibald Chisholm observed: "Nowhere during the last forty years have living conditions, money values, communications, political relations, oil exploration techniques, almost everything in fact except the climate, changed more radically than in the Gulf area."[106] Chisholm had participated in negotiating Kuwait's oil concession and later maintained ties to many of Kuwait's elite. The profound transformation of the Persian Gulf was a process that involved Western officials such as Chisholm, in large part because the discovery of oil incited great power competition for control of the region's resources. If motivated by geopolitical and economic factors, the transformation of the Persian Gulf ultimately altered the nature of urban and communal life throughout the region.

Disruptions in social life and patterns of migration and coexistence accompanied these monumental transformations. Merchants, pilgrims, travelers, beggars, and itinerants found themselves bound by new legal parameters intended to mold their identities and to contain their unobstructed passages. State infrastructure brought new

---

[104] I take the phrase "preponderance of power" from Melvin Leffler in his analysis of US Cold War objectives during the Truman era. As Leffler explains: "Preponderance did not mean domination. It meant creating a world environment hospitable to U.S. interests and values." Melvyn P. Leffler, *A Preponderance of Power: National Security, the Truman Administration, and the Cold War* (Stanford, CA: Stanford University Press, 1992), 19. Pertaining to the Persian Gulf, I would modify it to "U.S.-Saudi interests," if not values.

[105] NLAI File 297/51520: Vezārat-e Āmuzesh va Parvaresh, dated 30/4/1346 (July 21, 1967).

[106] Chisholm, *The First Kuwait Oil Concession Agreement*, 82.

regulations and modes of population control that imposed citizenship and property laws, which forced residents of different backgrounds to adopt the dominant ethnolinguistic character of the ruling dynastic families of the Gulf. Nations south of the Persian Gulf inherited the legacy of British policies, which aimed to reduce and limit Iran's influence there. Britain viewed Iran as the weak link in its defense of India, and in the course of the long nineteenth century it famously transformed the Persian Gulf into a "British lake."[107]

In the twentieth century, when the American presence and US state and corporate interests in Iran amplified, the United States initially attempted to adopt a somewhat even-handed stance in its Persian Gulf diplomacy. At times, the United States found itself frustrated with Britain's overbearing efforts to manage the region's oil through its treaty arrangements with various Arabian leaders. The creation of BAPCO and the discovery of oil in Bahrain gave the United States some independence and negotiating power, sources of leverage which increased with the fortuitous and lucrative discovery of oil in commercial quantities in Saudi Arabia.

At the same time, Britain shifted its attention away from Iran and toward Arabian communities—a point illustrated with the relocation of the Political Residency from Bushehr to Bahrain in 1946. Diplomatic historians, political geographers, and others had long perceived Britain's anti-Iranian tendencies in these waters.[108] I argue, however, that Britain's biases against Iran and its policies in the Persian Gulf incorporated a far more subtle and pervasive process of erasure and negation, or imperial cancel culture, going back to colonial policies and deeply embedded in Britain's many unfortunate interventions in Iran's boundary negotiation efforts.[109] This colonial process did not just efface Persianate communities from local histories of the Persian Gulf but also Africans and South Asians.

Anglo-American involvement in Iran assumed renewed significance in the Second World War and in the aftermath of the oil nationalization crisis of the early 1950s. These episodes seriously undermined Iran's relations with the United States and Great Britain and, at the same time, Persian culture and political influence south of the Persian Gulf. During the Cold War, the United States was no longer the honest broker that it seemingly was earlier in the twentieth century. An analysis of American strategy in the Persian Gulf reveals that the Twin Pillar policy of the 1960s and 1970s could not equally privilege Iran, contrary to common perceptions of this doctrine, because Iran had already lost the region's culture wars due to long-standing British practices.

The intent of this chapter—or project—is not to assert Iran's unequivocal right to Bahrain, Kuwait, or elsewhere, but rather to point to the discrepancies in colonial

---

[107] Sir Richard Temple, *India in 1880* (London: Murray, 1881), 417.
[108] Shahram Chubin and Sepehr Zabih, *The Foreign Relations of Iran: A Developing State in a Zone of Great-Power Conflict* (Berkeley: University of California Press, 1974), 141, 191; Pirouz Mojtahed-Zadeh, *Maritime Political Geography: The Persian Gulf Islands of Tunbs and Abu Musa* (Boca Raton, FL: Universal, 2015), 54.
[109] Kashani-Sabet, *Frontier Fictions*; Kashani-Sabet, "Colorblind or Blinded by Color"; and Darakcıoğlu and Kashani-Sabet, "Vagabond Routes." I have also given several public presentations on various aspects of these arguments: Columbia University (2008); University of Pennsylvania (2014); Princeton University (2015); Institute for Advanced Study (2016); and the London School of Economics (2018).

knowledge production and the limits of legal accommodation accorded to certain migrant and minority communities in the Persian Gulf from a historical perspective.[110] However, Persianate minorities, long silenced in these regions, deserve to have their stories recovered. Their perspectives must also be integrated into the region's historical narratives. I interrogate the notion of territorial belonging and "ownership" in the context of migratory communities.[111] This framework foregrounds the neglected struggles of beggars, prostitutes, and other nameless migrants lost in the region's battles for oil and political power.

The imposed and inherited negations, silences, and divisions overlook the cultural bonds that still join communities of Arab(ian)s and Iranians, especially in moments of crisis. This paradox should not escape any critic or proponent of these clashing nationalisms. In 1958 an individual claiming to be the cousin of King Faysal of Iraq sought shelter, or "asylum" (*panahandegi*), in Iran as a violent revolution erupted in Iraq.[112] Decades later, when the Shah of Iran, Mohammad Reza Pahlavi, had nowhere to turn, it was Anwar Sadat of Egypt who granted him refuge.

Anglo-American involvement in the Persian Gulf—whether of a competitive or collaborative nature—has given prominence to historical narratives that uncritically accept the inexorable divide between Arab and Ajam. This division has suited certain policymakers, especially since 1979 with the Islamic Republic's repudiation of the Anglo-American partnership. But Iran's current posture, and its perhaps unexpected support in certain communities, can only be understood within the context of systematic colonial erasures and enduring cultural connections throughout the Gulf.

---

[110] My forthcoming book, *Tales of Trespassing: Borderland Histories of Iran, Iraq, and the Persian Gulf* (under contract with Cambridge University Press), details this history from the late Ottoman period to 1971. This research project builds on my previous work on Iran's frontiers and boundary delimitation efforts. These subjects are absent from the bibliographies of historians of the Persian Gulf who do not adequately integrate Persian sources or perspectives, and therefore do not perceive the long-term impact of the boundary delimitation process, which necessitated information gathering and *creatio ex nihilo*. Nelida Fuccaro, for example, discusses Lorimer's *Gazetteer* as a quintessential example of Britain's engagement in knowledge production. But there is little mention oof Iran's negative experiences with border delineation efforts or of Lorimer's biases in recording his perspectives, which intended to privilege Britain's imperial objectives and alliances, often at the expense of Iran: Nelida Fuccaro, "Knowledge at the Service of the British Empire: *The Gazetteer of the Persian Gulf, Oman and Central Arabia*," in *Borders and the Changing Boundaries of Knowledge*, ed. Inga Brandell, Marie Carlson, and Önver A. Çetrez (Swedish Research Institute in Istanbul: Transactions, vol. 22, 2015), 17–34.

[111] For more on this concept, see the paper I delivered at the University of Pennsylvania's Perry World House Seminar Series, "(IL)Legal Borders: Narratives of Banning and Belonging in the Persian Gulf," February 3, 2021.

[112] NLAI File 290/002478: Vezārat-e Keshvar, dated 29/6/1337 (September 20, 1958).

5

De-Nationalized: Mohammad Reza Pahlavi, the Consortium, and Global Oil, 1954–64

Gregory Brew

In May 1962, the Shah of Iran, Mohammad Reza Pahlavi, met an executive from the Gulf Oil Company for dinner in San Francisco. The executive was no ordinary company man. One of the architects of Operation TPAJAX, the CIA coup that overthrew Iran's nationalist prime minister Mohammad Mosaddeq in August 1953, Kermit Roosevelt parlayed his experience in government into a lucrative second career as Gulf Oil's "vice president for governmental relations." That night, he plied the shah with questions regarding the Organization of Petroleum Exporting Countries (OPEC). The group, of which Iran was a founding member, hoped to pressure Gulf, Exxon, British Petroleum (BP), and other major oil companies into surrendering a larger percentage of oil's profits. There was even talk of cutting production or nationalizing local oil industries, as Mosaddeq had done eleven years before.

But the shah brushed aside such talk. His treasury depended on oil revenues generated by the companies that controlled the flow and sale of Iranian oil on a global market. "His country would benefit more from a world market for petroleum which was completely free," Roosevelt reported.[1] A year later, during a visit to Tehran, Roosevelt found that the shah had changed his tune. OPEC, the shah said, was on the verge of making history. Gulf had been too greedy. Either the companies would surrender a greater share of oil's vast profits, or the shah would join the rest of OPEC in taking unilateral action. There would be no peace in the global oil market, he declared. "Bargaining is what the companies and governments will have to live with" for the foreseeable future.[2]

Oil is an important part of modern Iranian history. Earnings from oil historically made up a large percentage of Iranian exports and formed a major contribution to state finances. Mohammad Reza Shah (r. 1941–79) embraced heavy state spending

---

[1] Foreign Office (FO) 371/164606 UES 1037/11, Rose to Eagers, May 11, 1962, UK National Archives (hereafter UKNA).
[2] FO 371/172530 UES 1037/94, Powell to Rose, December 4, 1963, UKNA; Memo of Conversation, December 6, 1963, *Foreign Relations of the United States, 1961–1963: Volume XVIII, Near East, 1962–1963* (Washington, DC: US Government Printing Office, 1995), document 381. Available online: https://history.state.gov/historicaldocuments/frus1961-63v18/d381 (accessed March 30, 2021).

after 1953 to advance Iran economically and consolidate his power.[3] The expansion of the Iranian state, the shah's ambitious economic development projects, and his military spending all depended on revenues realized from the sale of oil on the global market. Until OPEC seized control of price and production in the early 1970s—an event in which the shah himself played a major role—that market was controlled by a group of Western oil companies. Backed by the US government, the companies known as the "Seven Sisters" constructed an international energy system featuring oligopolistic suppression of production and joint control over foreign oil reserves in the Middle East and Latin America. Through this system, the companies delivered cheap oil to Western markets, feeding skyrocketing demand for fossil fuels while utilizing their oligopolistic power to realize massive profit, sharing only a portion with producing governments.[4]

Scholars studying the relationship between Pahlavi Iran and the oil companies tend to focus on disruptive episodes, such as the 1951–4 nationalization crisis.[5] Over the course of the 1950s and 1960s, oil's share of Iranian gross domestic product (GDP) increased, while oil's contribution to the state budget and the national development program rose exponentially. While these changes play an outsized role in the historiography of the Pahlavi period, the focus has tended toward what I have termed oil's "local integration," or the effect of oil revenues on the internal transformation of Iran. Outside of corporate histories, little attention has been paid to the "global integration" of Iranian oil, particularly the shah's relationship with the oil companies, which provided the bulk of Iran's oil earnings between 1954 and the 1970s.[6]

This chapter examines this relationship during the critical years between 1954 and 1964. It is based on research conducted in the archives of British Petroleum at the University of Warwick, the official archives of the US and UK governments, and personal memoirs and interviews accessible through the Foundation for Iranian

---

[3] Homa Katouzian, *The Political Economy of Modern Iran: Despotism and Pseudo-Modernism, 1926–1979* (London: Macmillan, 1981), 234–74; Ervand Abrahamian, *Iran between Two Revolutions* (Princeton, NJ: Princeton University Press, 1982), 427–8. For oil's importance to Iran's economic development during the Pahlavi period, see Julian Bharier, *Economic Development in Iran, 1900–1970* (New York: Oxford University Press, 1971); Kamran Mofid, *Development Planning in Iran: From Monarchy to Islamic Republic* (Outwell, UK: Middle East and North African Studies Press, 1987); Massoud Karshenas, *Oil, State and Industrialization in Iran* (New York: Cambridge University Press, 1990).

[4] For the construction of the postwar petroleum order, see Daniel Yergin, *The Prize: The Epic Quest for Oil, Money and Power* (New York: Simon and Schuster, 1991), 391–544. For the companies as an oligopoly, see Peter F. Cowhey, *The Problems of Plenty: Energy Policy and International Politics* (Berkeley: University of California Press, 1985); Neil H. Jacoby, *Multinational Oil: A Study in Industrial Dynamics* (New York: Macmillan, 1974); Anthony Sampson, *The Seven Sisters: The Great Oil Companies and the World They Shaped* (New York: Hodder and Stoughton, 1975).

[5] For the nationalization period, see Mary Ann Heiss, *Empire and Nationhood: The United States, Great Britain and Iranian Oil, 1950–1954* (New York: Columbia University Press, 1997); Mostafa Elm, *Oil, Power and Principle: Iran's Nationalization and Its Aftermath* (Syracuse, NY: Syracuse University Press, 1992); Malcolm Byrne and Mark J. Gasiorowski, eds., *Mohammed Mosaddeq and the 1953 Coup in Iran* (Syracuse, NY: Syracuse University Press, 2004).

[6] Ronald Ferrier, *The History of the British Petroleum Company, Volume I* (Cambridge: Cambridge University Press, 1982); J. H. Bamberg, *The History of the British Petroleum Company, Volume II* (Cambridge: Cambridge University Press, 1982); J. H. Bamberg, *British Petroleum and Global Oil, 1950–1975, Volume III* (Cambridge: Cambridge University Press, 2000).

Studies (FIS). These documents indicate that American oil companies worked with the US government to restart Iran's oil industry after the nationalization crisis. The companies were transnational actors, and while they observed a certain allegiance to Washington, their interests did not always align with those of the US government. For US policymakers, the goal was to strengthen the Pahlavi regime by increasing the flow of oil revenues. The companies exerted their power over Iran's oil industry, but were obliged to share profits with the shah, both to uphold industrial norms and to satisfy the US desire for an economically secure government in Tehran. The shah, initially a weak figure dependent on the companies' operations, grew bolder over time, as he sought to undermine the inequitable conditions of the 1954 Consortium Agreement. Rather than act as an "American stooge" or a tool of the companies, the shah practiced an independent foreign policy, albeit one influenced by his counselors and subject to his own whims, which were occasionally mercurial.[7] The mutually beneficial ties binding the Pahlavi government to the "Seven Sisters" precluded a complete break, but the late 1950s and early 1960s illustrated a subtle shift in the balance of power, one that the shah used to his advantage. This shift became more evident years later when the shah succeeded in subordinating the companies amidst the "oil shocks" of the early 1970s.

The Façade of Nationalization: The Consortium Agreement of 1954

Iran's oil history began with the D'Arcy concession, an agreement signed in 1901 between Mozaffar al-Din Shah Qajar and William Knox D'Arcy, an English industrialist. The agreement granted the British "the exclusive privilege to search for, obtain, exploit, develop, render suitable for trade, carry away and sell" any oil found within a 500,000 square mile area, in exchange for 16 percent "of the annual net profits."[8] The next fifty years revealed the imbalances between Iran and Great Britain, which owned a majority stake in the Anglo-Iranian Oil Company (AIOC). The company carved out an enclave in southwestern Iran, in the oil-producing province of Khuzestan. With support from the British government, AIOC grew into a state within a state, bribing politicians and interfering in Iranian politics. A document recovered from the company's archives illustrates the scope of these efforts. In March 1951, the company provided "entertainments" for Majles deputies and liberal payments to friendly editors who would publish stories emphasizing the company's contributions to Iran's economy.[9] These efforts, combined with Britain's more coercive tactics, were not enough to prevent the rise of a nationalist government in 1951, led by the popular

---

[7] This reflects growing appreciation of the shah as an independent actor, particularly in international affairs. See Roham Alvandi, *Nixon, Kissinger, and the Shah: The United States and Iran in the Cold War* (New York: Oxford University Press, 2014).

[8] "D'Arcy Concession," 1901, from Appendix 1.0 of Ferrier, *Vol. I*.

[9] British Petroleum Archive (BP) 126353, March 14, 1951, "Iranian Concessional Position—Means of Approach to Iranian Public Opinion." The BP Archive is located at the University of Warwick in Coventry, UK.

constitutionalist Mohammad Mosaddeq. He nationalized AIOC's assets in Iran that spring and formed a new company, the National Iranian Oil Company (NIOC), to assume control over the industry.[10]

While Iran had been dominated by the British, other oil-producing countries had concessions owned and operated by American oil companies. The five US majors—Jersey Standard (Exxon), Socony-Mobil, Socal (Chevron), Texaco, and Gulf—together with AIOC and Royal Dutch/Shell controlled 84 percent of global oil production, 90 percent of reserves, and 65 percent of refining.[11] Known collectively as the "Seven Sisters," the companies adopted oligopolistic practices by suppressing production through cooperative agreements in order to balance supply with demand and realize larger profits. Their position depended on the control of foreign oil reserves in the Middle East and Venezuela. Collectively, they worried that other oil-producing states would follow Mosaddeq's lead and nationalize foreign-owned oil assets. The companies, with the cooperation of the British government, embargoed Iranian oil. This cut off Mosaddeq's government from oil revenues, which at that point supplied three-quarters of foreign exchange and a significant portion of the state budget. Both the British government and the major oil companies hoped that such pressure would force Mosaddeq from power, while simultaneously deterring other oil-producing states from following his lead by nationalizing their oil industries.[12]

The US government attempted to mediate an end to the crisis. Though the United States balanced a number of concerns in its approach to oil nationalization, policymakers broadly agreed with the companies' position that the "contagion of nationalization" could not be allowed to spread.[13] Nevertheless, there was a constant concern in Washington over restarting the flow of Iran's oil revenues. The country was important to the Cold War strategy of containing the Soviet Union, and US officials feared that, without adequate support, Iran would collapse to communism, a development that would threaten other Western concessions in the Middle East. After years of failed negotiations, conditions in Iran in early 1953 appeared to be deteriorating. The US government worried that ongoing "oil-lessness" would lead to an economic and political cataclysm inside Iran, potentially leading to a communist government coming to power. The coup to remove Mosaddeq in August 1953 was meant to prevent this from happening.[14]

The coup installed a new government, led by General Fazlollah Zahedi and the shah, Mohammad Reza Pahlavi. The United States, which had orchestrated the coup with British support, offered the new government emergency aid. But such aid would only work on a temporary basis. "The most difficult problem confronting us," argued

---

[10] For the background of the nationalization crisis, see Heiss, *Empire and Nationhood*, 1–76.
[11] Charles P. Issawi and Mohammed Yeganeh, *The Economics of Middle Eastern Oil* (New York: Praeger, 1963), 61.
[12] Mary Ann Heiss, "The International Boycott of Iranian Oil and the Anti-Mosaddeq Coup of 1953," in *Mohammed Mosaddeq*, ed. Byrne and Gasiorowski, 178–200.
[13] Heiss, *Empire and Nationhood*, 78.
[14] Gregory Brew, "The Collapse Narrative: The United States, Mohammed Mossadegh, and the Coup Decision of 1953," *Texas National Security Review* 2, no. 4 (November 2019): 38–59. Available online: https://tnsr.org/2019/11/the-collapse-narrative-the-united-states-mohammed-mossadegh-and-the-coup-decision-of-1953/ (accessed March 23, 2021).

Secretary of State John Foster Dulles, "was how to develop revenues for Iran out of her oil."[15] Without oil, it was presumed Iran would not be able to maintain internal stability. Dulles told Ambassador Loy Henderson that the United States would move "at the earliest possible date" to secure an oil agreement "[that] would lessen the danger" of losing Iran.[16] In a speech in Washington in December 1953, Assistant Secretary Henry F. Byroade insisted that resolving the oil problem "is the most pressing need of the Iranian government."[17] At the same time, Dulles and Henderson believed the major oil companies would have to cooperate to reverse their embargo on Iran and reintegrate Iranian oil into the global market. The US government proposed a "Consortium" solution, with all seven of the major companies participating in restarting Iranian oil.

The companies, apart from AIOC, were not particularly enthusiastic about the idea of entering Iran. "From the strictly commercial viewpoint," wrote Exxon's Orville Harden to Dulles, "our company has no particular interest in entering such a group."[18] To understand this attitude, one must consider the state of the global oil economy. By 1953, production throughout the Middle East had increased to make up for the oil lost through the Iranian embargo. The companies owned concessions in Saudi Arabia, Iraq, Kuwait, and elsewhere, and they generally had good relations with local governments. While they might have been interested in retaking control of Iran's oil reserves—which, at 1.7 billion tons, ranked among the largest in the world[19]—they had little commercial interest in increasing Iranian production at a time when markets were in a state of oversupply. The US government eventually succeeded in cajoling the companies to participate through a combination of direct pressure and promises of favorable terms. Moreover, the US firms would not have to worry about potential antitrust action—they could work together to restart Iranian production for the sake of "national security."[20]

Once the companies agreed to participate, they had to determine on what basis to retake control of Iranian oil. Discussions held in December 1953 highlighted important issues. William J. Fraser, chairman of AIOC, argued that his company should return to its former position. As the US government felt this route was politically impossible and could trigger a revival of Mosaddeq-era nationalism inside Iran, Fraser pushed instead for a majority stake in the Consortium for AIOC. He argued that other companies, "interested in safeguarding their own concessions elsewhere," should join the Consortium to ensure control of Iran's oil reserves.[21] The US companies were

---

[15] Memo of Discussion at 160th Meeting of the National Security Council, August 27, 1953, *Foreign Relations of the United States, 1952-1954: Iran, 1951-1954, Second Edition* (Washington, DC: US Government Publishing Office, 2018), document 304. Available online: https://history.state.gov/historicaldocuments/frus1951-54IranEd2/d304 (accessed March 30, 2021).

[16] Record Group (RG) 59, Central Decimal File (CDF) Box 5511 888.2553/8-2553, Dulles to Henderson, No. 612, August 25, 1953, US National Archives and Records Administration II (hereafter NARA), College Park, MD.

[17] Henry Byroade, "The Present Situation in Iran," December 12, 1953, in *The United States and Iran: A Documentary History*, ed. Yonah Alexander and Allan Nanes (Frederick, MD: University Publications of America, 1980), 259–63.

[18] US Congress, Senate, Committee on Foreign Relations, *The International Petroleum Cartel, the Iranian Consortium, and U.S. National Security*, 93rd Cong., 2nd sess., 1974, p. 58.

[19] BP 66232 Note on Value of Existing Reserves, March 12, 1954.

[20] Mary Ann Heiss, "The United States, Great Britain, and the Creation of the Iranian Oil Consortium, 1953-1954," *International History Review* 16, no. 3 (1994): 511–35.

[21] BP 58246 Notes of Meeting, December 14, 1953.

uncomfortable with the idea of producing revenues solely for the stabilization of the shah's government. Orville Harden of Exxon, during a meeting on December 17, suggested that the World Bank offer Iran loans, "subject to an overriding condition that a satisfactory oil settlement was arrived at with the oil companies."[22] But this was also not acceptable to the US government, which wanted Iran's oil production to recover as quickly as possible. The companies eventually agreed to a formal increase in Iranian production, from ten million tons in 1955 to thirty million tons in 1957, after which point production would depend on "market conditions."[23]

By law, the Iranian government owned the oil industry. The companies agreed in December 1953 that "effective management" would have to be handed to the Consortium, but it was unclear how this could be accomplished.[24] The US companies offered their preliminary view in February 1954. At the very least, a new agreement would ensure that Iran "owns all of its oil in the ground and all of the physical assets."[25] But Sidney Swensrud of Gulf Oil, in a note sent to AIOC chairman William J. Fraser the previous October, felt that the question was not Iran's ownership of the oil but its ability to handle "the highly technical operations requiring vast amounts of capital, know-how, and access to markets" needed to render oil profitable.[26] The companies could not dispute Iran's ownership of the oil *in the ground*. They could, and did, dispute Iranian competence to manage that oil effectively.

Of course, the idea of Iranian inability to manage the industry—a point that Britain had raised again and again during the nationalization crisis—was itself a fiction. An inspection of AIOC's refinery at Abadan in February 1954 found that Iran's technicians had done an "excellent job" maintaining security and order.[27] The companies conducted their own technical survey of the oil industry. They concluded that Iranian nationalism and pride in ownership of the industry remained strong, and any final agreement would have to preserve "the façade of control of the oil industry by the Persian Government."[28]

The terms agreed to by all seven companies in early 1954 kept power with the foreign companies and away from the Iranian state. NIOC would retain title to the oil and the refinery, and eventually it would be granted management of "nonbasic" services in Abadan and the oil fields, including housing, medical services, training, and education. Control over production, however, would be placed in foreign hands, "even if nominal control remained in Persian hands."[29] Such control was needed to ensure the smooth reintegration of Iranian oil into world markets. Yet it also firmly reinstated foreign dominion over Iranian oil and strengthened the companies' hold over their other concessions. Even with a suitable "façade," such an imposition would undoubtedly stir up Iranian resentment. Neville Gass of AIOC noted that reinstating

---

[22] BP 58246 Notes of Meeting, December 17, 1953.
[23] BP 4592 Aide-Memoire for Negotiations, April 14, 1954.
[24] BP 58246 Memo: Agreement with Iran, December 17, 1953.
[25] BP 66232 "Preliminary Views of the American Companies," February 3, 1954.
[26] BP 58246 S. A. Swensrud, Gulf Oil, to William Fraser, AIOC, October 9, 1953.
[27] RG 59 CDF Box 5512 888.2553/2-1354, Henderson to State, No. 1768, February 13, 1954, 888.2553/2-2454, Aldrich to State, No. 3642, February 24, 1954, NARA.
[28] BP 67067 "Management—South Persian Oilfields and Refinery," Abadan Technical Mission, N. A. Gass, February 17, 1954.
[29] BP 66232 Meeting of Reconnaissance Party, February 23, 1954.

the original concession carried "grave political risks." While the companies were aware of this, they believed that their vision of management was necessary despite concerns about Iranian nationalism.[30] Iran could have managed its own industry, but the Consortium's terms concealed this fact in order to protect the international position of the companies.

The British recognized that the US companies had joined the Consortium out of "political considerations."[31] The Americans agreed to enter Iran "only at the request of the United States government, and for the primary purpose of assisting Iran."[32] This gave the US companies considerable leverage. AIOC accepted a 40 percent stake, with 40 percent going to the five US companies—Exxon, Socony-Mobil, Chevron, Texaco, and Gulf. Royal Dutch/Shell, an Anglo-Dutch firm, received 14 percent. The final 6 percent went to the French national firm Compagnie Française des Pétroles (CFP). The US companies, with the support of Shell, successfully rebuffed Fraser's attempt to win a large compensation award for AIOC, a demand that seemed "unrealistic … [without] any commercial basis," in their estimation.[33] AIOC ultimately accepted a smaller (though still considerable) compensation award from the Iranian government.[34] Such obvious corporate collusion violated US antitrust law, but on January 20, 1954, the US attorney general granted the companies protection from antitrust laws. "The national security of the United States requires that U.S. companies should be invited to participate" in the Iranian Consortium, he wrote.[35]

Negotiations with the Iranians began in April and concluded in August 1954. Howard Page of Exxon led the Consortium's team. The Iranian team featured experienced oil men Abdollah Entezām, Fuʿād Ruhāni, and Fathallah Nafisi, and was led by Ali Amini, the new minister of finance. Amini haggled, but by August 1954 he had agreed to most of the companies' terms. Dependent on US aid, the shah's government had little choice but to accept the Consortium's terms in 1954. Amini argued that the terms were the best they could obtain "under the circumstances" and that one day Iran could renegotiate the deal once it possessed the "technical, material and economic resources to compete all over the world."[36] The shah hailed the concession in public as "the best agreement yet made," admitting that Iran needed "know-how and outside help" in running its industry.[37] But this clearly did not sit well with the monarch, who chafed under the terms imposed upon his new government.[38] Though the CIA coup had returned the shah to power, the Consortium Agreement constituted a setback for

---

[30] BP 66232 Gass, Comment on Memo: Outline of Operating Agreement, February 4, 1954.
[31] BP 66232 AIOC Memo, March 17, 1954.
[32] BP 66232 "American Group Views on Basis for Settlement with Anglo-Iranian," March 16, 1954.
[33] Ibid.
[34] Heiss, "Creation of the Iranian Oil Consortium," 519–24.
[35] Attorney General Brownell to the National Security Council, January 20, 1954, *Foreign Relations of the United States, 1952–1954: Volume X, Iran, 1951–1954* (Washington, DC: US Government Printing Office, 1989), document 411. Available online: https://history.state.gov/historicaldocuments/frus1952-54v10/d411 (accessed April 7, 2021).
[36] RG 59 CDF Box 5513 888.2553/10-254, US Embassy No. 186, Dr. Amini's Speech, October 2, 1954, NARA.
[37] Records created or inherited by the Ministry of Power and of related bodies (POWE) 33/2121, Consulate Khorramshahr No. 1, March 29, 1955, UKNA.
[38] Abbas Milani, *The Shah* (New York: Palgrave Macmillan, 2011), 196–7.

Iranian nationalism. Iran's oil had been "denationalized."[39] Iran would soon enjoy the fruits of its reactivated oil industry, but it was only thanks to the active participation of the US government and the machinations of the foreign oil companies that such riches could be realized. The imbalance was visible in 1953–4, with the shah's government relatively prostrate. But the power dynamics between the Iranian state and the foreign companies would change as the shah grew more assertive.

Iran and the Consortium, 1954–60

The Consortium Agreement facilitated the return of Iranian oil to the international energy system (see Figure 5.1). It also accomplished what US policymakers had most hoped for: the rapid increase in revenues derived from oil production. Revenues to the Iranian government increased from $99 million in 1955 to $285 million in 1960. After the Consortium Agreement, oil was the bedrock of the Iranian government and covered 41.8 percent of total state expenditure.[40] Oil revenue funded the new development project, which the Second Seven-Year Plan budgeted at over $1 billion, while simultaneously acting as collateral for loans drawn from the World Bank and private investors in Europe and the United States.[41] Iran received more than $400 million in economic aid and $500 million in military aid from the United States between 1954 and 1963. Despite this aid, without oil revenues the "politics of promise," pushed by the Pahlavi government in the wake of the 28 Mordād Coup, would not have been possible.[42]

The companies managed Iran's reintegration through a sophisticated production and coordination system of aggregated program quantity (APQ). The system punished any company that bought more oil than was needed, which ensured that Iranian output did not increase too rapidly and thereby prevented a glut that could have depressed prices.[43] Iran's government received 50 percent of the profits derived from the sale of crude oil, according to the "fifty-fifty" principle that had become standard throughout the oil-producing world. The profit-sharing principle, combined with the increase in Iran's production after 1954, contributed to the rapid rise in oil revenues (see Figure 5.2).

The APQ functioned through the "bids" offered by each participant, the weight of which corresponded to their total membership stake. Generally, the highest "bidders"

---

[39] Ervand Abrahamian, *The Coup: 1953, the CIA and the Roots of Modern U.S.-Iranian Relations* (New York: New Press, 2013), 206–7.

[40] F. S. Smithers and Company, *International Oil Industry* (New York: F.S. Smithers, 1962), 51; Karshenas, *Oil, State and Industrialization*, 135; Benjamin Schwadran, *The Middle East, Oil and the Great Powers* (New York: Wiley, 1974), 161.

[41] Gregory Brew, "'What They Need Is Management': American NGOs, the Second Seven Year Plan and Economic Development in Iran, 1954–1963," *International History Review* 41, no. 1 (2019): 1–22.

[42] Cyrus Schayegh, "Iran's Karaj Dam Affair: Emerging Mass Consumerism, the Politics of Promise, and the Cold War in the Third World," *Comparative Studies in Society and History* 54, no. 3 (2012): 612–43; for aid statistics, see Mark J. Gasiorowski, *U.S. Foreign Policy and the Shah: Building a Client State in Iran* (Ithaca, NY: Cornell University Press, 1991), 93–5, 101–3, 109–26.

[43] Katayoun Shafiee, *Machineries of Oil: An Infrastructural History of BP in Iran* (Cambridge, MA: MIT Press, 2018), chapter 6; John Blair, *The Control of Oil* (New York: Pantheon Books, 1976), 104–5; Text of Participants Agreement, in US Congress, *The International Petroleum Cartel*, 95–117.

on the APQ—that is, those interested in maximizing Iranian output—were AIOC (renamed British Petroleum, or BP, in 1954), the French firm CFP, Shell, and Iricon (a group of small American companies invited into the Consortium in 1955). Combined with Socony-Mobil, a US major with large market outlets but less access to cheap crude, the high bidders commanded 72 percent of the Consortium, which brought the APQ *up* rather than down (see Figure 5.3). The remaining US companies—Exxon, Gulf, Socal, and Texaco—had little interest in increasing Iranian production. Yet their low bids were not enough to depress Iranian output, which rose at a more rapid rate than rivals Iraq or Kuwait.

Higher Iranian production helped meet rising demand for oil and oil products in the industrialized West. Oil demand rose from 11 million barrels per day (bpd) in 1950 to 57 million bpd twenty years later. As a share of world energy consumption, oil increased from 24 percent in 1949 to 43 percent in 1971. Oil from Iran, Kuwait, Saudi Arabia, Qatar, and Iraq was cheap relative to other sources, and the oligopolistic power of the majors meant that the oil could be sold at an artificially high price—the "posted price," as it was known. This made Middle East oil phenomenally profitable. At the same time, oil's importance to state finances increased. Oil funded 53 percent of the state budget in Iraq, 97 percent in Kuwait, and 71 percent in Saudi Arabia.[44]

The Consortium Agreement placed the Western companies in command of Iran's production, with NIOC operating as a junior partner. ʿAli-Naqi ʿAlikhāni, the shah's minister for the economy in the 1960s, noted that NIOC could provide Iran with better information on global oil than any other oil-producing country. Had it been charged with running the industry, there is little question NIOC would have performed admirably.[45] Given their experience, officials within NIOC bristled at their diminished status. While Iranian directors sat on the board of the operating companies and ostensibly had some say in setting policy, all they did was vote on directives issued from the Consortium partners in London. They "had no role in the decision," recalled engineer Parviz Minā.[46] The Consortium, an unwieldy corporate construction created for political purposes, lacked "company spirit," according to one British observer.[47] Unlike its counterpart in Saudi Arabia, the Arabian-American Oil Company (ARAMCO), which worked to ingratiate itself into local political and social life, the Consortium in Iran seemed artificial, "a foreign-owned enclave," and a reminder of the defeat of Iran's nationalization effort.[48]

Despite this, relations between the Consortium and NIOC were generally good. The companies formed close bonds with technical director Reza Fallah and chairman

---

[44] Jacoby, *Multinational Oil*, 49–55; Issawi and Yeganeh, *The Economics of Middle Eastern Oil*, 146, 170.
[45] Hossein Dehbāshi, ed., ʿAli-Naqi ʿAlikhāni, *Eqtesād va amniyat: tārikh-e shifāhi-ye zendegi va āsār-e ʿAli-Naqi ʿAlikhāni* (Tehran: Sāzmān-e asnād va ketābkhāneh-ye melli-ye Irān, 1393/2015), 56–7.
[46] Foundation for Iranian Studies (FIS) Development Series: Gholām-Rezā Afkhami, ed., *Tahavvol-e sanʿat-e naft-e Irān: negāhi az darun*, interview with Parviz Minā. Available online: https://fis-iran.org/fa/resources/development-series/oil (accessed April 19, 2017).
[47] POWE 33/2121, Beckett to FO, December 14, 1955, UKNA.
[48] FO 371/140857 EP 1533/5, British Consul, Khorramshahr December 9, 1958, UKNA; Robert Vitalis, *America's Kingdom: Mythmaking on the Saudi Oil Frontier* (New York: Verso, 2009).

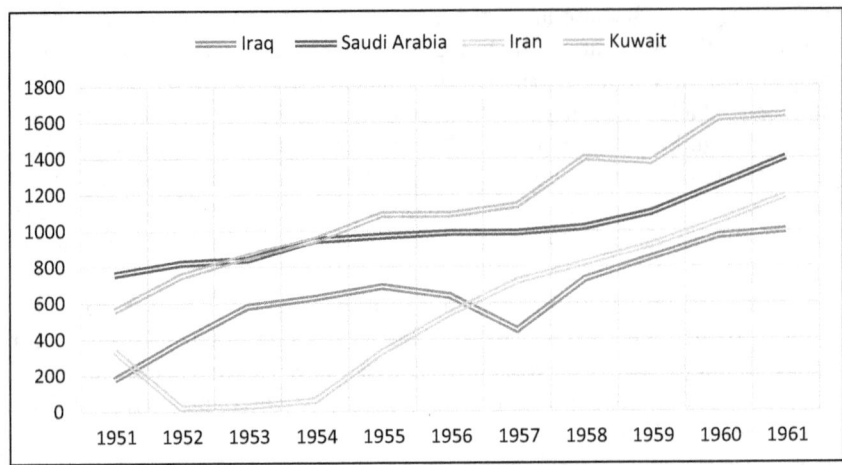

Figure 5.1 Middle East oil production, 1951–61.

Source: Smithers, *International Oil Industry*, 51; Schwadran, *The Middle East, Oil and the Great Powers*, 161–2.

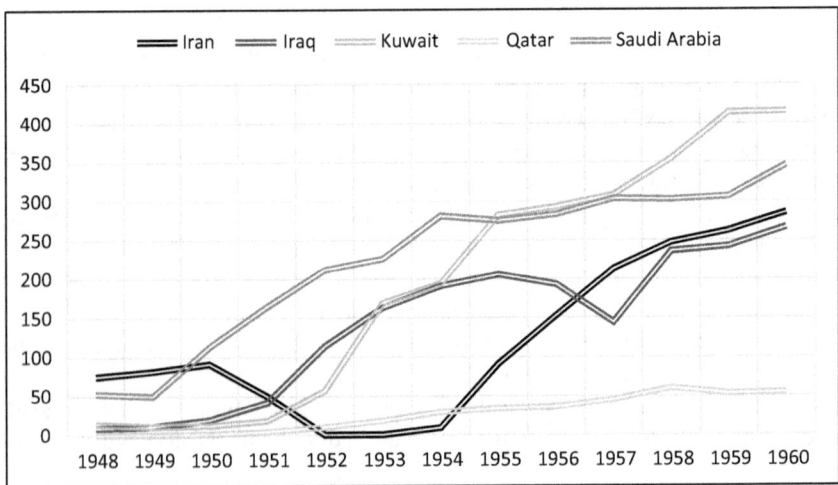

Figure 5.2 Revenues from oil (millions of US$), 1948–60.

Source: Issawi and Yeganeh, *Economics of Middle Eastern Oil*, 129.

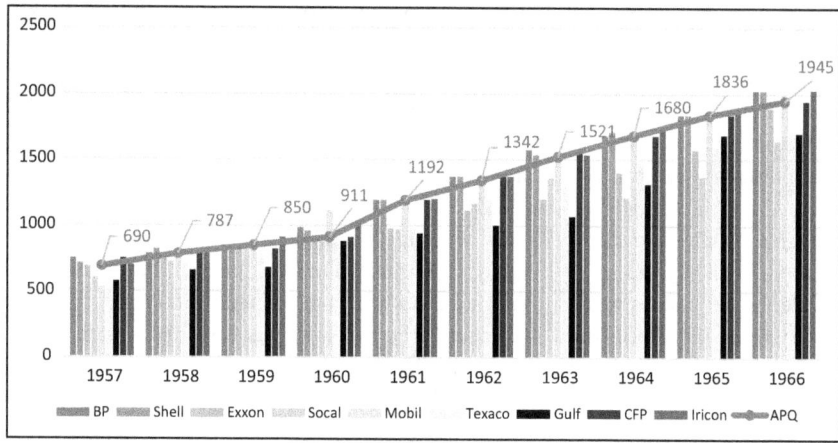

Figure 5.3 Consortium nominations (thousands bpd), 1957–66.

Source: US Congress, Senate, Committee on Foreign Relations, *Multinational Petroleum Companies and Foreign Policy*, Part 7, 93rd Cong., 2nd sess., 1974, p. 255.

Abdollah Entezām, an amicable politician regarded as their "friend at court."[49] While NIOC had little power over production, they met frequently with Consortium officials for vigorous debates over housing policy and nonbasic services.[50] The Consortium, for its part, respected the political imperative of managing Abadan, a city of 225,000 people in 1956, and endeavored to keep the city's enormous refinery in operation, despite commercial changes that had made it redundant. "Without the refinery," concluded one Consortium report, "Abadan cannot exist."[51]

Despite the working relationship it formed with NIOC, the Consortium was not a popular institution inside Iran. Speaking at a gathering of Iranian oil workers in Abadan in late 1954, Amini could not resist taking aim at the "foreign interests" in control of Iran's oil exports.[52] Though the finance minister measured his rhetoric in another speech in November 1955, emphasizing how Iran needed the "brains and practical guidance" provided by the Consortium's technicians, it was no secret that the shah and his ministers resented the terms of the oil agreement.[53] The Iranian

---

[49] FO 371/164221 EP 1532/24, Harrison to FO, No. 1168, October 24, 1962, UKNA.
[50] See BP 170608 Home Ownership, Part 1, May 1955–November 1960; BP 227604 Staff Housing and Labour, Part 2, January 1958–December 1960; and BP 227605 Staff Housing and Labour, Part 3, January 1961–December 1963.
[51] BP 4592 "Continuing Role of Abadan Refinery under the Government—Consortium Agreement of 1954/10/29," January 1958. While the massive Abadan refinery had been regarded as a major prize in 1951, by the late 1950s most refining had moved away from the site of production and into consuming countries. The market for Abadan's refined products shrank over the course of the decade. As a result, Iran shifted toward exporting crude oil, rather than refined products, rendering the Abadan refinery increasingly obsolete.
[52] RG 59 CDF Box 4971 888.2553/1-455, Amini Speech at Abadan, January 4, 1955, NARA.
[53] RG 59 CDF Box 4972 888.2553/11-855, US Consulate Khorramshahr No. 28, November 8, 1955, NARA.

government depended on oil revenues to fund its military and development program, but the shah hoped to tap new sources of income outside of Consortium control. He did this by two means: pursuing independent oil production and signing concession agreements with companies outside the Consortium.

In the late 1950s, NIOC undertook explorations of non-Consortium areas. The first major discovery came in 1956 near Qom. Hopes were high that Qom would prove as rich as the huge fields at Āghā Jari and Gach-Sārān in Khuzestan, and the shah talked eagerly of building a pipeline, known as the "Met-Line," from Tehran to the Mediterranean to market the oil to Europe.[54] While NIOC prospected in Iran's interior, the shah invited smaller oil companies into Iran through deals that undermined the fifty-fifty principle enshrined in the Consortium Agreement. The first agreement was made with AGIP-Mineria, an affiliate of the Italian firm Ente Nazionale Idrocarburi (ENI), led by Enrico Mattei. The deal, "better than all other existing oil contracts in the world," split profits 75-25 in Iran's favor, with ENI covering the initial investment and providing Iran a cash bonus.[55] The shah also reached deals with a Japanese company and with Pan American Oil, a subsidiary of Standard Oil of Indiana. According to Abdollah Entezām, the chairman of NIOC, Iran would develop its own oil in partnership agreements with the new companies, "and thereby receive a greater share of the revenue."[56] Iran's ultimate ambition, Entezām told *Petroleum Week*, was "to build up our markets and set up our own refineries abroad," in time matching the size and scale of the majors themselves.[57]

The shah's oil deals in 1957 marked a turning point in the history of the global oil economy. On paper, they broke the fifty-fifty principle and illustrated the autonomy of oil-producing governments. They indicated the gradual decline in the majors' domination, as smaller companies began to break into Middle East oil markets and undermine the oligopoly's hold over production. Despite their power on the international market, the majors could do very little to stop the shah from making side deals with smaller companies, though Howard Page did his best to "disillusion" the shah by warning him that flooding the world with more oil would only depress prices and reduce Iran's annual revenues.[58] The shah, who called the Pan American agreement "the most important achievement of his reign," thought it would give him greater leverage over the Consortium companies.[59]

His motivations were not only material but also political. "The Iranians want effective partnerships," wrote one British embassy official, "not only ... to get more money but mainly to develop their own oil industry." The shah, he continued, was hoping to tap into the same public sentiment "which for a time united the whole of Iran behind [Mosaddeq]."[60] While some observers worried the shah might let "his

---

[54] RG 59 CDF Box 4974 888.2553/1-1556, US Embassy Tehran, No. 628, Semi-Annual Petroleum Report, January 15, 1958, NARA; John Bowlus, "Connecting Midstream: The Politics and Economics of Oil Transportation in the Middle East" (PhD diss., Georgetown University, 2013), 51–5.
[55] FIS Oral History of Iran Collection: Reminiscences of Hushang Farkhān in an interview with Ardeshir Aqevli, 1983, 3–4.
[56] FO 371/127210 UES 1171/217, Russell to FO, No. 87, August 2, 1957, UKNA.
[57] *Petroleum Week*, March 15, 1957.
[58] RG 59 CDF Box 4974 888.2553/9-757, Chapin to Dulles, No. 466, September 7, 1957, NARA.
[59] RG 59 CDF Box 4974 888.2553/5-658, Chapin to State, No. 2056, May 6, 1958, NARA.
[60] FO 371/127212 UES 1171/275, Russell to Lloyd, October 11, 1957, UKNA.

greed get the better of his judgement," there seemed to be very little risk for Iran's monarch, "who felt confident he could count on support from the U.S. government."[61] His calculation proved accurate. The US ambassador in Tehran encouraged the shah to engage in more deals, "which would possibly provide immediate substantial revenue for … the hard-pressed budget."[62] While it furnished his government with military and economic aid, the US government studiously avoided direct involvement in the shah's negotiations with the companies. Yet for the United States, eager to preserve the shah as a Cold War ally, increasing Iran's earnings from oil made sense, even if it came at the expense of the companies.

The deals with non-Consortium companies might have been important symbolically, but in a commercial sense they changed very little. While NIOC engineer Hushang Farkhān noted that exploration in new concession areas was paid for by the newcomers, thereby saving Iran the cost, NIOC official Parviz Minā observed that exploiting Qom and other fields required capital, manpower, and technological skill, "none of which were available at that time to NIOC."[63] Exploiting oil outside the Consortium zone did not appreciably add to Iran's oil revenues, though the shah did benefit from signing bonuses attached to the new deals. In 1962, the Consortium produced 1.3 million bpd in Iran, compared to 18,000 bpd from the newcomers.[64] The companies continued to stand by the fifty-fifty profit-sharing provision, with one Socony-Mobil executive calling it the "most equitable and most advantageous rate for all concerned."[65]

But the shah's activities marked the beginning of a trend. The onerous terms of the 1954 Consortium Agreement, as well as the general pattern of control established by the companies throughout the oil-producing world, were unsustainable in a world of rising resource nationalism. Events like the shah's oil deals, the Suez Canal crisis of 1956, and the meeting of the first Arab Petroleum Congress in 1957 illustrated the rising discomfort in the Middle East with the oil status quo. The companies, warned the British ambassador in January 1959, would have to face such realities "if they are ever to come to terms with Iranian national pride and aspirations—and stay in Iran."[66]

The OPEC Challenge, 1960–4

In February 1959, the major companies cut the posted price of crude oil in the Persian Gulf. The move came after years of oversupply and was designed to align the posted price with the prices established in independent third-party exchanges. The companies followed the initial cut with a second cut in August 1960. In total, the price of oil fell

[61] FO 371/120742 EP 1536/3, FO to Stevens, No. 516, April 18, 1956, UKNA.
[62] RG 59 CDF Box 4974 888.2553/11-1257, Chapin to Dulles, No. 939, November 12, 1957, NARA.
[63] FIS Development Series: *Tahavvol-e san'at-e naft-e Irān*, interview with Minā; FIS Oral History of Iran Collection: Reminiscences of Hushang Farkhān, 4, 5–7.
[64] By 1971, these figures were 4.14 million and 392,000 bpd, respectively. See Jane Perry Clark Carey, "Iran and Control of Its Oil Resources," *Political Science Quarterly* 89, no. 1 (1974): 160.
[65] "Nationalism and Business Prospects in the Middle East," Siegel, Director, Socony-Mobil, September 30, 1958, ExxonMobil Collection, Box 2.207/E183, Folder 5, Briscoe Center for American History, Austin, TX.
[66] FO 371/140857 EP 1533/5, Harrison to Hiller, No. 6, January 15, 1959, UKNA.

20c in sixteen months, from $2.04 per barrel to $1.84 per barrel.[67] For Iran, the cut was equal to a $50 million reduction in revenues.

The decision to cut prices did not go unanswered. Nationalist opposition to the companies had been growing for years. At the Arab Petroleum Congress in 1957, Saudi oil minister Abdullah Tariki railed against Western control of Middle East oil. In September 1960, following the companies' unilateral price cut, Tariki and Venezuela's oil minister, Juan Pablo Pérez Alfonso, met in Baghdad and together with the oil ministers of Iran, Iraq, and Kuwait formed the Organization of Petroleum Exporting Countries. The new organization was designed to present a united front against the companies, yet OPEC was almost immediately pulled apart by divisions. While "gradualists" hoped to improve conditions through slow negotiations with the companies, "insurrectionists" like Tariki supported bolder action, including cuts in production and higher taxes on company operations.[68]

While the shah had tried for years to pressure the Consortium, he was hesitant to commit his government to the radical side. He told journalist Wanda Jablonski in November 1960 that Iran was opposed to production cuts, which Tariki had called for as a way to pressure the companies. The US embassy believed the shah's stance to be calculated, as Iran hoped for "preferential treatment by the oil companies."[69] Iran's prime minister, Ali Amini, expressed this position in a speech on October 23, 1961. "The world must realize it needs our oil," he said, "[and] supply can only be maintained if stability in producing countries prevails … Iran could not run the oil industry alone."[70] The shah did seek to influence policy within OPEC, which he saw as a potential tool for leveraging more revenue from the Consortium. Fortunately, his oil adviser, Fu'ād Ruhāni, was selected as OPEC's first secretary-general and served from 1960 to 1964.[71]

While scholars have downplayed OPEC's performance in its early years, the companies took the rise of a producers' organization very seriously.[72] The threat of resource nationalism remained acute. Moreover, the companies were not confident about support from Washington. Gulf Oil executive and former CIA operative Kermit Roosevelt complained in 1961 that State Department officials were "so tied up" with Cold War concerns like the Berlin Crisis that "they simply do not and will not take the time to look at any commercial aspects of our world problems, particularly

---

[67] Issawi and Yeganeh, *Economics of Middle Eastern Oil*, 68.
[68] Christopher Dietrich, *Oil Revolution: Anticolonial Elites, Sovereign Rights, and the Economic Culture of Decolonization* (New York: Cambridge University Press, 2017), 114–22; Giuliano Garavini, *The Rise and Fall of OPEC in the Twentieth Century* (Oxford: Oxford University Press, 2019).
[69] RG 59 CDF Box 2835 888.2553/12-560, US Embassy Tehran No. 158, December 5, 1960, NARA.
[70] RG 59 CDF Box 2835 888.2553/11-161, US Embassy to State No. 113, November 1, 1961, NARA.
[71] Dietrich, *Oil Revolution*, 110–11, Bamberg, *Vol. III*, 151. Ruhāni's diaries provide key insights into OPEC's early history. See FIS Development Series: Gholāmrezā Tājbakhsh and Farrokh Najmābādi, eds., *Yād-dāsht-hā-ye Fu'ād Ruhāni, nokhostin dabir-e kol-e sāzmān-e keshvar-hā-ye sāder-konandeh-ye naft (Upek) va nā-gofteh-hā-i darbāreh-ye siyāsat-e nafti-ye Irān dar daheh-ye pas az melli-shodan*, 1392/2013. Available online: https://www.fis-iran.org/fa/resources/development-series/Rouhani (accessed April 7, 2021).
[72] Garavini, *The Rise and Fall of OPEC in the Twentieth Century*, 145–53.

petroleum."[73] Officials were sympathetic to the companies but urged them to yield more to the Pahlavi regime, which by 1961 had entered a period of prolonged political strife and economic stagnation. The US companies resisted such pressure. "Gulf has not been an enthusiastic supporter for increasing Iran's production," stated the company's chairman, while an executive from Texaco "questioned the wisdom of any politically-motivated further production increases," noting that increases would anger other producers.[74] Ultimately, the US government chose to remain aloof, confident that the companies and Iran could come to an arrangement on their own.

In June 1962 OPEC voted on a set of resolutions designed to pressure the companies into raising the price of oil while increasing the share of profits for producers. Negotiations between Ruhāni and the Consortium members revolved around the question of royalty expensing. Rather than deducting the 12.5 percent royalty charge included in all oil agreements, Ruhāni argued that the companies should expense the charge, adding it to the producer "take" and effectively ending the fifty-fifty arrangement in Iran's favor. Ruhāni, a skilled and pragmatic negotiator, told Page of Exxon that this concession would boost Iran's revenues while allowing the shah to hold back the "wild men" in OPEC.[75]

Resolving the royalty expensing question divided the Consortium partners. Exxon, led by Howard Page, wanted to ditch the fifty-fifty arrangement and offer oil producers a guaranteed return per barrel. The idea was vigorously rebuffed by BP, which worried about the implications of such a plan on its domestic tax obligations. "It may be necessary," wrote one BP executive, "to give the Middle East governments a better take, but [we] are convinced that at this moment we cannot afford it."[76] The other US companies regarded Ruhāni's proposal as blackmail and therefore refused to budge. Iran had enjoyed higher production increases than its neighbors since returning to markets in 1954, and for that reason Gulf argued that the Consortium was under no obligation to reward the shah with additional revenue.[77]

Gradually, the Consortium partners set aside their differences and agreed on a strategy. They would offer minor concessions to the shah to deter him from taking action through OPEC, where Iran had emerged as a deciding vote between the gradualist and insurrectionist factions. Visiting Tehran in late October 1962, Page met with Entezām and Prime Minister Asadollah Alam, two moderates in the shah's government. Increasing payments to producer governments, Page said, would reduce the competitiveness of Middle East oil and pave the way for the development of cheaper nuclear power. His arguments were well received by Entezām and Alam, both of whom claimed they were working hard to restrain "hot-heads" like Ruhāni.[78] A month later,

---

[73] BP 58934 Whiteford to Bridgeman, Report on Conversation with K. Roosevelt, October 25, 1961.
[74] RG 59 CDF Box 2836 888.2253/6-1962, Memo of Conversation, June 19, 1962, 888.2553/7-2662, Memo of Conversation, July 26, 1962, NARA.
[75] BP 100334 Mitchell to Bridgeman, May 29, 1962, Note on Page's Meeting with Ruhāni, June 1962.
[76] BP 100369 Stockwell to Drake, OPEC, October 9, 1962, Note for Pattinson, OPEC, October 10, 1962.
[77] RG 59 CDF Box 2836 888.2553/6-1962, Memo of Conversation, June 19, 1962, 888.2553/7-2662, Memo of Conversation, July 26, 1962, 888.2553/8-962, Memo of Conversation, August 9, 1962, NARA.
[78] BP 100369 Talk by H. W. Page, Competitive Position of Middle East Oil, October 22, 1962, Meeting with the Prime Minister and Entezām.

BP chairman Maurice Bridgeman concluded a "gentleman's agreement" with Alam. The Consortium would increase Iranian production in future years, offer a concession on marketing expenses, and increase investment in Iranian oil infrastructure. In exchange, the shah agreed to delay punitive action through OPEC.[79] The deal was a sign that Iran, if properly motivated, would align with the companies against OPEC.

But within a few months, the fickle shah changed his mind. In 1963 he launched his "White Revolution," which included a land reform campaign and the suppression of Iran's Shia clerics and landowners to consolidate his position as supreme authority. Flush with confidence, by late 1963 the shah was once again ready to push the Consortium, particularly once it became clear that his government needed higher revenues to fund the land reform campaign and the new Third Plan. In November the companies succumbed to pressure from Ruhāni and agreed to partial royalty expensing, a decision that would have yielded Iran an additional 3.5c/barrel, or roughly $18 million in additional revenue.[80] But the shah did not accept this deal, and in December it looked as though he would side with the radicals in OPEC.

Moderates within the shah's own government resolved the crisis by working secretly with the companies. In early 1964 Prime Minister Asadollah Alam and NIOC's Reza Fallah successfully negotiated a compromise with the companies by working behind the scenes to agree on terms that fit the shah's desire for preferential treatment while defusing tensions between OPEC and Tehran. In his meeting with the Consortium partners, Fallah emphasized how the shah only wanted higher royalties; he had little interest in the political aspirations of OPEC, and he was dead set against measures to limit production. The final offer awarded Iran 6c/barrel in additional payments. In 1964 this amounted to $33 million, raising Iran's total revenues to nearly $400 million.[81] Iran's changed position tipped the scales inside OPEC, which agreed to accept the Consortium's offer in late 1964. Officials within the Consortium felt a crisis had been averted "thanks to the stand taken by Iran."[82]

OPEC remained divided for the rest of the decade, though the debacle over royalty expensing did result in slightly higher revenues per barrel for all producers. The companies, moreover, did not attempt to cut posted prices a second time.[83] The battle of the early 1960s thus marked a turning point. Over the course of the decade, the companies were gradually squeezed, both by producers and by market conditions. It was the energy crisis of the late 1960s and early 1970s that facilitated a revolution in the global oil economy that ended the companies' dominance and consolidated OPEC's power over price and production.[84]

---

[79] BP 100369 Details of Bridgeman's Trip to Tehran, November 8, 1962; Bamberg, *Vol. III*, 154–5.
[80] FIS Development Series: Tājbakhsh and Najmābādi, *Yād-dāsht-hā-ye Fu'ād Ruhāni*, 366–7; BP 100553 Record of the Meeting, November 11, 1963.
[81] BP 100553 Three P's Meeting with Fallah, December 17, 1963, Memo #3 "Effect of Small Increases in Costs on Outlets for Persian Gulf Oil"; FIS Development Series: Tājbakhsh and Najmābādi, *Yād-dāsht-hā-ye Fu'ād Ruhāni*, 187–94.
[82] POWE 61/297, WCC Rose, Report on OPEC Meeting in Geneva, July 17, 1964, UKNA.
[83] Garavini, *Rise and Fall of OPEC*, 135–78.
[84] Francesco Petrini "Eight Squeezed Sisters: The Oil Majors and the Coming of the 1973 Oil Crisis," in *Oil Shock: The 1973 Crisis and Its Economic Legacy*, ed. Elisabetta Bini and Giuliano Garavini (New York: I.B. Tauris, 2016), 60–73; Garavini, *Rise and Fall of OPEC*, 179–253.

Conclusion

Relations between major American oil companies and the shah's government between 1954 and 1964 were marked by considerable friction. Yet ultimately, both sides required the other to maintain stability and a favorable status quo. The shah pressured the companies, both directly and indirectly, for better terms. While prestige was important, he was more interested in maximizing Iran's oil production and increasing earnings from oil. He could only do this with the companies' cooperation, though he could also count on support from the US government.

The American companies, which had entered the Consortium grudgingly, were divided over how best to manage Iran's oil. While they recognized the growing power of Iranian resource nationalism and the shah's desire for revenues, they put up a stiff front against Iran's attempts to utilize pressure. The conclusion of the royalty expensing drama in 1964 represented a compromise. But it did not end the wrangling over profits or production. Throughout the rest of the 1960s, the shah never relented in his quest to squeeze the companies. The Pahlavi government filled the press between 1964 and 1967 with anti-company rhetoric, continually rejecting Consortium payments as too small and production levels as too low. The Consortium usually acquiesced to the shah's demands, promising to increase production and gradually surrendering an ever-increasing share of profits to the Pahlavi government.[85]

While the companies remained in control of Iranian oil in the early 1960s, the tide was beginning to turn. An important factor in this shift was the changing attitude of the US government. As Iran grew into a strong US ally, policymakers in Washington were determined to ensure that the shah received the revenues he needed to maintain his position of power in Tehran. A revealing episode came in June 1964, as Howard Page of Exxon and George Parkhurst of Socal visited the White House to meet with President Lyndon Johnson. The companies, he reminded the executives, had a duty to the so-called Free World to do everything possible to maintain amicable relations with the shah. "The President," noted Page, "could be very persuasive."[86]

---

[85] Bamberg, *Vol. III*, 171–84.
[86] Lyndon Johnson Presidential Library, Austin, TX, National Security File, Box 136, Memo of Conversation, June 5, 1964.

6

Alborz, Bethel, and Community: Missionary Institutions in Postwar Tehran

Matthew K. Shannon

American Presbyterian missionaries lived and worked in Iran during the 1940s, 1950s, and 1960s. These decades were marked by the arrival of "new" Americans in Iran, especially Peace Corps volunteers and aid workers with the Point Four Program. However, "older" forms of American influence were sustained after the Second World War through the Presbyterian Church of the United States of America (PCUSA). From New York, its Board of Foreign Missions funded, administered, and staffed the "Iran Mission" during two of these three decades. While Presbyterians shaped the landscape of postwar Iran, especially the national capital of Tehran, they are rarely discussed within the context of the Second World War and Cold War era.[1]

There are at least two reasons for this lacuna. The first is that the PCUSA's most active period in Iran was earlier. American missionaries first arrived in Iran in the 1830s, but Presbyterians took over and expanded the mission beginning in the 1870s. Religious studies scholars have unpacked the first wave of American missionary work in northwest Iran, and historians have examined the subsequent wave of Presbyterian activity during the late nineteenth and early twentieth centuries.[2] A landmark came when *Iranian Studies* published a special issue on the Alborz College of Tehran, the flagship

---

[1] The exception that proves the rule is Philip Hopkins, *American Missionaries in Iran during the 1960s and 1970s* (New York: Palgrave Macmillan, 2020). However, his emphasis is primarily on post-Presbyterian missionaries.

[2] Adam Becker, *Revival and Awakening: American Evangelical Missionaries in Iran and the Origins of Assyrian Nationalism* (Chicago: University of Chicago Press, 2015); Thomas S. R. O. Flynn, *The Western Christian Presence in the Russias and Qajar Persia, c. 1760–1870* (Leiden: Brill, 2017), chapter 8; Abraham Yeselson, *United States-Persian Diplomatic Relations, 1883–1921* (New Brunswick, NJ: Rutgers University Press, 1956). Michael Zirinsky's many articles include, but are not limited to: Zirinsky, "A Panacea for the Ills of the Country: American Presbyterian Education in Inter-War Iran," *Iranian Studies* 26, nos. 1–2 (1993): 119–37; and Zirinsky, "Render Therefore unto Caesar the Things Which Are Caesar's: American Presbyterian Educators and Reza Shah," *Iranian Studies* 26, nos. 3–4 (1993): 337–56. There are unpublished dissertations such as Matthew Mark Davis, "Evangelizing the Orient: American Missionaries in Iran, 1890–1940" (PhD diss., Ohio State University, 2001).

Presbyterian institution from 1925 to 1940.³ We now know that missionaries built churches, hospitals, and schools, and in the process they contributed to conversations about "modernity" in Iran through the interwar period.⁴ During this period, Reza Shah Pahlavi oversaw a series of nationalization measures that gave the Ministry of Education and the emerging "pedagogic state" greater authority over what had been a relatively freewheeling missionary enterprise.⁵ Then, on August 13, 1939, Reza Shah nationalized foreign schools, including the Presbyterian colleges for Iranian men and women in Tehran.⁶ At the close of the 1930s, there were approximately one hundred teachers and two thousand students in these and other Presbyterian schools throughout Iran.⁷ The schools closed in the summer of 1940, and the Iranian government paid 1.2 million dollars for the properties.⁸ Alborz College was placed under Iranian control and converted into an elite high school, and the missionary hospital in Tehran closed two years later in 1942.⁹

A second reason for the absence of American missionaries in histories of US-Iran relations is that scholars typically focus on the Allied occupation during the Second World War and the superpower competition during the Cold War. These developments, to be sure, disrupted a century of American missionary work in Persia. Yet the PCUSA's Iran Mission was altered rather than terminated. Other historiographies explore

---

³ Articles in the special issue include but are not limited to: Firoozeh Kashani-Sabet, "American Crosses, Persian Crescents: Religion and the Diplomacy of US-Iranian Relations, 1834–1911," *Iranian Studies* 44, no. 5 (2011): 607–25; Thomas M. Ricks, "Alborz College of Tehran, Dr. Samuel Martin Jordan and the American Faculty: Twentieth-Century Presbyterian Mission Education and Modernism in Iran (Persia)," *Iranian Studies* 44, no. 5 (2011): 627–46; John Lorentz, "Educational Development in Iran: The Pivotal Role of the Mission Schools and Alborz College," *Iranian Studies* 44, no. 5 (2011): 647–55; Michael Zirinsky, "Inculcate Tehran: Opening a Dialogue of Civilizations in the Shadow of God and the Alborz," *Iranian Studies* 44, no. 5 (2011): 657–69; Ali Gheissari, "The American College of Tehran, 1929–32: A Memorial Album," *Iranian Studies* 44, no. 5 (2011): 671–714; Houchang Chehabi, "Diversity at Alborz," *Iranian Studies* 44, no. 5 (2011): 715–29.

⁴ Jasamin Rostam-Kolayi, "From Evangelizing to Modernizing Iranians: The American Presbyterian Mission and its Iranian Students," *Iranian Studies* 41, no. 2 (2008): 213–40; Rostam-Kolayi, "Origins of Iran's Modern Girls' Schools: From Private/National to Public/State," *Journal of Middle East Women's Studies* 4, no. 3 (2008): 58–88; Lydia Wytenbroek, "Generational Differences: American Medical Missionaries in Iran, 1834–1940," in *Iran and the West: Cultural Perceptions from the Sasanian Empire to the Islamic Republic*, ed. David Bagot and Margaux Whiskin (London: I.B. Tauris, 2018), 179–94.

⁵ Afshin Marashi, *Nationalizing Iran: Culture, Power, and the State, 1870–1940* (Seattle: University of Washington Press, 2008), chapter 3.

⁶ Cornelius Van Engert (Tehran) to Secretary of State (Washington), August 13, 1939, *Foreign Relations of the United States, 1939: Volume IV, The Far East, Near East and Africa*, document 586. Available online: https://history.state.gov/historicaldocuments/frus1939v04/d586 (accessed March 23, 2021).

⁷ Samuel Martin Jordan to Reza Shah Pahlavi, [March 1940], Presbyterian Historical Society (hereafter PHS) 91-16-16. The PHS is located in Philadelphia, PA, and Record Group 91 contains the records of the PCUSA, Board of Foreign Missions, Secretaries' Files, Iran Mission, 1881–1968.

⁸ "Translation of Agreement between the American Mission and the Government of Iran Regarding the Transfer of School Properties," August 15, 1940, PHS-91-16-1.

⁹ Cady Allen, "Closed and Open Doors in Iran," in *The Crisis Decade: A History of the Foreign Missionary Work of the Presbyterian Church in the U.S.A. 1937–1947*, ed. W. Reginald Wheeler (New York: Board of Foreign Missions, 1950), 158–9. Outside of Tehran, mission hospitals remained open in Hamadan, Kermanshah, Mashhad, Rasht, and Tabriz. Missionaries ran clinics in Tehran and other cities. See also Homa Katouzian, "Alborz and its Teachers," *Iranian Studies* 44, no. 5 (2011): 743–54; Farzin Vahdat, "Alborz High School and the Process of Rationalization in Iran," *Iranian Studies* 44, no. 5 (2011): 731–41.

American missionary activity in the postwar world, including in the Arab Middle East.[10] However, histories of US-Iran relations tend to juxtapose prewar missionary work with Washington's postwar policies to portray the mid-twentieth century as a moment when US state power displaced other forms of American influence.[11] This framing is not entirely wrong, but the story is more complicated, especially when considering how missionary activity intersected with US and Iranian state power during the Cold War. The argument of this chapter is that Cold War dynamics and Mohammad Reza Shah Pahlavi's White Revolution amplified mission work in Iran's capital city. Some missionary institutions survived the early 1940s, and others were conceived and reimagined for the realities of the postwar decades. As a result, American Presbyterian missionaries remained carriers of US cultural influence in Iran for decades after their historiographic expiration date.

The most significant indicators of sustained missionary influence into the Cold War era were three educational institutions that sat astride the streets of Tehran. The first was the Alborz Foundation, a youth center for men and women that had no prewar precedent. Its establishment in the late 1940s signaled a shift in the nature of American influence in Iran, as the so-called social evangelism of missionaries paralleled the cultural programming of the US government during the Cold War. The second was Community School, a coeducational, English-language school for missionary children and international students. The third was Iran Bethel, Jane Doolittle's "finishing school" for young Iranian women that evolved into Damavand College. Although Iran Bethel and Community School were established prior to educational nationalization in 1939–40, both survived because of their liminal position between official and unofficial schools; their unique student bodies and alumni bases; and their connections to the United States. When the shah launched the White Revolution in the 1960s and expanded educational opportunities in the 1970s, these parochial institutions evolved with the support of broader internationalist networks and, in some cases, the Pahlavi state.

Community School and Iran Bethel carried forward the educational tradition of Alborz College, and the Alborz Foundation was its namesake.

Alborz Foundation

The "Alborz Foundation for Iranian Students" was established in 1947. The constitution described it as "a center for wholesome and creative social and recreational activities" and "informal Christian education for Iran."[12] Its mandate, as the flag-bearer of the

---

[10] Heather Sharkey, *American Evangelicals in Egypt: Missionary Encounters in an Age of Empire* (Princeton, NJ: Princeton University Press, 2008); Sharkey, ed., *Cultural Conversions: Unexpected Consequences of Christian Missionary Encounters in the Middle East, Africa, and South Asia* (Syracuse, NY: Syracuse University Press, 2013); Mehmet Ali Dogan and Heather Sharkey, eds., *American Missionaries and the Middle East: Foundational Encounters* (Salt Lake City: University of Utah Press, 2011).

[11] James Bill, *The Eagle and the Lion: The Tragedy of American-Iranian Relations* (New Haven, CT: Yale University Press, 1988); Barry Rubin, *Paved with Good Intentions: The American Experience and Iran* (New York: Oxford University Press, 1980). The first chapter of Rubin's book is titled, "A Friendship Is Born." Bill's first chapter discusses "early entanglements," and on p. 17 he credits the missionaries for establishing "a reputation for America that was positive and warm."

[12] "Constitution of the Alborz Foundation for Iranian Students," March 18/June 19, 1947, PHS-91-16-18.

"Alborz" name, was "to carry on ... in the tradition and spirit of the former Alborz College." The foundation had different homes until the late 1950s when it moved to the corner of Shah Reza and Farvardin avenues "with a view to greater service to the University of Teheran."[13] The Alborz Foundation's most popular draws were its study abroad counseling program and English-language classes. In these and other ways, it served the men and women of postwar Tehran before its conversion into the Armaghān Institute in 1967.

It was Arthur Boyce who, during the early 1940s, first found demand for a student-oriented center that was not a school. In January 1941, when most missionaries were departing Iran, Arthur and Annie Boyce returned from furlough. They had first taken up their posts in Iran decades earlier; Annie was a graduate of Wellesley College and Arthur had a doctorate in education from the University of Chicago. As longtime educators at Alborz College and contemporaries of its longtime principal, Samuel Martin Jordan, the Boyces lamented the school's closure. They wrote to friends that "the work of most of our life time" was "taken from our hands, never to be returned." In this unknown environment, however, Boyce was surprised to find "new openings on every side."[14]

Annie Boyce's letters reveal the nature of her husband's work during the 1940s. She saw that "the matter of reopening schools has not progressed," but she also saw that there was "an epidemic of young men wanting to go to the U.S.A." Arthur spent two busy mornings a week with aspiring students. According to Annie: "My husband is continually pounding his typewriter" writing letters "to some college or university." By the late 1940s, "the stream of students who went to study in the U.S.A. and come to Arthur for counsel keeps up amazingly."[15] In 1947–8 he assisted six hundred students. That year, as he neared retirement, Arthur Boyce decided it was time for a change of guard. "I am turning this part of my work over to Mr. Hulac," Boyce informed the board, "with the belief that his contacts with Y.M.C.A. and other Christian groups in American colleges will make this help to these students more and more effective."[16]

In the place of the Jordans and the Boyces was the generation that would increasingly define the work of the postwar Presbyterian mission. Charles Hulac was a Nebraskan with a divinity degree who was active in the YMCA. He was not a career missionary, but arrived in Iran as a short-termer with his family in 1947.[17] Upon arrival, he "quickly learned that all was not moonshine and honeysuckles on the mission field."[18] Challenges notwithstanding, in 1948 he began "getting under the load of helping the Iranian

---

[13] Program, "Dedication of the Alborz Foundation," April 28, 1959, PHS-91-17-22; Alborz Foundation, "The Order of Service for the Dedication of the Chapel," May 29, 1966, PHS-91-17-22.

[14] Annie Boyce report, 1941, PHS, Annie Stocking Boyce (ASB) biographical file 360-18-31. See also Arthur Boyce, "Alborz College of Teheran and Dr. Samuel Martin Jordan," in *Cultural Ties between Iran and the United States*, ed. Ali Pasha Saleh (Tehran: Her Imperial Majesty's National Committee for the American Revolution Bicentennial, 1976), 155–234.

[15] Annie Boyce letter, January 19, 1944, PHS-ASB-360-18-31; Annie Boyce letter, December 7, 1944, PHS-ASB-360-18-31; Annie Boyce letter, October 25, 1947, PHS-ASB-360-18-31.

[16] Arthur Boyce report, 1948, PHS, Arthur C. Boyce (ACB) biographical file 360-18-30.

[17] Charles Hulac to P. Hewison Pollock, December 27, 1962, PHS, Charles Rolvin Hulac (CRH) biographical file 360-69-27.

[18] Hulac to H. C. Coleman Jr., July 18, 1949, PHS-91-17-12.

Students who are interested in studying in America." Hulac was convinced that he could, like Boyce, help "prepare the way for a cordial reception for these Iranian Students and also for a wholesome time of it while they go to an American College."[19] So it was that Hulac "fell heir to the job of counselling with students who desire to study in the United States."[20] More broadly, it fell to Hulac to channel the reservoir of goodwill that some Iranians had toward Alborz College in the direction of the Alborz Foundation.

Hulac received assistance from many sources, and this line of work brought him into the orbit of the official American colony in Tehran.[21] US consular officials relied on the Alborz Foundation to administer the English-language examination to students who sought to go abroad. This was one of the reasons why many missionaries never accepted the Alborz Foundation and other forms of social evangelism as legitimate missionary work. In the late 1940s, some of Hulac's colleagues charged him with being "a functionary of the American Consulate."[22] They were not entirely wrong, and Hulac departed Iran in 1950.[23] In 1951 the US government's Iran-America Society (*Anjoman-e Irān-Āmrikā*) took over the Alborz Foundation's counseling program for US-bound students. During the last half of 1951 alone, nearly two thousand students visited the Iran-America Society.[24] Despite the transference of student counseling services from the PCUSA's Iran Mission to the US government's public diplomacy apparatus, the 1950s and 1960s brought new vistas for the Alborz Foundation as a cultural representative of the United States in Iran.[25]

In addition to their religious inspiration, most Alborz Foundation directors were committed to promoting American culture in a cosmopolitan environment. This was true for Hulac's successor, a West Virginian named Thomas McNair. He found that students came to the Alborz Foundation "not because we are Christian but because we are Americans." Amid the superpower competition, he continued, "America is a great utopia to them."[26] While skepticism predominated among the missionary community, McNair believed that the Alborz Foundation might as well "make hay while the sun shines."[27] In this mission, most directors acknowledged that "the cosmopolitan nature of our staff is a definite asset." Individuals from Iranian Christian families served as administrators, and many of the younger members of the American missionary

---

[19] Hulac, Alborz Foundation annual report, [1948], PHS-91-16-16.
[20] Hulac to William M. Spence, February 3, 1949, PHS-91-17-12.
[21] Hulac report, August 22, 1949, PHS-91-16-16.
[22] John Elder to J. L. Dodds, July 5, 1950, PHS-91-17-1.
[23] Hulac to J. L. Dodds, February 4, 1950, PHS-91-17-1. It is interesting to note, given Alborz College's historic connection to Lafayette College, that the Alborz Foundation's first director, Charles Hulac, took an administrative position at Lafayette upon his brief return to the United States in the early 1950s. "Lafayette Aide Named," *New York Times*, June 25, 1950.
[24] "Special Report on the Educational Counselling Service," July–December 1951, Record Group (RG) 306, Records of the United States Information Agency, P74, box 2, folder: Reports 1951, US National Archives and Records Administration II (hereafter NARA), College Park, MD.
[25] [Frank Woodward] to Paul Seto, December 18, 1958, PHS-161-3-23. Record Group 161 contains the records of PCUSA/UPCUSA, Board of Foreign Missions/COEMAR, Secretaries' Files, Iran Mission, 1956–73.
[26] Thomas McNair report, February 1950, PHS-91-17-1.
[27] Thomas McNair to Herrick Young, June 20, 1949, PHS-91-16-17.

community were "veteran" English teachers by the late 1950s.[28] An American from San Francisco named Sherman Fung directed English programming for many years, and an Iranian woman moonlighted from her job with the Ministry of Education to run Boyce Memorial Library when it opened in 1960.[29]

Hulac's directorship marked "years of tentative, uncertain, experimental existence."[30] However, in the 1950s and 1960s the Alborz Foundation offered a wide and steady palette of cultural programming. It included everything from chapel services and religious study groups to recreational activities and film screenings. But it was the English classes that sustained the foundation's "involvement in the ongoing life of this metropolitan center."[31] The foundation's per-term capacity was 200 in 1956, but that number grew to 375 in 1961 and 500 in 1966. With four terms per year, Alborz serviced two thousand young Iranians annually in the mid-1960s. At this point, the majority of students were under the age of twenty-four; 37 percent were enrolled in an institution of higher education and 71 percent were women. A cross-section of Tehran came through the doors. One director recalled working with "mostly students but also cooks of the royal family, a consul general of one of the embassies, [and] an atomic research scientist."[32]

An important development came in 1957 when the Alborz Foundation moved to a property across from the University of Tehran. According to director Frank Woodward, the move marked "the biggest forward step in its history." To the missionaries, this was important because it meant that "the Foundation will be able to concentrate on serving and winning those for whom the former Alborz College existed and for whose sake this present venture was begun." The new building was spacious and, so the missionaries believed, fostered "an atmosphere of friendly exchange and of mutual respect for individual differences of opinion." The directors of the 1960s led cultural initiatives designed to expand the Alborz "circle of friends" in the university neighborhood.[33] Durwood and Barbara Busse were deeply integrated into the missionary community, and "Woody" was Alborz Foundation director from 1959 to 1963.[34] He found that, whether in the classroom "or while on a bus, or in a sandwich shop, or waking in the university area—friendships arise."[35] Stanley Hollingsworth was the final director

[28] "The Alborz Foundation," 1948–9, PHS-91-17-8; Frank Woodward, Alborz Foundation annual report 1956, PHS-161-2-12; Woodward, Alborz Foundation annual report 1957, PHS-161-2-13; Durwood Busse, Alborz Foundation annual report 1961, PHS-161-2-15; Busse, Alborz Foundation annual report 1962, PHS-161-2-16.
[29] Durwood and Barbara Busse letter, December 5, 1959, PHS, Durwood A. Busse (DAB) biographical file 360-23-29.
[30] Frank Woodward, Alborz Foundation annual report 1958, PHS-161-2-14.
[31] Durwood Busse, Alborz Foundation annual report 1962, PHS-161-2-16.
[32] Frank Woodward, Alborz Foundation annual report 1956, PHS-161-2-12; Durwood Busse, Alborz Foundation annual report 1961, PHS-161-2-15; Stanley Hollingsworth, Alborz Foundation annual report 1965, PHS-161-2-19; Hollingsworth, Alborz Foundation annual report 1966, PHS-161-2-20.
[33] Frank Woodward, Alborz Foundation annual report 1956, PHS-161-2-12; Woodward, Alborz Foundation annual report 1957, PHS-161-2-13; Woodward, Alborz Foundation annual report 1958, PHS-161-2-14; Program, "Dedication of the Alborz Foundation," April 28, 1959, PHS-91-17-22.
[34] Barbara Busse report, 1962, PHS-DAB-360-23-29.
[35] Durwood Busse, Alborz Foundation annual report 1961, PHS-161-2-15.

of the Alborz Foundation, and he was considered by colleagues to be the "keenest evangelist with university students and professional people."[36]

It was less the changes in Iran than those in the United States that compelled American Presbyterians to repurpose their foreign missions and, by extension, institutions such as the Alborz Foundation. In the United States, Presbyterians reconciled an intra-denominational schism with a 1958 merger that created the United Presbyterian Church in the United States of America. In place of the PCUSA's Board of Foreign Missions, but still in New York, was the Commission on Ecumenical Mission and Relations (COEMAR), and a Christian Service Board took over on the ground from the Iran Mission. As the number of congregants in "mainline" denominations declined in the United States, many Americans simultaneously developed a critical view of missionaries, seeing them as Christian crusaders and agents of empire. Still other Americans opted to do international work on behalf of their government or secular nongovernmental organizations rather than missionary societies.[37] In Iran these forces led to calls for "integration" between the Presbyterian Mission, which took marching orders from New York, and the Evangelical Church of Iran, which American missionaries had established a century earlier. It was reported that, on New Year's Day 1965, "the Church here in Iran ... has at long last taken the great stride forward ... of absorbing the work of our Presbyterian Mission."[38]

However, Presbyterian decolonization was incomplete in Iran. The Alborz Foundation and both mission schools in Tehran evaded integration and remained nominally independent from the church. Although the Iran Mission was phased out in the mid-1960s, all three Presbyterian institutions were sustained by broader ecumenical and internationalist networks and, in some cases, the Iranian government. In 1967, twenty years after Charles Hulac established the experimental student center, the Alborz Foundation was converted into the Armaghān Institute. Its English-language section continued to offer courses, but under the purview of Iran's Ministry of Education. Meanwhile, the student center facilitated outreach in the university community.[39] Paul Seto directed the institute.[40] Under his leadership, Presbyterians

---

[36] Frank and Jean Woodward letter, November 15, 1958, PHS, Frank T. Woodward (FTW) biographical file (2 of 2) 360; Durwood and Barbara Busse letter, December 5, 1959, PHS-DAB-360-23-29.

[37] David Hollinger, *Protestants Abroad: How Missionaries Tried to Change the World but Changed America* (Princeton, NJ: Princeton University Press, 2017); William Hutchison, *Errand to the World: American Protestant Thought and Foreign Missions* (Chicago: University of Chicago Press, 1987), chapter 7; Sharkey, *American Evangelicals in Egypt*, 204–5; James Smylie, *A Brief History of the Presbyterians* (Louisville, KY: Geneva Press, 1996), chapter 11; John C. B. Webster, "American Presbyterian Global Mission Policy: An Overview of 150 Years," *American Presbyterians* 65, no. 2 (1987): 78.

[38] Alice Johnson letter, January 16, 1965, PHS, Alice Eaton Johnson (AEJ) biographical file 360-72-43; William H. Hopper Jr., "A Program of Work for the Evangelical Church in Iran" (MA thesis, Louisville Presbyterian Theological Seminary, 1959).

[39] Memorandum to Christian Service Board Members, "A Recommendation Concerning an Adjustment of CSB Action 67-63," November 1, 1967, PHS-161-3-31.

[40] Paul Seto, "Armaghān Institute," [November 1967], PHS-161-3-31; Alexa Smith, "Middle East Missionary Dies—Paul Seto," *Reformed Online*, January 3, 2004. Available online: http://www.reformiert-online.net/aktuell/details.php?id=1750&lg=span (accessed January 21, 2021).

cooperated with local Christians and other American denominations, including Baptists, to carry on the program that Boyce and Hulac introduced during the 1940s.[41] The Armaghān Institute worked through the entirety of the 1970s, and Seto was the last American missionary to leave Iran in late July 1980.[42]

Community School

Community School was a fixture on Tehran's educational landscape from the mid-1930s to 1980.[43] It was originally an elementary and middle school for missionary children and other English-speaking students. Unlike its sister schools, Community School "escaped the general closing order that affected all the Mission schools for Iranians."[44] It grew in size and notoriety during the postwar years, enrolling Iranians and students of dozens of other nationalities in a liberal arts program that ran through the high school level. Without Alborz College, the Presbyterians thought that Community School was "the next best thing."[45]

Building on the work of Maud Rowlee, Commodore B. Fisher and J. Richard Irvine were the two headmasters of Community School from 1940 to 1967. Irvine acknowledged that it was Fisher who "had given the school its essential form."[46] Born in 1894, this "tall, gentle Tennessean" had no familial ties to the missionary network.[47] He and his wife, Franke Sheddan Fisher, first arrived in Hamadan in the early 1920s.[48] "The opening of the school for the missionary children," Franke Fisher wrote from Hamadan in the summer of 1930, "was one of the outstanding events of the year." Eleven students attended the "little Hamadan school" and took classes in a "pleasant schoolhouse" during the first year. Amid these beginnings, "We hope that this station school will develop into a mission school eventually."[49] This ad hoc arrangement evolved into the more formal "School for Missionary Children" in Hamadan by 1932.[50]

---

[41] George Braswell Jr., *To Ride a Magic Carpet* (Nashville, TN: Broadman, 1977); Philip Hopkins, "An Overview of the Missions Activities of the Southern Baptist Convention's Foreign Mission Board in Iran," *Iran and the Caucasus* 22, no. 2 (2018): 168–76, especially 171.

[42] Iran Missionaries [sound recording], recorded July 31, 1980, New York, Cassette 333, PHS.

[43] J. Richard Irvine, "Iranzamin, Tehran International School," *Encyclopaedia Iranica*. Available online: http://www.iranicaonline.org/articles/iranzamin-tehran-international-school (accessed January 21, 2021).

[44] John Elder, *History of the Iran Mission* (Tehran: Literature Committee of the Church Council of Iran, [1960]), 82.

[45] Commodore Fisher, "Alborz Foundation—Community School: An Explanation," [1947] PHS-91-16-17.

[46] J. Richard Irvine, Community School Report: "An Open Letter to Mr. Commodore Fisher," June 1962, PHS-161-2-16.

[47] Program Agency Board Memorial Minutes, February 26–28, 1987, "Commodore B. Fisher," PHS, Commodore B. Fisher (CBF) biographical file 424.

[48] Commodore Fisher to Orville Reed, December 1, 1919, PHS-CBF-360; Commodore B. Fisher personnel file, November 1947, PHS-CBF-424.

[49] Franke Fisher letter, July 1, 1930, PHS, Franke Sheddan Fisher (FSF) biographical file 360-47-35.

[50] Sarah McDowell, "Early History of Community School," n.d. Thank you to the members of the Community School Facebook group, and to Andrew Waterhouse for sending me this source in an email on July 19, 2020.

That July, the US legation in Persia reported to Washington about this and other "scraps of news." They noted that, with the school's opening, "one of the most serious problems facing missionary parents in this country is apparently solved to the general satisfaction of all concerned."[51] Not exactly. Some missionaries wanted the school to be located in Tehran. William Wysham recalled that he "argued for the capital city because we could draw on all the foreign community." Other missionaries "presented an idealistic picture of a country school without big city distractions." Hamadan was the initial host. But to Wysham's telling, "realism" ultimately prevailed, and in 1935 the school moved to Tehran. That is where it remained "anchored," and within a year it was rechristened "Community School." To the recollection of another missionary who was present at the creation, "community" was chosen because it conveyed "the concept of serving other than missionary children."[52] As Franke Fisher had hoped, the Hamadan station school became a mission school, but in Tehran.

Unlike Alborz College and most other foreign schools, Community School avoided educational nationalization in 1939–40 because, at the time, it catered to non-Iranian populations, mainly the children of missionaries. Iranian officials explained that institutions like Community School were spared "from motives of leniency and purely temporarily," but they "had no standing or legal status."[53] They were essentially rogue schools, and the missionaries preferred it this way. With memories of Reza Shah's nationalization decree and uncertainties about Mohammad Reza Shah's policies, most of the older missionaries who ran the schools wanted to avoid "the strait jacket of the Ministry of Education."[54] In the mid-1940s the remaining mission educators were "in exact agreement on one point that is … the all-important one." They "would never favor the expenditure of one dollar on any educational effort that would once more put us in competition with Government schools and with our students required to take Government examinations."[55] They, therefore, had to develop a unique educational program to remain relevant.

In 1940 Community School was located at the Iran Mission's Central Compound, located just south of the Soviet embassy on Qavām al-Saltaneh, a historic road in Tehran that was renamed Stalin Avenue during the Second World War.[56] It was also in 1940 that Commodore Fisher took over as principal of Community School. Franke Fisher taught classes and helped run the boarding house. As other foreign schools closed, the Fishers enjoyed "absolute freedom." The couple informed friends in the fall

---

[51] Charles C. Hart (Tehran) to Secretary of State (Washington), June 17, 1932, RG 59, Records of the Department of State, Central Decimal File, 391.1163/43, NARA.

[52] William Wysham, *My Life and Times*, 1976, pp. 170-1, 184, PHS, FOLIO BX 9225.W97 A3; McDowell, "Early History of Community School"; Pat Peck, ed., "Community School Alumni Bulletin," 2nd ed., December 1977, PHS, Commodore B. Fisher Papers, clippings and pamphlets.

[53] Translation of letter from Iranian foreign minister to British ambassador, April 17, 1947, PHS-91-17-12.

[54] J. D. Payne to Walter Groves, October 29, 1946, PHS-91-16-17.

[55] Walter Groves to Commodore Fisher, February 12, 1946, PHS, Commodore B. Fisher Papers, correspondence and reports.

[56] Walter McClennen, *Remembering Clem: A Good American in Iran* (Harwich, MA: Bogastow Books, 2017), 29–35; McDowell, "Early History of Community School"; Elizabeth C. Kay Voorhees, *Is Love Lost? Mosaics in the Life of Jane Doolittle* (Pasadena, CA: William Carey, 1988), 26–7.

of 1940 that "our own future was very uncertain until we were asked to take charge of this sole remaining Mission school."[57] Prior to the Anglo-Soviet invasion of 1941, Commodore Fisher found that it was "quite a League of Nations that we have every day." In 1948 he wrote in an education journal about "uniting nations in Iran."[58] During the 1940s, Community School evolved from a school for American missionary children to one for English-speaking students of all nationalities. As the missionaries understood the situation, "The rapid development of Iran has brought in engineers and specialists from other countries, and its isolation and freedom from European quarrels have made it a haven for refugees."[59] These trends began during the Second World War and picked up during the Cold War. As a result, there was a pressing demand for seats and an increasingly cosmopolitan student body at Community School as the 1940s came to a close.

When the Fishers retired in 1950, Community School was left in the hands of Richard Irvine. He was a North Carolinian by birth who relocated to New Jersey and earned a graduate degree in education from Rutgers. When "Dick" and Mary Ann first arrived in Tehran in 1951, they were immediately struck by the school's distinctiveness. During his first year on the job, Irvine noted that "Community School occupies a unique position in Iran, perhaps in the world. It was organized by missionaries ... for their children. It has become a project in international education."[60]

Irvine and the faculty—which included full-time missionaries and short-term teachers from the United States, professional educators from across Europe and Asia, and high-powered Iranian women such as Parvin Amin and Nayereh Ebtehāj-Samii—cultivated an international student body and crafted a curriculum to match that ran through the high school level. Throughout the 1940s, enrollments were consistently in the two hundreds, with Americans in the minority.[61] The students came "from all over the earth," Irvine wrote in the early 1950s, "from both sides of the Iron Curtain." In January 1952, as other Americans worried about the nationalization of Iran's oil industry, Irvine reported that "the school is now engaged in a program looking toward the complete revision of curriculum so that pupils graduating will ... have acquired a world cultural background."[62] The objective was to produce graduates who, as Irvine put it, "will be better able than their predecessors to solve the problems of international relations ... because they possess a wholesome nationalism coupled with a mature sense of membership in the community of nations."[63] To that end, the students recited an international pledge to three flags—those of Imperial Iran, the United States, and the United Nations. Anyone familiar with Community School is quick to recall its "big annual fete" that was held each October to celebrate the school's diversity on "United Nations Day."[64]

---

[57] Commodore and Franke Fisher, October 25, 1940, PHS-CBF-424; Profile of Mrs. Commodore B. Fisher, November 1961, PHS-CBF-424.
[58] Commodore Fisher, March 2, 1941, PHS-CBF-424; Commodore Fisher, "Uniting Nations in Iran," *Journal of Education* 131, no. 1 (1948): 18–19.
[59] Adelaide Frame, "Adaptation of the Narrative of the Iran Mission," 1941, PHS-91-16-17.
[60] J. Richard Irvine letter, January 1952, PHS, J. Richard Irvine (JRI) biographical file 360-70-31.
[61] Irvine, Community School Report, June 1961, PHS-161-2-15.
[62] Irvine letter, January 1952, PHS-JRI-360-70-31.
[63] Irvine, Community School Report: "An Open Letter to Mr. Commodore Fisher," June 1962, PHS-161-2-16.
[64] McClennen, *Remembering Clem*, 72–3; Wysham, *My Life and Times*, p. 171.

The aim of maintaining a diverse student body was threatened during the early 1950s because the "American colony" in Tehran was expanding rapidly.[65] At Community School, the American population skyrocketed from 52 to 179 between 1950 and 1953.[66] Writing in 1954, Irvine surmised that students began to "crowd our school plant" approximately "three years ago, when Point Four first came to Iran and when military missions here began to grow."[67] To relieve the pressure, in 1954 the US embassy sponsored a school for American dependents, the Tehran American School. This school's enrollments grew from 156 in 1954 to 860 in 1963.[68]

Community School experienced growth and transformation during the 1950s and 1960s. Early in Irvine's tenure, the school moved to a new campus-compound farther east in the city on the site of the old American Mission Hospital.[69] The school remained there until the revolution of 1979, and it was after the move to this campus that Iranians began to outpace other nationalities among enrolled students. A significant portion of the student body were Jewish refugees from Iraq who settled in Tehran and, for generations, sent their children to Community School.[70] Enrollments hovered in the four hundreds throughout the late 1950s, and in 1961 there were just over five hundred students—35 percent Iranian, 33 percent American, and 17 percent Iraqi, in addition to others. Religiously speaking, just under half were Christian in 1961, with 30 percent Jewish and 18 percent Muslim. In 1966-7 there were 642 students, about half of whom were Iranian. By that point, there were only twenty-nine students from fourteen missionary families. Graduates were regularly placed in the world's leading universities, and the school's track record earned the respect of the Iranian elite at the height of the developmentalist moment in Pahlavi Iran. As educational standards rose around the world in the 1960s, Irvine boasted that "Community is not running to catch up."[71] In the 1960s outside observers were startled to find that "Community School is in a very real sense a private parochial school sponsored and maintained by the Presbyterian Church."[72]

Community School lived two lives after 1967. It was then that Irvine and the school parted ways.[73] The Irvines did not leave Iran, however. They would "work with another school," announcing that "our motivation and concern continue to be essentially what they were when we were first sent to Tehran."[74] In summer 1967 Irvine

---

[65] McClennen, *Remembering Clem*, 38.
[66] Irvine, Community School Report, June 1961, PHS-161-2-15.
[67] Irvine letter, July 14, 1954, PHS-JRI-360-70-31.
[68] "The American School, Tehran, Iran," RG 59, Records of the Department of State, Records of American Sponsored Schools, box 31, folder: American School of Tehran, Iran, FY 1964, NARA.
[69] McClennen, *Remembering Clem*, 109, 177; Joan Rankin letter, February 5, 1955, PHS-486-1-2 Joan Rankin Papers, Correspondence January–November 1955.
[70] Victoria Rabbie, "Iraqi Jews in Iran," *The Scribe* 59 (September 1993): 2–3.
[71] Irvine, Community School Report, June 1961, PHS-161-2-15; Jackson Bird, Community School Report, 1956–7, PHS-161-2-13; Mary C. Thompson and Frank T. Wilson, "Report of Evaluation Consultants to the Policy Committee of Community School Teheran," November 1966, PHS-161-2-20.
[72] "The Community School, Tehran, Iran," RG 59, General Records of the Department of State, Records of American Sponsored Schools, box 31, folder: Iran, Tehran, the Community School, NARA.
[73] R. Park Johnson to Rodney Sundberg, June 20, 1966, and attached letter, "To the members of the Christian Service Board," June 18, 1966, PHS-JRI-360-70-30.
[74] Richard and Mary Ann Irvine to Rodney Sundberg, June 24, 1967, PHS-JRI-360-70-30.

obtained a license from Iran's Ministry of Education to open a coeducational K-12 school for Iranian and international students in Tehran.[75] Also known as the Tehran International School, "Iranzamin" was one of the few schools in the world that offered an International Baccalaureate in 1968. A decade later, Iranzamin had nearly 1,500 students from 50 countries and an international faculty of 112 members.[76] Upon its establishment, the American community in Tehran noticed that "Community School, missionary-sponsored, has a new competitor."[77]

The creation of Iranzamin and the transformation of Community School resulted from a revolution in expectations that swept through Iranian society. Those expectations grew in the late 1960s as the swelling number of students strained Iran's national education system.[78] In light of the educational demands, Community School and Iranzamin adapted their missions to the new context. US diplomats in Tehran were pleased that, after 1967, "both private schools now accept Ministry of Education supervision." For that reason, "their graduates are eligible at last to compete for entrance into Iranian universities." Looking toward the 1970s, US officials were impressed with Community School and Iranzamin. They predicted that "those two schools are in a position to set examples and standards for other local schools and possibly for the Ministry of Education itself."[79]

Community School remained under Presbyterian guidance after 1967, but it adopted a more inclusive board structure and sought funding and leadership from outside of the mission network.[80] The school continued to grow during the 1970s, reaching 1,500 students in 1977. During the twilight years of the monarchy, Empress Farah Pahlavi visited the school, which was still located at the former compound of the American Mission Hospital—the hospital where she was born nearly forty years prior. In her speech in 1977, Farah used the language of Fisher and Irvine in describing the school as "a mini United Nations."[81]

Interestingly, Community School's self-perception mirrored that of royal elites during the late Pahlavi era. A prerequisite for this harmony of interests and pedagogical notoriety occurred a decade earlier, in the late 1960s, with "the resolution of difficulties between the long-established Community School and the Ministry of Education."[82]

---

[75] Irvine letter, December 4, 1967, PHS-JRI-360-70-31.

[76] Irvine, "Iranzamin, Tehran International School," *Encyclopaedia Iranica*. See also "Iranzamin School Co-Founder Mary Ann Irvine Passes Away," *Kayhan Life*, June 25, 2017. Available online: https://kayhanlife.com/people/valentine-founders-iranzamin-celebrate-seven-decades-marriage-remember-iran/ (accessed January 21, 2021).

[77] Airgram A-197 from American Embassy Tehran to Department of State, October 14, 1967, Manuscript Collection 468: Bureau of Educational and Cultural Affairs Historical Collection, group 16, box 318, file 7, University of Arkansas Libraries Special Collections, Fayetteville, AR.

[78] David Menashri, *Education and the Making of Modern Iran* (Ithaca, NY: Cornell University Press, 1992).

[79] Airgram A-415 from American Embassy Tehran to Department of State, September 27, 1969, Bureau of Educational and Cultural Affairs Historical Collection, group 16, box 318, file 7. The 1966 Community School yearbook announced on p. 97 that, "Those planning for college were delighted to hear the recognition of the C.H.S. diploma by the Ministry of Education."

[80] Julian Cole Phillips, "Missionary Education in the American Century: The Changing Mission of the Tehran Community School, 1932–1980" (MA thesis, New York University, 2016), 13–16.

[81] Peck, ed., "Community School Alumni Bulletin," 2nd ed., December 1977, PHS, Commodore B. Fisher Papers, clippings and pamphlets.

[82] Airgram A-956 from American Embassy Tehran to Department of State, December 18, 1968, Bureau of Educational and Cultural Affairs Historical Collection, group 16, box 318, file 7.

Those difficulties were resolved as the residual caution from the Reza Shah years evaporated amid Mohammad Reza Shah's oil-fueled developmentalism and educational spending. Whatever plans were laid in the late 1970s were interrupted by the revolution. Community School and Iranzamin held their last graduation ceremonies in 1980.[83]

Iran Bethel

Iran Bethel is inextricably tied to the life of Jane Doolittle. She was a Pennsylvanian by birth and New Yorker by upbringing with an undergraduate degree from Wells College and a graduate degree from Teacher's College at Columbia University. Doolittle engaged in a range of work during her six decades in Iran, which spanned the entirety of the Pahlavi period. Among the most impactful and least studied was her educational work at Iran Bethel from 1940 to 1966.[84] While the Alborz Foundation and Community School were coeducational, Iran Bethel was a women's school that, like the other Presbyterian institutions, at once contributed to and reflected state-society dynamics in Pahlavi Iran.

In the late 1960s Iran Bethel became Damavand College. But American support for Iranian women's education began nearly a century earlier in 1874.[85] "Bethel" means "House of God," and Iran Bethel was intended to be a "House of God" in Iran, Doolittle explained. "At least we attempt in various ways to approach that high calling."[86] After decades in existence, the school was, from 1935 to 1940, known as Nurbakhsh, or the "light-giving" school. It had a relationship with Sage College, a Presbyterian junior college for Iranian women in the 1930s.[87] Doolittle knew that, whatever its name, the institution was "always in the eyes of the Iranians known as 'The American School for Girls.'"[88] She described the mission thusly: "Superficially it is a finishing school for girls. ... Fundamentally it is an institution where we seek to find and use all opportunities which will make Iranian women ... better fitted to meet their problems in life, to share in others' needs, and to build a better world."[89] In other words, "our aim has been to teach them to live, and to live abundantly."[90]

After the nationalization of Sage College and Nurbakhsh, "Miss Doolittle was staying on, starting a school ... in her own home." As one former student wrote of

---

[83] Irvine, "Alborz to Iranzamin," August 9, 1998, PHS-JRI-360-70-31.
[84] Foundation for Iranian Studies (FIS) Oral History of Iran Collection: Reminiscences of Jane Doolittle in an interview with Behruz Nikzat, September 30, 1983. See also Rostam-Kolayi, "From Evangelizing to Modernizing Iranians"; Vorhees, *Is Love Lost?*
[85] Doolittle, Iran Bethel annual report 1964, PHS-161-2-18.
[86] Doolittle, Iran Bethel annual report 1957, PHS-161-2-13.
[87] Sattareh Farmanfarmaian with Dona Munker, *Daughter of Persia: A Woman's Journey from Her Father's Harem through the Islamic Revolution* (New York: Three Rivers Press, 1992), 56–60, 108–9; Rostam-Kolayi, "From Evangelizing to Modernizing Iranians," 219, 229; Voorhees, *Is Love Lost?*, 71, 79–80n. 1, 84.
[88] Doolittle, Iran Bethel annual report 1966, PHS-161-2-20; Doolittle personal report 1945, PHS, Jane E. Doolittle (JED) biographical file 360-39-12.
[89] Doolittle, Iran Bethel annual report 1963, PHS-161-2-17.
[90] Doolittle, Iran Bethel annual report 1966, PHS-161-2-20.

her mentor: "after so many years she could not imagine a life that did not include teaching Persian children."⁹¹ After educational nationalization, Doolittle was in a situation comparable to those of the Boyces and the Fishers. "What the coming year— or month, or week—will bring forth none of us know," Doolittle wrote in August 1941. Like her colleagues, she found that "there is work to do, and plenty of it."⁹² After Reza Shah's abdication and the US entry into the Second World War, Doolittle interpreted her surroundings in these terms: "What wide, wide fields there are here untouched. So many hearts longing for just the human touch, the love and fellowship which this world so desperately needs."⁹³

The Iranian Ministry of Education allowed Iran Bethel to continue its work despite the fact that, unlike Community School, Doolittle's audience had always been Iranian students. Recalling the unusual arrangements, Doolittle mused that, by 1946, "I'd been running this illegal school for some years." In 1948–9 the school used money from the Sage College settlement to secure a new property at 27 Khiābān-e Dibā.⁹⁴ By 1950 Doolittle spoke in her reports of the "Bethel Project." She secured an operations permit each year and, twenty years after Reza Shah's nationalization decree, she was still "hoping to get something more permanent than a personal permit requiring annual renewal." Most years, according to Doolittle, "Inspectors from the Ministry of Education come to see what we are doing, heartily approve, and tell us to continue unhampered."⁹⁵

Given that it was a women's school, women ran Iran Bethel. Doolittle recalled that, early upon her arrival in Iran, "The women missionaries finally revolted at having a man as the head of their school committee."⁹⁶ In the mid-1960s there were sixteen instructors, seven of whom were full-time. Doolittle described it as "a fine loyal staff, half American and half Iranian, all working together for the progress of the girls." Like Community School, Iran Bethel relied on career and short-term missionaries from the United States. Missionary women taught classes, as did everyone from the "wives of businessmen" to the daughters of US embassy employees. The school also had "staunch national teachers who carry heavy loads," with Akhtār Āzādegān working by Doolittle's side for most of the postwar years. Whatever their background, Doolittle appreciated that they all "have given their time and talents to us most graciously."⁹⁷

As for the students, most were daughters "of the privileged classes" who "for one reason or another do not wish to continue in the regular program of the Ministry of Education." They were "educated, cultured young women," Doolittle wrote, "with ideals and great ability, who long to be of use in the world."⁹⁸ Religion was taught during the

---

[91] Farmanfarmaian, *Daughter of Persia*, 119–20.
[92] Doolittle letter, August 15, 1941, PHS-JED-360-39-12.
[93] Doolittle letter, January 22, 1942, PHS-JED-360-39-12.
[94] FIS Oral History of Iran Collection: Doolittle, 23–5.
[95] Doolittle personal report, 1950, PHS-JED-360-39-12; Doolittle, Iran Bethel annual report 1958, PHS-161-2-14; Doolittle, Iran Bethel annual report 1961, PHS-161-2-15.
[96] FIS Oral History of Iran Collection: Doolittle, 12.
[97] Information from the following Iran Bethel reports: 1957, PHS-161-2-13; 1958, PHS-161-2-14; 1961, PHS-161-2-15; 1962, PHS-161-2-16; 1963, PHS-161-2-17; 1964, PHS-161-2-18.
[98] Doolittle, Iran Bethel annual report 1964, PHS-161-2-18; Doolittle, personal report, 1950, PHS-JED-360-39-12; Doolittle, personal report, 1951, PHS-JED-360-39-12.

final year, and the faculty taught "the word in season" through the humanities, sciences, and vocational classes. There were also extracurricular programs, including work twice per week at a clinic that was related to the school and served the underprivileged of Tehran. The total program was geared toward producing the "Ideal Iran Bethel Girl"— an annual award given to a student who excelled in "all phases of Iran Bethel life." That "ideal" was defined by the gender-specific priorities of Presbyterian missionary schools for women, which in Iran dated to the late nineteenth century, and it was imbued with the American-style "domesticity" that reached Iran through home economics programs, consumer connections, and other mechanisms of US influence during the Cold War. By the mid-1950s, the curriculum was popular enough that Iran Bethel had "reached capacity" with two hundred students beginning each year.[99] The attrition rate was high, yet Iran Bethel enjoyed a small but significant base of 550 alumnae when Doolittle graduated her final class in 1966.[100]

Many of the graduates were members of the Iran Bethel Alumnae Association. It was among the oldest women's organizations in the country, having been established in 1915.[101] Outside of the Iran Bethel community, there was a proliferation of women's organizations during the 1950s. In 1959 Ashraf Pahlavi, the shah's sister, gathered seventeen of them under the umbrella of the High Council of Women's Organizations, which in 1966 became the Women's Organization of Iran.[102] The Iran Bethel Alumnae Association was not among those initial seventeen organizations. The association's status was similar to the school's in that it was not formally recognized by the Iranian government. Still, Doolittle studied the scene as women's organizations "were encouraged to unite under one head," and she realized that "a large percentage of the leaders of the various groups is drawn from among our graduates."[103]

Iran Bethel graduates and US-educated Iranians were at the center of the activity surrounding women's suffrage—a hallmark of the shah's White Revolution. Iranian women secured the right to vote in early 1963.[104] In April the Committee of Correspondence, an organization that championed "the contributions women can make to their community and nation," held one of its "most notable"

---

[99] Sarah McDowell, Iran Bethel annual report 1956, PHS-161-2-12. See Pamela Karimi, *Domesticity and Consumer Culture in Iran: Interior Revolutions of the Modern Era* (New York: Routledge, 2013); Rostam-Kolayi, "From Evangelizing to Modernizing Iranians"; Rostam-Kolayi, "Origins of Iran's Modern Girls' Schools."
[100] Doolittle, Iran Bethel annual report 1966, PHS-161-2-20.
[101] Doolittle, Iran Bethel annual report 1961, PHS-161-2-15. See also Michael Zirinsky, "Harbingers of Change: Presbyterian Women in Iran, 1883–1949," *American Presbyterians* 70, no. 3 (1992): 182–3; Zirinsky, "A Presbyterian Vocation to Reform Gender Relations in Iran: The Career of Annie Stocking Boyce," in *Women, Religion and Culture in Iran*, ed. Sarah Ansari and Venessa Martin (Richmond, Surrey: Curzon, 2002), 51–69.
[102] Mahnaz Afkhami, "The Women's Organization of Iran: Evolutionary Politics and Revolutionary Change," in *Women in Iran: From 1800 to the Islamic Republic*, ed. Lois Beck and Guity Nashat (Champaign: University of Illinois Press), 112–14. See also Stephanie Cronin, ed., *The Making of Modern Iran: State and Society under Riza Shah, 1921–1941* (New York: Routledge Curzon, 2003), chapters 9–11.
[103] Doolittle, Iran Bethel annual report 1957, PHS-161-2-13.
[104] Parvin Paidar, *Women and the Political Process in Twentieth-Century Iran* (New York: Cambridge University Press, 1995), 140–6.

international "workshops" in Tehran.[105] At this moment, US officials determined that "any attempt to help Iranian women must be in a low key and should in general be based on individual contacts."[106] One set of contacts were the recipients of the US government's Foreign Leader Grants. Reporting on the Committee of Correspondence, US diplomats found that "most of our women grant returnees ... took an active role in this conference which was termed as 'highly successful.'" One returnee was Effat Samiian.[107] In the early 1960s she was a participant in the national women's movement and the president of the Iran Bethel Alumnae Association.[108] This was a second source of American influence. The alumnae were always active, but "especially in this year of women's emancipation in Iran," Doolittle reported in 1963. She also stressed the importance of the Committee of Correspondence workshop, writing that "it was gratifying to find that over half of the Iranian delegates were Iran Bethel graduates who continue to play their leading role in working for the progress of women."[109]

In late 1963 two Iran Bethel graduates were elected to the twenty-first Majles.[110] One was Nayereh Ebtehāj-Samii, a longtime instructor at Community School and "one of the first women graduates of the American School in Tehran."[111] With new friends in high places, Doolittle reported in 1965 that the alumnae association "has finally become an officially recognized organization, engaged in activities for the advancement of women in society."[112] In 1966 Doolittle signed off from educational work, hoping that the "Iran Bethel School may have a new and inspiring future under the direction of Miss [Frances Mecca] Gray."[113]

Doolittle continued to run her clinic, but it was up to Gray, the former president of the Beirut College for Women, to determine whether "the school should be either upgraded or closed."[114] Gray discovered that "this school has had a notable record of achievement and has gained a position of prestige in the country." She concluded her initial report by writing that "the light in the field of women's education," while already bright, could burn "with a brighter flame." Rather than close Iran Bethel, she would transform the finishing school into a world-class university.[115] Gray expressed her logic in 1967:

---

[105] Hugh Wilford, *The Mighty Wurlitzer: How the CIA Played America* (Cambridge, MA: Harvard University Press, 2008), 155; Helen Laville, *Cold War Women: The International Activities of American Women's Organisations* (Manchester: Manchester University Press, 2002).
[106] Farian Sabahi, "Gender and the Army of Knowledge in Pahlavi Iran, 1968–1979," in *Women, Religion and Culture in Iran*, ed. Ansari and Martin, 105.
[107] Airgram A-133 from American Embassy Tehran to Department of State, August 28, 1963, Bureau of Educational and Cultural Affairs Historical Collection, group 16, box 318, file 6.
[108] Doolittle, Iran Bethel annual report 1961, PHS-161-2-15.
[109] Doolittle, Iran Bethel annual report 1963, PHS-161-2-17.
[110] Doolittle, Iran Bethel annual report 1964, PHS-161-2-18.
[111] Haleh Esfandiari, "The Role of Women Members of Parliament, 1963–88," in *Women in Iran*, ed. Beck and Nashat, 140–1.
[112] Doolittle, Iran Bethel annual report 1965, PHS-161-2-19.
[113] Doolittle, Iran Bethel annual report 1966, PHS-161-2-20.
[114] Frances Mecca Gray profile, PHS, Frances Mecca Gray (FMG) biographical file 360-56-20.
[115] Frances Mecca Gray, "A Preliminary Evaluation of Iran Bethel," December 1, 1966, PHS-FMG-360-56-20.

Since Iran Bethel was the first and ... finest school for young women in this land, it would be easy to rest on past laurels and recount the flow ... of the year as one more bead on a lovely rosary of memory. In our era, however, time does not flow ... it catapults in torrents, and one must look sharply ahead or suffer shipwreck.[116]

In fall 1968 Iran Bethel opened as Damavand College, a four-year liberal arts college with a license from the Ministry of Education to offer BA degrees to Iranian women. The curriculum was based on a global liberal arts program, the president reported to a board of trustees, and the college was supported by an array of donors from Iran and abroad.[117] In 1971, a half-decade before her visit to Community School, Empress Farah Pahlavi broke ground near Niavaran Palace on the new Damavand campus "dedicated to the humane studies and the liberating arts."[118] Damavand graduated its first class in 1972, and the new campus opened in 1975. At the end of Gray's tenure as president, there were 670 students, 37 full-time faculty, and 12 administrators. Before departing, she reflected on the school's place in the landscape of 1970s Tehran: "Last evening I rode out along Jordan Boulevard ... to the site of Damavand College. In a sweeping arc like the form of an historic Iranian caravans[e]rai the walls and towers of the new College are rising."[119]

Fittingly, the first Presbyterian college in Iran since the closure of Alborz College was located on a road named for its principal, Samuel Martin Jordan. When compared to Jordan, Jane Doolittle's educational legacy in Iran was equally as significant. When asked about her "greatest achievement," Doolittle said this: It was "the fact that I re-opened classes for the girls in 1940, after the schools were closed.... If I hadn't kept the girls' school open, there wouldn't have developed any Damavand College."[120]

Conclusion

Most historians of the Cold War treat the missionaries as relics from a bygone age that faded into obscurity with educational nationalization in 1939–40 and the subsequent US state interventions that transformed Iranian life in innumerable ways. The point here is that, despite important societal and geopolitical changes, missionary institutions survived educational nationalization, on the one hand, and total war and superpower competition on the other. Presbyterian institutions—forgotten in the historiography and buried amid the debris of US government interventions in Iran—informed the cultural project between Americans and Iranians from the 1940s to the 1960s.

---

[116] Frances Mecca Gray, Iran Bethel annual report, October 1967, PHS-161-2-21.
[117] Damavand College President's Report to the Board of Trustees 1974–5, PHS-FMG-360-56-20; D. Ray Heisey, "Reflections on a Persian Jewel: Damavand College, Tehran," *Journal of Middle Eastern and Islamic Studies (in Asia)* 5, no. 1 (2011): 19–44.
[118] Frances Mecca Gray letters, May 18, 1970, and November 13, 1971, PHS-FMG-360-56-20.
[119] Frances Mecca Gray, personnel development interview report, September 28, 1974, PHS-FMG-360-56-20.
[120] FIS Oral History of Iran Collection: Doolittle, 36–7.

The Presbyterian institutions of postwar Tehran operated within the context of the Cold War and White Revolution. In the Alborz Foundation one sees how the missionaries contributed to the "cultural cold war" in Iran.[121] Its first director, Charles Hulac, left missionary service to work for the American Friends of the Middle East. The nongovernmental organization became the most reputable agency dedicated to advising Iranian students who wished to study in the United States, and it was later discovered to be a front organization for the Central Intelligence Agency.[122] At the same time, the Alborz Foundation served as a weigh station between Tehran's postwar urbanites and their tangible and intangible encounters with America. In Community School one sees an internationalist expression that functioned as a source of US power and, in various ways, shaped the American-Iranian encounter. This form of international education, rooted in English-language instruction and a liberal arts curriculum, helped the missionaries repurpose their evangelical network for the postwar world. While the school was undoubtedly cosmopolitan, its very existence was due to the large colony of "privileged Americans" and other foreigners who were, for whatever their reasons, residing in Cold War Iran. In that setting, Community School and Iranzamin were "pioneer international schools" that paved the way for International Baccalaureate programs across Cold War blocs.[123] In Iran Bethel one sees how Presbyterian institutions contributed to the dynamic between Iranian citizens and their state. More specifically, Jane Doolittle and her school were part of the conversation about women's rights and suffrage in Iran. Yet, as had been the case with American missionary education since the nineteenth century, Iran Bethel provided emancipatory opportunities for Iranian women within the bounds of traditional "womanhood." Boundaries that were not set by the missionary curriculum were determined by the "patriarchal paternalism" of the Pahlavi state. In some ways, Iran Bethel and Damavand College brought about "revolutionary change." In other ways, the schools promoted the kind of "evolutionary politics" that revolutionaries later derided as apolitical bourgeois feminism.[124] Such was the mixed legacy of the American intervention in Iran.

[121] G. J. Breyley, "From the 'Sultan' to the *Persian Side:* Jazz in Iran and Iranian Jazz since the 1920s," in *Jazz and Totalitarianism*, ed. Bruce Johnson (New York: Routledge, 2017), 297–324; Houchang Chehabi, "Sport Diplomacy between the United States and Iran," *Diplomacy and Statecraft* 12, no. 1 (2001): 89–106; Hadi Parandeh Gharabaghi, "'American Mice Grow Big!': The Syracuse Audiovisual Mission in Iran and the Rise of Documentary Diplomacy" (PhD diss., New York University, 2018); Esmaeil Haddadian-Moghaddam, "The Cultural Cold War and the Circulation of World Literature: Insights from Franklin Book Programs in Tehran," *Journal of World Literature* 1, no. 3 (2016): 371–90; Louise Robbins, "Publishing American Values: The Franklin Book Programs as Cold War Cultural Diplomacy," *Literary Trends* 55, no. 3 (2007): 638–50. For broader perspectives, see Frances Stonor Saunders, *The Cultural Cold War: The CIA and the World of Arts and Letters* (New York: New Press, 1999); Hugh Wilford, *America's Great Game: The CIA's Secret Arabists and the Shaping of the Modern Middle East* (New York: Basic, 2013).

[122] Matthew K. Shannon, *Losing Hearts and Minds: American-Iranian Relations and International Education during the Cold War* (Ithaca, NY: Cornell University Press, 2017), 34–9.

[123] Guive Mirfendereski, *The Privileged American: The U.S. Capitulations in Iran, 1856–1979* (Costa Mesa, CA: Mazda, 2014); Tristan Bunnell, "The International Baccalaureate and the Role of the 'Pioneer' International Schools," in *International Education and Schools: Moving Beyond the First 40 Years*, ed. Richard Pearce (London: Bloomsbury, 2013), 167–82. See also Betty Anderson, *The American University of Beirut: Arab Nationalism and Liberal Education* (Austin: University of Texas Press, 2011).

[124] Liora Hendelman-Baavur, *Creating the Modern Iranian Woman: Popular Culture between Two Revolutions* (New York: Cambridge University Press, 2019), 54–5, 99; Afkhami, "The Women's Organization of Iran: Evolutionary Politics and Revolutionary Change"; Nima Naghibi, *Rethinking Global Sisterhood: Western Feminism and Iran* (Minneapolis: University of Minnesota Press, 2007), chapter 3.

7

American Academics and US Technical Aid for Iranian Modernization

Richard Garlitz

American universities contributed to Iran's modernization from the beginning of the Point Four Program in 1950 through the closing of the Agency for International Development (USAID) missions in 1967.[1] That Iran became the first country to receive such assistance speaks to its importance in American strategic thinking during the early Cold War.[2] American universities, for their part, became significant partners for the new US technical assistance program. They employed top scientists and sponsored research in fields that were important to economic development. Many academics proved eager to attack the world's poverty problems, especially within the context of combating international communism.[3] Scientists from Utah State University (USU) were early arrivals who worked on projects designed to enhance Iranian agricultural production as part of Point Four's rural improvement initiative beginning in the fall of 1951.[4]

By the middle of the 1950s, university projects shifted from low-level agricultural development to the modernization of higher education in Iran and other recipient countries. In Iran, the University of Tehran was an important target of the US aid program and its academic contractors. Three American universities sent advisers to strengthen colleges within the University of Tehran and train Iranians in the technical skills necessary for national development. USU had already begun assisting the

---

[1] Much of this chapter is revised from Richard Garlitz, *A Mission for Development: Utah Universities and the Point Four Program in Iran* (Logan: Utah State University Press, 2018). See especially chapters four and five. Point Four was the popular name for the US government's technical assistance to countries outside of Europe threatened by international communism during the 1950s. President Harry Truman first proposed the idea as the fourth foreign policy point of his January 1949 inaugural address. Congress enacted it the following spring as part of the Foreign Economic Assistance Act of 1950. President John F. Kennedy created the US Agency for International Development, or USAID, in 1961.
[2] "Point Four Project in Iran Announced," *Department of State Bulletin* (October 30, 1950), 703.
[3] Walter Adams and John Garraty, *Is the World Our Campus?* (East Lansing: Michigan State University Press, 1960).
[4] The official name of Utah State University was Utah State Agricultural College until 1957. For simplicity's sake, I use Utah State University or USU throughout this chapter.

expansion and modernization of Karaj Agricultural College, a branch of the university located just outside of Tehran. The improvement of that college was the sole focus of the USU contract from 1958 until the last Utahns left in the summer of 1964. A team of education professors from Brigham Young University (BYU) assisted the Teacher Training College in Tehran between 1957 and 1961. Finally, between 1954 and 1961 specialists from the University of Southern California (USC) helped establish the Institute (later College) of Business and Public Administration within the University of Tehran to promote efficiency and civic virtue in the Iranian government and to inspire American pedagogical reforms at the university.

This chapter situates these technical assistance projects within recent historiographical trends. Historians have, for example, increasingly emphasized how the Iranian government tailored economic development toward mass consumption, especially following the coup that overthrew Mohammad Mosaddeq in August 1953. The Pahlavi state attempted to mold an "alternative materialist vision" to Mosaddeq's liberal constitutionalism. Raising living standards would, presumably, help restore internal stability in the wake of the tumultuous oil nationalization crisis and augment public support for Mohammad Reza Shah Pahlavi's monarchy, which showed signs of floundering during the coup. Thereafter, an influx of US foreign aid encouraged "an American model of modernization" that would, in the words of one historian, "inoculate the country against communism through economic development."[5] David Collier has similarly written that American economic aid was "tasked with rejuvenating Iran's economy in such a way that Iranian citizens would directly benefit and more greatly appreciate the shah's regime."[6] Cyrus Schayegh has called this turn in Iran's modernization the "politics of material promise."[7] The projects under consideration here, especially Utah State's contributions to Iranian agriculture and rural development, further illustrate how the Iranian government attempted to use American foreign aid to improve material prosperity for Iranians. Yet, aid programs often produced truncated or ephemeral results. Some shortcomings reflected Point Four's narrow scope and the limitations of Iranian infrastructure; others happened because of the US government's proclivity to phase out financial support for many of its projects before they became self-sustaining.

The impact of Western science on the modernization of Iran has been another pertinent area of historical inquiry. Schayegh, for example, found that state sponsorship of formal training in Western science played a prominent role in shaping the Iranian middle class during the first half of the twentieth century.[8] Recent work on Point Four in Iran has described the ways in which the aid program attempted to channel "scientific

---

[5] Roham Alvandi, "Introduction: Iran in the Age of Aryamehr," in *The Age of Aryamehr: Late Pahlavi Iran and its Global Entanglements*, ed. Roham Alvandi (London: Gingko Library, 2018), 3.

[6] David Collier, *Democracy and the Nature of American Influence in Iran, 1941–1979* (Syracuse, NY: Syracuse University Press, 2017), 167.

[7] Cyrus Schayegh, "Iran's Karaj Dam Affair: Emerging Mass Consumerism, the Politics of Promise, and the Cold War in the Third World," *Comparative Studies in Society and History* 54, no. 3 (2012): 615.

[8] Cyrus Schayegh, *Who Is Knowledgeable Is Strong: Science, Class, and the Formation of Modern Iranian Society, 1900–1950* (Berkeley: University of California Press, 2009), 2–5.

progress" toward building "a future as mankind has never dreamed."⁹ Modernization theorists of the 1950s took this faith even further by asserting that American "technical expertise and social-scientific knowledge could rapidly solve the most trenchant societal problems, despite context, condition, or history."¹⁰ The BYU and USC projects indicate how Point Four attempted, with limited success, to transplant American pedagogies and administrative practices into Iran.

American assistance played a significant role in Iran's postwar modernization, but Iranians were hardly passive recipients. Scholars have traced the ways that Iranians "contested and negotiated" American approaches to modernization.¹¹ These projects demonstrate that Iranians were often ambivalent toward, and sometimes opposed to, American technical advisers. Attempts by American academics to introduce pedagogical reforms at the University of Tehran, in particular, illustrate how Iranian academics either resisted American practices or adapted them to fit their own purposes. The limits of transferability, therefore, proved to be more than technical. They were also cultural, especially when applied to education. What had worked in an American context did not necessarily prove adaptable to Iran, despite Point Four's abundant optimism in the transformative power of American expertise.

Agricultural Improvement Projects

Point Four Program officials looked to USU for agricultural advisers in part because of the school's preexisting connections in the country. Franklin Harris, who first directed Point Four's Iranian rural improvement initiative, served as president of USU between 1945 and 1950. He spent eleven months during 1939 and 1940 surveying Iran's agricultural challenges for the Ministry of Agriculture.¹² Upon returning to the United States, he recommended two USU faculty members, agronomist Don Pittman and irrigation engineer Luther Winsor, to continue his work. Winsor stayed in Iran through 1946 to work on irrigation problems for the Ministry of Agriculture, a position that gave him access to important government leaders. He even accompanied the young shah, who had shown an interest in agricultural improvements, on a three-day horseback tour of irrigation facilities.¹³ USU agronomist George Stewart traveled

---

[9] Jacob Shively, "'Good Deeds Aren't Enough': Point Four in Iran, 1949–1953," *Diplomacy and Statecraft* 29, no. 3 (2018): 416. The quotation is from Henry Bennett.
[10] Christopher T. Fisher, "'Moral Purpose is the Important Thing': David Lilienthal, Iran, and the Meaning of Development in the US, 1956–1963," *International History Review* 33, no. 3 (2011): 432.
[11] Ramin Nassehi, "Domesticating Cold War Economic Ideas: The Rise of Iranian Developmentalism in the 1950s and 1960s," in *The Age of Aryamehr*, ed. Alvandi, 40.
[12] Franklin Harris Diaries, 1908–54, vol. 4, 1061–1161, MSS 1611, Church History Library, Salt Lake City, UT. Harris had previously served as president of BYU from 1921 until 1945 and was respected around Utah and in the Latter-day Saints Church.
[13] Bob Parson, "International Students and Programs," folder 16, box 4, University History Materials, Utah State University Special Collections and Archives, Logan, UT (hereafter USU). See also the photos in folder 18, box 15, Luther Winsor Collection, USU.

to Iran in 1949, along with other American experts, to start laying "practical plans" for the country's rural development.[14]

USU's agricultural work anticipated the shah's emphasis on material promise in at least two ways. First, it concentrated on raising the standard of living for ordinary Iranians, an important departure from Reza Shah's interwar emphasis on building the army and modernizing infrastructure, cities, and manufacturing.[15] While much of the existing scholarship on material promise has focused on Iran's increasingly sophisticated urban and technocratic classes, Point Four shifted the focus to Iran's impoverished rural peasantry.[16] Scholars refer to Point Four's methodology as "low modernization" because it focused on small-scale rural improvement without relying on expensive technology or challenging existing social structures.[17] Its first director, Henry Bennett, described Point Four as a "down-to-earth" program of collaboration and demonstration that "deals directly with villages and with people ... who are barefooted, diseased, and hungry."[18] Second, Point Four was designed to foster stability within recipient countries, another important component of material promise. Bennett presented coordinated economic growth as the best antidote to the "false philosophy" of international communism.[19] USU livestock specialist Farrell Olson added that, by helping "the [Iranian] people adopt new and better practices," rural development could "instill in them a healthy philosophy of faith in their country."[20]

Agricultural improvement became more important to the Iranian government after the Second World War. While peasant farmers accounted for nearly 80 percent of the population, most lived at or near the subsistence level. The Iranian government took halting steps to improve land use and water conservation during the interwar years, but rural development was not a high priority then. Officials lacked both the political will and the means to enforce the halting measures that did pass through the Majles.

---

[14] George Stewart, "Iran: Pathway of the Middle East," *Improvement Era* (October 1950): 790–2.

[15] Amin Banani, *The Modernization of Iran, 1921–1941* (Stanford, CA: Stanford University Press, 1961), 120–2; Stephanie Cronin, "Riza Shah and the Paradoxes of Military Modernization in Iran," in *The Making of Modern Iran: State and Society under Riza Shah, 1921–1941*, ed. Stephanie Cronin (New York: Routledge, 2003), 38–66; Eckart Ehlers and Willem Floor, "Urban Change in Iran, 1920–1941," *Iranian Studies* 26, nos. 3-4 (1993): 251–75; Homa Katouzian, *The Political Economy of Modern Iran: Despotism and Pseudo-Modernization, 1926–1979* (New York: New York University Press, 1981), 111–16.

[16] A recent overview is Nassehi, "Domesticating Cold War Economic Ideas," 35–49. Two exceptions that emphasize American contributions to Iran's rural development are Sara Ehsani-Nia, "'Go Forth and Do Good': US-Iranian Relations during the Cold War through the Lens of Public Diplomacy," *Penn History Review* 19, no. 1 (2011): 10–18; and Victor V. Nemchenok, "'That So Fair a Thing Should Be So Frail': The Ford Foundation and the Failure of Rural Development in Iran, 1953–1964," *Middle East Journal* 63, no. 2 (2009): 261–84.

[17] Amanda McVety, "Pursuing Progress: Point Four in Ethiopia," *Diplomatic History* 32, no. 3 (2008): 385.

[18] Henry Bennett, Memorandum by the Technical Cooperation Administrator to the Director of the Management Staff, April 20, 1951, *Foreign Relations of the United States, 1951: Volume I, National Security Affairs, Foreign Economic Policy* (Washington, DC: US Government Printing Office, 1979), p. 1644, document 733. Available online: https://history.state.gov/historicaldocuments/frus1951v01/d733 (accessed March 30, 2021).

[19] Henry Bennett, "Workshops of Liberty," *Department of State Bulletin* (April 9, 1951): 585–7.

[20] Farrell Olson, Completion of Tour Report, undated, folder 3, box 7A, University Participation in Iran (UPI), USU.

As large landlords became more politically powerful, they blocked reforms that could threaten their own control of agricultural income and rural society.[21] "The villagers are in the grips of destitution and ignorance," explained Mostafā Zahedi, deputy minister of agriculture, in the spring of 1953. "They are totally lacking health and education, and they live for the most part a very hard life."[22]

Agricultural techniques had advanced little throughout much of the country, and Iran lacked a modern extension service to help farmers solve technical problems. Few small farmers could afford modern equipment or commercial fertilizers; irrigation practices ranged from inefficient to nonexistent. A vast network of underground tunnels, *qanats*, provided water from mountain sources to some dry areas of the interior, but Iran had fewer than three hundred deep irrigation wells in 1950. Many farmers used a method of lightly flooding fields, which wasted scarce water and washed away seeds. On top of it all, insects reduced the annual harvest by 15 percent on average. "The soil yields a small quantity of product," sighed one ministry official, "which is barely enough to keep flesh and bones together."[23] All told, the average Iranian farmer's standard of living in 1950 was not significantly better than it had been in 1900.[24]

Harris pressed his USU colleagues to participate in Point Four's rural improvement initiative even before it began. He wrote to the dean of agriculture, Rudger Walker, in early 1951 that he was "thoroughly convinced" that USU was "better suited to sponsoring Iran than any other institution."[25] To the university's president, Louis Madsen, Harris wrote that "Utah and the college are known very favorably in this country ... I know of no other institution that can carry on the work ... as well."[26] Following a summer of recruitment and preparation, USU sent its first five agricultural advisers and their families to Iran in the fall of 1951. The university had fourteen advisers in the country by the end of 1952, all of whom held some form of leadership position within Point Four's agricultural division.[27] Their first task was to establish credibility with farmers and village leaders. "The important job," observed Roy Bunnell, who spent nearly five years in Iran, "was to gain the confidence of the people." Progress, he explained, was measured "first by attitudes, followed by confidence, trials, observation, further trials, then eventually by introducing a new practice."[28]

The USU scientists' early efforts yielded mixed results. Initial research emphasized the development of higher-yield seeds that would better resist drought and insects, especially in cereal crops. Grains accounted for almost 95 percent of land under

---

[21] Gideon Hadary, "The Agricultural Reform Problem in Iran," *Middle East Journal* 5, no. 2 (1951): 185–6.
[22] Mostafā Zahedi, "Problems and Difficulties Facing Extension Work in Iran," [March 1953], folder 19, box 6, UPI, USU.
[23] Ziauddin Behravesh quoted in Andrew J. Nichols, "Development of the Iranian Agricultural Extension Service," May 1957, folder 9, box 26, Richard Welling Roskelley Papers, USU.
[24] Julian Bharier, *Economic Development in Iran 1900–1970* (London: Oxford University Press, 1971), 12, 139; Keith McLachlan, *The Neglected Garden: The Politics and Ecology of Agriculture in Iran* (London: I.B. Tauris, 1988), 39, 105–6.
[25] Franklin Harris to Rudger Walker, February 14, 1951, folder 2, box 2, University Participation, International Cooperation Administration (UPICA), USU.
[26] Franklin Harris to Louis Madsen, February 25, 1951, folder 2, box 2, UPICA, USU.
[27] "Ostan Agricultural Programs," draft, May 16, 1960, folder 5, box 7a, UPI, USU.
[28] LeRoy Bunnell, "Utah State Agricultural College-ICA Contract," folder 11, box 7, UPICA, USU.

cultivation in 1950.[29] Iran's varied climate and topography complicated the work, and in some cases the Utahns' lack of familiarity with local conditions and water rights undermined promising starts. The USU advisers learned a great deal from these early failures, but they inspired little confidence in village leaders.[30] Projects designed to improve livestock breeding also required time and modification before they produced consistently positive results. Point Four introduced new breeds of bulls, donkeys, and chickens, but many succumbed to local diseases. The donkeys, in particular, inspired mockery from skeptical Iranians.[31] Crossbreeding helped improve dairy production by 1958, however, and Utah scientists assisted the Tehran Veterinary Department in vaccinating more than eleven million farm animals between 1952 and 1956.[32] Neither the crop trials nor the livestock program had much impact, however, outside of the immediate regions where Point Four advisers served.

Creating a modern agricultural extension service that could disseminate better techniques to Iranian farmers was another high priority for the Iranian government. Training extension agents fit naturally into Point Four's low modernization approach, and it was probably the most successful USU contribution to Iranian agriculture. Nevertheless, the program had to be built almost from scratch. A small Iranian service existed in 1950, but it functioned more as a regulatory agency than as an educational body. With Point Four help, Deputy Minister Zahedi began organizing training seminars for Iranian extension agents in the summer of 1952, but it soon became clear that "working with villagers to solve their problems [was] not emphasized in their previous experiences."[33] The USU advisers worked with Iranian counterparts to manage a host of extension challenges. D. C. Purnell, for example, taught farmers how to control insects that ravaged wheat fields around Isfahan and how to apply sulfur spray to control mildew on grapes.[34] Melvin Peterson helped Qashqā'i tribal leaders in Fars develop a pasture rotation system that doubled the amount of grass available to their horses.[35] However, their main priority was teaching Iranian extension agents to engage villagers on terms they could understand, and in ways that would allow them to see how better techniques could improve their livelihoods.

Methods of demonstration varied. The USU advisers helped the Ministry of Agriculture organize community fairs and field days to demonstrate new techniques in produce and livestock. Audiovisual technicians from Syracuse University assisted the Utahns in producing informational posters and simple filmstrips about insect

---

[29] Richard Welling Roskelley, "Program of the Agricultural Division of TCI (Point IV in Iran)," April 1952, folder 4, box 26, Richard Welling Roskelley Papers, USU.
[30] Bruce Anderson, Terminal Report, November 5, 1951–March 15, 1954, folder 10, box 7, UPICA, USU.
[31] William Warne provides a more favorable description of these efforts in his memoir, *Mission for Peace: Point Four in Iran* (Bethesda, MD: Ibex, 1999). See especially chapters three and six.
[32] Bunnell, "Utah State Agricultural College—ICA Contract," UPICA, USU.
[33] Zahedi, "Problems and Difficulties Facing Extension Work in Iran," folder 19, box 6, UPI, USU.
[34] D. C. Purnell, Terminal Report, undated, folder Isfahan Agricultural Reports, Record Group 286, Records of the Agency for International Development, box 14, entry 486, US National Archives and Records Administration II (NARA), College Park, MD.
[35] Melvin Peterson, Completion of Tour Report, August 1, 1957, folder 1, box 7A, UPI, USU.

and disease control.³⁶ The Iranian government initiated a home extension program in 1958 to help rural families improve basic sanitation and methods of food preservation. Because home extension worked mostly with housewives, it provided a rare professional opportunity for rural women in a society that observed a high level of gender segregation. A youth program modeled on the American "4-H" taught adolescents about horticulture, health, and handicrafts.³⁷

Agricultural engineering concentrated on irrigation and mechanization, two areas that stretched the limits of Point Four's low modernization philosophy. Of the two, improving irrigation was the higher priority. Few Iranian agricultural officials had been trained in water management, and the ministry had little reliable information on groundwater supplies and usage throughout much of the country. USU adviser Cleve Milligan supervised the drilling of twenty deep wells in 1952, but the country lacked sufficient equipment and trained engineers to sustain a program of nationwide irrigation research and development. Instead, Milligan and Bruce Anderson focused on more fundamental forms of assistance, such as helping their Iranian counterparts design simple equipment for leveling and corrugating fields. They also conducted a series of irrigation demonstrations and short courses designed to help farmers maximize their usage of scarce water.³⁸

Iranian officials were often drawn toward mechanization because large equipment promoted the appearance of modernization. However, in this case the introduction of more advanced technology often created more problems than solutions. Point Four's modest budget included funds for just a handful of scattered machinery demonstrations, the utility of which was questionable given how few Iranian farmers could afford large machinery. The country's underdeveloped road network left many areas inaccessible to such equipment, and peasant plots were often too small to accommodate it.³⁹ Iran lacked enough trained mechanics and suppliers of spare parts. USU electrical engineering professor Bertis L. Embry observed many cases in which poorly trained operators and mechanics did more harm than good to machines.⁴⁰ Parts ordered abroad were expensive and caused lengthy delays. Fuel supplies and distribution were also inadequate, despite Iran's status as a burgeoning petroleum producer. Anderson reported in 1954 that "every region is plagued with machinery problems," and he noted that several landlords had abandoned their tractors or sold

---

[36] International Cooperation Administration, "Technical Cooperation through American Universities," no date, folder 2 University Contracts, box 101, John Ohly Papers, Harry Truman Presidential Library, Independence, MO. For more on the Syracuse University project, see Hadi Parandeh Gharabaghi, "'American Mice Grow Big!': The Syracuse Audiovisual Mission in Iran and the Rise of Documentary Diplomacy" (PhD diss., New York University, 2018).
[37] Government of Iran, Ministry of Agriculture, *Agricultural Extension in Iran* (Tehran: Iranian Ministry of Agriculture, 1959), 8–15.
[38] Bruce Anderson, Terminal Report, November 5, 1951–March 15, 1954, folder 10, box 7, UPICA, USU.
[39] "Ostan Agricultural Programs," UPI, USU.
[40] Bertis L. Embry, interviewed by Jessie Embry, undated, Utah Universities in Iran Oral History Project (UUIOHP), L. Tom Perry Special Collections, Brigham Young University, Provo, UT (hereafter BYU).

them for more oxen.[41] He, therefore, advised that agricultural mechanization should take "a long range view" in Iran.[42] Iran's first national survey of agriculture found that almost 90 percent of farms still relied exclusively on human labor and draft animals at the close of the 1950s.[43]

Nor did peasant farmers necessarily embrace mechanized agriculture, even though it might reduce their workloads. Some were reluctant to use machinery if they believed landlords would realize most of the benefits. Small farmers who owned their oxen, for example, risked losing a portion of their harvest and sliding deeper into debt if they had to rent more expensive equipment. Tractors and harvesters also increased efficiency, which threatened to deprive the poorest families of the traditional gleaning that took place after the harvest was finished. This was a significant loss for peasant households because such supplemental income could yield as much as six weeks' worth of bread.[44] The introduction of smaller horticultural equipment, such as garden planters and ox-pulled cultivators, proved more successful and helped increase the amount of land under vegetable cultivation.[45]

American officials shifted administrative control of Point Four agricultural programs to the Iranian Ministry of Agriculture in the mid-1950s. The change was designed to integrate the projects into Iran's national development plan while reducing American involvement to technical advice and training. A US congressional investigation that uncovered waste and corruption surrounding development aid to Iran probably hastened the process.[46] Integration, as this process became known, seemed like a natural step to Rudger Walker. "The program must be ... Iranian," he wrote in 1956, "not an American program."[47] Farrell Olson thought the change would create "more time for teaching the technicians, for holding demonstrations, and doing all those things needed for the lasting improvement of agriculture in Iran."[48]

Some Americans, however, felt that the transition was premature and triggered a decline in agricultural progress. Odeal Kirk, one of USU's longest serving extension advisers in Iran, wrote in 1958 that he did not believe the ministry "had sufficient experience" to keep Point Four's agricultural projects "moving ahead."[49] Nationwide, only two-thirds of the American projects had been completed by 1956. Many floundered amid the uncertainty surrounding the transfer of responsibilities. "If the

---

[41] Bruce Anderson to Rudger Walker, November 11, 1954, folder 3, box 3, UPICA, USU. See also "Present State of Cooperatives," pp. 17–19 of an untitled document, folder 6, box 2, UPI, USU.
[42] Bruce Anderson, Terminal Report, July 1954–May 1956, folder 3, box 6, Bruce Anderson Papers, USU.
[43] Bharier, *Economic Development in Iran*, 141.
[44] Banani, *The Modernization of Iran*, 126.
[45] Gwen Haws, ed., *Iran and Utah State University: Half a Century of Friendship and a Decade of Contracts* (Logan: Utah State University Press, 1963), 70–2.
[46] Fred Cook, "The Billion Dollar Mystery," *The Nation* (April 12, 1965): 381.
[47] Walker quoted in Jessie Embry, "Utah Universities in Iran, 1950–1964," *Journal of the Utah Academy of Sciences, Arts, and Letters* (2002): 172.
[48] Olson, Completion of Tour Report, UPI, USU.
[49] Odeal Kirk to Harry A. Brenn and Ray G. Johnson, April 8, 1958, folder 8, box 3, UPI, USU.

Iranians were not able to carry out their economic development program without Point Four during the early years of the 1950s," reasoned economist and cabinet minister Jahangir Amuzegar, "there was no reason to believe they were suddenly prepared to do so in the middle of 1956."[50]

Without question, Point Four's modest scope and low modernization approach left some Iranian officials wanting more, especially prior to the massive expansion of American development aid in 1954. The American financial commitment between 1951 and 1953 was far smaller than what Iranian leaders wanted, and many favored larger "prestige-giving" projects over community-level rural improvement.[51] William Warne, Point Four's first director in Iran, recalled how Prime Minister Mosaddeq "half-jokingly" likened the aid program to a tarantula that "jumps up and down and scares everybody, but it has never been known to bite." When Warne first met Ayatollah Abol-Qasem Kashani in the summer of 1952, the influential cleric inquired about doing "something substantial," such as building a hydroelectric dam on the Karun River to promote development in Khuzestan. Warne protested that such a project would cost ten times the entire Point Four budget for Iran, and he concluded that "the Ayatollah was completely unrealistic" in his approach to rural development.[52] Again, Amuzegar writes that what Iranians really wanted were "true symbols of economic progress" such as "large buildings, automated factories, and mountain-piercing roads."[53]

The efforts of the Utah advisers to bring material promise to Iranian peasant farmers proved modest when stacked against the country's overall needs. One Iranian observer acknowledged that Point Four's rural improvement initiative "introduced certain revolutionary measures which would have otherwise been very difficult, if not impossible, for the Iranian government to undertake."[54] Amuzegar likewise ranked agricultural research, especially on disease-resistant seed, among Point Four's most remarkable contributions, though he also noted that other areas such as irrigation produced less impressive results.[55] Bertis L. Embry was more despondent. "It was very difficult to change these people from the agriculture of two thousand years ago into the agriculture of the twentieth century," he recalled in a condescending tone. "You don't change things very fast."[56]

---

[50] Jahangir Amuzegar, *Technical Assistance in Theory and Practice: The Case of Iran* (New York: Praeger, 1967), 239.
[51] Mark Gasiorowski provides a financial overview of US foreign aid to Iran, including technical assistance, in *US Foreign Policy and the Shah: Building a Client State in Iran* (Ithaca, NY: Cornell University Press, 1991), 101–5. On the Iranian desire for "prestige-giving" modernization, see Matthew K. Shannon, "American-Iranian Alliances: International Education, Modernization, and Human Rights during the Pahlavi Era," *Diplomatic History* 39, no. 4 (2015): 678.
[52] Warne, *Mission for Peace*, 43, 68–9.
[53] Amuzegar, *Technical Assistance*, 127.
[54] Gholam Hossein Kazemian, *Impact of US Technical Aid on Rural Development in Iran* (New York: Theo Gaus' Sons, 1968), 20, 23.
[55] Amuzegar, *Technical Assistance*, 10.
[56] Embry interview, UUIOHP, BYU.

Karaj Agricultural College and the Teacher Training College

Dwight Eisenhower overhauled the foreign aid program that he inherited from Harry Truman, including Point Four technical assistance. In the mid-1950s the Eisenhower administration shifted the emphasis of university projects to modernizing and expanding higher education through direct partnerships with counterpart institutions in host countries. This new focus was designed to allow American universities to marshal their expertise in teaching and research in order to make higher education more responsive to the developmental needs of host countries.[57] American advisers found, however, that while Iranian academic leaders appreciated US financial and material support, they were often much less receptive to American ideas, especially those that challenged existing practices.

Higher education emerged as an important vehicle for Iran's modernization by the 1950s. From their earliest inception in the second half of the nineteenth century, modern Iranian state-supported schools aimed to infuse scientific knowledge into national institutions, especially the army and nascent foreign service. Reza Shah prioritized higher education over lower levels of public education during the interwar years, largely to meet the need for a more skilled workforce in the government's expanding bureaucracy. The Majles consolidated several existing colleges into the University of Tehran, Iran's first modern public university, in 1934.[58] While higher education emerged as "an essential part of the modern middle class's cultural capital," it struggled to meet the demands of a modernizing society.[59] The government chartered five new universities in the decade following the Second World War, but they were "set up with little planning and with scant regard for the availability of teaching and research staff."[60] Iranian universities also tended to reflect scholastic French influence from the nineteenth and early twentieth centuries. Learning relied heavily on rote memorization and a cycle of annual examinations that ended with the *konkur*; curricula observed rigid standardization with little allowance for innovation or specialization within fields of study.[61] Even the University of Tehran showed deficiencies in several of its colleges, including Karaj Agricultural College and the Teacher Training College.

Karaj Agricultural College had been located, since 1927, on the grounds of a former royal garden some twenty-five miles west of Tehran. The college, which became part of the University of Tehran in the mid-1930s, was intended to mark a "stride toward the introduction of modern agricultural methods." Its immediate impact, however, was slight. Its physical campus was insufficient for growth, and few of its approximately 125

---

[57] John Richardson, *Partners in Development: An Analysis of AID-University Relations, 1950–1966* (East Lansing: Michigan State University Press, 1959), 53–9. See also "Basic FOA Policy on University Contracts," June 13, 1955, folder 7, box 2, Dean Peterson Collection, BYU.
[58] David Menashri, *Education and the Making of Modern Iran* (Ithaca, NY: Cornell University Press, 1992), 53–8, 117, 146–7; Josheph Szyliowicz, *Education and Modernization in the Middle East* (Ithaca, NY: Cornell University Press, 1973), 172, 241–2.
[59] Schayegh, *Who Is Knowledgeable Is Strong*, 60–1.
[60] Menashri, *Education and the Making of Modern Iran*, 213.
[61] Szyliowicz, *Education and Modernization*, 235–6.

students showed much interest in agriculture. Rather, most students saw the college as a ticket into the Ministry of Agriculture's professional bureaucracy.[62] Teaching, in the view of USU adviser Richard Welling Roskelley, was "not service oriented," and courses did "not relate to the problems of rural people." According to the dean, the college had not supported field research since 1940.[63]

The Teacher Training College, also part of the University of Tehran since 1934, languished in a similar condition. It had been reduced to renting a collection of converted homes in Tehran that were "very inadequate" for classroom use.[64] The faculty consisted mostly of part-time professors who, in the view of BYU advisers, brought "various degrees of dedication" to their teaching.[65] Many of the students were not particularly interested in teaching, especially at the elementary level, where salaries were low and Iran's need for qualified teachers was most acute. Rather, they saw the college as a springboard into a more lucrative career in secondary education or administration.[66]

Iranian and American development planners believed that strengthening higher education would augment the nation's material prosperity. They wanted to expand access to meet rising expectations among young Iranians and thereby reduce the number who had to seek a university education abroad. American advisers also sought to make universities more responsive to the country's development needs by placing more emphasis on problem solving, experimentation, and practical applications of knowledge. The Americans, therefore, promoted subjects that had previously enjoyed little or no standing within Iranian universities. For example, USU advisers encouraged the development of home economics and home extension programs at Karaj Agricultural College. College leaders appeared interested and even hired a home economist, but inadequate housing for female students and a lack of classroom space prevented the program from progressing.[67] Home economics fared better at the Teacher Training College. There, BYU adviser Malno Reichert applauded the pioneering spirit of two young home economists, Nāhid Farzād and Vidā Daftari, the latter of whom was a graduate of USU. They previously served as Point Four extension agents and now undertook the responsibility of building a home economics department out of a dilapidated basement. Though neither held faculty rank, they prepared classrooms, developed course materials, procured equipment, and established a training program for home extension agents.[68]

The Americans also urged Iranian academics to incorporate hands-on practical applications of knowledge. USU advisers, for example, helped develop a 500-acre research and demonstration farm at Karaj into a "blooming enterprise" that "everyone

---

[62] Banani, *The Modernization of Iran*, 124–5.
[63] Richard Welling Roskelley, "Some Notes on Institution Building at Karaj Agricultural College, 1951–1967," folder 16, box 26, Richard Welling Roskelley Papers, USU.
[64] A. Reed Morrill, End of Tour Report, 1961, folder 1, Point Four Program Files (PFPF), BYU.
[65] Brigham Young University Contract Team, "Evaluation and Recommendation for Danesharaye Ali Prepared by a Committee of Iranian Professors and the Brigham Young University Contract Team, 1960–1961," 11.
[66] John Ord, Terminal Report, June 1961, folder 1, PFPF, BYU.
[67] J. Clark Ballard, Monthly Report, April 1963, folder 1, box 3, UPICA, USU.
[68] Malno Reichert, End of Tour Report, 1959, folder 1, PFPF, BYU.

could point to with pride."⁶⁹ By 1961, the farm included a large machinery shed, four deep wells, and modern irrigation pumps.⁷⁰ Still, American methods cut against Iranian social conventions that eschewed manual labor for educated professionals. William Carroll observed that the students "consider any job that requires them to put down their briefcase, or put on work clothes, or to get their hands soiled, to be beneath the dignity of the educated man."⁷¹ The Utahns did make some progress in this area. Horticulturalist J. Clark Ballard, who worked at Karaj Agricultural College in 1960 and 1961, noted that a cadre of "progressive as well as aggressive faculty members," many of whom had advanced degrees from USU, began to incorporate farm work into their teaching and research.⁷² Horticulturalist Odeal Kirk observed that Iranians who received training on the farm "found themselves quite in demand" and secured profitable employment.⁷³ The USU advisers urged college officials to recruit more students from rural communities who showed an interest in farming. They also lobbied the Ministry of Agriculture to allow graduates of agricultural high schools to compete in the annual entrance examinations.⁷⁴

Many American pedagogical reforms either met resistance from Iranian academic leaders or proved ephemeral. Richard Welling Roskelley noted that Karaj Agricultural College officials were "very secure" in their curriculum and teaching methods; they "weren't about to make any great changes."⁷⁵ He added that the Iranians were "very appreciative of the dollars that were spent" as long as Americans did not challenge "how they felt they should operate."⁷⁶ Mohammad Hassan Mahdavi, who served as dean of the college from 1954 until 1962, acknowledged that Iranian professors "did not always indicate that they were interested in having Americans on campus." He conceded that "the only reason the Iranian professors put up with Americans is that they brought so much money with them."⁷⁷ Roskelley was disappointed when he visited Karaj Agricultural College in 1967, three years after the last Utah advisers left and thirteen years after his own work in Iran had ended. The dynamic Mahdavi had been replaced by a political appointee who lacked a background in higher education. The curriculum retained little evidence of practical application. Roskelley thought that, perhaps, the advisers had pushed too hard to impose their ideas too quickly.⁷⁸ It might have been better to encourage Iranians to *adapt* American concepts to an Iranian context rather than expecting them to *adopt* those methods outright.

BYU advisers encountered similar difficulties in their attempt to transplant American educational concepts to the Teacher Training College. They advocated for

---

[69] "Interview with Dr. M. Mahdavi," June 12, 1967, folder 16, box 16, Richard Welling Roskelley Papers, USU.
[70] Haws, *Iran and Utah State University*, 98–101, 106–7, 109–11.
[71] William Carroll, Terminal Report, March 26, 1957, folder 13, box 7, UPICA, USU.
[72] J. Clark Ballard, Completion of Tour Report, June 3, 1962, folder 1, box 3, UPICA, USU.
[73] Odeal Kirk, Completion of Tour Report, undated, folder 5, box 2, UPI, USU.
[74] Carroll, Terminal Report; Ballard, Completion Report, both in UPICA, USU.
[75] Richard Welling Roskelley, "A Development of Karaj Agricultural College," folder 15, box 26, Richard Welling Roskelley Papers, USU.
[76] Roskelley, "Some Notes on Institution Building," Richard Welling Roskelley Papers, USU.
[77] "Interview with Dr. M. Mahdavi," Richard Welling Roskelley Papers, USU.
[78] Ibid.

a more comprehensive approach to general education by arguing that a good teacher had to be "a well-educated person in the broad sense of the word."[79] They also pushed for more development in elementary education because Iran faced an acute shortage of professional teachers. John Ord recalled that enthusiasm for elementary school teaching was low when he arrived in 1957. Few university students considered it a worthy profession, in part because of the low pay and low social prestige that came with it. By 1961, however, he reported that the importance of professional elementary school teachers "is slowly being realized by the people of Iran." Ord noticed that a "favorable attitude toward educating all children is now evident" at the Teacher Training College.[80] The emphasis on training more elementary school teachers and the professionalization of practicing teachers were probably BYU's most important contributions to the modernization of Iranian public education.[81]

Yet, other BYU initiatives proved less successful. Golden Woolf, who led the BYU team, complained that senior Iranian academic leaders continued to treat the college "like an unwanted child."[82] The country needed more physical education teachers to help improve public health.[83] David Geddes tried to develop that specialty but noted with frustration that, in 1961, physical education still had no full-time teachers or permanent facilities of its own. Students "received much poor instruction" as a result.[84] Like the USU advisers at Karaj Agricultural College, BYU professors at the Teacher Training College thought that the curricula and teaching methods were too rigid and that senior faculty members were unresponsive to innovation. "Individual professors see us as a threat," concluded audiovisual adviser Morris Shirts, "and refuse to work with us."[85] Malno Reichert observed that some junior professors wanted "to make changes in their courses to make them more meaningful." But, she grumbled, they were too shackled "by rules and traditions and older professors who cannot change." Her greatest disappointment was that female education had not made more progress. "At the end of four years in Iran," she lamented, "my opinions of the educational prospects for the women of this country are not bright."[86]

The American experience at Karaj Agricultural College and the Teacher Training College in Tehran illustrates that Iranians were far from passive recipients of American technical aid. Iranian professors and administrators wanted American material assistance, but they tried to limit American pedagogical influence. While they gradually moved toward greater emphasis on development-centered fields, such as home economics and elementary education, they often rejected reforms that attempted

---

[79] "Education in Iran with Special Reference to Teacher Education and to Daneshsraye Ali," July 29, 1961, folder 1, PFPF, BYU.
[80] Ord, Terminal Report, PFPF, BYU.
[81] For more on an earlier BYU project to help professionalize practicing teachers, see Garlitz, *A Mission for Development*, 115–20.
[82] Golden Woolf, Terminal Report, 1961, folder 1, PFPF, BYU.
[83] Reza Arasteh, *Education and Social Awakening in Iran* (Leiden: E. J. Brill, 1962), 84.
[84] David Geddes, End of Tour Report, July 1961, folder 1, PFPF, BYU.
[85] Morris Shirts to family, December 27, 1957. I am grateful to Jessie Embry for sharing her transcription of this letter with me.
[86] Malno Reichert, Completion of Tour Report, 1959, and End of Tour Report, 1961, PFPF, BYU.

to Americanize teaching practices. Indeed, the Utahns' experience reflects a common pattern in American technical aid to Iranian education. A team of academics from the University of Pennsylvania encountered a similar situation at Pahlavi University in Shiraz between 1962 and 1967. Senior Iranian professors and administrators welcomed American resources and financial support but resented American influence in teaching, the curriculum, and the administration of the university.[87]

The College of Business and Public Administration

American university advisers also tried to improve Iran's public administration. In 1900 the Iranian government consisted of four ministries that exercised little control over most of the countryside and contributed little to the nation's economic development. Reza Shah greatly expanded the national bureaucracy during the interwar years, and by the mid-twentieth century the national government comprised eleven ministries with broad regulatory powers and employed more than a quarter of a million Iranians.[88] Yet, the state suffered from a lack of properly trained managers and poor intragovernment coordination.[89] Bureaucratic inefficiency undermined Iran's first two national development plans between 1949 and 1962.[90] Low salaries and arcane methods of tax collection encouraged corruption at all levels. American officials thought that increasing civic mindedness among government employees would instill public confidence in the state, especially in the wake of the chaotic Mosaddeq years. They also saw civic virtue as an important weapon against "red infiltration."[91]

Point Four officials recruited USC to help the University of Tehran create an Institute (later College) of Business and Public Administration between 1954 and 1961. USC organized one of the first American colleges of public administration in 1929 and had provided similar training in Turkey and Brazil. US officials hoped the institute would incubate both democratic values in the Iranian government and American reforms within the University of Tehran.[92] In shaping the new institute, the USC advisers

---

[87] See Richard Garlitz, "U.S. University Advisors and Education Modernization in Iran, 1951–1967," in *Teaching America to the World and the World to America: Education and Foreign Relations since 1870*, ed. Richard Garlitz and Lisa Jarvinen (New York: Palgrave Macmillan, 2012), 204–7. A contemporary American account of the University of Pennsylvania collaboration with Pahlavi University can be found in W. A. Copeland, "American Influences on the Development of Higher Education in Iran" (PhD diss., University of Pennsylvania, Philadelphia, 1973). See especially chapter 5.

[88] Ervand Abrahamian, *A History of Modern Iran* (Cambridge: Cambridge University Press, 2008), 67, 70–1. See also Bharier, *Economic Development in Iran*, 7–9.

[89] Jahangir Amuzegar, *The Dynamics of the Iranian Revolution: The Pahlavi's Triumph and Tragedy* (Albany: State University of New York Press, 1991), 195–6.

[90] George Baldwin, *Planning and Development in Iran* (Baltimore, MD: Johns Hopkins University Press, 1964), 26–34; Kamran Mofid, *Development Planning in Iran: From Monarchy to Islamic Republic* (Wisbech, UK: Middle East and North African Studies Press, 1987), 34–41. Other constraints included the fiscal impact of the British-led boycott of Iranian exports during the oil nationalization controversy and the government's tendency to emphasize showy projects of questionable utility. See Katouzian, *The Political Economy of Modern Iran*, 202–5.

[91] Matthew K. Shannon, *Losing Hearts and Minds: American-Iranian Relations and International Education during the Cold War* (Ithaca, NY: Cornell University Press, 2017), 27.

[92] William B. Storm and Richard W. Gable, "Technical Assistance in Higher Education: An Iranian Illustration," *Educational Record* 41, no. 2 (1960): 175–8.

tried to create a more flexible system of transferable credits and regular assignments that would allow students to apply what they learned. They also wanted to make the university more accessible by creating evening classes and an open-stacks library with circulating books. Finally, the USC advisers urged the university to hire full-time professors whose complete professional attention would be focused on teaching and practical research into the country's administrative challenges.[93]

USC also brought thirty Iranians to Los Angeles to study during the seven-year life of the project. This aspect of technical assistance was commonly called "participant training." In selecting the participants, the USC advisers considered each candidate's intellectual ability, practical experience, and ability to use English. Because the training would prepare Iranians for meaningful work within the Iranian government, the USC professors chose candidates of an "appropriate social standing" and disqualified those whose "sympathy for the western position in the Cold War" was uncertain.[94] USC took this aspect of the contract very seriously. In addition to providing standard courses and research guidance, the university sponsored field trips to allow the Iranians to see how state and local government, as well as courts and municipal police departments, operated in California. USC also created an International Public Administration Center to provide special services to international students, including academic support and counseling.[95]

The USC advisers clearly saw the participant program as the most successful aspect of their project. Of the thirty Iranians who studied at USC, twenty-four earned doctorates and one completed a master's degree. USC's final report concluded that those Iranians achieved an "amazingly high standard of performance" and would become "one of the most significant pillars of strength in the future of public administration." While such praise was hardly objective, it did have some merit. USC-trained participants went on to work for major banks and financial institutions, ministries of the Iranian government, and the National Iranian Oil Company. ʿAli-Naqi Farmanfarmaian and ʿAli Asghar Vahābzādeh achieved high-level positions within the Plan Organization—Iran's central agency for coordinating economic development plans. Mostafā ʿElm distinguished himself as a diplomat and academic. He represented Iran on the Economic Committee of the United Nations and later served as ambassador to Sudan. Iraj Ayman became a distinguished professor of psychology and international education consultant.[96]

By the time the project ended in 1961, the USC team could point to tangible accomplishments. The College of Business and Public Administration employed seventy-five full-time professors when Iranians took over from their American colleagues. An independent American review of the USC project found evidence that the new college would "help generate important new ideas, questions, and hopes."[97] The USC advisers could also point toward improvements in police administration, tax collection, and

---

[93] Copeland, "American Influences on the Development," 137–8.
[94] Storm and Gable, "Technical Assistance in Higher Education," 176–7.
[95] University of Southern California (USC), School of Public Administration, "Seven Years in Iran: The Final Report of a Technical Assistance Project in Public Administration under US Contract No. ICAC-1299" (Los Angeles: University of Southern California School of Public Administration, June 1962), 2–7, 11–12.
[96] Ibid.
[97] James R. Watson, "A Review of the Program." This review is included as Part Two of USC, "Seven Years in Iran."

public finance—all of which had been objectives of the larger US aid mission in Iran. One professor helped found a municipal association to improve relations between government workers and the public, while others worked to enhance the sense of service among provincial and local officials. The USC advisers also helped create a social science research center to facilitate systematic analysis of the country's administrative challenges.[98]

Despite some notable successes, the new college had a limited impact on the Iranian government and very little influence on Iranian business outside of the oil industry in the late Pahlavi period. Its influence on Iranian higher education reform was likewise modest. As with the American experience at Karaj Agricultural College and the Teacher Training College, many senior Iranian professors objected to American initiatives at the College of Business and Public Administration. They were prepared to accept the American advisers as "part of a bigger package" that included financial support, but they proved much less receptive to American academic influence.[99] Another review in 1969 found that, university-wide, USC's reforms were "more shadow than substance."[100]

The USC advisers overestimated how well American public administration concepts would work in Iran. William Storm and Richard Gable wrote in 1960 that "the basic elements of administration are applicable in any organization, regardless of … the culture to which it is a part." The USC project, therefore, was based on the assumption that "the ideas and programs which work in Southern California will work in Iran."[101] The argument paralleled the universalist thinking of many modernization theorists, but it turned out to be a fallacy. Twenty years later, John Seitz found that American public administration advisers lacked sufficient knowledge of Iranian political and economic culture to adapt American methods to the Iranian context. "Adapt not adopt," he concluded, was "more a slogan than a set of tested practices."[102]

Conclusion

American technical advisers from USU, BYU, and USC went to Iran with an expectation to contribute to the country's modernization. Their work fit generally within the Iranian government's attempt to use American foreign aid to enhance material promise. While most of the agricultural projects aimed to improve the quality of life for the impoverished rural peasantry, attempts to expand and modernize Iranian higher education primarily benefited the urban middle class. The Americans attempted to improve, or develop from scratch, colleges of the University of Tehran to make them more responsive to the country's modernization needs. However, their efforts often

---

[98] USC, "Seven Years in Iran," 8–12.
[99] John L. Seitz, "The Failure of US Technical Assistance in Public Administration: The Iranian Case," *Public Administration Review* 40, no. 5 (1980): 408–9.
[100] Joel B. Slocum, *Iran: A Study of the Educational System and a Guide to the Admission and Academic Placement of Iranian Students in Colleges and Universities in the United States* (Washington, DC: American Association of Collegiate Registrars and Admissions Officers, 1970), 62.
[101] Storm and Gable, "Technical Assistance in Higher Education," 176, 180.
[102] Seitz, "The Failure of US Technical Assistance," 409–10.

met with resistance from Iranian academic leaders, a reality that fits a larger pattern in the history of American technical assistance during the Cold War era. Writing in 1962, historian of education Reza Arasteh noted how Iranian educators "nominally accepted" input from foreign advisers "only to circumvent it by devising their own modification."[103] In many instances, Iranians expressed interest in material support, but they resented American influence in curricular and pedagogical matters. These projects, therefore, illustrate how Iranians "contested and negotiated" the American vision for modernization. Finally, American university advisers had to confront the limits of transferability. The much-vaunted faith in American scientific know-how often proved to be a mirage that gave way to frustration and underwhelming results. Advisers learned that the cultural context really did matter, especially when negotiating pedagogical reforms. What had worked well in the United States could rarely be transplanted seamlessly into Iran, especially to an institution as symbolically important as the University of Tehran.

---

[103] Arasteh, *Education and Social Awakening*, 114.

8

"We Learned How to Be Friends": What Oral History Tells Us about the American Peace Corps in Iran

Jasamin Rostam-Kolayi

We who have had the opportunity to experience Iran and the world from perspectives unimaginable to most Americans, possess a special quality that we should not take lightly. Though we were once Peace Corps Volunteers, we can always be Peace Corps Volunteers … We can bring about change in America by providing understanding of Iran.[1]

When former American Peace Corps Iran volunteers Tom Klobe and Jackie Spurlock wrote the words above in late 2019, Iranians were turning out into the streets to protest government-sponsored oil price increases and being subjected to a harsh crackdown leading to the deaths of hundreds.[2] Since then, these words became even more urgent. The years 2020 and 1398/99[3] have been turbulent for both Americans and Iranians. January 2020 saw the United States and Iran on the brink of war after the US-sponsored assassination of a top Iranian general at a Baghdad airport in retaliation for alleged Iranian-sponsored rocket attacks and the death of an American contractor on a US military base in Iraq. As Iran's economy continued to struggle under the weight of crippling US-imposed sanctions, a previously unknown virus, known as COVID-19, hit the Iranian population, making Iran an early epicenter of the coronavirus in

---

[1] Tom Klobe and Jackie Spurlock, "Community Outreach and Advocacy," *KhabarNameh* 8 (December 2019): 25–6.
[2] The exact death toll of the November/December 2019 protests is in dispute. In early December 2019, Amnesty International claimed at least two hundred Iranians had been killed by domestic security forces, whereas the US State Department claimed the casualties were more than one thousand. Recent numbers provided to Reuters by several Iranian Interior Ministry officials corroborate the US figures. "Special Report: Iran's Leader Ordered Crackdown on Unrest," December 23, 2019, Reuters. Available online: https://www.reuters.com/article/us-iran-protests-specialreport/special-report-irans-leader-ordered-crackdown-on-unrest-do-whatever-it-takes-to-end-it-idUSKBN1YR0QR (accessed January 19, 2021).
[3] For Iranians, the year 1399 started on March 21, 2020, the first day of spring.

the Middle East and in urgent need of medical supplies and assistance. By March 17, 2020, when Iran had almost 16,200 confirmed cases and 2,000 recorded deaths, the contagion had spread to the United States.[4] The pandemic knew no borders, reflecting the nature of our entwined existence. The story of the American Peace Corps in Iran brings this contemporary mutuality into relief.

Spurlock and Klobe were among the almost 1,800 Americans, referred to as "volunteers" according to Peace Corps lingo, who participated in the Iran program. Known in Persian as the *Sepāh-e Solh-e Āmrikā*, the Peace Corps sponsored American volunteers from 1962 to 1976 in all corners of the country—from remote villages to the capital—who worked in English instruction, vocational education, agriculture, community development, city planning, and other fields. As a hallmark of President John F. Kennedy's "New Frontier," the Peace Corps Act of 1961 set forth three objectives: to provide trained American manpower to the world, promote a better understanding of Americans in the world, and increase Americans' knowledge of the world.[5]

This chapter will show how these goals—especially the second and third—still inform, if not inspire, Peace Corps volunteers who once served in Iran. Through the use of oral history interviews with former volunteers and the Iranians who knew them, this chapter reconstructs the events and structures of daily life in Iran during the 1960s and 1970s, as well as the narrators' reflections on how their participation in Peace Corps Iran shaped the personal trajectory of their lives.

Perspectives on Peace Corps Iran

The Peace Corps program in Iran is one of the many forgotten episodes in the history of US-Iran relations. In both Iran and the United States, the transnational and cross-cultural engagement of the 1960s and 1970s is scarcely known or remembered. Rather, it has been eclipsed by the tragic events of the Iranian Revolution, the taking of American hostages, the resulting hostilities between the Iranian and US governments, and decades of devastating US sanctions on Iran. For these reasons, since 1979, American narratives of exceptional US-Iran cooperation, exchange, and partnership have been overshadowed by images of Iranian anger, fanaticism, and anti-Americanism. Likewise, Iran experienced traumatic and largely negative postrevolutionary entanglements with the United States, leaving little room for memories of a positive past association.[6]

---

[4] Arash Azizi, *The Shadow Commander: Soleimani, the US, and Iran's Global Ambitions* (London: Oneworld, 2020). See also Tara Kangarlou and Joseph Hincks, "'People are Dying Left and Right': Inside Iran's Struggle to Contain Its Coronavirus Outbreak," *Time*, March, 17, 2020; "Coronavirus: Iran Told to Take Threat Seriously as Death Toll Passes 1,000," BBC, March 18, 2020; "Coronavirus updates from March 17, 2020," CBS News. Available online: https://time.com/5804706/iran-coronavirus/; https://www.bbc.com/news/world-middle-east-51945468; https://www.cbsnews.com/live-updates/coronavirus-disease-covid-19-latest-news-2020-03-17/ (all accessed January 19, 2021).

[5] US Congress, Peace Corps Act, September 22, 1961. Available online: http://research.archives.gov/description/299874 (accessed April 8, 2021).

[6] William O. Beeman, *The "Great Satan" vs. "The Mad Mullahs": How the United States and Iran Demonize Each Other* (Westport, CT: Praeger, 2005).

Nevertheless, a stream of contemporary references to Peace Corps Iran bears testimony to the unique and exceptionally meaningful experience that the program provided young Americans at the height of the Cold War. In the twenty-first century, narratives written by former volunteers are appearing as books and short stories.[7] On the other side, existing records show that even Iranians opposed to the shah and US foreign policy during the 1960s and 1970s tended to have a favorable view of the Peace Corps, and still do today. Though the Iranian opposition to Mohammad Reza Shah Pahlavi vehemently denounced his regime's military, political, and economic ties to the United States, there is little to no evidence of it maligning the Peace Corps. For example, Iran's leading literary figure and quintessential public intellectual of the 1960s, Jalal Al-e Ahmad, famous for his condemnation of cultural imperialism in his 1962 publication *Gharb-zadegi* (Westoxication), was apparently oblivious to the Peace Corps' presence in Iran until the mid-1960s. Then, in a dismissive reference to its altruistic goals, he offered a relatively benign assessment of the program.[8] Another example is found in the unequivocally positive impression of individuals involved with the program, most notably in the friendship between Iran's renowned oppositionist cultural critic, Ali Shariati, and Michael Hillman, a Peace Corps volunteer at the University of Mashhad from 1965 to 1967. Shariati accepted Hillman as a colleague and friend, and he even acted as an intermediary facilitating Hillman's marriage to a local woman.[9] Similarly positive interpretations of Peace Corps volunteers are found in testimonies of Iranians who knew them.[10]

It is certainly easy to be cynical about America's Cold War foreign policy and international adventurism, and there is much to critique. The bulk of scholarship in the field of US-Iran relations focuses on the problematic CIA-supported coup of 1953 and the fraught relationship between Jimmy Carter and the shah, leading to the 1979 revolution. Beyond these two flashpoints, scholars of foreign relations turn to the subsequent tensions between the Islamic Republic of Iran and the United States in the aftermath of the 1979–81 Hostage Crisis. The Peace Corps program in Iran originally supported US Cold War aims to contain the communist threat looming along Iran's

---

[7] For recently published memoirs by former Peace Corps Iran volunteers, see David Devine, *Persian Mosaic: Getting Back to Iran after 25 Years* (Lincoln, NE: Writer's Showcase, 2001); Arlene Elle Gray, *Letters from Iran: Memoirs of a Peace Corps Volunteer, 1970–1972* (Port Saint Lucie, FL: Westwood, 2020); John Krauskopf, *Iran: Stories from the Peace Corps* (San Francisco, CA: John Krauskopf, 2013); Tom Klobe, *A Young American in Iran* (Oakland, CA: Peace Corps Writers, 2014); Mary Marks, *Walled In, Walled Out: A Young American Woman in Iran* (Oakland, CA: Peace Corps Writers, 2017); Paul Pitzer, *Hello Mister* (San Francisco, CA: Blurb, 2015). For novels inspired by the Peace Corps Iran experiences of their authors, see Rea Keech, *A Hundred Veils* (Baltimore, MD: Real Nice Books, 2015); and Jennifer Seaver, *Journeys: A Novel of Iran* (New York: iUniverse, 2004). For the short stories of Peace Corps Iran volunteers, see the website of the Peace Corps Iran Association (PCIA). Available online: https://www.peacecorpsiran.org/cpages/stories (accessed January 19, 2021).
[8] Jalal Al-e Ahmad, *Kārnāmeh-ye Seh-Sāleh* (Tehran: Ketāb-e Zaman, 1968).
[9] Roland Elliot Brown, "Peace Corps Memories: Love and Learning in Mashhad," *IranWire*, November 25, 2016. Available online: https://iranwire.com/en/features/4222 (accessed January 6, 2021).
[10] Recently published accounts by Iranians expressing favorable attitudes toward the Peace Corps and its volunteers in Iran include Hamid Ekbia, "The Moon, the Corps, and the War," *Los Angeles Review of Books*, October 13, 2019; and Saied Saiedi, ed., *Alam High School* (Bijou, 2018).

northern border with the Soviet Union and was, most likely, received favorably by the shah to acquire the American military armaments and weaponry he so desperately desired.[11] Interestingly, the most comprehensive Persian-language analysis of Peace Corps Iran, published in the Islamic Republic of Iran, relies on English-language sources to depict the program primarily as an instrument of US foreign policy. Nevertheless, it is somewhat ambivalent in its overall evaluation of the Peace Corps' actual performance in Iran.[12]

While ultimately a Cold War program, however, the Peace Corps was unique in emphasizing and prioritizing people-to-people interactions, reciprocity, and exchange between Americans and communities in what was the Third World. As this chapter shows, Peace Corps Iran contributed to the making of strong personal bonds and friendships that transcended political, national, and religious boundaries. Personal testimonies of former Peace Corps Iran volunteers reveal an American perspective consisting of genuine emotional connections to Iran and an affinity toward its people, languages, and cultures.

It is therefore essential to understand the story of Peace Corps Iran from the perspective of the human interactions and social relationships that defined it, that is, the Iranians who came into contact with the Peace Corps program and the American volunteers who served in it. Archival documents, such as Peace Corps Agency publications and reports contained in Record Group 490 at the US National Archives and elsewhere, along with US State Department telegrams and memoranda, provide a substantial amount of information. But they reflect the perspectives of state-centered organizations and bureaucrats. They therefore fall short of capturing the nature and contours of the relationships on the ground that made the Peace Corps a Cold War innovation *and* deviation.[13] As this chapter shows, oral history narratives are vital primary sources to help unpack the tangled layers of the Peace Corps experience that are missing from government archives.

Using oral history narratives to examine US-Iran relations and, more specifically, the Peace Corps in Iran conjures both facts and subjectivities. How do oral histories shed light on the processes, events, structures, and individual lives involved in the Peace Corps Iran experience? What trends and anomalies do they uncover that are missing in archival material or existing scholarly work? Casting new light on unexplored areas of daily life, oral history evidence reveals "unknown events or unknown aspects of known

---

[11] For more on the geopolitical context of the Peace Corps program in Iran, see Jasamin Rostam-Kolayi, "The New Frontier Meets the White Revolution: The Peace Corps in Iran, 1962–1976," *Iranian Studies* 51, no. 4 (2018): 587–612.

[12] Vida Hamraz, "Tahlili bar faʿāliyat-e sepāh-e solh-e Kennedy dar Irān 1962–1976," *Tārikh* 4, no. 13 (Summer 1388/2009): 97–114, http://fa.journals.sid.ir.

[13] Record Group (RG) 490, Records of the Peace Corps, US National Archives and Records Administration II (hereafter NARA), College Park, MD. *Peace Corps Volunteer*, the Peace Corps Agency's monthly newsletter, is available online: peacecorpsonline.org. US State Department records are available via the *Foreign Relations of the United States (FRUS)* series and available online: https://history.state.gov/historicaldocuments. Ideally, these sources should be studied alongside comparable official records of the Iranian government. Documents related to Iran-US relations are cataloged in the archives of the Foreign Ministry of Iran. However, those from 1953 to 1979 are classified and inaccessible. I thank Rezā Āzar Shahrestāni, a leading archives-based researcher in Iran, for this information.

events."[14] However, just as important is the narrator's subjectivity. As oral historian Alessandro Portelli argues: "Oral sources tell us not just what people did, but what they wanted to do, what they believed they were doing, and what they now think they did." This kind of subjectivity is as much the fabric of historical narration as archival evidence or established "facts."[15] Though memory is partial, selective, and sometimes faulty, it also unfolds in the present context to create meaning about the past.

Thus, Peace Corps Iran stories are remembered and reconstructed within broad and immediate frames. They often focus on the Iranian Revolution, the Iran-Iraq War, September 11, and the US "war on terror" and military presence in the Middle East. Even more immediate is the current status of postrevolutionary Iran's Islamist regime, heated rhetoric between the United States and Iran, US sanctions on Iran, and the so-called Iran nuclear agreement, or Joint Comprehensive Plan of Action. Awareness of how such contexts frame historical memory does not diminish its significance. It means that historians must be alert to the complexities of what oral history reveals and balance it alongside other types of evidence and source material.

This chapter's case study is constructed on the basis of what is remembered from various sides in Peace Corps Iran oral histories. The range of narrators is varied. They include an Iranian assistant to the first Peace Corps Iran director, who helped get the program off the ground in 1962; several American volunteers who joined the first group sent to Iran; many who served during the program's peak in the mid-1960s; and some of the last American participants on the eve of its closure in 1976. I also interviewed Iranian trainers employed by the Peace Corps and Iranian students of Peace Corps teachers. Nevertheless, most narrators cited here were American volunteers, with the bulk of those serving in the mid-1960s. I used the directory and network of the Peace Corps Iran Association (PCIA) to reach these women and men, most of whom were septuagenarians at the time of the interview. To conduct the interviews, I traveled throughout the United States and to one European locale to meet with them face-to-face.[16]

My reconstruction of Peace Corps Iran history is therefore based on two historical approaches—oral history's focus on the memories of individuals and communities, and transnational history's attention to broader conceptualizations of non-state structures, actors, and events. The combination of oral history methods and transnational history complements diplomatic history's reliance on the archival records of state actors and institutions. Therefore, using oral history does not mean ignoring national archives. As I have shown elsewhere, US State Department and other government documents reveal how the Peace Corps carried out and managed its programs, not only in Iran but also around the world, along with domestic and internal debates about its role and priorities.[17] By contrast, oral histories with

---

[14] Alessandro Portelli, *The Death of Luigi Trastulli and Other Stories* (Albany: State University of New York Press, 1991), 50.
[15] Ibid.
[16] One of the almost sixty interviews was conducted on Skype and two via handwritten responses to questions. Only two narrators wished to remain anonymous.
[17] Rostam-Kolayi, "The New Frontier Meets the White Revolution"; Rostam-Kolayi, "'Beautiful Americans': Peace Corps Iran in the Global Sixties," in *The Routledge Handbook of the Global Sixties: Between Protest and Nation-Building*, ed. Chen Jian, Martin Klimke, Masha Kirasirova, Mary Nolan, Marylin Young, Joanna Waley-Cohen (New York: Routledge, 2018), 303–14.

American volunteers and the Iranians with whom they worked shed light on the grassroots encounters and relationships between ordinary Iranians and Americans. They were, after all, the individuals who made up the cultural exchanges that were embedded in the larger geopolitical context.

This chapter argues that, while Peace Corps Iran oral histories expose important details of daily life and interactions between Iranians and Americans in a bygone era, it is ultimately their emotional content that conveys what the program accomplished. Indeed, the oral histories indicate that the program brought together strangers from vastly different national, cultural, and religious backgrounds and enabled them to forge friendships that crossed these boundaries.

Representing America or Making Friends?

It is important to remember that Kennedy's Peace Corps built on earlier American development efforts in Iran, namely President Harry Truman's Point Four Program and Kennedy's own Agency for International Development (USAID). Point Four, established in 1950, called for the United States to assist Third World countries to develop and modernize industrially and economically in order to contain the communist threat. Its Iran programs provided medical, educational, community development, agricultural, and public health services, which USAID continued when it took over in Iran in 1961.[18] The totality of Point Four and USAID funds to Iran amounted to $118.4 million by 1965, the last year of USAID technical assistance to Iran.[19] However, the innovation of the Peace Corps was to build on the material assistance elements of previous Cold War development programs and inject them with new idealism and optimism. The new direction was mandated by the last two of the three objectives of the Peace Corps Act—to promote a better understanding of Americans in the world and increase Americans' knowledge of the world. Taken seriously, this meant a reciprocal learning process based in a grassroots people-to-people exchange, which diverged from the top-down Cold War efforts of previous American foreign aid programs. In practice, cultural transmission, rather than cultural imperialism, is a more apt description of the dynamics of Peace Corps activities in Iran. Iranians selected what they wanted and needed from Peace Corps Americans in the context of a "fluid cross-cultural process of mutual fertilization, reinforced by mass communication, cultural exchange, and international economic and political cooperation."[20]

The first Peace Corps Iran contingent of forty-three Americans—ranging in age from nineteen to forty-seven years[21]—arrived in Tehran in September 1962. Interestingly,

---

[18] For more on Point Four in Iran, see Richard Garlitz, *A Mission for Development: Utah Universities and the Point Four Program in Iran* (Logan: Utah State University Press, 2018).

[19] Sara Ehsani-Nia, "'Go Forth and Do Good': US-Iranian Relations during the Cold War through the Lens of Public Diplomacy," *Penn History Review* 19, no. 1 (2011): 93.

[20] Jessica C. E. Gienow-Hecht, "*Shame on US?* Academics, Cultural Transfer, and the Cold War—A Critical Review," *Diplomatic History* 24, no. 3 (2000): 487–8.

[21] Genna Wangsness, unpublished manuscript. In the 1960s, Wangsness worked as staff in Peace Corps Iran offices in Tehran and later Shiraz. She is completing a history of each Peace Corps Iran group that served between 1962 and 1976.

though the first group was overwhelmingly white and male, a quarter were split evenly between men of color and women, making it the most diverse contingent sent to Iran in the program's fourteen years. Iran-2 and Iran-3, as the Peace Corps referred to volunteer groups, overlapped with Iran-1 and started their two-year terms of service the following year. During the mid-1960s, the heyday of the Peace Corps worldwide, the Iran program supported a peak of between 200 and 400 volunteers per year. Though in many cases official assignments diverged from what volunteers actually did on the ground, most taught English to middle and high school students during the day and adults in the evenings.

As Iranian state-sponsored development and planning priorities changed, the nature of Peace Corps work did, too. Thus, while the 1970s saw many volunteers still teaching English, a larger number worked in municipal, urban planning, and architectural projects to meet the needs of a state with greater industry and a growing population. Given Iran's growing oil revenue and ability to pay top dollar for American technical expertise, along with simmering popular unrest against the shah, it appeared that the program could no longer serve its original purpose. For these reasons, the last Peace Corps Iran director, Quentin Fleming, and the then-active volunteers, voted to close it in 1976, two years before protests and demonstrations turned into a revolution that overthrew the shah.[22]

As mentioned above, Peace Corps Iran was at once a Cold War innovation and deviation. It is well documented that the Cold War rhetoric of countering communism and Leftist insurgencies abroad pervaded the internal communications and public pronouncements of Peace Corps officials.[23] As an agency of the American government, the Peace Corps worked in tandem with USAID and was indeed an arm of American foreign policy. Nevertheless, evidence shows that, in practice, Peace Corps Iran volunteers distanced themselves from unpopular US policies and the taint of the Cold War. In fact, many Peace Corps volunteers deliberately separated themselves from other Americans, especially those involved in the military and USAID missions in Iran. The gap between these various groups of Americans in Iran widened considerably by the 1970s.[24] Most volunteers recounted that they joined after college because they were motivated by the ethos to serve one's country through peace, a sense of adventure and longing to live abroad, and, for men, the desire to delay the Vietnam War draft. The rhetoric of hope, idealism, and altruism of the Kennedy era and the lingering memory of his presidency throughout the 1960s and early 1970s inspired interest in the Peace Corps. Therefore, its Cold War priorities did not appeal to would-be volunteers, and none mentioned a yearning to combat communism in the Third World when discussing their motivations for joining the Peace Corps. Nor did volunteers recall any

---

[22] For an account of the shuttering of the program written by the son of the last country director, see Sheldon Fleming, "The Peace Corps Leaves Iran, 1976." Available online: https://silkstart.s3.amazonaws.com/0d772ea8-4b16-4382-9761-39f389c3a4b3.pdf (accessed January 19, 2021).
[23] Glenn Francis Sheffield, "Peru and the Peace Corps, 1962–1968" (PhD diss., University of Connecticut), 17–20.
[24] John McKee, interview with author, Scottsdale, AZ, January 8, 2015; Hossein Moftakhar, interview with author, Sacramento, CA, December 27, 2015; Marks, *Walled In, Walled Out*; and Thorburn Reid, "Overseas Evaluation: Iran," March 20–April 12, 1963, RG 490, A120, Box 5, NARA.

language about an anti-communist crusade in their Peace Corps orientation materials, a fact that speaks to the discrepancies between the official goals and actual training.

These divergences were related to the fact that the Peace Corps was Janus-faced. The Kennedy administration officials who conceived the program were indeed motivated by countering Leftist ideas and creating US geostrategic alliances in the Third World. But they also sought to cultivate interdependence and partnerships among peoples, in contrast to old-fashioned imperialism or one-sided development assistance.[25] During a 1962 meeting with Peace Corps officials, US Under Secretary of State George McGhee asserted that the Peace Corps had the potential to be a "builder of ties, governmental, institutional, and personal ... to promote that interdependence."[26] US officials hoped that the Peace Corps would help align and harmonize American and Third World interests at all levels, from the state at the top to the grassroots on the bottom. Indeed, Peace Corps Iran played some role in aligning the government interests of both the United States and Iran during the 1960s and 1970s. The program, however, succeeded neither in cultivating a pro-American strain of Iranian political ideology nor in trumping other US policies, particularly in the area of foreign policy, deemed problematic by Iranians.[27] Yet it did foster friendships and understanding between ordinary Americans and Iranians that have withstood the test of time and significant political hostility between two governments. Its more lasting achievement, then, was on the interpersonal front.

Peace Corps Iran personnel were indeed participants in a US state-sponsored program, but they were also classified as volunteer employees of the Iranian government. Because Iranian government ministries selected and oversaw Peace Corps work assignments, volunteers were responsible as well to the host government. Significantly, they were known as "volunteers," rather than "technical advisers," a term that applied to USAID employees. Oral history interviews make it clear that individual volunteers did not think of themselves as agents, or even representatives, of the US government. Jeffrey Curtis, who served in Rasht in the late 1960s, drew a distinction between official Peace Corps rhetoric and his identity as a volunteer:

> The Peace Corps office would have said ... you're a representative of America ... I mean we are representatives in this country, but ... we've got so much to learn, but what we can show them, if we can show them anything, is ... that we're real people, that we make mistakes, that we ... mess up their language and laugh about it.[28]

Nevertheless, Curtis' desire to distance the volunteer from US state interests and highlight the intimate, everyday interactions between people was certainly in line with the Peace Corps mission.

---

[25] Elizabeth Cobbs Hoffman, *All You Need Is Love: The Peace Corps and the Spirit of the 1960s* (Cambridge, MA: Harvard University Press, 1998).
[26] George C. McGhee, cited in Sheffield, 52.
[27] For example, the Status of Forces Agreement (SOFA) was received critically by the Iranian media, the Shia clerical leadership, and the general population. See James Bill, *The Eagle and the Lion: The Tragedy of American-Iranian Relations* (New Haven, CT: Yale University Press, 1988), 156–61.
[28] Jeffrey Curtis, interview with author, Austin, TX, May 29, 2015.

To accomplish its unique objectives, Peace Corps Iran emphasized cultural and language immersion during training and in the field. The mandatory six-week training, though sometimes of uneven quality, prioritized intensive Persian-language instruction and included lessons on Iranian history and culture, as well as actual social interaction with Iranians. Peace Corps training took place exclusively in the United States until 1967, when it was split between the United States and Iran, and then shifted exclusively to Iran in 1970.[29] Wherever the training, once in Iran, volunteers were placed in work settings alongside Iranians. They were encouraged to integrate into the local community by offering evening classes for adults and socializing with townspeople and their colleagues. Living conditions varied widely. While some volunteers found housing with Iranian families or lived in close proximity to Iranian neighbors, and thus quickly integrated into a social unit, others lived alone and felt isolated. For example, Dennis Briskin lived with an Iranian Jewish family in Arak, while Jeanette Gottlieb was the sole tenant in a house in Nowshahr. Both faced challenges particular to their different living arrangements. For Briskin it was lack of privacy, while for Gottlieb it was loneliness.[30]

If volunteers were culturally and politically uneducated or naive before joining the Peace Corps, after settling in they received an immediate dose of reality. Many narrators admitted that they had to consult a map when they first learned Iran was their Peace Corps assignment, and most had no prior knowledge of or interaction with Iranians. They were traveling to a foreign, faraway place not yet so entrenched in the American consciousness. On the other hand, for many Iranians in the 1960s, *Āmrikā* had already made its mark on Iran. The US government had, only a decade earlier, overthrown Iran's popular nationalist leader Mohammad Mosaddeq and restored the shah to his throne. Iranians with whom volunteers socialized in villages and towns tended to be more circumspect in discussing Iranian politics, and they rarely criticized the shah in public.

Some volunteers described developing a political consciousness in Iran. For example, Elizabeth Gay, who taught at Pahlavi University in Shiraz from 1966 to 1968, recalled witnessing Iranian university students and faculty on strike. Students spoke with her about "the Shah being a dictator and about how he had people murdered and … that [Iran] wasn't a democracy." Though she did not believe that the monarchy's overthrow would lead necessarily to a better alternative, her visits to the countryside revealed the underdevelopment and sporadic efforts of the White Revolution's Health and Literacy Corps.[31] Another case of political education was the 1966 arrest and three-week detention of Iran volunteer Thomas Dawson by Soviet authorities. They accused him of crossing into the USSR when he was wading in the Aras River near the town of Astara along the Iran-Soviet border. His Peace Corps traveling companion was taken into Iranian custody and held briefly before being released. Still, while

---

[29] Wangsness, unpublished manuscript; Roger Wangsness, "TEFL Training Plans for 1969," *Sholuq Nāmeh* 1, no. 3 (1969): 7–10.

[30] Dennis Briskin, interview with author, San Diego, CA, October 7, 2019; and Jeannette Gottlieb, interview with author, Austin, TX, May 30, 2015.

[31] Elizabeth Gay, interview with author, Austin, TX, May 28, 2015.

the incident made it onto the front page of the *New York Times* and threatened to end Peace Corps Iran, it also revealed that the Soviets were indeed interested in this American project.[32]

Part of the cultural context pervading the reception of Peace Corps volunteers was a new exposure in Iran to American popular culture during the 1960s. The new media of television and radio were beginning to enter Iranian homes to further shape perceptions of the United States as a place not only of curiosity and menace but also of excitement and change. American volunteers, told by the Peace Corps that they were ambassadors of goodwill, were at first surprised when they learned that Iranians perceived them as CIA agents; they were equally as surprised to learn that SAVAK informants kept tabs on them.[33] Volunteerism and choosing to live far from one's family seemed to strike ordinary Iranians as strange and suspicious behavior. Volunteers admitted that the doubts that some Iranians harbored toward them never wavered. However, an Iranian narrator—who identified as a politicized, Leftist teenager of the 1960s—explained that over time he developed a warm and trusting friendship with the Peace Corps men housed by his family. As a result, he developed a better understanding of Americans and an appreciation for how they often opposed their own country's policies.[34] Another young Iranian, with a budding Leftist political identity, recalled almost fifty years later being struck by his Peace Corps teacher's public criticism of the Republican candidate, Richard Nixon, during the 1968 US presidential election. The Iranian students in this class learned from their American teacher that "Nixon, is a crook."[35]

Eventually, as a consequence of this group of Americans living in Iran, both sides came to learn much more about each other and developed understandings that stretched beyond their first assumptions. Ironically, in fulfilling the mission of being a people-to-people venture, the Peace Corps program produced political results in Iran that diverged widely from its Cold War goals.

The "Facts" of Daily Life in Peace Corps Iran

Oral histories reveal that Peace Corps experiences varied depending on a range of factors. Those factors include where and when volunteers lived in Iran, the nature of their work and living conditions, their personal temperament and attitudes, and

---

[32] Brent Ashabranner, *A Moment in History: The First Ten Years of the Peace Corps* (New York: Doubleday, 1971), 153-4, 331; Jennifer Seaver, interview with author, San Diego, CA, October 6, 2019; and Braymond H. Anderson, "American Seized at Soviet Border," *New York Times*, September 15, 1966, 1.

[33] Officially, the Peace Corps denied association and collaboration with the CIA in accordance with an agreement between the intelligence agency and President Kennedy, Peace Corps director Sergeant Shriver, and the State Department. However, this did not preclude US consular officials from consulting with Peace Corps Iran volunteers as sources of information, as is clear from oral history interviews with former State Department officials located in the collection of the Association for Diplomatic Studies and Training and available online: https://adst.org/oral-history/.

[34] Mostafa Rahbar, interview with author, Annapolis, MD, October 30, 2017. See also Rea Keech, "A Semnan Friendship," *KhabarNameh* 8 (December 2019), for an account of the fifty-year friendship between the Rahbar family of Semnan and three Peace Corps volunteers.

[35] Afshin Matin-Asgari, interview with author, December 30, 2019.

whether they were married or single, man or woman. While teaching English was the most common Peace Corps Iran assignment throughout the program's fourteen-year duration, a brief experiment in rural community development took place from 1965 to 1967. Peace Corps Iran also assigned volunteers to work in lesser-known fields, such as urban planning, animal conservation, library sciences, and even the national orchestra. While interviews with volunteers tended to convey satisfaction with social and recreational life in Iran, accounts of work experiences tended to be less glowing.

Teaching English as a Foreign Language (TEFL) occupied most volunteers' working hours. In 1952 the Iranian Ministry of Education replaced French with English as the foreign language requirement in secondary schools.[36] By the 1960s, American English was Iran's language of "development" and "progress." The shah's desire to have a population of workers who read and spoke English drove the Peace Corps' recruitment of hundreds of TEFL volunteers. Initially working as "advisers" to Iranian teachers, volunteers taught their own classes starting in 1966. This somewhat alleviated tensions with Iranian teachers and filled empty positions in provincial sites.[37] Many volunteers also taught adults English in evening classes and in small, private gatherings. Teaching English did not require more than a bachelor's degree and some basic training from the Peace Corps. However, the work was far from easy. Narrators remember facing a host of challenges in the classroom. Most were first-time teachers in charge of multiple sections of fifty or more students, and they sometimes worked at more than one school. Students often took advantage of their young age and inexperience with Iranian-style disciplinary methods to misbehave. Frustration with student unruliness and apathy was common.[38] Volunteers posted in towns where Persian was not the first language of their students faced additional pedagogical and communication mishaps. For example, Mary Hegland and Tom Ricks taught English in a Kurdish-speaking region, though they had learned only Persian in Peace Corps training.[39] Though teaching English could be physically taxing and emotionally draining, community development assignments of the mid-1960s presented daunting challenges.

Work in community development often proved complicated and could lead to politically compromising outcomes. For instance, Tim Thomas, who served in a Gilan village from 1965 to 1966, was tasked with overseeing and certifying elections in various surrounding hamlets to verify that they were done fairly and "democratically," in accordance with local governance reforms that were introduced as part of the White Revolution. Despite the fact that he witnessed fraudulent procedures, such as vote rigging, he felt compelled to certify the results and participate in the ceremonial signing of documents, take photographs with local officials, and attend the celebratory feasts. Thomas recalled:

---

[36] Gertrude Nye Dorry, *Forty-Five Years in Iran: A Memoir* (Wareham, MA: Dorry, 1998), 18.
[37] Park Teter and Richard Wandschneider, "Overseas Evaluation: Iran," April 30, 1968, RG 490, P89, Box 4, NARA.
[38] Mary Mitchell, interview with author, Scottsdale, AZ, January 10, 2015; and Stephen Kafoury, interview with author, Portland, OR, October 11, 2014.
[39] Mary Hegland, interview with author, Vienna, Austria, August 5, 2016; and Thomas Ricks, interview with author, Vienna, Austria, August 5, 2016.

They would have a picture every time with me, and the picture would be with me, a representative of the government of the United States [who] congratulates the newly elected *kadkhodā* [chief] of this village. And, I would be shaking his hand, standing there ... so there's no ambiguity in the villagers' mind that I was a member of the White Revolution. Plus all my friends were in the Literacy Corps.[40]

Thomas was eventually pulled from Gilan and transferred to Isfahan to teach at the university level.

Even though this type of politically sensitive work was atypical, volunteers in other forms of community development work became immersed in local struggles to differing degrees, and sometimes with more positive results. Barkley Moore, a legendary Peace Corps volunteer touted by the agency in publicity and recruitment efforts beyond the Iran program, worked in community development in the mid-1960s in the small town of Gonbad-e Kāvvus in Khorasan province. Many achievements were attributed to his efforts, which included building a kindergarten, library, and sports club, and adjudicating disputes among locals.[41] Tom Klobe's account of community development in Mazandaran also documents a constructive experience involving integration and acculturation into village life.[42]

The social lives of volunteers took various forms. Some mingled exclusively with Iranians by choice or necessity, as the only American or foreigner in a small town or village, whereas others tended to stay closer to their compatriots. David Devine, who served in Zahedan, a town in the remote province of Baluchistan, in the early 1970s, lived, worked, and socialized exclusively with single Iranian men. He experienced local life through their interests, hobbies, and perspectives, including their solicitation of prostitutes.[43] High school students and fellow teachers sought out the company of Bob Erikson, the only Peace Corps volunteer in Bojnord, Khorasan in the early 1970s.[44] Those living in larger towns or cities with other volunteers often mixed comfortably in both Iranian and American social circles. Kathleen McLeod, who served in Gorgan from 1964 to 1966, shared a residence with a local midwife and split her recreational time with her Iranian roommate and two other Peace Corps volunteers who lived nearby.[45] By contrast, some volunteers spent downtime in the company of fellow Americans or other foreigners due to shared housing arrangements or personal preferences.[46] Married volunteer couples were often invited to local Iranian homes for meals where they would split up into separate rooms according to gender-segregated

---

[40] Tim Thomas, interview with author, Austin, TX, May 30, 2015.
[41] Thomas, interview with author; Jim Hampton, "The Beautiful American," *Peace Corps Volunteer* (March/April 1971): 12; and Barkley Moore, "The World as a Classroom," *Peace Corps Volunteer* (Summer 1971): 17.
[42] Klobe, *A Young American in Iran*.
[43] David Devine, interview with author, Tucson, AZ, January 10, 2015.
[44] Bob Erikson, interview with author, Austin, TX, May 30, 2015.
[45] Kathleen McLeod, interview with author, San Diego, CA, October 7, 2019.
[46] McKee, interview with author.

norms.⁴⁷ A treasured pastime for Peace Corps men was accompanying their Iranian friends during the evening walk around town, known in Persian as *gardesh*.

Annual program evaluations carried out by the Peace Corps office in Washington, DC, feared that Iran was a hardship post for female volunteers. A 1967 report, shaped by Orientalist assumptions, noted that single women had not fared well due to "Islamic fanaticism." It recommended the Peace Corps restrict Iran assignments to single and married men and married women only.⁴⁸ Oral history accounts counter such dim assessments of the time. Mary Hegland, who lived in Mahabad in western Kurdistan province as a single woman from 1966 to 1968, remembered being happily immersed in the life of the town, especially the gatherings of the local Kurdish women, who took her under their wing. Hegland maintained that participating in all-female rituals and activities and witnessing women's agency were a source of her own budding feminism.⁴⁹ Another single volunteer, posted in Shahr-e Kord in the late 1960s, often spent lunchtime discussing life with the widow of a Bakhtiāri khān. She was befriended as well by other townswomen for whom the young American was a source of "great curiosity and brainstorming." The women of Shahr-e Kord showed enthusiastic interest in her Sears catalog and would complain to her about their financial dependence on men.⁵⁰ Though female volunteers remembered being pinched, fondled, or gawked at by Iranian men or boys in public spaces, such offenses did not appear to be the norm. Nor were they socially acceptable, as other Iranians sometimes came to their defense.⁵¹

Male volunteers tended to socialize exclusively with Iranian men in deference to local practices and norms, though there were exceptions. For example, Jeffrey Curtis, stationed in Rasht from 1967 to 1969, enjoyed platonic friendships with local teenage girls. His status as an adopted son and brother in two Iranian families gave him an entrée into the world of young women. Curtis recalled staying up late chatting with the daughters of his landlord—who was a school custodian—and with a physician's daughter, having "fairly comfortable conversations … talking … about a lot of things."⁵² Such friendships became the linchpin of the Peace Corps Iran experience on the ground. As Curtis reflected further:

> I think we tried to teach some, but I really think … we tried to understand stuff, too. And I don't know how well we did it, and I think we were arrogant sometimes … but I wish that they would remember us as people who came to learn as much

---

⁴⁷ Susan Downey, interview with author, Tucson, AZ, January 10, 2015; Mitchell, interview with author; and Kafoury, interview with author.

⁴⁸ Russell Chappell, "Overseas Evaluation: Iran," January 30, 1967, RG 490, P61, Box 24, NARA. Interestingly, a handwritten note by an agency official on the cover page of the evaluation suggested that the "single female problem … [was] overstated."

⁴⁹ Hegland, interview with author.

⁵⁰ Anonymous, written communication with author, 2015.

⁵¹ An article published in the volunteer-led Peace Corps Iran newsletter outlined the complaints of female volunteers in the late 1960s. See Chris Langley, "Iran as a Peace Corps Host Country," *Sholuq Nāmeh* 1, no. 1 (1968): 2–14; "Peace Corps Women's Experience in Iran," panel presentations, Peace Corps Iran Association Reunion/Conference, Austin, TX, May 28, 2015.

⁵² Curtis, interview with author. This account also fits with the general knowledge of Rasht and Gilan provinces as renowned for their relative openness and tolerance of fluid gender barriers.

as to teach and that … we did … we learned how to be friends with people who were different from us.[53]

These American experiences in Iran were profoundly shaped by meaningful personal relationships with Iranians. Oral history reveals these hidden details of daily life, common experiences shared by Americans and Iranians alike, and other historical anomalies of the Cold War era.

Memory as Poignant and Empowering

Narrators were eager to discuss their past experiences—their motivations to join the Peace Corps, what they did during their service, whom they befriended, and where they lived and traveled. Yet these stories were told with a poignancy framed by the current state of Iran-US relations. Vivid memories of their Iran years called forth sights and smells, meals eaten, and clothes worn. Such memories made Iran a tangible reality, rather than the abstraction that it often is for policymakers, the public, and even some scholars. Quite often, remembering the past proved emotionally wrenching. It was not uncommon for narrators to break down in tears when recounting the people they knew in Iran, the regret for paths not taken, and the discomfort that negative attitudes toward Iran caused them when they returned to the United States. They showed distress when discussing how American Iranophobia and Islamophobia contrasted with their own lived realities, and they stressed that their culturally immersive experiences in late Pahlavi Iran changed their thinking about how to live, act, and feel in the world.

Some viewed the act of relaying their memories of Iran as a mission to recover the humanity of their Iranian friends and acquaintances. Keith Kendall, who lived in a village near Shiraz from 1974 to 1976, remembered the anger he felt when he was "on the internet and Facebook with friends … and they're talking about ragheads and … all these disparaging comments about Iranians or Arabs … You know I can get pretty aggressive at times because they have no clue."[54] Volunteer Kerry Segel, who served in Khānsār in Isfahan province from 1969 to 1971, made a commitment to introduce to an American audience the scholarship and life's work of his Iranian friend and mentor, Dr. Mohammad Hossein Tasbihi.[55] Narrators were moved and gratified when the Iranians they once knew contacted them decades later to reconnect.[56] Oral histories reveal the individual narrator's emotions, their participation in the story of the Peace Corps in Iran, and how it shaped their own life and personal trajectory.

Indeed, oral histories reveal that former Peace Corps Iran volunteers exhibit exceptional affinity toward Iranian language and culture. Some incorporate Persian cuisine into their cooking repertoire, and others chose Persian names for their children.

---

[53] Ibid.
[54] Keith Kendall, interview with author, Austin, TX, May 29, 2015.
[55] Kerry Segel, interview with the author, San Diego, CA, October 7, 2019.
[56] Ibid.; and Erikson, interview with author.

Their recollections were peppered with Persian words and phrases, as some are still fluent or near-fluent speakers of Persian. And, as often happens when people cross national boundaries, many married Iranians and stayed in Iran beyond their service in the Peace Corps. They also sponsored the migration to the United States of Iranians whom they met while serving in the Peace Corps, and these acts of care changed the trajectory of those Iranian lives. Upon their immediate return to the United States and in the following years, former volunteers gave presentations on Iranian culture and history to their churches, children's schools, and community groups. A number have traveled to Iran since the revolution, especially in recent years. Some sought advanced degrees in Iranian, Middle East, Islamic, or Persianate studies, and many pursued work in academia, education, foreign service, politics, law, and business. Many of their children have followed them into the Peace Corps and, in one case, a daughter was inspired to write a play informed by the Iran stories and Persian culture she was exposed to growing up.[57]

Examples abound. Stephen Kafoury, who served in Azerbaijan from 1964 to 1966, remembered an American friend asking him why he talked about Iran all the time. "Because," he said, "it's something so big … that changed my life, and it was the biggest thing that ever happened to me … aside from getting married."[58] Though not all former volunteers should be classified as romantic Iranophiles, none expressed indifference toward Iran even as they went on with their busy lives of working and raising families. Susan Downey, who served in Golpayegan from 1968 to 1970, revealed that she carried her Iran experience with her back to Detroit. "Went to Iran, had my eyes opened and got used to working with a variety of other people … [I was] dropped in … the middle of inner city Detroit. A lot of people couldn't handle it and left. I just thought it was an extension of Iran … I was well-suited to adapt."[59] Such reflections on the transformative nature of the Peace Corps Iran experience are a common refrain in oral history accounts.

In addition to these emotional reflections, oral history inevitably veers into the present. Though most of the dialogue between the narrators and interviewer was based on recollections of the past, stories were told in the present. Recent events and current contexts inevitably intervened to shape the meaning that a narrator constructed out of the past. Former volunteers often noted that their post-Peace Corps mission was to counter American misperceptions about and prejudices toward Iran, and to urge policymakers and elected representatives to restore diplomatic ties with Iran. As Peace Corps volunteer Jackie Spurlock, who served in Abedeh and Zarrinshahr from 1974 to 1976, wrote in 2019: "I am highly conscious of this unique perspective I've been given and I see, for all of us, the opportunity to lean in, follow events, look for opportunities to speak up, and hold our friends in Iran in our hearts and front and center in the minds of our fellow Americans."[60] Such sentiments have found an organizational home.

---

[57] Downey, interview with author; and Gail Doughty, interview with author, Vienna, VA, November 24, 2015. Joanna Garner, daughter of Peace Corps Iran volunteer Steve Horowitz, wrote "The Orange Garden," a theatrical play set in 1970s Iran and the United States featuring a fictional Peace Corps volunteer named John.
[58] Kafoury, interview with author.
[59] Downey, interview with author.
[60] Jackie Spurlock, "Front and Center in Our Hearts," *PCIA Board Newsletter*, December 19, 2019.

First formed in 1986, on the twenty-fifth anniversary of the Peace Corps, and revived in 2011, Peace Corps Iran Association is today one of the most active returned Peace Corps volunteer organizations. In its early years, the organization took cues from the aftermath of the Iranian Revolution and the ensuing Hostage Crisis, which threw into disorder US-Iran relations. PCIA was thus formed in the context of the mid-1980s, during Ronald Reagan's presidency and as the Iran-Iraq War and the Iran-Contra Affair were raging. A 1988 PCIA newsletter quoted Iran-1 volunteer Jerome Clinton as saying: "The need for returned PCVs [Peace Corps volunteers] to put their expertise to use in waking Americans up to what Iran really is has never been more pressing."[61] Three decades later, PCIA is still promoting "peace and understanding between Americans and Iranians through education, outreach and advocacy, and upholds the legacy of the Peace Corps in Iran."[62] Its organizational capacity today includes producing a triannual newsletter and monthly bulletins from its board and advocacy circle. PCIA has also built a directory of Peace Corps Iran volunteers and staff, organized biennial conferences and reunions, published editorials in newspapers, lobbied elected representatives, established an archive of personal accounts and artifacts, reconstructed the history of volunteer groups, and collaborated with other like-minded organizations. For example, a 2019 PCIA-sponsored reunion featured panels on traveling to Iran, writing a personal narrative, refreshing Persian language skills, and conducting community outreach. PCIA's efforts channel private and individual memories into a collective platform with a broader goal to educate and advocate.[63]

Though not all former Iran volunteers are necessarily politically aligned to favor US-Iran diplomatic engagement, they agree on the fundamental point that their Peace Corps experience changed them. The knowledge of Iran and ordinary Iranians they gained in the Peace Corps placed them in a unique role to help revise American narratives.

Conclusion

Though the Peace Corps initially appeared successful in serving state interests in Iran and the United States, it was most effective in the long term on the people-to-people front. It would be foolhardy and facile to assume every American volunteer formed deep connections to Iran and its people, or that the thousands of Iranians who came into contact with the Peace Corps had invariably positive interactions. Nevertheless, the cumulative memory of Peace Corps Iran is quite favorable, even when one steps outside the circle of American volunteers and those Iranians who knew and worked with them.

The value of Peace Corps Iran oral history testimonies is in their illumination of the encounters, engagements, and connections between non-state actors during the Cold War. Oral history accounts, I argue, give a nuanced and complex relational picture

---

[61] Jerome Clinton, quoted in Joe Truskot, "IPCA News," *Iran Peace Corps Association Newsletter*, no. 1 (April 1988): 2.
[62] PCIA Mission Statement. Available online: https://www.peacecorpsiran.org/cpages/our-mission (accessed January 19, 2021).
[63] More details on PCIA's activities and initiatives are available online: https://www.peacecorpsiran.org/cpages/home (accessed January 19, 2021).

of a long-standing American engagement with Iran that complements what State Department records and other government documents convey. Using oral history sources to examine US-Iran relations in this historical moment produces denser analyses of the contexts, processes, and layers of American and Iranian histories.

Oral histories with Americans and Iranians who worked with the Peace Corps raise the question of where "Iranian history" stops and "American history" begins. This chapter suggests that such boundary lines are porous, if not arbitrary. American national identity has been shaped by engagement with Iran, despite the harshness of contemporary rhetoric and policy. Peace Corps Americans and their Iran experiences are another facet of American identity that needs to be analyzed contextually in relation to Iranian history and identity. Furthermore, the story of American relations with Iran "ought not be a story prepared for only American historians, nor should it be narrated only or primarily as an aspect of American history."[64] The story of the Peace Corps in Iran is part of Iranian history as well.

---

[64] Ussama Makdisi, "After Said: The Limits and Possibilities of a Critical Scholarship of U.S.-Arab Relations," *Diplomatic History* 8, no. 3 (2014): 684.

9

"Support the 41": Iranian Student Activism in Northern California, 1970–3

Ida Yalzadeh

On June 26, 1970, forty-one unarmed Iranians entered the Iranian consulate at 3400 Washington Street in San Francisco, California. After entering, they secured the building and held the employees hostage in their offices. While some of the forty-one made sure that the employees did not move, others took down and slashed through the pictures of the Shah of Iran that adorned the consulate walls. In their place, the protesters painted slogans in English and Farsi denouncing the leader. A few went into the office of Vice Consul Mortezā ʿAli-Akbar and ordered him to remain seated. From his office, they called reporters, telling them to come to the consulate for a press conference. It was only after police saw a banner, which hung outside of the building and read "Down with the Shah puppet of U.S. imperialism," that the Tactical Squad of the San Francisco Police Department was called to the scene.[1]

Upon entering, the police began restraining the protesters, who fought back by throwing office supplies and furniture. Despite the violent altercations that ensued, the Tactical Squad regained control of the consulate and arrested the instigators. This was the first mass arrest of Iranians in the United States, and all forty-one were held with a bail of between two thousand and four thousand dollars.[2] Television stations captured the scene that took place outside the consulate, as police officers escorted the Iranians—men and women—out of the building and into the back of a police truck. The "Tac Squad"—whose members wore helmets and leather gloves with nightsticks in their hands and guns in their holsters—dragged out the forty-one as they continued to protest.[3] In the aftermath, the students were charged with conspiracy, burglary, false

---

[1] Transcript of 41 Trial, July 13, 1970, Parviz Shokat Personal Collection, Berkeley, CA, accessed October 2019. All documents hereafter cited from the Parviz Shokat Personal Collection were accessed in October 2019.

[2] Female demonstrators were given a bail of two thousand dollars while male demonstrators were given a bail of three thousand to four thousand dollars. "Mounting Pressure to Release Iranian Students," CBS5 KPIX-TV, Bay Area Television Archive, June 30, 1970. Available online: https://diva.sfsu.edu/collections/sfbatv/bundles/238283 (accessed January 21, 2021).

[3] "Arrests at the Iranian Consulate," CBS5 KPIX-TV, Bay Area Television Archive, June 6, 1970. Available online: https://diva.sfsu.edu/collections/sfbatv/bundles/238287 (accessed January 21, 2021).

imprisonment, assault with a deadly weapon against a police officer, and malicious mischief. In the following months, a trial was held to prosecute the forty-one, where they were sentenced to thirty-five days in jail, given three years of probation, and ordered to pay a fine.[4]

The Iranians who took over the consulate—most of whom had middle- and upper-class social backgrounds in Iran—acted under the leadership of the Northern California branch of the Iranian Student Association in the United States (ISA-US, or ISA). The ISA served the objectives of the Confederation of Iranian Students National Union (CISNU), whose activities and international reach were integral to the 1979 Iranian Revolution.[5] However, in the early 1970s, organized Iranian students were working to bring awareness to the atrocities committed under Mohammad Reza Pahlavi while bringing the working masses of the Third World together. As such, the consulate occupation was meant to accomplish these two goals. The forty-one hoped the occupation would lead to a press conference, where Iranian Consul Parviz ʿĀdel and Ashraf Pahlavi—the shah's sister, who happened to be in town for a United Nations celebration—would hear their grievances. A press conference would have given the students a forum in the United States from which to issue their support to the many Kurds, oil workers, and university students who were imprisoned in their Iranian homeland for agitating against the regime. While the CISNU's main outpost abroad was West Germany, the ISA kept the international organization—with branches in cities such as Paris and Vienna—informed about its efforts within the United States.[6]

This oppositionist activity in the United States was particularly vital considering the country's importance to Iran during the prerevolutionary era. As other scholars have noted, throughout the 1950s, 1960s, and 1970s, the United States was at the helm of modernization efforts in Iran, as the shah's "elite-driven" White Revolution attempted to show the global community, especially the West, that Iran had achieved parity with the developed nations of the Cold War era.[7] Furthermore, the Pahlavi era was

---

[4] Sentencing Documents, December 12, 1972, Parviz Shokat Personal Collection.
[5] Afshin Matin-Asgari, *Iranian Student Opposition to the Shah* (Costa Mesa, CA: Mazda, 2002).
[6] This act, however, was planned by the Northern California chapter of the ISA without the CISNU's prior knowledge. The Northern California group sent letters to Farhād Samnar, a member of the CISNU Board of Directors, trying to explain the events and why the larger organization should support the efforts of the forty-one individuals who were arrested. The correspondence between the Northern California branch of the ISA and the Board of Directors of the CISNU illustrates the messiness of this organization, as well as its underground and ad hoc nature. Parviz Shokat Personal Collection.
[7] The White Revolution, which was developed as a six-point reform program in 1963 by the shah, consisted of the following policies: "(1) land reform; (2) sale of government-owned factories to finance land reform; (3) a new election law including woman suffrage; (4) the nationalization of forests; (5) a national literacy corps, mainly for rural teaching; and (6) a plan to give workers a share of industrial profits." Its construction and implementation emerged from the Imperial Government of Iran's need to appease the increasing politicization of the general public to avoid "the danger of a bloody revolution from below." Ultimately, Iranians were concerned about the shah becoming a demagogue, and saw the White Revolution as a program designed to consolidate royal power and promote Western consumption rather than to help the people. Ali M. Ansari, *Modern Iran since 1921: The Pahlavis and After* (London: Pearson Education, 2003), 198–206; Ali M. Ansari, "The Myth of the White Revolution: 'Modernization' and the Consolidation of Power," *Middle Eastern Studies* 37, no. 3 (2001): 1–24; Nikki R. Keddie, *Modern Iran: Roots and Results of Revolution* (New Haven, CT: Yale University Press, 2003).

characterized by the dissemination of the myth of Aryanness—that Iranians were part of an "Aryan" racial group—through which Iranians were able to claim that they were racially "white."[8] Imbued with this foundational myth of "Aryanness" and encouraged by Iran's progression toward a "modern" state, Iranians came to the United States by the thousands as temporary student sojourners to study at universities throughout the country. After their Western education, they were expected to go back to Iran and develop the nation in the US image. As a result of this relationship, both countries worked to minimize the presence and profile of Iranian political dissenters.

However, the context of the Third World and anti-war movements in the United States was equally as important to the ISA and its oppositionist activity. The Iranian consulate's occupation, after all, took place around two months after the Kent State shootings at the height of the anti-war movement. Student protests were par for the course during the late 1960s and early 1970s, as organizers worked within university spaces to bring about change, whether in response to the Vietnam War or US neocolonialism in Iran.[9] There was a large number of Iranian students—both within the homeland and abroad—involved in agitating against the Imperial Government of Iran. Although Iranian political activism was present abroad in earlier decades, the 1970 Iranian consulate takeover was particularly significant because it resulted in the first mass arrest of Iranian student protesters in the United States. As a CISNU booklet put it at the time, "the case of the 41 was perhaps the single most successful endeavor by Iranian students in the U.S. to bring the issue of political repression in Iran to the attention of the American public."[10]

Despite their numbers, oppositionist students were dismissed by Iranian and US policymakers as a small, outspoken minority that did not represent Iranian opinion on the shah's rule or US foreign policy. Instead, the US government overlooked these individuals to position Iranian non-immigrant migrants broadly as international "model minorities."[11] Particularly when compared to other communities of color, the allegedly tolerable treatment of Iranians in the United States was framed as an example of American benevolence and a celebration of racial pluralism that would, so the Cold

---

[8] Neda Maghbouleh, *The Limits of Whiteness: Iranian Americans and the Everyday Politics of Race* (Stanford, CA: Stanford University Press, 2017); Reza Zia-Ebrahimi, "Self-Orientalization and Dislocation: The Uses and Abuses of the Aryan Discourse in Iran," *Iranian Studies* 44, no. 4 (2011): 445–72.

[9] Roderick A. Ferguson, *We Demand: The University and Student Protests* (Berkeley: University of California Press, 2017); Christopher P. Loss, *Between Citizens and the State: The Politics of American Higher Education in the 20th Century* (Princeton, NJ: Princeton University Press, 2012), 217–19; Laura Pulido, *Black, Brown, Yellow, and Left: Radical Activism in Los Angeles* (Berkeley: University of California Press, 2006), 73.

[10] "Political Repression in Iran," Confederation of Iranian Students National Union, March 1971, p. 43, Labadie Collection, University of Michigan.

[11] This conception is distinct from model minority subjects more commonly written on in Ethnic Studies and Asian American Studies. Scholarship on the model minority subject in the United States has emphasized how this figure, particularly attached to Asian Americans, is read against blackness to represent assimilation, political quiescence, and hard work. Similarly, the figure of the international model minority is constructed as one that is read against communities of color in the United States to represent modernization, racial liberalism, and global uplift. However, international model minorities are presumed to return home without much change to the fabric of the US national landscape. Wendy Cheng, "'This Contradictory but Fantastic Thing': Student

War logic went, move the Third World away from the prospects of communism.[12] Iranians like the forty-one were thus constructed as exceptions to the large number of students who, it was assumed, would support the alliance and contribute to the prosperity of Iran and also the United States.

Rather than focus on the impact that the 1970 San Francisco occupation—and other demonstrations organized by the ISA—had on the Iranian homeland, I am interested in examining how this occupation and its aftermath can serve as a microcosm for understanding the relationship between US-Iran foreign policy and Iranian racialization in the United States, both before and after the revolution of 1979. Specifically, I understand this moment within the context of the US war in Vietnam and international student protest. In this situation, American allies were expected to be cooperative and grateful "client states." Moreover, Iran and Iranians were assumed to be proximate to whiteness through the myth of Aryanness.[13] In rejecting these expectations, Iranian students instead positioned themselves as part of US protest culture, Third Worldism, and the larger legacy of the global 1968 movements. It is through this lens that the significance of the forty-one within the United States emerges.

This chapter argues that the case of the forty-one and its aftermath exhibited two dynamics central to Iranian racial formation in the United States. First, these events make a case study for understanding the nascent disciplinary powers that would come to racialize Iranians in the United States after the revolution of 1979. Second, the case of the forty-one shows how Iranian political oppositionists themselves strategized to acquire visibility and solidarity while agitating for political change. The splinters within the diaspora thus reflected an intra-class conflict that transposed Iranian political affiliation onto the US color line. While the alliance between the United States and Iran placed Iranians within an international model minority status that would later be officially read as "white," these two dynamics punctured what was, in the late 1960s and early 1970s, an amicable neocolonial relationship.[14]

Networks and Political Activism in Cold War Taiwanese/America," *Journal of Asian American Studies* 20, no. 2 (2017): 161–91; Takashi Fujitani, *Race for Empire: Koreans as Japanese and Japanese as Americans During World War II* (Berkeley: University of California Press, 2011); Robert G. Lee, *Orientals: Asian Americans in Popular Culture* (Philadelphia, PA: Temple University Press, 1999); Manijeh Moradian, "Neither Washington, Nor Tehran: Political Cultures of Iranian American Un/Belonging" (PhD diss., New York University, 2014); Naoko Shibusawa, *America's Geisha Ally: Reimagining the Japanese Enemy* (Cambridge, MA: Harvard University Press, 2006); Chih-ming Wang, *Transpacific Articulations: Student Migration and the Remaking of Asian America* (Honolulu: University of Hawaii Press, 2013); Ellen D. Wu, *The Color of Success: Asian Americans and the Origins of the Model Minority* (Princeton, NJ: Princeton University Press, 2014); Henry Yu, *Thinking Orientals: Migration, Contact, and Exoticism in Modern America* (New York: Oxford University Press, 2001).

[12] Shibusawa, *America's Geisha Ally*; Penny M. Von Eschen, *Satchmo Blows Up the World: Jazz Ambassadors Play the Cold War* (Cambridge, MA: Harvard University Press, 2004).

[13] Mark J. Gasiorowski, *U.S. Foreign Policy and the Shah: Building a Client State in Iran* (Ithaca, NY: Cornell University Press, 1991).

[14] Maghbouleh, *The Limits of Whiteness*.

Iranian Activism and the US Disciplinary State

The mass arrest of the forty-one signaled that the US state felt the need to determine a course of action—namely, deportation—to deal with a group of non-immigrant migrants who were political oppositionists to one of America's most important allies. The aftermath of the consulate occupation speaks, then, to the way in which the United States was able to discipline these individuals (in the Foucauldian sense) while still maintaining Iranians more generally as international model minorities in the eyes of the US state and general public.[15] Because all eyes were on Southeast Asia during the Vietnam War, Iran was a country that did not attract much attention from the American people. While US policymakers were making Iranians more deportable, the Iranians themselves used the momentum of the global situation to change their relationship to the United States.

Critical to this development was the relationship between US state disciplinary powers—such as the police, the judicial system, and the media—and US immigration policy. As news cameras documented the scene of police hauling Iranians out of the consulate, they trained their many silver microphones on the police supervisor, Captain Jerimiah Taylor, who gave his own account of the events that occurred within the building. As he broke down the charges against the dissenters, Taylor mentioned the other institution that would take "interest" in the incident: "We'll en route them upon the Immigration Department on the assumption that most of them are foreign born and will be interested in by the Immigration Department."[16] By calling upon the Immigration and Naturalization Service (INS), Taylor implied the potential deportation of some if not all of those arrested based on their actions in the consulate. Though he tried to couch his threat in bureaucratic jargon, the threat of deportation loomed all too clearly for most of the students who participated in the occupation, as only four (Jaleh Behzādi, Jaleh Pirnazar, Nasrin Pirnazar, and Parviz Shokat) were permanent residents of the United States.[17]

The Iranian students themselves were quick to pick up on this dynamic, as many of their public appeals took note of the disciplinary action taken by the INS after the occupation of the consulate. Days after the incident, the ISA published a letter in *The Daily Californian*, the school paper at the University of California (UC), Berkeley. Before listing their demands to the Iranian and American governments, they mentioned the consequences of the consulate occupation. The students informed the Berkeley community that members of the ISA were still in custody at a San Francisco jail while also "being harrassed [sic] by the Immigration Office (Immigration Office has threatened to deport them)," even though they all had valid visas.[18] As the ISA saw

---

[15] Michel Foucault, *Society Must Be Defended: Lectures at the Collège de France, 1975–76* (New York: Picador, 2003).
[16] "Arrests at the Iranian Consulate."
[17] List of Arrested ISA Members, Parviz Shokat Personal Collection.
[18] "Letters to the Ice Box: Iranian Protest," *The Daily Californian*, June 30, 1970, Parviz Shokat Personal Collection.

it, the INS "made every effort to deport them." Once in Iran, they would face a jail term of three to ten years for their political opposition activities.[19]

These allegations about the INS spread internally and internationally throughout the branches of the ISA and the CISNU. Internal organization documents from the Northern California branch of the ISA that summarized the aftermath of the occupation noted that the forty-one were under investigation by authorities for "their visa status and other immigration matters."[20] In letters to the CISNU Board of Directors in West Germany, Firuz Pejman and Farāmarz Vaziri—two leaders of the ISA in Northern California— wrote that the INS was working in San Francisco with the Iranian consul and local police to "put pressure" on the arrested students.[21]

Within the broader context of US histories of racialization and race making, the connection between state discipline and US population management through migration controls is nothing new, particularly for Asian and Latinx diasporic populations.[22] The case of the forty-one in the early 1970s speaks to later iterations of deportation based in exceptional immigration procedures for Middle Eastern Americans, including for minor student visa violations during the Iran Hostage Crisis of 1979–81 and because of the PATRIOT Act after September 11, 2001. However, I see the case of the forty-one as more critically evocative of racial scripts inherent in the biopolitical management of marginalized bodies in the United States. I use Natalia Molina's concept of racial scripts, which signifies the way in which racialized groups are linked across time and space through the experience of common discriminatory practices by other people, institutions, and states. This theoretical framework also shows how the management of Iranian political oppositionists fits into the longer history of Asian American surveillance and exclusion.[23] Seen in this light, the police captain's remark on deportation in the summer of 1970 indicated a nascent racial formation based within the politics of foreign policy and allyship.

Mainstream media additionally served as an unofficial arm of US state power, as it worked to discredit ISA concerns. Similar to previous instances of political dissent from Iranian students in the early 1960s, US media used language that masked the

---

[19] *Defend the 41* (Berkeley, CA: Iranian Student Association in the United States, Defense Section, January 1973), Social Protest Collection, BANC MSS 86/157 c, The Bancroft Library, University of California, Berkeley.
[20] Occupation of Iranian Consulate Summary, June 29, 1970, Parviz Shokat Personal Collection.
[21] Firuz Pejman and Farāmarz Vaziri to Farhād Samnar, Parviz Shokat Personal Collection.
[22] Moon-Ho Jung, *The Rising Tide of Color: Race, State Violence, and Radical Movements Across the Pacific* (Seattle: University of Washington Press, 2014); Lee, *Orientals*; Natalia Molina, *How Race Is Made in America: Immigration, Citizenship, and the Historical Power of Racial Scripts* (Berkeley: University of California Press, 2014); Wu, *The Color of Success*.
[23] Elena Tajima Creef, *Imaging Japanese America: The Visual Construction of Citizenship, Nation, and the Body* (New York: New York University Press, 2004); Fujitani, *Race for Empire*; Erika Lee, *At America's Gates: Chinese Immigration During the Exclusion Era, 1882–1943* (Chapel Hill: University of North Carolina Press, 2003); Erika Lee, *America for Americans: A History of Xenophobia in the United States* (New York: Basic Books, 2019); Mae M. Ngai, *Impossible Subjects: Illegal Aliens and the Making of Modern America* (Princeton, NJ: Princeton University Press, 2004).

grievances of the ISA in 1970.[24] In the weeks after the occupation, as the jailed forty-one students were awaiting trial, the *San Francisco Chronicle* reported on the July demonstrations and called for the release of the ISA members. But when referring to the initial occupation of the Iranian consulate, the articles described the incident as a "wild invasion."[25] One article in particular, titled "Angry Students: Iran Consulate Picketed Again," quotes Iranian Consul Parviz ʿĀdel as calling them "illogical" and "professional troublemakers." The consul described the group as a "very, very insignificant minority of 7000 Iranian students in the Bay Area."[26] In contrast to the apolitical students, the San Francisco Tactical Squad "kept a cool eye" on the protesters who were demonstrating against the consul and his US partners.[27] The stark difference in the way these parties were portrayed highlights how the media caricatured the ISA's actions in order to delegitimize their political concerns over the treatment of dissenters in the homeland.[28] That the police officers were depicted as calm and rational actors in the face of "illogical" students and their "wild invasion" only added to the implication that the ISA was causing unnecessary trouble.

Moreover, Parviz ʿĀdel muddled the ISA's message through his testimony to the *San Francisco Chronicle*. He characterized the actions and demands of the ISA as part of a plan to "undermine [the] democracies" of the United States and Iran.[29] Given that this was during the Cold War era—a time when the United States practiced a policy of containment—ʿĀdel was implying that these students were communist threats to democracy and the so-called Free World. The statement itself is quite ironic, given the dictatorial actions of the Pahlavi government in Iran, which the United States

---

[24] In the early 1960s, Ali Fatemi and Sadeq Qotbzadeh were two students in leadership positions of the ISA who came under criticism by the Iranian government for their vocal opposition to the Shah of Iran. Pro-shah students, for instance, called Qotbzadeh an "agitator" in the *Washington Post*, with the Iranian government eventually suspending their visa renewals. Although at this time, the US government (through the "benevolence" of specific policymakers) took the side of the two students to get their visas renewed, this delegitimizing language was directed time and time again at Iranian students abroad who opposed the Pahlavi regime in Iran. Matthew K. Shannon, *Losing Hearts and Minds: American-Iranian Relations and International Education during the Cold War* (Ithaca, NY: Cornell University Press, 2017), 51.

[25] "Angry Students: Iran Consulate Picketed Again," *San Francisco Chronicle*, July 9, 1970, Parviz Shokat Personal Collection; "Iranians Protest Indictment of 41," *San Francisco Chronicle*, July 17, 1970, Parviz Shokat Personal Collection.

[26] "Angry Students: Iran Consulate Picketed Again." Moreover, when he and a US diplomat got together in Tehran a year later, documents note him stating the following to his American colleague: "You should be more strict in issuing visas to Iranians. I have far too many over there who shouldn't be there. Please don't let them go." Memorandum of conversation, May 3 / June 22, 1971, Record Group (RG) 59, Records of the Department of State, Records Relating to Iran 1965–75, box 6, POL 13-2, US National Archives and Records Administration II (hereafter NARA), College Park, MD.

[27] "Angry Students: Iran Consulate Picketed Again."

[28] For a discussion of the US media's coverage of Iran, see William A. Dorman and Mansour Farhang, *The U.S. Press and Iran: Foreign Policy and the Journalism of Deference* (Berkeley: University of California Press, 1987). While both scholars make the similar case that media is integral to public understandings of who is friend or enemy, I argue that this was done through racialized rhetorics of othering in the case of Iranian students.

[29] "Angry Students: Iran Consulate Picketed Again."

supported as it created the conditions conducive to its brand of modernization.[30] However, the United States portrayed its modernization efforts in Iran as efforts to stabilize the country. As a result, the media characterized Iranian dissidents as trying to destabilize Iran's progress toward becoming a "developed nation."[31] The implications of ʿĀdel's accusation not only villainized the ISA's actions and consequently discredited the concerns of the student community but also masked the atrocities committed within Iran by the Imperial Government.

The legal documentation, especially the trial's transcript, employed discursive frames to harness the disciplinary state in service of delegitimizing the Iranian protesters. Such discursive frames can be read through the testimony of those called to the witness stand. In the transcript of the trial of the forty-one, as lawyers questioned the police officers present at the occupation, the prosecution referred multiple times to the "battle" that took place in the basement of the Iranian consulate.[32] The word choice that the prosecution used turned the scene into an equal playing field in which police officers and the students—characterized as "invaders" through media narratives—faced off. Whereas some protesters in the United States were given the benefit of the doubt as to their peaceful intentions and legitimate grievances, ISA members were flagged as enemy combatants. However, the students were unarmed during the occupation and had to resort to using office supplies and furniture to defend themselves against bodily harm and personal injury.[33]

Furthermore, when police officer Gregory Alan Beatty was asked to describe the actions of the students during the altercation, his court testimony evoked the same sort of sentiment present in the media reports of the event. He described Forud Pāyandehju, one of the ISA members, as "very wild" and "[frantically] shouting," and the officer stated that, upon corralling them into a corner, the students "[chanted and sang] … several things over and over. 'Down with the Shah,' many times … Shaking fists, jumping up and down and yelling."[34] The description of the students as allegedly fanatical reinforced the portrayal of the occupation as a "wild invasion," rather than a means of airing grievances to Parviz ʿĀdel, Ashraf Pahlavi, and the press about the social and political issues plaguing their home country. Thus, the way in which the US legal and media apparatuses described the actions of the students made it seem as though their concerns were not valid and that they composed a minority opinion among the many Iranian student sojourners studying in the United States.

---

[30] The United States gave this kind of support to dictatorships under the pretext that they were helping to stabilize a country before it could become democratic. David F. Schmitz, *Thank God They're on Our Side: The United States and Right-Wing Dictatorships, 1921–65* (Chapel Hill: University of North Carolina Press, 1999).

[31] Lyndon B. Johnson officially designated Iran a "developed nation" in 1967. Shannon, *Losing Hearts and Minds*, 90–1.

[32] Transcript of 41 Trial, July 13, 1970, Parviz Shokat Personal Collection.

[33] The students' lack of weapons was something that was additionally downplayed in the media. For instance, the CBS broadcast of the incident only mentioned that the students were unarmed in the last sentence of the report before the broadcaster signed off the segment. Prior to that, Jerimiah Taylor talked at length about the fight that ensued between the police officers and the protesters. "Arrests at the Iranian Consulate."

[34] Transcript of 41 Trial, July 13, 1970, Parviz Shokat Personal Collection.

A couple years later, in 1973, the forty-one faced additional obstacles when the Iranian consulate refused to renew their student visas under "orders from the Iranian Government."[35] Ali Taheri—one of the students who was hospitalized due to the violent encounter with police—was still appealing for political asylum status even though the United States denied his request the prior year.[36] While the United States was not directly implicated in the second round of deportation threats to the students (though it did not make staying any easier), the ISA saw the visa revocations as an example of the United States allowing Iran to "extend its dictatorship abroad" in order to "stifle every movement by the Iranian people for democracy and independence."[37]

However, Iranian students and members of the ISA were not without their privileges in the prerevolutionary era, as illuminated through their country's relationship with the United States as well as their own class status. Indeed, by constructing the ISA's views as a minority opinion, US and Iranian state actors were able to uphold the notion that Iranians generally supported the neocolonial relationship between the United States and Iran and were working to modernize their home country. By constructing Iranian students as international model minorities, then, the United States attempted to legitimize its Cold War foreign policy and, in particular, the modernization project in Iran. And, by the same hand, these Iranian students retained some privileges during the occupation that may not have been so easy for other communities of color to have enjoyed in a similar situation. For instance, the occupation of the consulate did not get widespread coverage nationally—it remained a local news story that seemed not to get beyond the *San Francisco Chronicle*. It is likely that this remained local news because the United States was in the midst of the Vietnam War, and the issue of Iranian political opposition was, despite its growing visibility throughout the country, still on the back burner. By treating the case of the forty-one as a local issue that did not gain widespread attention, Iranian students were able to go on with their daily lives in the United States without facing the same sort of discrimination that came after the occupation of the US embassy in Tehran in 1979. The lack of national mobilization—either on the part of the United States or Iran—against Iranian students allowed them to continue their oppositionist work in the public sphere without much uproar from the American public.

In order to dive deeply into the ways in which the members of the ISA were able to retain some privileges that maintained their international model minority status, I look to the personal papers of Parviz Shokat, one of the forty-one who participated in and was arrested during the occupation of the Iranian consulate. While Shokat first came to the United States for secondary school, he became heavily involved in ISA activities as a college student at UC Berkeley. Of particular note is the fact that his family knew the shah, and prior to leaving Iran, Shokat had a conversation with Mohammad Reza

---

[35] *Defend the 41*, Social Protest Collection.
[36] Aide memoire, April 30, 1973, RG 59, Records Relating to Iran 1965–75, box 9, POL 30–1, NARA; List of Arrested ISA Members, Parviz Shokat Personal Collection.
[37] *Defend the 41*, Social Protest Collection.

Pahlavi about what he planned to study in the United States.[38] Perhaps it was because of these sorts of backgrounds and connections that members of the ISA were able to deftly navigate the US legal system and communicate their Third Worldist position effectively, albeit with some privilege. Despite this, materials relating to Shokat's arrest and prosecution go into 1973, as his participation in the 1970 protest caused trouble for his visa renewal in later years. Through his legal documents, we can glean the ways in which Iranian students managed to get reduced sentences and their records expunged during this time.

For example, in the time leading up to and after the trial of the forty-one, Shokat's charges were reduced with the help of legal counsel. In July 1970, the forty-one were charged with "Section 182 P.C. (Conspiracy), 459 P.C. (Burglary), 237 P.C. (False Imprisonment), 245b P.C. (Assault with Deadly Weapon against Peace Officer), and 596 P.C. (Malicious Mischief)." Court documents enumerated the criminal counts. However, in December 1970, all charges except false imprisonment were dismissed. Shokat spent thirty-five days in prison and received three years of probation.[39] Although still convicted of false imprisonment, ISA members such as Shokat did not face more severe consequences from the incident—and none of the forty-one were deported.

Moreover, the law seemed to work to their advantage when they were challenged in the US judicial system by members of the Iranian consulate. In August 1970 the Iranian government and Parviz ʿĀdel brought charges against the forty-one—as well as up to five hundred additional members of the ISA—for continuing to demonstrate outside of the consulate in San Francisco.[40] In response, attorneys John Murko and Ronald Yank invoked the First and Fourteenth Amendments in defense of the ISA's right to continue protesting in front of the Iranian consulate against the imprisonment of their compatriots. Indeed, they based their legal argument on the fact that the protesters were "citizens of Iran and have a right to enter the Iranian Consulate in San Francisco to transact matters with consulate officials."[41] The way in which the American legal system worked in their benefit, then, allowed them to continue protesting in the United States against the Iranian government under Mohammad Reza Pahlavi.

Additionally, two years later, Parviz Shokat's probation officer worked to get his probation terminated early and the guilty verdict expunged from his record. He was, in 1972, described as "a mature person, not the type of person who would engage in the activities as described in the police report, a person of superior intelligence, highly motivated to obtain a good education and accept his family responsibilities." Note was also made of his permanent resident status and his role as a father, husband, and provider: "The defendant states that he is no longer actively involved with the Iranian Association, and that he is not in school. He has plans of starting his own business

---

[38] Author Interview with Parviz Shokat, October 15, 2019.
[39] Sentencing Documents, December 12, 1972, Parviz Shokat Personal Collection.
[40] Statement of Intended Decision, Government of Iran, et al. (plaintiff) vs. Abdol Aflakeih, et al. (defendants), March 26, 1971, RG 59, Records Relating to Iran 1965–75, box 9, POL 23–8, NARA.
[41] Defendant Responses, July 30, 1970, Parviz Shokat Personal Collection.

in the field in which he is employed."[42] Ironically enough, Shokat did begin his own business in printing, and he worked to print radical, Iranian oppositionist documents to be taken back to Iran and distributed in the United States. The way in which the probation officer described Shokat was based on the model minority trope. Based on this logic, he had assimilated to become a subject worthy of citizenship and the rights that come with it.

Despite these caveats that reflect the privilege that Iranian migrants had as international model minorities because of the US-Iran alliance, the US state and media dealt with the occupation through systems that were already in place for minoritized subjects in the United States. The relationship between the US judicial system and the politics of immigration and deportation exemplifies the scripts used to racialize Iranians and other communities of color in the United States, particularly Asian Americans. Similarly, the words that journalists and litigators used to describe the forty-one functioned to delegitimize the grievances that were behind the occupation of the consulate in the first place.

Meanwhile, members of the ISA were working to publicize their occupation of the Iranian consulate through local and global connections. While this section examined the disciplinary mechanisms of state power that racialized and delegitimized the forty-one within the United States, the next section explores the agency of the ISA in confronting these systems of minoritization.

Solidarity and Coalition-Building in the Occupation's Aftermath

Prior to the 1979 revolution, the Northern California branch of the ISA was tied formally to the transnational network of the CISNU and informally to the local network of Leftist student communities in San Francisco and the East Bay. The ISA relied on both levels of connection to get the word out about the occupation of the consulate and the arrest of the forty-one, and to create solidarity around revolutionary anti-imperialism. While student activism was nothing new to the history of Iranians abroad, its form in the United States resulted in coalition-building with other communities of color under a Third Worldist rhetoric that spoke to the particular brand of US racialization.[43] Through interactions with other student groups in the United States and their European counterparts, the Northern California branch of the ISA reflected the strategies that Iranian students would continue to use, in the 1970s and far past the revolutionary era, to create Third World solidarity with their compatriots.

California was a particularly critical location to the construction of the Iranian diaspora, both before and after the revolution. The most well-known location of the Iranian diaspora is Los Angeles—or "Tehrangeles," as it is called by certain members of the diaspora—because it has historically maintained the largest number of Iranians

---

[42] Sentencing Documents, December 12, 1972, Parviz Shokat Personal Collection.
[43] Student opposition to Reza Shah originated with Iranians who had been educated in England, France, and Germany. Matin-Asgari, *Iranian Student Opposition to the Shah*.

in the world outside of Iran itself.[44] The Southern California chapter of the ISA was very active during the prerevolutionary era, and its members protested outside of the Federal Building in Los Angeles with the same grievances as their Northern California counterparts. While the Bay Area may not be as visible in the current representation of the Iranian diaspora as Los Angeles, the former was a critical hub for activist circles that enabled Iranians to connect with other major organizing communities—the Black Panthers, for instance—through their shared urban space.[45] Also critical was the fact that the Iranian consulate had its office in San Francisco, which allowed political oppositionists to make direct appeals to the Iranian government. The Bay Area was therefore an important space for making local connections to other communities of color in the United States that were fighting against US imperialism and colonialism.

The members of the ISA were conscious of what these connections would allow them to accomplish on behalf of their home country. This consciousness was on display during a broadcast on June 30, 1970, that covered the picketing that began in San Francisco in reaction to the arrest of the forty-one. When a reporter asked an ISA spokesman whether they feared being deported, the latter responded: "I think we are basically relying on the people in this country to show the collaboration between the consulate here and the U.S. immigration office to put political pressure on us when we want to represent our just views and demands in this country." Behind him, Iranians and Americans demonstrated and held signs that read "Support the Just Struggle of the 41 Students."[46] In another venue, a letter from the ISA in *The Daily Californian* appealed to "progressive forces" to "join" the fight to release the forty-one imprisoned students.[47] The ISA regarded these local connections to other Leftist organizations as critical to their effort to secure the release of the forty-one students from jail.

That being said, the ISA saw its local ties to Leftist organizations as serving causes larger than the specificity of this incident. In many English-language flyers, the ISA remarked on the points of convergence between Iranians and other communities of color in the United States and abroad. For example, in an ISA flyer the students related their own struggles with the US justice system to "our American fellow-captives of Imperialism—the black and third-world people."[48] Given the rise of Third Worldism, Civil Rights, and the anti-war movement in the United States during the decades prior, this form of coalition-building was based within the longer histories of racial

---

[44] Mainstream accounts continue to illustrate that Los Angeles holds the greatest number of Iranians in the diaspora, and this has been historically corroborated by studies conducted in the 1980s and 1990s, which attribute this growth in Los Angeles to the aftermath of the Iranian Revolution. Melissa Etehad, "They Can't Go Back to Iran. So L.A. Persians Built 'Tehrangeles' and Made It Their Own," *Los Angeles Times*, February 24, 2019. Available online: https://www.latimes.com/local/california/la-me-ln-iranian-revolution-anniversary-20190224-story.html (accessed January 21, 2021); Mehdi Bozorgmehr and Georges Sabagh, "High Status Immigrants: A Statistical Profile of Iranians in the United States," *Iranian Studies* 21, no. 4 (1988): 5–36; Mehdi Bozorgmehr, "Internal Ethnicity: Iranians in Los Angeles," *Sociological Perspectives* 40, no. 3 (1997): 387–408.

[45] Author Interview with Parviz Shokat, October 15, 2019; Moradian, "Neither Washington, Nor Tehran: Political Cultures of Iranian American Un/Belonging."

[46] "Mounting Pressure to Release Iranian Students."

[47] "Letters to the Ice Box: Iranian Protest."

[48] "On Friday, June 26 …" [Untitled], no date, Parviz Shokat Personal Collection.

formation and social protest in the United States.⁴⁹ By situating their own struggles within frameworks of judicial discrimination and mechanisms of colonialism, Iranian students consciously sought out local connections as they became increasingly embedded in radical networks in the United States.

The occupation and arrests made at the consulate triggered a wave of demonstrations among Iranian and American Leftist student groups. Internally, the ISA distributed flyers issuing the call to "Support the 41" to branches across the country. In the Bay Area, Iranian students and the Arab Student Association, the Progressive Labor Party, Students for a Democratic Society, various Asian student organizations, and the Black Student Union demonstrated outside of the consulate "voicing anti-imperialist slogans" and distributing leaflets to onlookers about releasing "the forty-one."⁵⁰ The buy-in from other student groups was critical to generating awareness about Iranian issues and creating a space for cross-coalitional liberatory agendas.

The ISA hosted events meant to bring organizations together under common values and objectives. In early July 1970 the Northern California branch organized a screening at UC Berkeley of "East Is Red," a film that discusses the Chinese Revolution through a context that suits many anti-imperial struggles: "A true representation of the potential of the peoples' culture achieved through an uncompromising political and cultural revolution of the Chinese people." After advertising the event, the bottom of the flyer stated, "Support the Struggle, Defend the 41 ... By coming to this picture—which is an exemplary manifestation of a revolutionary people—let's show our support for the struggle of the 41."⁵¹ In late July another leaflet advertised a screening of a film on the Russian Revolution, with the same rhetoric written at the bottom of the publicity flyer.⁵² These calls for support were placed within a cross-coalitional framework, as the ISA worked to link its goals with those of others in the Third World. Furthermore, in ISA reports, the "East Is Red" screening was said to have been attended by seven hundred people and became a demonstration site.⁵³ By showcasing to the rest of the organization that these events were well attended and sparked agitation, the Northern California branch of the ISA emphasized the importance of understanding Iranian political goals through a broader framework.

Aside from demonstrations, cultural events, and expressions of solidarity, ISA members benefited materially from non-Iranians looking to support their cause. The bail that the forty-one had to pay was covered through donations earmarked

---

[49] Mary L. Dudziak, *Cold War Civil Rights: Race and the Image of American Democracy* (Princeton, NJ: Princeton University Press, 2000); Vijay Prashad, *Everybody Was Kung Fu Fighting: Afro-Asian Connections and the Myth of Cultural Purity* (Boston, MA: Beacon Press, 2001); Vijay Prashad, *The Darker Nations: A People's History of the Third World* (New York: New Press, 2007).

[50] "41 Iranians Face Deportation," Demonstration Flyer, Parviz Shokat Personal Collection; Report of Activities of American Defense Organization related to the arrest of 41 Fighting Friends of Northern California Organization, July 1, 1970, Parviz Shokat Personal Collection. Translated by author.

[51] "East is Red," Reel 99 Social Protest Collection, BANC MSS 86/157 c, The Bancroft Library, University of California, Berkeley.

[52] "Ten Days That Shook the World," Social Protest Collection, BANC MSS 86/157 c, The Bancroft Library, University of California, Berkeley.

[53] [Open] Letter regarding bail reduction by court and freeing 41, July 20, 1970, Parviz Shokat Personal Collection.

specifically for their support. According to different ISA documents, about $18,000 (elsewhere categorized as 50,000 marks out of a total of 500,000 marks) were collected by the "mass support of progressive and democratic individuals not only in Northern California but from various cities throughout the U.S. as well."[54] This monetary investment was integral to the students' ability to pay their bail and subsequent legal expenses.

By raising support for the forty-one, the ISA was able to "forge new ties with the anti-Imperialist forces of the Bay Area, the United States, and Europe."[55] The framing is notable, as it attempted to tie together local connections with globalized, transnational networks. While this was common to other Third Worldist organizations in the United States, the Northern California branch also spoke to the particular organizational dynamics of the ISA and the CISNU. Because the ISA was a branch of the larger CISNU—which represented Iranian students in Iran, Europe, and the United States—the students in Northern California corresponded regularly about the situation of the forty-one with the CISNU Board of Directors in West Germany.

The local ties between the Northern California Iranians and other communities of color in the United States were at times highlighted in their correspondence with the CISNU. In letters to the CISNU Board of Directors in the aftermath of the forty-one's arrest, the leaders of the Northern California ISA Defense Division recounted their public gatherings and protests to highlight the support they received from members of the community. They reported, for instance, that during a major demonstration in San Francisco on July 1, 1970, a member of the Progressive Labor Party and a member of an Asian students' organization gave speeches in support of the forty-one in front of the local immigration office. The demonstration march also consisted of members of the Socialist Revolutionary Party, the Organization of Arab Students, and the Black Student Union. Similar organizations professed their support of the forty-one at an ISA demonstration on the same day in New York.[56] In another report distributed widely to branches of the ISA in the United States and the CISNU in Europe, the Northern California members commented that the July 1 demonstration had an "impressive" number of Black students sharing their support for the release of the forty-one.[57] These remarks in the reports underscore that local buy-in by radical organizations bolstered the case of the forty-one. Moreover, such remarks spoke to the sense of solidarity present between the people of the Third World and those oppressed within the United States. Thus, it was necessary not only to report on the large numbers of people at the demonstration, but also to show that the crowd was diverse and reflected the larger anti-imperialist stance of Iranian political oppositionists. Ultimately, this cross-coalitional solidarity between radical student organizations proved to be one of the facets that allowed the ISA to gain a solid holding in the Northern California activist milieu and continue to agitate for change in their home country.

---

[54] *Defend the 41*, Social Protest Collection.
[55] Leaflet, "Rely on 'masses' not on 'imperialist justice,'" Parviz Shokat Personal Collection.
[56] Report of Activities of American Defense Organization related to the arrest of 41 Fighting Friends of Northern California Organization, July 1, 1970, Parviz Shokat Personal Collection. Translated by author.
[57] [Open] Letter regarding bail reduction by court and freeing 41.

Just as critical to their organization was the cohesion between different geographical branches of the ISA. Indeed, the forty-one consisted of not only members from the Northern California chapter but also students from Missouri, Illinois, and Kansas.[58] That these members were from the larger national organization is indicative of the relatively easy and systematic communication between ISA regional branches. In fact, the July 1 protests were not confined to the San Francisco Bay Area. The ISA organized large demonstrations in support of the forty-one that took place simultaneously in San Francisco, New York, and Chicago, all of which were reported to have a significant turnout.[59] Moreover, the ISA's cross-regional organizing contributed to the fundraising that bailed out the forty-one and covered their legal fees.[60]

Additionally, a couple years later in 1973, when the Iranian government refused to renew the passports of the forty-one, the organization launched "a nation-wide campaign to secure the renewal" of their passports, with "all of the ISA chapters [publicizing] the case to gain support from progressive and democratic public opinion."[61] By working together nationally, the ISA was able to gain petition signatures against the Pahlavi regime's passport policy, not only from the Bay Area and Greater Northern California but also from professors in Southern California and Oklahoma, attorneys in Los Angeles, and a director of a Black cultural center at Purdue University.[62] The cohesive campaign, then, garnered deliverables for the Iranian student movement.

Through ISA reactions to the mass arrest of the forty-one, we can identify the two main dynamics that continue to be the backbone of Iranian political opposition in the United States. First, the organized national response by the ISA signals the ways in which Iranian students were able to amplify their voices against the oppression of the shah. Second, the cross-coalitional movement, which included non-Iranian student groups, was critical to the Iranian student movement and in line with the Third Worldist ideological underpinnings of its organizing work.

Conclusion

The 1970 arrest of the forty-one is illustrative of two emerging dynamics that came to define Iranian diasporic representation and lived experience in the 1970s and early 1980s. While the United States broadly positioned Iranian non-immigrant migrants as international model minorities who formed part of their client state, Iranian political opposition was nonetheless present as a force that had to be reckoned with. As a result, US state powers delegitimized ISA grievances through deportation tactics and media bias, showing how racial scripts previously used to silence other communities of

---

[58] Occupation of Iranian Consulate Summary, June 29, 1970, Parviz Shokat Personal Collection. Translated by author.
[59] [Open] Letter regarding bail reduction by court and freeing 41.
[60] For this particular case, the CISNU in West Germany did not understand the objectives of the consulate occupation, as it had not been discussed with them beforehand. As a result, the CISNU did not provide monetary support to the ISA for their actions.
[61] *Defend the 41*, Social Protest Collection.
[62] Letters Regarding Visa Renewal, Parviz Shokat Personal Collection.

color were applied to Iranian dissenters. In turn, Iranians in support of ISA activities strategized through the transnational networks of the CISNU and the cross-coalitional solidarity movements tied to the Third Worldist, Civil Rights, and anti-war movements in the Bay Area. These two dynamics can be understood as nascent articulations of US state racialization and ISA solidarity work that would crystalize with the Iran Hostage Crisis of 1979–81.

In thinking through Chih-ming Wang's work on the "Asian/American" foreign student, a term that captures the transnational flows and struggles of national belonging, this chapter similarly seeks to place Iranian student sojourners in a larger conversation that recognizes the importance of Asia—in this case, West Asia—as a political and social site of significance to the formation of race and the process of racialization in the US nation-state more broadly.[63] Indeed, the history of Iranian migrants in the United States during the prerevolutionary period follows along the lines of other Asian/American groups through a shared geopolitical and imperial project brought on by the United States. In engaging with the international model minority figure and its permutations, this chapter expands the conversation beyond national borders and thinks through how imperial projects produce these subjects.

---

[63] Wang, *Transpacific Articulations*, 12–14, 16.

10

Professional Transnationalism and Iranian-American Im/mobility in Michigan

Camron Michael Amin

There are several windows through which researchers can peer to understand the historical and present state of cultural intimacy between Iran and the United States. In addition to the journalistic, literary, and academic approaches,[1] there are insights to be gained from travelogues, memoirs, and oral histories.[2] This is especially true for scholars of the postwar years. As the Second World War came to a close, the US government took an interest in enhancing its image in Iran by showing "America" to "influential" Iranians.[3] The cultural intimacy between Iran and the United States, of course, did not emerge *ex nihilo* in the twentieth century. The history of social, political, and economic engagement between the two countries is built on Iran's sustained engagement with the West since the eighteenth century—one that penetrated private homes and wove itself into public spaces.[4] However, Cold War imperatives shifted and intensified US efforts to cultivate relations with young Iranians through educational and professional opportunities.

---

[1] Amy Motlagh, "*Black Light*, White Revolution: Translation, Adaptation, and Appropriation in Galway Kinnell's Cold War Writings on Iran," *Comparative American Studies* 13, no. 4 (2015): 220–35; Matthew K. Shannon, "Reading Iran: American Academics and the Last Shah," *Iranian Studies* 51, no. 2 (2018): 289–316.

[2] Sattareh Farmanfarmaian with Dona Munker, *Daughter of Persia: A Woman's Journey from Her Father's Harem through the Islamic Revolution* (New York: Crown, 1992); Nasrin Rahimieh, *Missing Persians: Discovering Voices in Iranian Cultural History* (Syracuse, NY: Syracuse University Press, 2001); Nile Green, "Fordist Connections: The Automotive Integration of the United States and Iran," *Comparative Studies in Society and History* 58, no. 2 (2016): 290–321.

[3] Camron Michael Amin, "An Iranian in New York: Abbas Masudi's Description of the 'Non-Iranian' on the Eve of the Cold War," in *Rethinking Iranian Nationalism and Modernity*, ed. Kamran Scot Aghaie and Afshin Marashi (Austin: University of Texas Press, 2014), 161–78.

[4] Pamela Karimi, *Domesticity and Consumer Culture in Iran: Interior Revolutions of the Modern Era* (London: Routledge, 2012).

The view offered in this chapter is through the window of oral history, more specifically, the Michigan Iranian-American Oral History Project (MIAOHP).[5] The interviews explore the transnational experiences of Iranians and Iranian-Americans, and they point to how both state and non-state factors facilitated their mobility. The interviews featured here are mainly with Iranian-Americans in Michigan who arrived in the United States between 1955 and 1979, at the height of the US relationship with Mohammad Reza Shah Pahlavi's Iran. Their recollections highlight the role of the American Friends of the Middle East (AFME, established in 1951),[6] and, in one interview, the Educational Commission for Foreign Medical Graduates (established in 1958), in facilitating their educational and professional opportunities. Many of those interviewed did not intend to stay in the United States. But a mix of historical upheavals in Iran and personal reasons changed their trajectory. Many MIAOHP interviewees returned to Iran or visited regularly—before and after the revolution of 1979. Six returned to Iran in an effort to establish lives there, two before the revolution and four after the revolution.

That said, the binational intimacy between the United States and Iran is not a mere by-product of macro-historical trends. There were multiple durable transnational social networks that encouraged individual Iranians and Americans to achieve a level of familiarity with the complexities of both societies. In each case, their unique blend of professional experiences in Iran and the United States facilitated mobility between the countries and, despite the changing state of US-Iranian relations, reinforced their agency regarding where to settle and build their lives in Michigan. In each individual's narrative are vignettes that clarify their agency in moving physically or imaginatively between Iranian and American contexts. In these ways, state-facilitated mobility intersected with the interpersonal and professional networks of Iranian-Americans in Michigan.

Oral History and "Regimes of Im/mobility": Situating the Michigan Iranian-American Oral History Project in the Literature

The MIAOHP is unique in its conceptualization. Unlike the Harvard Iranian Oral History Project, which focuses on former Pahlavi elites and participants in the revolution of 1979, it does not seek to understand a particular event.[7] Nor is it focused

---

[5] The MIAOHP was funded by the Michigan Council for the Humanities and the University of Michigan-Dearborn Office of Research. I want to gratefully acknowledge the efforts of student research assistants (Tina Nelson, Muhammad Ali Mojaradi, Deanna Burrows, Abdelrahman Abdelhaq, Graham Liddell, and Marlaine Magewick) and staff (Patrick Armatis, Julia Daniel Walkuski, Tim Streasick—at the Mardigian Library—and Greg Taylor at the JASS Studio) over the years since work began in 2016.

[6] Matthew K. Shannon, *Losing Hearts and Minds: American-Iranian Relations and International Education during the Cold War* (Ithaca, NY: Cornell University Press, 2017), 34–41.

[7] Michigan Iranian-American Oral History Project (https://library.umd.umich.edu/miaohp/index.php); Iranian Oral History Project, Harvard University (https://curiosity.lib.harvard.edu/

on historical actors from a particular institution, as is the case with Jasamin Rostam-Kolayi's interviews with former Peace Corps volunteers in Iran.[8] Rather, the MIAOHP is focused on the experience of the Iranian Diaspora in relation to a particular place, rather like Persis Karim's oral history project on Iranian-Americans in the Bay Area of California.[8]

For methodological good or ill, the very choice to share a story with the MIAOHP can be understood as a way of creating a version of Iran for an American context. There is always a performative aspect to oral history and an awareness of unseen audiences. For this reason, interpreting these oral history narratives requires familiarity with Iran, America, and the cultural spaces between. It also means accepting that some topics—politics and religion, in particular—are often quite sensitive and must be approached obliquely, if at all. MIAOHP interviews are, first and foremost, about the experience of settling (or growing up) in Michigan while maintaining a connection to Iranian heritage or Iran itself. The recorded conversations are otherwise open ended and transparent. Thus, they accord us a chance to see which themes in diaspora and Iranian history resonate with individual lives. Oral history reminds us that macro-level ideological, social, political, and economic trends rest upon more dynamic quanta of individual psyches. Oral history is not the only methodology that provides this window, of course. Anonymized field interviews, often supplemented by surveys, are essential sources in analyses of Iranian-Americans in Texas, Iowa, and California, as well as in Neda Maghbouleh's analysis of race and Iranian-American identity.[9]

Michigan, like the American Midwest generally, has not figured much in the literature on Iranian-Americans or the Iranian Diaspora. The number of Iranian-Americans in Michigan stands around 10,000 and is, therefore, much smaller than the communities in Texas, California, or the Washington, DC area. The Iranian-American community in Michigan is also small relative to the Arab Americans who, like Iranian-Americans, live and are culturally visible in the southeastern part of the state. But, if Iranians are a micro-minority, they are not new to the cultural landscape of Michigan. One can find traces of immigrant "Persians" in the local press as early as 1890.[10]

---

iranian-oral-history-project); Foundation for Iranian Studies Oral History Collection, Bethesda, MD (https://fis-iran.org/en/oralhistory).

[8] Chapter 8 in this volume; Iran/America Project, Oakland, CA (http://iranamericaproject.org); Iranian American Voices of Silicon Valley, San Jose State University (http://www.sjsu.edu/persianstudies/videogallery/iranianamericanvoicesofsiliconvalley/index.html). See also Iranian-American Foreign Policy Oral History Project, Hoover Institution Archives, Stanford University (https://oac.cdlib.org/findaid/ark:/13030/kt5n39r844/entire_text/); and Research Association for Iranian Oral History, Berlin, Germany (http://www.iranianoralhistory.de/English/Englich-free/Home.html).

[9] Mohammad A. Chaichian, "First Generation Iranian Immigrants and the Question of Cultural Identity: The Case of Iowa," *International Migration Review* 31, no. 3 (1997): 612–27; Patricia J. Higgins, "Interviewing Iranian Immigrant Parents and Adolescents," *Iranian Studies* 37, no. 4 (2004): 695–706; Neda Maghbouleh, *The Limits of Whiteness: Iranian Americans and the Everyday Politics of Race* (Stanford, CA: Stanford University Press, 2018); Mohsen Mobasher, *Iranians in Texas: Migration, Politics, and Ethnic Identity* (Austin: University of Texas Press, 2012).

[10] Charles Barnes, "ROFEIGNERS [sic] IN MICHIGAN ... ," *Detroit Free Press (1858–1922)*, December 21, 1890. *Detroit Free Press* available via the ProQuest Historical Newspapers database.

From the Great Game to the Cold War to the War on Terror, this intimacy has not been immune from Orientalizing and Occidentalizing discourses—even in the American Midwest. Long before Iranians came to Michigan in significant numbers, the *Detroit Free Press* lumped "Persia" together with "Asiatic" and "Mohammedan" countries that were portrayed as rife with corruption, disease, and moral laxity, a view often filtered through the perspective of American missionaries.[11] Events in Iran were followed more closely and sympathetically beginning with Iran's Constitutional Revolution, with Iran's turn toward "democracy" being seen as a turn toward a modernity that Americans should support.[12] Iranian travelers abroad, including in the United States, did register the material and sociopolitical gaps between Iran and the West as Iranian deficiencies. But this was not uncritical "Westoxication," as twentieth century Iranian commentators such as Sadeq Hedayat (d. 1951) and Jalal Al-e Ahmad (d. 1969) would have savaged it. Rather, these perceptions derived from a more complex Occidentalism along the lines first identified by Mohammad Tavakoli-Targhi.[13] There are echoes of that dynamic in the oral history narratives of the MIAOHP, and they tend to highlight the cultural boundaries navigated as part of their experience as Iranian-Americans. It is important to note that, in the late nineteenth and early twentieth centuries, framings of "Persia" in the American press coincided with litigation in US courts in which Middle Eastern and Muslim immigrants argued for recognition as "white," if not out of a sense of conviction then to navigate America's racist immigration and naturalization laws. As Neda Maghbouleh points out, Iranians were largely categorized as non-white even before their rate of immigration reached significant levels during the Cold War and after the Immigration and Nationality Act of 1965.[14] As we shall see, understandings of race and ethnic difference, both in the United States and Iran, inform the experiences of the interviewees.

Iranian-Americans in Michigan have been taking steps since the 1990s to document and institutionalize their presence. These steps included an informal, apparently short-lived, effort to have the Detroit Public Library acquire Persian-language books. The most durable of these efforts has been the *Khāneh-ye Irān-e Mishigān*, or (as the organization translates it) the Persia House of Michigan. Since 1999, it has, through

---

[11] "A ROYAL CONFIDENCE MAN.: REUTER AGAIN THE VICTIM OF THE KING OF KINGS. THE SHARP GAME PLAYED BY THE OF PERSIA [sic]. HIS PERSIAN BANK CONCESSION AND HOW IT IS BEING MANIPULATED… ," *Detroit Free Press (1858–1922)*, October 27, 1889; "IN DARKENED LANDS: SUCCESSFUL MEETING OF THE PRESBYTERIAN FOREIGN MISSIONS BOARD TALES OF DISTRESS FROM JAPAN, CHINA, INDIA AND OTHER BENIGHTED COUNTRIES … ," *Detroit Free Press (1858–1922)*, May 28, 1891; and "PEMININE [sic] FOLLY.: HOW WOMEN OF VARIOUS NATIONS DISFIGURE THEMSELVES," *Detroit Free Press (1858–1922)*, July 10, 1892. For more on the origins of American academic and popular views of Muslims generally, see Firoozeh Kashani-Sabet, "Before ISIS: What Early America Thought of Islam," *Sociology of Islam* 8, no. 1 (2020): 17–52.

[12] "'FREE PERSIA': ANCIENT ORIENTAL EMPIRE IS GRANTED MODERN GOVERNMENT BY THE SHAH. TO HAVE A CONSTITUTION … ," *Detroit Free Press (1858–1922)*, August 11, 1906; and "MAKE PLEAS BY PHONE: SUBJECTS PETITION OF PERSIA IN NOVEL MANNER. SPECIAL BOOTH FOR THE PURPOSE ERECTED IN PUBLIC SQUARE AT TEHERAN–LINE KEPT BUSY FROM DAYBREAK TO SUNSET," *Detroit Free Press (1858–1922)*, December 9, 1907.

[13] Mohamad Tavakoli-Targhi, *Refashioning Iran: Orientalism, Occidentalism and Historiography* (London: Palgrave, 2001).

[14] Maghbouleh, *The Limits of Whiteness*, chapter 2.

modest membership dues ($25/year) and donations, sponsored holiday celebrations (like *Nowruz, Mehregān,* and *Shab-e Yaldā*), monthly "Iran Nights," and a weekend Persian school for the children. Since 2004, it has circulated the bilingual *PHoM Newsletter* (or *Faslnāmeh*) on a quarterly basis, which is a rich source of cultural and social history for the Iranian-American community in southeast Michigan.[15] Many MIAOHP interviewees were former and current members of the Persia House of Michigan.

Despite its significance, it is important to stress that Persia House of Michigan does not encompass the entirety of the Iranian-American experience in Michigan. Many live outside of the Detroit metropolitan area. Furthermore, many in Detroit are what M. G. S. Hodgson might have called "piety-minded," and the Persia House is avowedly secular and non-political.[16]

In addition to these differences within Michigan's Iranian-American community, MIAOHP interviewees reflect the regional diversity of Iran itself. Their families came from different parts of Iran—Tehran, Azerbaijan, Fars, Isfahan, Yazd, and Mazandaran provinces—and reflect some of the ethnic and religious pluralism of the country. They are mostly of Muslim background but include Armenians and Zoroastrians. They are mostly of Persian-speaking background, but there are interviewees of Azeri Turkish, Mazandarani, and Dari-speaking backgrounds.[17] Except for one person who was born in Kalamazoo, Michigan, and another who was born in Mumbai, India, all interviewees were born in Iran. Despite many personal variations, the data from the interviews track with both the scale of immigration and the educational motivations behind much of it.

The number of Iranian students in the United States increased steadily from 570 in the 1949–50 academic year to a peak of 51,740 in 1979–80. The number of Iranian students steadily declined until the turn of the twenty-first century and sat at 12,142 in the 2019–20 academic year. Between 1950 and 1977, only 8,997 Iranians became naturalized US citizens, but that number increased between 1978 and 1995 to 82,465.[18] Most Iranian-Americans came to Michigan amid the waves of Iranian visitors at the height of Iran's Cold War alliance with the United States. During the 1960s and 1970s, Western observers and the Iranian government worried about a "brain drain" of Iranian professionals, particularly in STEM fields, as a percentage of the thousands of Iranian students in American institutions opted not to return home for political, economic, or personal reasons. From 1958 to 1975, 14,443 of the 21,124 Iranian immigrants to the United States, or 68.4 percent, adjusted to permanent resident status upon arrival. In addition, in 1975 alone there were 21,299 temporary visitors and 7,795 students

---

[15] Some issues are archived digitally and available online: https://persiahousemi.wildapricot.org/Newsletter (accessed June 20, 2021). The Mardigain Library at the University of Michigan-Dearborn is developing a bilingual index and search engine for the PHoM Newsletter and digitizing earlier issues.

[16] Reference, of course, to Marshall G. S. Hodgson, *The Venture of Islam: Conscience and History in a World Civilization, Volume One* (Chicago: University of Chicago Press, 1974).

[17] Here Dari refers not to the Persian spoken in Afghanistan but to the very local dialect spoken by Zoroastrians in a village near Yazd. See Saloumeh Gholami, "Remnants of Zoroastrian Dari in the Colophons and Sālmargs of Iranian Avestan Manuscripts," *Iranian Studies* 51, no. 2 (2018): 195–211.

[18] Mehdi Bozorgmehr, "From Iranian Studies to Studies of Iranians in the United States," *Iranian Studies* 31, no. 1 (1998): 5–30.

from Iran in the United States.[19] This professional exodus continued after the rise of the Islamic Republic.[20] Ten of the fourteen interviewees first came to the United States as "temporary" visitors, nine as students and one as the family member of a student.

The data from the interviews also indicate that many migrants came *through* Michigan for educational purposes. Most attended the University of Michigan-Ann Arbor (UM), Michigan State University (MSU), and Wayne State University. Eight of fourteen MIAOHP interviewees have graduate degrees; this is higher than the average among Iranian-Americans of 34.3 percent and 22.8 percent of men and women, respectively.[21] With decades-old ties to Iran and countries around the world, UM and MSU consistently place among the top US institutions that draw international students.[22] Then as now, UM, MSU, and Wayne State have been powerful draws for international students. Thus, even though Michigan was not a prime destination for Iranian-Americans, its institutions of higher learning ensured that many Iranians spent some time in Michigan, with enough settling in the state to support cultural societies like the Persia House of Michigan.

The "nonpolitical" nature of the Persia House of Michigan, like the aversion to discussing politics among MIAOHP interviewees, may be a legacy of the pre-1979 "student diaspora" and the wider post-1979 Iranian Diaspora that grew out of it.[23] Iranian student activism in the United States, no less than Iranian seminary student activism in Iraq in the 1970s, shaped the course of the revolution of 1979. But political activism from a variety of ideological positions was not the only organizing feature of pre-1979 Iranian student life in the United States; there was also an effort to participate in American society *and* share with American allies highlights of Iranian culture.[24] In the wake of the revolution, a sense of community in the diaspora may have required an obscuring of political difference. The absence of overtly political narratives among MIAOHP interviewees, though it is a loss, does allow other aspects of the immigration experience, including the importance of informal and professional networks, to come into view.

---

[19] Hossein Aksari, John T. Cummings, and Mehmet Izbudak, "Iran's Migration of Skilled Labor to the United States," *Iranian Studies* 10, nos. 1–2 (1977): 3–35; Hossain A. Ronaghy, Elaine Zeighami, and Bahram Zeighami, "Physician Migration to the United States—Foreign Aid for U.S. Manpower," *Medical Care* 14, no. 6 (1976): 502–11.

[20] Mazyar Lotfalian, "The Iranian Scientific Community and Its Diaspora after the Islamic Revolution," *Anthropological Quarterly* 82, no. 1 (2009): 229–50.

[21] Mehdi Bozorgmehr and Eric Ketcham, "Adult Children of Professional and Entrepreneurial Immigrants: Second-Generation Iranians in the United States," in *The Iranian Diaspora: Challenges, Negotiations, and Transformations*, ed. Mohsen Mostafavi Mobasher (Austin: University of Texas Press, 2018), 39, Table 1.4.

[22] Statistics from Institute of International Education, *Open Doors*. Available online: https://www.iie.org/en/Research-and-Insights/Open-Doors (accessed November 30, 2019).

[23] Susannah Aquilina, "Common Ground: Iranian Student Opposition to the Shah on the US/Mexico Border," *Journal of Intercultural Studies* 32, no. 4 (2011): 321–34. Aquilina follows the characterization of Iranian students by Nilou Mostofi and Mitra K. Shavarini as constitutive of a "diasporic identity," that per the analysis of Afshin Matin-Asgari was bound to be politicized by the oppressive conditions in Iran. See Mostofi, "Who We Are: the Perplexity of Iranian-American Identity," *Sociological Quarterly* 44, no. 4 (2003): 681–703; Matin-Asgari, *Iranian Student Opposition to the Shah* (Costa Mesa, CA: Mazda, 2002); and Shavarini, *Educating Immigrants: Experiences of Second Generation Iranians* (New York: LFB Scholarly, 2004).

[24] Aquilina, "Common Ground," 329. Of course, the cultural was being politicized as a reclaiming of traditions from the ruling class behind the shah's regime.

Anticipating America

Long before the living memories of MIAOHP interviewees, Iranians encountered Americans through missionaries, entrepreneurial adventurers, nonprofit organizations, consultants, and diplomats. "America" itself was something they read about in the Iranian press, going back to the earliest official gazettes in the nineteenth century. But after the Second World War, America reached out to recruit Iranians as local employees of programs like Point Four and through semiofficial organizations such as AFME.[25]

AFME was decisive in the account of the earliest Iranian visitor to the United States to record an interview with the MIAOHP, Dr. Mohammad Amin. Born in 1936 in Tabriz, he was raised in Tehran after his father was killed during the Second World War during failed government attempts to reestablish control of Kurdistan province in early 1942. Dr. Amin came to America in 1955, in circumstances that were not random but serendipitous. It is also clear that he was thinking about studying overseas:

> **Q:** [When] did you decide to come to the US?
> **Amin:** [*Laughs*] This is very interesting because I really, I had a friend, we were studying to take the entrance exam to the university system. And I had this friend that, he had planned to come to US. But I did not know, I wasn't sure whether financially was possible for my family to go. So, we had agreed to go to a movie at four o'clock or something, so he came to my house, and we came out and then he said, "I have to talk to my adviser at the Iran-America Society before we go." So, we ended up there. And he went to see his adviser, and I was sitting in the—just the entrance place. And there were two secretaries there. At least, I assume they were secretaries. So, after a while, they told me—these ladies—one of them told me, "What is your business here?" I said, "No. I'm just waiting for my friend, I don't have any business." And right at that time this friend walked out of his adviser's office and once he heard the discussion, he said, "You know this guy is the second ranked student in all of Tehran." And then these ladies became kind of interested and so on. And they told me if I fill out an application they may be able to get a scholarship for me. So, I think they gave me the forms and I filled it out. I returned it to them the next day, and then I got admission to Worcester Polytechnic Institute in Worcester, Mass.
> **Q:** Were the forms in English or in Persian?
> **Amin:** They were in English.
> **Q:** So, you knew English already.
> **Amin:** Yeah, because in addition to English in my high school, I used to go to private lessons for English.[26]

---

[25] Although no MIAOHP interviewees had direct experience with Point Four, one of the friends of Dr. Amin (and thus, the author) worked as a local contractor for Point Four. For more on Point Four, see Gregory Brew, "'What They Need Is Management': American NGOs, the Second Seven Year Plan, and Economic Development in Iran, 1954–1963," *International History Review* 41, no. 1 (2019): 1–22.

[26] Mohammad Amin, interviewed by Camron Michael Amin, May 28, 2016, Berkley, Michigan. *Michigan Iranian-American Oral History Project*, University of Michigan-Dearborn, 2–4 (hereafter MIAOHP Transcript or Recording).

Although it was something of an accident that he discovered an opportunity to travel to the United States, he was ready for that opportunity. His journey in April 1955 involved a train trip from Tehran to Abadan followed by a series of flights to New York. There he was met by AFME personnel, who put him on a train to Ann Arbor, Michigan, where he was to study English further before going to Worcester Polytechnic Institute to study civil engineering. Amin finished his studies of English ahead of schedule and was permitted to take engineering classes at the University of Michigan. The program focused on not only language but also orientation to "the American way of life." Amin was permitted to work in an automobile plant as a substitute for a vacationing worker in August 1955; he learned of the opportunity from a fellow Iranian student who was a couple of years into his studies at the University of Michigan. Every night, he was expected to watch television in order to learn colloquial English phrases and the nuances of popular American culture. Day trips to Detroit were organized, and Amin visited Chicago with an American friend he had made. Amin was also taught a version of "American Government 101," which he described this way:

> **Amin**: They would explain things. One of the things that happened, they explained a lot of things about US to us.
> **Q**: What kinds of things did they explain to you?
> **Amin**: Just how the government is, how the elections are.
> **Q**: Did you find their explanations to be true as you got to know things on your own?
> **Amin**: I think so, yeah.
> **Q**: Anything in particular you remember from their explanations that struck you as, "Yeah that is how it works."
> **Amin**: I think the election process. Yeah, that was very …
> **Q**: How did you think about the election process as you came to understand it?
> **Amin**: Well, I mean, in here … In Iran, maybe they had elections—I was, first of all much, younger—I never got involved. But in here, I had the sense that a lot of people got involved with the elections.
> **Q**: Did you think that was a good thing?
> **Amin**: I thought it was … The whole business of campaigning and so on, this was all very new to me.[27]

In his recollections, Amin consistently recalled that he never had any intention of staying in the United States, as much as he came to like the country. He knew America's political system was more open than Iran's, both from observation and from questions Americans asked him about "tight" government control in Iran. Beyond the question of political liberty, Amin recalled being conscious of Iran's underdevelopment. He was particularly struck by municipal water systems in America and the fact that there was "nothing comparable" in Iran.[28]

---

[27] Ibid., 27–30.
[28] Ibid., 36–7.

Amin was able to visit home once between 1955 and 1971. In 1971 he returned to start a career at the Aryamehr University of Technology (now Sharif University). There his career progressed. He served as a deputy minister in the Ministry of Science and Higher Education and became the chancellor of the Aryamehr University of Technology in Isfahan before his career was cut short by the revolution.[29] The Isfahan campus, which Amin helped to build, was originally conceived as a branch of the Tehran Aryamehr campus; it was "spun off" as an independent campus shortly before the revolution. Though he had let his Green Card lapse, Amin was able to return to the United States in the summer of 1979 by virtue of having an American wife and family (you are welcome, Dad). He also had the sponsorship of an engineering firm in Chicago where he had worked in the summers during his graduate studies in the 1960s. He was exactly the kind of person that AFME was trying to cultivate: a successful professional with a basically positive impression of, and multiple connections to, the United States.

Dr. Hasan Alizadeh first came to the United States in 1972. He was very much a beneficiary, not just of the American Cold War alliance with Iran but of the later stages of the White Revolution and the various alternatives to military service that were provided to Iranian college students. Unlike Amin, Alizadeh returned to Iran just before the revolution to begin his career. He worked in his home province of Azerbaijan during the Iran-Iraq War. He remembers this time as being difficult, and he eventually decided that, if possible, his career would be better served outside of Iran. He was able to return to the United States, in part, through the sponsorship of his American alma mater—MSU—for graduate work. As in the case of Dr. Amin, the professional connections to the United States that made it possible for him to emigrate from the Islamic Republic began with friends and stretched beyond organizations such as AFME. Because of his scores on the *konkur*,[30] Dr. Alizadeh studied mechanized agriculture at the University of Tabriz. After he completed his degree in 1971, he fulfilled his eighteen months of required military service via the Development Corps (*Sepāh-e Tarvij va Ābādāni*). When that service concluded, he decided to go to the United States for further study. His account lays out the mix of interpersonal, official, and semiofficial factors that facilitated his choice and course of action:

---

[29] For more on this chapter of Amin's life and the university in Isfahan, see Camron Michael Amin, "Blurring Private and Public Lives by Design: Isfahan University of Technology, 1977–2005," *Comparative Studies of South Asia, Africa and the Middle East* 26, no. 2 (2006): 279–302.

[30] The Iranian university entrance exam is known as *konkur* in Persian, from the French "concours." The *konkur* can only be taken once a year and ranks all students nationally according to their performance. This determines which students can actually attend state-subsidized universities at little or no cost. The acceptance rate is typically around 10 percent. The demand for such opportunities routinely exceeds supply. See Keith Watson, "The Shah's White Revolution—Education and Reform in Iran," *Comparative Education* 12, no. 1 (1976): 23–36; and Keiko Sakurai, "University Entrance Examination and the Making of an Islamic Society in Iran: A Study of the Post-Revolutionary Iranian Approach to 'Konkur,'" *Iranian Studies* 37, no. 3 (2004): 385–406.

> **Alizadeh:** My friends actually called me that, "Okay, you got—you are first and some ... [*do*] you want to come and you want to go to United [*States and get a*] scholarship." And I said "Okay."
>
> **Q:** A friend simply told you?
>
> **Alizadeh:** Yeah, they called me because they were getting ready. And they were, those three people. So, we, all four, got on the plane and came to Illinois
>
> **Q:** That sounds, ...
>
> **Alizadeh:** O'Hare Airport.
>
> **Q:** That sounds, that sounds super easy ...
>
> **Alizadeh:** Well, it was like, uh, super easy [*shrugs*], we had an American embassy [i.e., *consulate*] in Tabriz. So, you know, around there. The American Friends of the Middle East—they had all these things arranged.[31]

Before his trip to the United States, Alizadeh and his friends traveled to Tehran to meet with representatives of AFME and have their student visas and other arrangements processed. This included placements at Mundelein College in Chicago to study English before continuing on to MSU to study engineering. But his experience in Chicago was also mediated by another network. A Peace Corps worker based in his hometown of Miandoāb was from Chicago and put him in touch with his family. He met the Peace Corps worker through an English teacher renting a room from his parents. They only met once or twice, but that was enough to produce a useful connection in the United States.

Medicine was another important professional route for Iranians that came to the United States. For Dr. Shapoor Ansari, a pioneering cardiologist and medical entrepreneur, medical school and his early professional network in Iran informed his decision to come to America, and Michigan specifically. As he recalled:

> **Q:** You're a doctor training in Iran, you're from a family that's doing fairly well, Iran would be a place that you would have a career potentially. What brought you to America, or out of Iran?
>
> **Ansari:** I had started French as a second language in high school. And in the university, I studied French again. At the time after World War II, the Americans they started having footprint in Iran. They opened a lot of opportunities. I saw people who they were doctors, graduating trying to go to America, become specializing in surgery or whatever. And I couldn't. So, I wanted to go, because I went I saw one doctor who came from Johns Hopkins and he was a gynecologist. He talked to me about medicine is so much better in America. I said "I have to go to America." So, the best way to go? I better learn English. So, I went ... at night I used to go to English classes.
>
> **Q:** Where did you ... was that at a university or was it a private place?
>
> **Ansari:** It was [at the] *Anjoman-e Irān-Āmrikā* [Iran-America Society].[32]

---

[31] Hasan Alizadeh, interviewed by Camron Michael Amin, May 22, 2018, MIAOHP Recording, Time 5:20–6:12 (Segment 1).

[32] Shapoor Ansari, interviewed by Camron Michael Amin and Deanna Burrows, July 31, 2018, MIAOHP Transcript, 20.

Of course, it was not just transnational professional connections but an application process facilitated by the US embassy that contributed to Ansari's professional mobility:

> **Ansari:** [America] didn't have enough doctors, America become more prosperous after World War II, and they wanted more doctors to get from Europe. Many doctors came from Europe here, but they didn't discriminate against Muslims. [*Laughs*] They had an exam called the ECFMG. Education[*al*] Council [*Commission*] for Foreign Medical Graduates [*sic*]. So, it was a whole-day exam. Multiple choice questions, so US embassy was conducting once a year, that exam. And I had studied enough English to be able to read some of the sentences. I remember many of them I didn't understand but I used my common sense and answered them, turned out to be correct.[33]

The US embassy and also the Iran-America Society facilitated the recruitment of Iranian doctors. But why did he choose Michigan? This choice was informed by a French pharmaceutical company. During the "gap year" between finishing medical school and coming to the United States, Ansari took a position as a traveling pharmaceutical representative. It was in the course of that work that Michigan became his first choice. In Isfahan, he met a pediatrician who had spent time in Grosse Point, Michigan, a wealthy Detroit suburb:

> **Amin:** So, this doctor in Isfahan, you interacted with him while you were being a representative?
>
> **Ansari:** Yes, just about five or ten minutes in his office, his patients are waiting in the waiting room. I said, "I don't know where to go." He said, "Go to Michigan, there are so many beautiful lakes over there, a lot of water, and green." In Iran we are very dry country, so love lakes. So, I didn't think about asking about temperature. When I was traveling going to different provinces [*in Iran*], coming back, I was so much letters coming from America, some of them ten letters, some of they sent me brochures, even my roommate had opened them, he used to open read for me say that, "Such and such hospital approve you, you need to go." One of them had sent a nursing school picture which is next to the doctor's residency quarter, there was a swimming pool, the nurses and the residence swimming in the swimming pool.[34]

Dr. Ansari was actively recruited to come to America. Like Amin and Alizadeh, his initial intention was always to return to Iran. The revolution, the success of his career in the United States, and long-standing issues over his required military service in Iran kept him from retuning to Iran. Such difficulties notwithstanding, he was able to regularly visit Iran before and after the revolution. After he finally became a US citizen, he almost moved back to Iran permanently in the 1990s to open a government-sponsored clinic. This fascinating episode is beyond the scope of this study, but what ultimately kept

---

[33] Ibid., 20–1.
[34] Ibid., 23–4.

Ansari in the United States was bias in Iran against his Azeri Turkish background. While he certainly had to contend with prejudice in the United States, he felt free to be himself as an Iranian of Azeri background. This sense of alienation from Persian-speaking Iranians is something he shared with the Miandoāb-born Alizadeh but not with the Tabriz-born, but Tehran-raised, Amin.[35] Because he had become an American citizen, Dr. Ansari was able to extricate himself from an uncomfortable attempt at return to Iran in the 1990s. His mobility to and from Iran had been assured by settling in Michigan, but it was initiated and sustained by his professional standing and networks.

Anticipating Returns to Iran

Mahmoud Mark Moallemian launched the Persia House of Michigan and served on its board, as its president, and as a regular columnist for its newsletter. His career began on Radio Tehran shortly after finishing high school and long before he considered going to the United States. At Radio Tehran, he was involved in translating American culture into the Iranian context. Among his first assignments was to adapt an American detective show, recalled as "Johnny Dollar," into a series for an Iranian radio audience.[36] Moallemian earned a BA in English Literature and Language at the University of Tehran. As his career progressed, National Iranian Radio and Television gave him an opportunity to earn a master's degree in the United States to gain expertise in broadcasting. While at MSU in 1978, he decided to switch to a PhD program in educational technology. Despite the revolutionary turmoil, the Pahlavi government still functioned well enough to require him to return to Iran for three months before being authorized to change his program of study abroad. He completed that requirement just before the revolution climaxed in February 1979. Moallemian was able to return to the United States with his family, but he was soon cut off from further Iranian state assistance:

> **Q:** So, you were back in seventy-nine before February?
> **Moallemian:** Yeah, before. Otherwise, I couldn't be back here. And then for the three or months, or no maybe six months or so, they didn't bother people who were out. And then they figure out there are a whole bunch of people out there which are getting scholarship and so they wrote that, "You have to come back." I said, "I will, provided you tell me I come over there what would I do." So, they wrote me a letter that before that, of course there were articles in the papers, some of them were printed here in *Iran Times*.[37] It said, "All those who are on

---

[35] For fuller expression of Ansari's views, see his remarks at a Human Rights Council event on March 20, 2015. Available online: https://www.youtube.com/watch?v=BWF1cxoTtMI (accessed April 12, 2021).

[36] Mahmoud Moallemian, interviewed by Camron Michael Amin, Dearborn, Michigan, November 7, 2016, MIAOHP Transcript, 3–4. More on the series that was actually called *Yours Truly, Johnny Dollar* and ran from 1932 to 1948 is available online: http://www.yourstrulyjohnnydollar.com/index.html (accessed March 23, 2021).

[37] *Iran Times* is a bilingual newspaper published in Washington, DC by Javād Khākbāz. It has been in operation since 1970, survived a firebombing by pro-Islamic Republic militants in 1980, and continues now online and in print as *Iran Times International*. Available online: http://iran-times.com/about-us/ (accessed March 23, 2021).

a scholarship from National Iranian Radio and Television or those people who had had connections here. And all scholarships should be cut off."

Q: When were you cut off? Were you cut off in the fall of seventy-nine?

Moallemian: I would say I think, I'm not recalling it exactly when. But it was cut off anyway. So, my [*laughs*]—now I have to go and find a source of income because before that time I didn't have to go. I was not even looking for graduate assistantship of any kind. So, I started talking to profs here and there and finally I was able to get some graduate assistantship in osteopathic medicine. And I was just creating for them overheads, slides, and all kinds of instructional aids that they needed. And I was there for more than two and a half years or so.[38]

After 1979, Moallemian did not return to Iran for thirty-five years, but he had both financial and family connections to Iran. This highlights another socioeconomic factor for Iranian students abroad. The Iranian government required collateral to ensure that students would return to Iran. If they did not, the funds they received became a loan. For many students, the collateral was not their own property but that of a relative. Moallemian recalled:

Moallemian: Because during the time I was studying here, I had to pay back to the National Iranian Radio and TV whatever they paid for my scholarship.

Q: So, you owed them for the previous education then?

Moallemian: I did owe them but there was, I think they passed in the parliament there that they abolished their compulsory coming back and working for the government. I referred to that and said, "This is the case. So why do I have to pay?" And, of course, I could just ignore it, and not pay it. But because my brother was my sponsor and his property in Tehran was at their mercy, they had a lien on it. So, I said, "Okay, I'll pay you." But I don't have to pay you all in once, but I can pay you monthly installments. So, for a while, I can't remember how long, but it was very long. We paid each month three-hundred and fifty dollars.

Q: You had to give money back to the Iranian government?

Moallemian: Yep … I was sending it to my brother in Tehran. And he would go and put it in the bank get the receipt and go over there, and get a receipt from them. This month's payment has been received. So, we got all the receipts piling up.

Q: So, you had this kind of connection back to Iran in that sense, right?

Moallemian: Yes.[39]

Moallemian is entirely comfortable with the "American" parts of his life. But he was also committed to staying connected culturally to Iran. This began with informal efforts to celebrate traditional, nonreligious holidays like *Nowruz* and *Shab-e Yaldā*. This, in turn, led to his active role in shaping and leading the Persia House of Michigan. Moallemian

---

[38] Moallemian, MIAOHP Transcript, 5–7.
[39] Ibid., 11–12.

saw no contradiction between enjoying tailgate parties and participating in Persia House's monthly *Shab-e Irān* [Iran Night], in which the whole purpose is to speak Persian for an hour or two while sharing a potluck dinner of (mostly) Persian cuisine. But for others who felt traumatized or simply conflicted about how they came to leave Iran and resettle in the United States, Persia House was a haven and social network built to recreate and share a depoliticized, nonsectarian vision of Iran.

Moallemian highlighted the role of Taraneh Rahmanifar in creating the Persia House of Michigan. A lifelong fascination with devices motivated her to study engineering. A number of her siblings had already attended MSU, and she followed the same trajectory. The revolution happened just as she was getting started with her studies, and she made the decision to return. In Iran she was impacted by the closure of universities and new restrictions placed on women. In the mid-1980s she returned to the United States to resume her study of electrical engineering at MSU. After graduation, Rahmanifar became a project engineer for Ford Motor Company in Michigan. Even as she achieved professional success in the United States, she felt the separation from Iran keenly—more painfully, it seems, than Moallemian. In this, she was more typical of other interviewees. Rahmanifar was motivated to create something durable after seeing that other cultural groups "faded away" due to, in her view, a lack of formal organization. It was also important to her to create a "fun" but definitely "Persian-speaking" cultural space for Iranians in Michigan. She drew upon her wider family and professional networks to accomplish this, describing her role in creating the Persia House of Michigan this way:

> **Rahmanifar:** [Everybody] wanted it, and the only thing people were wary about is, "Don't make it one religion or another. Because we are all of different religions here. And if you want all of Iranians to belong to the same thing, it needs to be independent of all of that." Well, I believed in that anyway ... I started researching it. *And I had connections with a really, really old family friends that I have high respect for. A professor that I know, in Portland. They have a Persian House of Michigan in Portland. ... He was the president of the [Portland] club at the time [1997 or 1998]. He basically told me a lot of his history, what works, what doesn't work. Kind of, his lessons learned. What you could or couldn't do* [emphasis added]. And then I basically said, "This all sounds good." Actually, I went and used most of their bylaws to create the bylaws of the Persia House of Michigan, currently. Basically, part of that by-law is that this is a non-profit organization. This is not religious, political, or have any type of inclination of any kind, the whole soul of the group is culture, education. And that's basically the whole goal. ... Some of the members of the group right now, were extremely against it, they didn't want it. They thought well, it needs to be more of an American community. "Why would it be an Iranian community? Because most of the people here are Iranian-Americans." I said "Well, you have access to all of the American related documentation, education. But you don't have access to anything Persian. So that's what's missing."[40]

---

[40] Taraneh Rahmanifar, interviewed by Camron Michael Amin and Tina Nelson, Dearborn, Michigan, September 22, 2016, MIAOHP Transcript, 5–10.

The impulse here was clearly to build an aspect of community through culture—to transform informal social and personal networks into something more institutional. The idea was to create something durable and with legal standing in the United States; an American nonprofit organization devoted to promoting a particular version of Iran in a primarily Persian-speaking milieu. Rahmanifar's narrative also highlights how the Persia House of Michigan served as an interprofessional network for local Iranian-Americans to cultivate socioeconomic mobility and success. The tension between being "Iranian American" versus being a Persian-speaking Iranian in America is unresolved in this narrative. There is a clear sense of membership in multiple social networks because she talks to "everybody." There is a local community context, replete with differences of opinion on what Persia House of Michigan should be. But there was also, in this case, a "trans-diasporic" professional network—an Iranian professor she knew in Portland—that could be drawn upon to promote Iranian heritage in Michigan.

For Rahmanifar, Persia House of Michigan neither realized her original ambition nor salved her sense of being among the postrevolutionary "lost generation." She expressed her ambivalence this way:

> **Rahmanifar**: I don't belong in either place. I don't feel like I belong here, or I belong there. Because I am a mix. They call us the lost generation. And that is a true statement. We are the lost generation.
> **Q**: So, you feel out of place here and there?
> **Rahmanifar**: Yeah, kind of. But if I was to place myself I feel more of a belonging here than I do there. Though last time I was there, I felt like the culture changed so much, even the language, I couldn't understand some people. And I write poetry, and I read books. And I'm pretty versed in Persian; I don't have a problem with the language. But a lot of the way people talk or the words that they have used have changed. The common words, every country has common words people use in their normal, natural language. And I feel like I'm so far away, I've kind of lost touch with those natural changes in a language ... Life in Iran changed. Right? But I feel like I didn't, I didn't feel like I recognized a lot of it. I loved it; don't get me wrong, because it's from where I'm from. People spoke my language; I felt belonging from that perspective. I look like them; I talk like them. I didn't walk like them; it seems like, because everyone knew I wasn't from there. Everybody walked up to me and: "You're not from here are you?" I don't know why [*looks surprised*]. I am walking, but you're figuring it out from my walking. But I didn't feel like I understood the culture like I used to. I didn't feel like I could do anything and nobody recognized. Everybody recognized I wasn't from there, *everyone* [emphasis added].

"Everyone" in this passage connotes a group from which she is excluded. This sense of cultural liminality is well documented in Iranian Diaspora and Iranian-American studies, and it is a potent theme is diasporic literature and memoirs.[41] To Rahmanifar,

---

[41] Amy Motlagh, "Towards a Theory of Iranian American Life Writing," *MELUS* 33, no. 2 (2008): 17–36; and Amy Malek, "Memoir as Iranian Exile Cultural Production: A Case Study of Marjane Satrapi's 'Persepolis' Series," *Iranian Studies* 39, no. 3 (2006): 353–80.

this liminality seems connected to a sense of *thwarted mobility*. She cannot recreate the vision of Iran she wants in the United States, and when she visits Iran she realizes that she cannot fully return as an Iranian. Michigan is a less-imperfect home, but a high degree of virtual and actual mobility between Iran and America is, in fact, happening, even if not to the extent desired. In her dissatisfaction with efforts to create a version of Iran to "visit" in America, Rahmanifar's narrative resonates with interviews described in Mohsen Mobasher's study of Iranians in Texas, particularly those under the pseudonyms "Cindy" and "Kevin."[42]

The Persia House of Michigan can facilitate a sense of "home," at least for some, by creating an *accessible* connection back to "Iran." Another well-traveled interviewee, Zohreh Raein (Rā'in), shared the feeling that Michigan, eventually, felt like home. Her sense of America was informed, in part, by relatives who were already there, and from a Sears catalog that she got from a friend who worked at the US embassy.[43] She first came to the United States with her husband in the late 1970s when he pursued an educational opportunity. Her initial feeling about Michigan was that the people there were biased against Middle Easterners. When her husband's work took them to Texas, she found that environment more welcoming.

The revolution in Iran disrupted her life severely. Her father was Esmāʻil Rā'in (1919–1979), a famous researcher and dissident who was killed in the early wake of the revolution. She and her husband returned to Iran in 1980, and during the course of the Iran-Iraq War their Green Cards lapsed. It was her husband who wanted to return to the United States once the war was over. They managed to reestablish their legal residency and return to southeast Michigan where family members now lived. Ms. Raein's graduate education (an unfinished master's degree in Persian literature) in Iran had lapsed in the aftermath of the revolution. In 1990, after settling in the Detroit suburb of Farmington, she resumed her studies at Wayne State University in library science. This led to a position at Marygrove College and, after a fourteen-year career there, to Georgetown University in Qatar. She eventually found her way back to Michigan:

> **Raein**: Actually, [Michigan is] my home now because when I returned from Qatar I went to Virginia, I stayed there for a few years, because my mother was old and I felt that I was never with her because I left the house when I was twenty years old I married and I never went back to my mom. So, I thought that I owe her, to be with her. And it was a good decision because I stayed there for four years and she was very sick and I left Virginia when she passed away. So, it's about few months that I came back to Michigan, which is home now. And I had a house here and I was renting it for a while and then I thought, "Why don't I go back?"

---

[42] Mobasher, *Iranians in Texas*, 92–132. These interviews were presented in his analysis of "second-generation" Iranian-Americans, which highlights, I think, some caution that should be employed in making firm distinctions between generations as a point of departure for analysis.

[43] Zoreh Raein, interviewed by Camron Michael Amin, April 13, 2017, Troy, Michigan, MIAOHP Transcript, 14.

And here I am more happy because I have friends that I used to know, and, I'm very involved in Persia House of Michigan.[44]

At the time of the interview, Ms. Raein was the principal of the weekend Persian school run by the Persia House of Michigan. She was encouraged into that position by Ms. Mahin Shad Oveis.

Oveis' own immigration to the United States occurred in 2005, well after the period of cozy relations between the United States and Iran and the subsequent rise of the Islamic Republic. That timing notwithstanding, her mobility had its origins in the late Pahlavi period. Like many other MIAOHP interviewees, members of her family were in the United States in the 1970s as part of the rising tide of Iranian students in the country. She was sponsored by her younger sister, who came in the midst of the revolution, and then managed to navigate the path to naturalization and professional success. Oveis had a career as a podiatrist in Birmingham, Michigan, an affluent suburb along the M-1 "Woodward Corridor" between Detroit and Pontiac. Before the revolution, Mahin Shad accompanied a niece, who was planning to attend university in America, on visits to the US consulate in Shiraz. She actually balked at the suggestion that she, too, should study in the United States. She acquired a negative image of the country from the portrayals of Native Americans that she saw in American Western films. Mahin Shad had to wait until the next millennium for her next chance to leave Iran. When it came, she had to abandon all her professional success as a high school educator and principal in Shiraz to start from scratch in America. For her, the Persia House of Michigan was something of an emotional lifesaver. As she recalled:

> **Oveis**: When I first came [to America], I don't know, I felt … I wasn't a child when I came here, I wasn't young like this man [*gestures to my student assistant Muhammad Ali Mojaradi*]. I missed Iran terribly. Believe me, when I heard an Iranian song I would start to cry intensely—it was to this extent. [Now,] I had dreamed of [coming here to America], I was waiting for years to come here. I had wished to throw my head covering [i.e., the veil] away and to [*be free to*] to do whatever I wanted. Now I could do these things. But this did not make me happy at all. I began searching everywhere for an Iranian circle. Because my sister's husband is American and they mostly are in contact with Americans. One day my sister told me she saw a flier for a *Mehregān* event.[45] I saw the flier, and I called.
>
> **Q**: When was this?
>
> **Oveis**: About twelve and a half years ago [*c*. 2005]. I called and found them. The first person who I was in contact with, was the late Farrokh [Nassirpour]. He reached out to me. He reached out to me and told me "You must come to Iran

[44] Ibid., 8.
[45] *Mehregān* is a pre-Islamic Iranian autumn festival that once was on par with the spring new year's festival (*Nowruz*) on the vernal equinox. It is a holiday that has enjoyed particular revival in the Iranian Diaspora but also received some renewed official attention in twentieth-century Iran under the Pahlavi Dynasty.

Night [*Shab-e Irān*]," he came and picked me up [to take me]. I went and became acquainted with them. During the time that Farrokh was there, I founded the first Persian class. We started the Persian class and I became the teacher. And we started the Persian [*language*] school.[46]

Like Rahmanifar, Oveis is neither completely at home in America nor in Iran. Her hopes that America might have a more enlightened and modern cultural landscape were tempered by seeing her own identity racialized by American peers, and through the process of coming to terms with the racist realities of the profoundly segregated Detroit metropolitan area. Part of her motivation to come to the United States was frustration at the lack of opportunities in Iran, especially for women. She dreams of returning to Iran after she "achieved her goal" of earning a doctorate at Wayne State University. Another interviewee, Dr. Farideh Freedom Hosseini, a psychiatrist who came to America in the 1970s for a medical residency and subspecialty training, saw no place for herself as a professional woman in the Islamic Republic and never countenanced a return. Nonetheless, she spoke with great satisfaction about an invitation to participate in a conference on child psychiatry in Tehran in 2005.[47] The version of "Iran" that she and other members of the Persia House of Michigan recreate in the United States is, perhaps, a placeholder for the Iran they wish was a reality. That Iran would welcome them in triumph and value the professional odyssey each as taken.

Conclusion: Agency, Mobility, and Cultural Intimacy

Hassani: I feel I have actually changed the view of Iran for a lot of different people I've met in my life. I've made a lot of people that grew up in a family [*that thinks*], "Oh Iran is evil and don't deal with those Iranians." And I've changed them to be like, "Oh my God, can I go to Iran with you?" I've had that impact on people, I think it's very important for people to understand that.[48]

Sarah Hassani was born in Kalamazoo, Michigan to Iranian immigrant parents. She shared her oral history in 2018 as she was completing her senior year at the University of Michigan-Dearborn. She visits Iran regularly and follows not just diasporic Iranian culture but also television programs produced in Iran. Her connection to Iran is a very comfortable part of her American life. For her, the "regimes of im/mobility"[49]

---

[46] Mahin Shad Oveis, interviewed by Camron Michael Amin and Muhammad Ali Mojaradi, December 14, 2016, MIAOHP Translated Transcript, 20-2.
[47] Farideh Freedom Hosseini, interviewed by Camron Michael Amin, September 29, 2016, Bloomfield Hills, Michigan, MIAOHP Transcript, 9.
[48] Sarah Hassani, interviewed by Camron Michael Amin and Deanna Burrows, February 21, 2018, MIAOHP Transcript, 38.
[49] Nina Glick Schiller and Noel B. Salazar, "Regimes of Mobility across the Globe," *Journal of Ethnic and Migration Studies* 39, no. 2 (2013): 200. For my first use of regimes of im/mobility in studies of the

that facilitated and then complicated the transnational lives of Alizadeh, Amin, Ansari, Hosseini, Moallemian, Oveis, Rahmanifar, and Raein do not seem to apply in the same manner.

Iranians who first came to the United States before 1979 had every reason to expect that mobility. That expectation derived in part from their professional networks and education, and in part from the friendly official relationship between Pahlavi Iran and the United States. Post-1979 circumstances interrupted and restricted that mobility. Limited mobility can be felt acutely, so much so that I have almost come to expect that an interviewee will broach the issue even if I do not raise it directly in my questions.

Each oral history featured in this analysis articulated a desire to enjoy full mobility between the two cultures in some form. All but one of the interviewees has been able to visit Iran since the rise of the Islamic Republic. In a recent survey of all Iranian-Americans, 90 percent had family or friends in Iran and only 20 percent said that they rarely or never had contact with family and friends in Iran. Moreover, 76 percent opposed the Trump administration's "Muslim Ban."[50] Thus, the enduring motivation to stay connected to Iran among MIAOHP interviewees mirrors that of Iranian-Americans generally. In the case of many interviewees, conceptual mobility—even hypermobility—to Iran meant more than simply escaping into Persephone texts or digital environments.

For Iranian-Americans who visit Iran frequently, however, there are concerns about having this kind of visibility to Iranian authorities who unpredictably seize dual nationals and, sometimes, imprison them for extended periods of time. The case of Amir Mirzā Hekmati, whose parents live in Flint, Michigan, was a regular feature of the local and national press after his 2011 arrest in Iran while visiting his grandmother.[51] He was convicted of espionage with a sentence of death, which was commuted to a prison term in 2012 before he was finally released in January 2016. The Iranian government released him and other Iranian-Americans in the context of the brief quasi-rapprochement that resulted from the Joint Comprehensive Plan of Action of 2015. That slight thaw in official relations shaped the optimistic cultural and political context in which the MIAOHP commenced work in the summer of 2016.

The election of Donald Trump and the subsequent souring of official relations between Iran and the United States was reflected in the oral histories recorded after November 2016. This introduces another point of hesitation for potential interviewees, namely, visibility as people of Iranian descent in America. Indeed, a number of

---

Iranian Diaspora, see Camron Michael Amin, "Gender, Madness, Religion, and Iranian-American Identity: Observations on a 2006 Murder Trial in Williamsport, Pennsylvania," *Social Sciences* 6, no. 3 (2017): 85. See also, "Bounded Mobilities: An Introduction," in *Bounded Mobilities: Ethnographic Perspectives on Social Hierarchies and Global Inequalities*, ed. Miriam Gutekunst, Andreas Hackl, Sabina Leoncini, Julia Sophia Schwarz, and Irane Götz (Bielefeld: Transcript Verlag, 2016), 19–34.

[50] James, Elizabeth, and Sarah Zogby, *The Public Affairs Alliance of Iranian Americans 2019 National Public Opinion Survey of Iranian Americans*, 3, 5–6. Available online: https://paaia.org/wp-content/uploads/2019/10/PAAIA-2019-Survey.pdf (accessed November 24, 2019).

[51] Amir Hekmati, *Crossfire: Trapped in the US-Iran Covert War* (Independently Published, 2020); Jason Rezaian, *Prisoner: My 544 Days in an Iranian Prison* (New York: Harper Collins, 2019). There is also a running total of "foreign nationals" in captivity in Iran, and most of the US citizens in that tally have Iranian names. "Dual Nationals and Foreigners Held in Iran," *Iran Primer*, United States Institute of Peace. Available online: https://iranprimer.usip.org/blog/2016/jul/25/dual-nationals-and-foreigners-held-iran (accessed April 12, 2021).

interviewees identify themselves as "Persian" to fellow Michiganders, reasoning that it "softens" the truth of their Iranian heritage. Still, even in the face of post-1979 and more recent stresses, there is evidence of positive cultural interaction and hybridity in each of the oral history narratives, and not only in Ms. Hassani's interview.

MIAOHP interviews give voice to multiple generations of Iranian Diaspora history. The interviews speak to the resilience of the intercultural intimacy that was deliberately cultivated by state action and non-state actors during the Cold War, along with the role of informal professional and interpersonal networks in facilitating transnational mobility. While MIAOHP interviews help us better understand the networks that encouraged movement between the United States and Iran in the late Pahlavi period, they also point to how those very networks survived the revolution of 1979 and continue to bolster intercultural intimacy in transnational, trans-diasporic, and local contexts.

Conclusion: Third Parties, Non/State Actors, and the Ambiguities of US Imperial Power

Cyrus Schayegh

This volume is an innovative contribution to an issue that is as politically sensitive as it is historically fascinating. Many of the chapters' protagonists are not the top-level elite actors around whom a good part, though far from all, of the scholarship on US-Iranian relations turns. What is more, the volume's authors study a wide range of aspects of US-Iranian relations, including identity formation, cultural diplomacy, and political economy, among other themes.[1] The present text concludes this volume with a few exploratory notes on three points that concern all chapters, matter also to scholars not specialized in US-Iranian relations, and correlate with my interests.[2] These points are the role of third parties in bilateral US-Iranian relations, the overlap between state and non-state actors, and the ambiguous nature of US imperial power. I would add that, certainly from the 1950s to the 1970s, the US-Iranian relationship is an excellent case for reflecting on the US imperial-postcolonial field.[3]

---

[1] For a recent literature overview, see Gregory Brew, "State of the Field >> United States-Iranian Relations," H-Diplo Essay 234, May 22, 2020. Available online: https://hdiplo.org/to/E234 (accessed June 15, 2020).

[2] Cyrus Schayegh, "Foreign Gifts and US Imperial Ambiguities: The Kennedy Years," in *Globalizing the U.S. Presidency: Postcolonial Views of John F. Kennedy*, ed. Cyrus Schayegh (London: Bloomsbury, 2020), 130–49; Cyrus Schayegh, "The Man in the Middle: Developmentalism and Cold War at AUB's Economic Research Institute in-between the U.S. and the Middle East, 1952–1967," in *150 Years AUB*, ed. Nadia El Cheikh and Bilal Orfali (Beirut: AUB Press, 2016), 105–19; Cyrus Schayegh, "'Seeing Like a State': An Essay on the Historiography of Modern Iran," *International Journal of Middle East Studies* 42, no. 1 (2010): 37–61.

[3] All while taking into account third parties:

> this approach can build on Ann Stoler and Frederick Cooper's by now classic call to "treat [European] metropole and colony in a single analytic field." ... [The U.S. imperial-postcolonial field] emerged at the intersection of two equally historic postwar developments, the crystallization of anti-imperial liberation and the rise of a truly worldwide US empire. ... [Such] a symbiotic view of "the postcolonial/American" and "the domestic/foreign," through the concept of "the joint field," ... backs critiques of postwar US transnational history as a field that, while fruitfully undermining US exceptionalism, too often eschews empire. Moreover, it goes one step further than concepts like "circuits" or "two-way street" that

Third Parties

All chapters united here mention not only Americans and Iranians but third parties, too. John Ghazvinian shows that many US consular representatives of late Qajar Iran were Ottoman Armenian residents of the United States with ample commercial experience in carpets, the arts, and antiquities. The very title of the book Kelly J. Shannon discusses, Morgan Shuster's *The Strangling of Persia*, references a third party: European imperialist powers. The two powers that, at the time, were directly meddling in Iran were the Russians, who engineered Shuster's dismissal as Iran's treasurer-general in 1911, and the (to Shuster) somewhat less odious British. Kyle Olson demonstrates that US archaeologists were allowed to excavate in Iran from the 1930s only after Tehran and Paris agreed, partly due to persistent US mediation, to cancel the French archaeological monopoly signed in 1900. Firoozeh Kashani-Sabet argues that in British imperial eyes, and later those of the United States, the Persian Gulf was divided into two halves, with Iranians belonging only to the northern, not southern, shore. Gregory Brew shows that it was through contracts, in 1957, not only with US Pan American Oil but first with an Italian and a Japanese company, that Mohammad Reza Shah started to chip away at the domineering structure of the US-led 1954 oil consortium. Matthew Shannon, in his chapter on postwar US missionary-led educational institutions in Tehran, quotes headmasters Commodore B. Fisher and J. Richard Irvine as noting, respectively, that in the late 1930s their Community School was "quite a League of Nations" and that in the early 1950s pupils came "from all over the earth ... [including] from both sides of the Iron Curtain." Elite Iraqi Jewish residents of Tehran for decades enrolled their children, too. Richard Garlitz, writing on American technical assistance and educational modernization in Iran, states that the University of Southern California (USC) had run public administration training programs similar to that in Iran in Brazil and Turkey. Also, the other two US universities he focuses on, Utah State and Brigham Young, were active in yet other Third World countries. Jasamin Rostam-Kolayi notes that Peace Corps (PC) volunteers engaged in "people-to-people interactions ... [in many] communities in what was the Third World." Ida Yalzadeh mentions European-based Iranian anti-shah activities and their direct connection to opposition activities in the United States. While Camron Amin's discussion of professional transnational Iranians living in Michigan naturally keeps to Iranians and Americans, the US institutions that his interviewees mention, primarily the American Friends of the Middle East as well as the Educational

---

historians use to finesse our understanding of the United States' postwar nature as a great power that, however, was influenced by others, too. (Cyrus Schayegh, "Introduction and a Note on U.S. Imperial-Postcolonial Relations," in *Globalizing the U.S. Presidency*, ed. Schayegh, 8, 11.)

A related approach can be discerned in Robert McGreevey, Christopher T. Fisher, and Alan Dawley, *Global America: The United States in the Twentieth Century* (New York: Oxford University Press, 2018), for instance, when they argue on pp. 58 and 60 that "the more the United States embraced racial justifications for rule over others abroad, the more entrenched Jim Crow became at home," and that hence, "desegregation and decolonization would only arrive together."

Commission for Foreign Medical Graduates, were active not only in Iran but also in other Middle Eastern countries. Moreover, one interviewee, Dr. Shapoor Ansari, whose first foreign language growing up in Iran was French, explains that he came to Michigan, not another US state, because the French pharmaceutical company for which he early on worked as a traveling representative in the United States sent him there.[4]

The presence of third parties in the bilateral US-Iranian relationship is not exceptional. They factor into all bilateral relationships, certainly between countries. Take France and Germany. They are neighbors, fought three wars in seventy odd years (1871, 1914–18, and 1939–45), and formed an engine for the creation of the European Coal and Steel Community, in 1951, and the European Economic Community, in 1957, both of which are at the root of today's European Union. Also, their dense sociocultural ties inspired *histoire croisée* in the 1990s, which was soon used to conceptualize transnational relationships more broadly.[5] Even so, many aspects of the Franco-German relationship—not only military and political ones related to alliance building but also social, cultural, and economic ones—involve third parties.

Third parties matter doubly for a bilateral relationship like that between Iran and the United States. Not only are these two countries not neighbors, but they are not even part of the same region or continent, to reference two admittedly imprecise spatial categories. In consequence, what happens *en route* between Iran and the United States forms part of their relations.[6] Who exists in between has an impact as well—even on perceptions. Thus, Iranians visiting and working in the United States, like Hossein-Qoli Khān Nuri, Tehran's first ambassador to Washington in 1888-9, and Hajj Mirzā Mohammad-Ali Mo'in al-Saltaneh, who toured the country in 1893, routinely compared what they saw in the United States to Europe, and what they saw in Europe, *en route* to or from America, to the United States.[7] And when "by the early twentieth century more reports on American current affairs were appearing in Iranian newspapers, … they appear to have been mainly translations from the European press."[8] What is more, third parties mattered to US-Iranian relations because some were situated between the two countries. Some third parties were regional or world

---

[4] Quotes from this book on pp. 122, 152.
[5] Michael Werner and Bénédicte Zimmermann, "Beyond Comparison: *Histoire Croisée* and the Challenge of Reflexivity," *History and Theory* 45, no. 1 (2006): 30–50, building on an article of theirs in *Annales HSS* 58, no. 1 (2003): 7–36. The concept was initially developed in Michael Werner, "Le prisme franco-allemand: à propos d'une histoire croisée des disciplines littéraires," in *Entre Locarno et Vichy: Les relations culturelles franco-allemandes dans les années 1930*, ed. Hans Manfred Bock, Reinhart Meyer, and Michel Trebisch (Paris: CNRS, 1993), I, 303–16; Claude Didry, Peter Wagner, and Bénédicte Zimmermann, eds., *Le travail et la nation: Histoire croisée de la France et de l'Allemagne* (Paris: Editions de la Maison des sciences de l'homme, 1999).
[6] An example is police officer Abdollah Bahrāmi's 1925 journey to the United States. Nile Green, "Fordist Connections: The Automotive Integration of the United States and Iran," *Comparative Studies in Society and History* 58, no. 2 (2016): 290–331.
[7] Mohammad Ghanoonparvar, "Nineteenth-Century Iranians in America," in *Society and Culture in Qajar Iran: Studies in Honor of Hafez Farmayan*, ed. Elton Daniel (Costa Mesa, CA: Mazda, 2002), 239–48; Hossein Kamaly, "HĀJI VĀSANGTON," *Encyclopaedia Iranica*. Available online: https://iranicaonline.org/articles/haji-vasangton (accessed June 23, 2020).
[8] Green, "Fordist Connections," 295.

powers. Thus, they were not just present in US-Iranian relations. They helped shape and hence explain them, which also holds for some non-state actors like Ghazvinian's Armenians, one should add.

Looking at the flow of time covered in this volume from the viewpoint of third parties, one may distinguish between three periods.⁹ Through the 1910s, the most consequential third parties were the Ottoman Empire, the European empires, and their imperial visions and policies.¹⁰ Through most of the nineteenth century, "American missionaries collaborated with Great Britain. Until the establishment of diplomatic relations in 1883, U.S. interests in Iran were represented by the U.K. Even afterwards, U.S. missionary relations with nearby British consuls were close, especially in the absence of American consular representation."¹¹ By the 1910s Russian and British imperialist meddling in Iran exemplified to Shuster a broader issue, as Kelly Shannon points out: the issue of a global order dominated by European powers in which Washington did not play a primary role, at least until after the First World War.¹² As for Tehran, trying to keep London and Moscow from further encroachment made it turn to Washington, not only in 1911 but also unsuccessfully in 1919 at the Paris Peace Conference. In addition to Washington, Tehran contacted others, for instance, Italy (in vain) and Sweden (successfully), for a gendarmerie mission in 1911–15.¹³ In the interwar years, especially the 1930s, as Washington gingerly deepened its engagement in the Middle East, it did so not the least—and in Iran first—by associating itself with bodies wielding soft power instruments like archaeology.¹⁴ This step barely bothered the largest foreign presence in Iran, Britain, but did concern France, as Olson shows. Other third parties evidently figured into

---

⁹ A rapidly emerging body of literature that helps conceptualize the issue of third parties concerns inter-imperial relations. See, e.g., Simon Potter and Jonathan Saha, "Global History, Imperial History and Connected Histories of Empire," *Journal of Colonialism and Colonial History* 16, no. 1 (2015): doi:10.1353/cch.2015.0009; Daniel Hedinger and Nadine Hée, "Transimperial History—Connectivity, Cooperation and Competition," *Journal of Modern European History* 16, no. 4 (2018): 429–52; Kristin Hoganson and Jay Sexton, *Crossing Empires. Taking U.S. History into Transimperial Terrain* (London: Duke University Press, 2020).

¹⁰ It was not by chance that when the Iranian Ministry of Foreign Affairs was reorganized in 1881, its four departments covered Britain, Russia, the Ottoman Empire, and all other countries. Willem Floor, "Foreign Affairs," *Encyclopaedia Iranica*. Available online: https://www.iranicaonline.org/articles/foreign-affairs (accessed June 23, 2020).

¹¹ Michael Zirinsky, "A Panacea for the Ills of the Country: American Presbyterian Education in Inter-War Iran," *Iranian Studies* 26, nos. 1–2 (1993): 119–20. In Ottoman Beirut, to add another example, US missionaries got very close to European powers by the 1860s: Ussama Makdisi, "Reclaiming the Land of the Bible," *American Historical Review* 102, no. 3 (1997): 704.

¹² A recent restatement of this view is Katherine Epstein, "The Conundrum of American Power in the Age of World War I," *Modern American History* 2, no. 3 (2019): 345–65.

¹³ Oliver Bast, "La mission persane à la Conférence de Paix et l'accord anglo-persan de 1919," in *La Perse et la Grande Guerre*, ed. Oliver Bast (Louvain: Peeters, 2002); Markus Ineichen, *Die schwedischen Offiziere in Persien (1911–1916): Friedensengel, Weltgendarmen, oder Handelsagenten einer Kleinmacht im ausgehenden Zeitalter des Imperialismus?* (Bern: Peter Lang, 2002).

¹⁴ Two other cases are Ludovic Tournès, *Sciences de l'homme et politique: les fondations philanthropiques américaines en France au XXe siécle* (Paris: Classiques Garnier, 2011); Cyrus Schayegh, "The Interwar Germination of Development and Modernization Theory and Practice: Politics, Institution Building, and Knowledge Production between the Rockefeller Foundation and the American University of Beirut," *Geschichte und Gesellschaft* 41 (2015): 649–84.

this history. Think of, among others, Germany, Iran's Soviet neighbor, or British India, where US actors had sociocultural interests.[15] Finally, after the Second World War, in which Washington was London's junior partner in the Middle East, and with the coming of the Cold War, the overwhelming third party became the Soviet Union. At the same time, other third parties continued to matter. Three of many examples are Iran's CENTO partners; US allies like Britain and Israel; and Egypt, about whose President Nasser Washington and Tehran from the late 1950s had considerable differences. The Iranian establishment feared and loathed Nasser so much that Foreign Minister Ardeshir Zahedi once called him "a whore."[16] At the latest from the 1960s, Iranian Leftists saw Tel Aviv and Tehran as US "imperialism's two principal bases in the region. ... It is the duty of all anti-imperialist forces in the region to unite against and fight this Iranian-Israeli sinister axis."[17] As for Moscow, it cast a long shadow on matters both large and small. As is well known, it was basically for fear of a communist takeover that Washington led a coup in 1953. The coup turned Tehran into a US client state and has influenced US-Iranian relations ever since. On the ground in Iran, US advisers were concerned about how the Soviets related to Iranians and what this meant for Washington's interests. Thus, in 1951, a US Point Four delegation visiting Iran's border area with the Soviet Union reported that "it is one of the propaganda tricks of the Communists to show to the population living in these border areas that life is pleasant and enjoyable on the other side."[18] Meanwhile, Iranian officials habitually invoked Leftist dangers to try to get their way with their US patron.[19] Iranians understood well that their country, as others, was a playground of the US-Soviet symbolic-political competition, as the below caricature and car advertisement demonstrate (see Figures C.1 and C.2).

In sum, for interwoven geographical, perceptional, and geopolitical reasons, third parties have always helped shape US-Iranian relations.[20]

---

[15] Harald Fischer-Tiné, "Fitness for Modernity: The YMCA and Physical Education Schemes in Late Colonial South Asia (c. 1900–1940)," *Modern Asian Studies* 53, no. 2 (2019): 512–59; Heather Curtis, *Holy Humanitarians: American Evangelicals and Global Aid* (Cambridge, MA: Harvard University Press, 2018), chapter 4, on the *Christian Herald*'s intervention in the 1899 famine in India.

[16] Quote: Letter, Ardeshir Zahedi to the shah, February 3, 1967, reprinted with an English translation in Abbas Milani, ed., *A Window into Modern Iran: The Ardeshir Zahedi Papers at the Hoover Institution Library and Archives* (Stanford, CA: Hoover Institution Press, 2019), 178.

[17] "Bāyāniyeh-ye Cherik-hā-ye Fedā'i-ye Khalq darbāreh-ye naqsh-e imperialism va sahiyunism va sāyer-e mortaje'in va zarurat-e ettehād-e niru-hā-ye enqelābi dar manteqeh," *Nabard-e Khalq: Nashriyeh-ye Dākheli* 1 (Bahman 1352s [1973]): 7, 9.

[18] C. S. Stephanides, "Report to Trip to Azerbaijan and Kurdistan, Iran, September 17–28, 1951," p. 9, Iran/U.S. Joint Commission: box 1, Executive Office Subject Files (central files) 1951, Mission to Iran, Record Group 469, Records of US Foreign Assistance Agencies, US National Archives and Records Administration II (NARA), College Park, MD.

[19] Cyrus Schayegh, "Iran's Karaj Dam Affair: Emerging Mass Consumerism, the Politics of Promise, and the Cold War in the Third World," *Comparative Studies in Society and History* 54, no. 3 (2012): 612–43.

[20] A parallel case was the simultaneous presence and mutual impact of multiple development agencies from several countries in India. Corinna Unger, *Entwicklungspfade in Indien: eine internationale Geschichte, 1947–1980* (Göttingen: Wallstein, 2015); David Engerman, *The Price of Aid: The Economic Cold War in India* (Cambridge, MA: Harvard University Press, 2018).

Figure C.1 "Netayej-e siasi-ye mah-e masnu'i" [The political consequences of the satellite (Sputnik)], *Ettelā'āt*, October 20, 1957, p. 13. The caption on Khrushchev's chest reads "Pishraft-hā-ye 'elmi-ye shoravi" [the scientific advances of the Soviet Union]. The caricature was copied from the *New York Herald Tribune*, mentioned just above the main caption.

Figure C.2 "Har do bi-raqib-and. Eshkoda dar zamin va qamar-e masnuʿi dar āsemān" [Both are peerless: the Škoda on earth and the satellite (Sputnik) in the sky], *Ettelāʿāt*, October 17, 1957, p. 11. On the bottom, the contact details of the Tehran dealer. Škoda was a Czechoslovak, not Soviet, manufacturer, but basked in the glow of its patron's success.

The Overlap between State and Non-State Actors

State and non-state actors are not neatly separated in this volume's chapters. The Armenians whom the Iranian minister in Washington from 1900, Ishāq Khān Mofakhkham al-Dowleh, appointed as consuls were, and remained, merchants; Dikran

Kelekian even used his art gallery on New York's Fifth Avenue as his consulate. Morgan Shuster was not a US government employee while serving as Iran's treasurer-general in 1911. But President William Howard Taft personally recommended the ex-colonial officer, who had worked in Cuba and the Philippines from 1899 to 1909. This suggests that Tehran found him by contacting Washington rather than a private firm. In sum, he and his team were "conceivably informal representatives of the United States" in Iran, neither simply a private citizen nor a formal government employee. The University of Pennsylvania Museum of Archaeology sent Frederick Wulsin to Iran in 1930 on the advice of the US legation in Tehran, and he and other US archaeologists worked hand in glove with the legation to establish themselves in Iran. Archaeological "American institutions, through their prestige, financial clout, and personal connections to State Department officials, were able to extract concessions from the Persian government." To US *chargé d'affaires* Hugh Millard, "archaeology was the most effective means by which the United States could increase its prestige in Iran." In the late 1940s "the so-called social evangelism of missionaries paralleled the cultural programming of the US government during the Cold War" to the point that colleagues of Charles Hulac, the first head from 1947 to 1950 of the Alborz Foundation, derided him as a "functionary of the American Consulate." The foundation *inter alia* administered the English examination for Iranians interested in studying in the United States on the consulate's behalf. Although the official Iran-America Society assumed this task in 1951, the foundation's "most popular draws were its study abroad counseling program and English-language classes." It thus remained a "cultural representative of the United States in Iran." Meanwhile, the surge after the 1953 coup of Americans working in Iran boosted enrollment in another missionary institution, Tehran's Community School, which helped keep it attractive for non-Americans, too. Again postcoup Washington cited government-defined "national security" interests—keeping the shah afloat—when using "direct pressure and promises of favorable terms" to force US companies into the 1954 oil consortium. Overriding US antitrust legislation to legalize this move, the US Attorney General invoked national security as well. Others took note: Britain knew that US oil companies were in Iran for "political considerations." From the 1950s, US academics in departments as varied as agriculture, education, and public administration worked for shorter or longer stints for the Point Four Program, later the Agency for International Development. The PC, present in Iran from 1962, was "an arm of American foreign policy" whose activities, for instance, teaching English, *prima facie* buttressed the US position in the Third World. Meanwhile, PC volunteers were "classified as volunteer employees of the Iranian government." Many "deliberately separated themselves from other Americans, especially those involved in the military and USAID missions," and most if not all refused to see themselves as cogs in a bureaucratic wheel. Rather, they were individuals with ideals and a thirst to experience the world—and not its rich, but its poor, nations. Last, the American Friends of the Middle East and the Educational Commission for Foreign Medical Graduates, while not government entities, worked hand in hand with US diplomatic and consular representatives in Iran to help execute US policies. As Camron Amin's interviewee Hasan Alizadeh noted: "Well, it was like, uh, super easy [to get to the United States from Iran] [*shrugs*], we had an American embassy [i.e., *consulate*] in Tabriz. So, you know, around there. The American Friends of the Middle East—they had all these things arranged."[21]

One can sort this vast and varied gray zone between state and non-state actors in various ways. For our purposes, the best approach pivots around the question of how that gray zone illuminates bilateral relations.

Let us start by observing the gray area chronologically. The last section distinguished between three periods (as covered by chapters in this volume) regarding third parties to US-Iranian relations: the years up to the 1910s, the interwar decades, and the early post-Second World War years through the 1960s. This tripartite periodization characterizes the development of the gray zone between non-state and state actors. This was not by chance. In each period, the broad environment of US-Iranian relations that third parties helped create was a factor in shaping the gray zone.

From about the 1850s a sizable American (and European) upper-middle and upper class bought increasing numbers of Iranian carpets, helping to augment, change, and diversify the international demand for that good.[22] Even so, Tehran had a very limited official presence in Washington. As noted, its first ambassador there served during 1888-9; from then until 1900, Iran did not have permanent diplomatic representation. The use, from 1900, of Ottoman Armenian US merchants helped bridge the gap between commerce and political representation. As for Washington, it had a very limited footprint in Iran, although Protestant US missionaries had arrived in 1834. Its first diplomat to Tehran, Samuel Benjamin, arrived in 1883. In constitutional revolutionary Iran, Washington did not want to officially torpedo Russia and certainly not Britain, the world's largest empire with which good relations mattered in the Western Hemisphere. Then again, the post-Spanish War United States, now master of considerable imperial possessions farther away from home and from its Central American glacis, sought to unobtrusively sharpen its presence in Asia. The Shuster Mission reflected this situation. Shuster was a known entity in Washington and, given Taft's recommendation, US officials knew that Tehran understood this. Thus, an opening to Tehran was made. But this was a low-stakes move because Shuster was the only American working for Tehran, and he was not an official US representative. By operating in this manner, Washington did not directly challenge the formal post-1907 accord between British and Russian stakeholders in Iran. When Moscow killed Shuster's job, Washington could afford *not* to protest without losing face. This gray zone between state and non-state actors differed from the case of Tehran's Armenian consular representatives. These were useful, presumably because they shared the US majority's Christian faith, and more importantly because they were mediators *par excellence*. They were well networked in the Middle Eastern Ottoman Empire as well as in the United States and probably—empirical study would clarify—elsewhere, too. That is, these US-based Armenian merchants of the modern period "worked" in two senses of the word. They worked for Tehran because their lives and businesses

---

[21] Quotes from this book on pp. 37, 70, 72, 99, 101, 115–17, 155–6, 192.
[22] Annette Ittig, "CARPETS xi. Qajar Period," *Encyclopaedia Iranica*. Available online: http://www.iranicaonline.org/articles/carpets-xi (accessed June 24, 2020).

descended from multigenerational world-embracing diasporic networks: a reach that Qajar Iran, squeezed by European pressures, lacked and evidently hoped to tap into.[23]

In the interwar period the gray zone between US state and non-state actors present in Iran shifted. There were more actors. Besides the archaeologists were also the 1922–7 Arthur Millspaugh finance mission and an ultimately aborted interest, by US engineering companies, in helping build the Trans-Iranian Railway, among others. The overlap with the US state tended to be tighter during the interwar period. Recall the archaeologists' relationship with the US legation. Millspaugh, too, was more directly linked to Washington than Shuster had been. However, it seems that US missionaries did not really become more directly intertwined with the US legation than before the 1910s, in part because they nurtured direct relations with high-ranking Iranian officials.[24] In parallel, even by 1934 the US State Department still judged that "American interests in Persia today center largely around the activities of the Presbyterian Board of Foreign Missions."[25] This limited shift occurred for three intertwined reasons: Washington's interest in Iran was creeping up; Europeans stopped directly meddling in Iranian politics, though Britain remained formidable due to the Anglo-Iranian Oil Company; and Tehran became more fully sovereign.

Another change occurred from the later 1940s,[26] turning into a real jump following the coup of 1953. In the Cold War, Washington's stakes became sky-high in Iran, for it was a large Soviet neighbor and hence a frontier in the US strategy of Soviet containment, whose two key pillars were situated in East Asia and Western Europe. As a result, the gray area between state and non-state actors involving the United States and Iran grew and ties became inextricable.

Let us look at three dimensions of this reality. The first is Washington's. To hold the line in Iran, the US government brought into its orbit a massive range of existing and new non-state institutions, including many discussed in this volume. I say "range" on purpose, for the Cold War was in many ways a total war because it involved all aspects of human life. At the latest from the Korean War it took place not only in the First and Second but also in the Third World, to use the period's own terminology. Even when some US officials until the early 1960s believed this war could be won (by 1949 both superpowers had nuclear weapons), Washington understood that soldiers and spies alone

---

[23] It'd be interesting to compare these moves by Qajar Iran to the Ottoman Empire's endeavor to assert its presence worldwide as a means to counteract European pressures and assert its equality—internationally and in terms of formal diplomatic presence—to Europe from the later nineteenth century. See, e.g., Mostafa Minawi, *The Ottoman Scramble for Africa* (Stanford, CA: Stanford University Press, 2016); Renee Worringer, *Ottomans Imagining Japan* (New York: Palgrave, 2014), which includes discussion of Ottoman officials in Japan; and Azmi Özcan, *Pan-Islamism: Indian Muslims, the Ottomans, and Britain* (Leiden: Brill, 1997).

[24] Jasamin Rostam-Kolayi, "From Evangelizing to Modernizing Iranians: The American Presbyterian Mission and its Iranian Students," *Iranian Studies* 41, no. 2 (2008): 236.

[25] Quoted in Zirinsky, "Panacea," 121. Some US missionary organizations even criticized Washington. Thus, the Committee of Cooperation in Latin America and the Fellowship of Reconciliation opposed interwar US policy in Latin America: Geneviève Dorais, "Missionary Critiques of Empire, 1920–1932: Between Interventionism and Anti-imperialism," *International History Review* 39, no. 3 (2017): 377–403.

[26] One may posit roots in the Second World War. Consider the second Millspaugh mission, in 1942–5, which was more formally US government sponsored than the first one.

would not do. Neither did diplomats. Many more and different experts were needed. But the US government, as big as it had become in the Second World War, did not possess them all. Hence, it urgently needed to bring a plethora of non-state actors into its orbit, some for the first time and others closer than before. Cold War historians focused on the United States have studied this story, often field by field. Studies exist regarding area studies, missionaries, the PC, oil, and the press, to just name a few. They have shown that all fields and actors were in some form affected by Washington's (however changing and heterogeneous) national security considerations.[27]

There was another side to this coin: our second dimension. The US non-state actors whom Washington recruited and pulled closer kept their own identities, idea(l)s, goals, and forms of capital, to however varying degrees. This was the exact reason why they interested Washington: a fascinating paradox. Not being feeble, inexperienced, and shallowly rooted in American society and economy, they could deliver, Washington hoped. But this selfsame fact, their relative strength, also meant that their selves did not simply dissolve when getting closer to Washington, though they certainly shifted. Many of these actors partook in a sweeping US consensus, until the mid-1960s, about what the Cold War was at its core—a fight between right and wrong if not good and evil—and about the need to win over the world. Moreover, as they differed from each other and from US state officials, positions could vary. Two examples from this volume's chapters are missionaries calling their peer Hulac a "functionary of the American Consulate" and many PC members socially avoiding other US functionaries. At the same time, some US actions on the ground and even some policies were partly shaped by non-state actors. They did not just reflect a presumably monolithic and purely "political" Washingtonian interest. For example, Washington did not simply use pressure to force US oil companies into the 1954 consortium but, as noted, offered carrots through the terms of the consortium deal. These in turn contributed to persistent tensions between Iran (and other non-Western oil producers) and Western oil companies. By the 1970s these tensions were "solved" in a way that shook US domestic life and politics, a development that symbolically peaked in President Jimmy Carter's so-called malaise speech of July 1979.[28] All told, the US presence abroad on the ground was exceptionally complex, certainly in a country like Iran, the playground of so many different US actors.

What made this situation even more complex was the fact that Iranian state actors could, and did, deal with US non-state actors directly: our third dimension. An example is the relationship that Abol-Hassan Ebtehāj, the head of Iran's Plan Organization in 1954–9, built with the US company Development and Resources (D&R). This company was cofounded in 1955 by David Lilienthal and Gordon Clapp, high-level

---

[27] Zachary Lockman, *Field Notes: The Making of Middle East Studies in the United States* (Stanford, CA: Stanford University Press, 2016); David Hadley, *The Rising Clamor: The American Press, the Central Intelligence Agency, and the Cold War* (Lexington: University Press of Kentucky, 2019); Elizabeth Cobbs Hoffman, *All You Need Is Love: The Peace Corps and the Spirit of the 1960s* (Cambridge, MA: Harvard University Press, 1998); William Inboden, *Religion and American Foreign Policy, 1946–1960: The Soul of Containment* (Cambridge: Cambridge University Press, 2008).

[28] Daniel Horowitz, *Jimmy Carter and the Energy Crisis of the 1970s: The "Crisis of Confidence" Speech of July 15, 1979* (Boston, MA: St. Martin's Press, 2005).

ex-officials of a signature New Deal project, the Tennessee Valley Authority. In Iran and elsewhere, including South Vietnam, D&R formed part of a broad Washingtonian Cold War consensus. But at the same time it nurtured its own image and pursued its proper interests;[29] was subject to Republican critique in the 1950s;[30] and in 1962 was summoned to a hearing at the Senate. The US Senate demanded a "reasonably full and accurate picture of the way in which the D&R Corporation carries on its contractual relationships with, and on behalf of, the Government of Iran—one of the largest recipients of American aid. We believe this is a legitimate concern of the Committee on Foreign Relations."[31] Moreover, while US non-state and state actors abroad saw and even cherished their differences, these looked less consequential to Iranian officials and private citizens. As *Āmrikā* was Iran's patron, any *Āmrikāi* who was in Iran in any institutional capacity was by definition a representative of that country. This viewpoint, while perhaps crude from a US perspective, reflected a real geopolitical inequality between the two countries. When Fakhri Garakani, a woman who in 1961 sent a beautiful needlework image to President John F. Kennedy, requested a missionary in her birthplace of Rasht to ask an ex-missionary Princeton professor who had come through to inquire about the parcel's fate in Washington, she ignored the distinction between non-state and state actors. She was right. The professor, T. Cuyler Young, made the inquiry successfully and without effort.[32]

Two notes can be added to the above chronologically ordered observations. One concerns perspective. Iranians and Americans perceived the gray zone differently. Consider two examples. When Shuster was Tehran's treasurer-general, Iranian officials tried to tighten their relationship with Washington through him. He "demurred." And PC member Tim Thomas likely thought of himself as a volunteer with some ideals independent from Washington's state interests, or Tehran's for that matter. But he was squarely a representative of US state power to the Iranians who "tasked [him] with overseeing and certifying elections" that turned out to be shot through with "fraudulent procedures" and who cajoled him to nonetheless "certify the results and participate in the ceremonial signing of documents, take photographs with local officials, and attend the celebratory feasts." Also, Iranian officials were able to exploit Thomas for their own political ends in the Gilaki area in which he worked. Although on a macro-political scale Iran was a US client, the situation on the ground was more complex.[33]

The second note regards location. In this volume's chapters the gray zone, for the most part, concerns US actors and institutions in Iran. In a sense this is a selection bias. Most chapters study Americans in Iran rather than Iranians in the United States or encounters in third locations. Could this balance have been different? In principle, yes.

---

[29] Christopher T. Fisher, "'Moral Purpose is the Important Thing': David Lilienthal, Iran, and the Meaning of Development in the US, 1956–63," *International History Review* 33, no. 3 (2011): 431–51.
[30] David Ekbladh, "'Mr. TVA': Grass-Roots Development, David Lilienthal, and the Rise and Fall of the Tennessee Valley Authority as a Symbol for U.S. Overseas Development, 1933–1973," *Diplomatic History* 26, no. 3 (2002): 355–6.
[31] Quote: Letter, Gordon Clapp to committee chairman Senator J. W. Fulbright, January 26, 1962, folder 2, box 564, MC014 (Development and Resources), Princeton University Archives, quoting a letter from January 11, 1962 by Fulbright to Clapp.
[32] Schayegh, "Foreign Gifts," 133.
[33] Quotes from this book on pp. 47, 159.

Third locations existed at institutions such as the American University of Beirut and in international organizations like the United Nations.[34] And while the American population in Iran spiked during the Second World War with the arrival of tens of thousands of US noncombat troops, and again in the 1970s during the oil and defense contract boom, the volume of Iranian movement to the United States increased steadily during the postwar decades and warrants more attention from scholars. In fact, Iranian migration to, and settlement in, the United States began much earlier. It began as early as the years covered by Ghazvinian, who mentions Assyrian Iranians arriving from the 1880s and numbering over one thousand by 1910 in Chicago alone. Then again, there were more individual US institutions in Iran than there were Iranian institutions in the United States. They included not only the legation/embassy and consulates but also missionaries, museums, translation offices, oil companies, and university academics, to only mention some.

The Ambiguous Nature of US Imperial Power

The last two notes, about varying perspectives and institutional imbalance, share a key trait: inequality. As a matter of fact, the modern-time relationship between the United States and Iran as countries and between American and Iranian individuals has never been that of equals. Until 1953, that inequality was not structurally imperial. Not all unequal relationships involve empire, after all. But all relationships involving an empire are unequal.[35] The US-Iranian relationship from 1953 to the early 1970s is a good example. There are, however, different kinds of inequality. That characterizing US-Iranian relations in those two decades was truly intricate and provides a beautiful case on which to reflect.

Let me start with a note that draws on Brew's chapter. In 1957 Washington encouraged the shah to sign the aforenoted two contracts with an Italian and Japanese oil company, whose terms were better for Iran than those of the 1954 consortium. Moreover, 60 percent of the latter was controlled by non-US oil companies, including 40 percent by British Petroleum (the former Anglo-Iranian Oil Company), 14 percent by Royal Dutch/Shell, and 6 percent by the Compagnie Française des Pétroles, despite the postcoup Iranian government's initial existential dependence on Washington. Thus, after the Second World War the US empire was "international" not only in that it operated through and with other nation-states like Iran, undermining while also accepting and in some aspects buttressing their sovereignty.[36] It was "international" also because in many countries in Asia (from the 1940s and 1950s) and in Africa (from the late 1950s and 1960s), Washington did not operate on its own.[37] To be clear, Washington habitually set policy terms and overall

---

[34] Farzin Vejdani, "The Iranians of AUB and Middle Class Formation in the Early Twentieth-Century Middle East," *British Journal of Middle Eastern Studies* 43, no. 4 (2016): 486–506; for an account during the First World War, see *Yād-dāsht-hā-ye Doktor Qāssem Ghāni* (London: Ithaca Press, 1980), vol. 1.

[35] For inequality framed as difference, see Jane Burbank and Frederick Cooper, *Empires in World History: Power and the Politics of Difference* (Princeton, NJ: Princeton University Press, 2011).

[36] Paul Kramer, "Power and Connection: Imperial Histories of the United States in the World," *American Historical Review* 116, no. 5 (2011): 1366.

[37] Furthermore, in some places Washington let others take the lead into the late 1950s. Classic: William Louis and Ronald Robinson, "The Imperialism of Decolonization," *Journal of Imperial and Commonwealth History* 22, no. 3 (1994): 462–511.

frameworks, implemented policy, and made sure that US non-state actors got their due. But it did not try to keep all the spoils and it often tried to tie in its closest allies such as Britain, other key NATO members, Japan, New Zealand, Australia, and often South Africa. It did so because those allies—many of which had been empires, still had imperial possessions, or had been key parts of an empire, like ex-British white dominions— were deeply networked in African and Asian areas and hence helped contain the Soviet Union and its camp. By this point, Washington's fear of being associated with European imperialism ultimately weighed less in the minds of policymakers.[38] In sum, the Cold War international setting of the US empire differed substantially from that of, say, the high European imperialism of the late nineteenth century. In consequence, imperial Washington quite often acted as an overbearing and commanding team leader, something that imperial London or Paris never did.[39]

A second note concerns the question of how structural inequalities that are internationally political—here, imperial—in origin become manifest in personal relations. Rostam-Kolayi provides particularly useful points because she conducts searching oral history interviews with former members of the US Peace Corps. They likely were the Americans working in 1960s–1970s Iran furthest away from an imperial mindset. She demonstrates "strong personal bonds and friendships that transcended political, national, and religious boundaries" and reminds us that a good number of PC members married Iranians, stayed in Iran, and/or helped Iranians to move to the United States, among other things. Still, structural inequalities mattered. Let me pick out three. One concerned the knowledge conditions under which Iranians met American PC members. Most of the latter knew very little about Iran, whereas "for many Iranians in the 1960s, Āmrikā had already made its mark on Iran." Moreover, some PC members had what we may call a developmentalist imperial mental map of the world that included poor non-white areas of the United States. As one recalls: "Went to Iran, had my eyes opened and got used to working with a variety of other people … [Later] [I was] dropped in … the middle of inner city Detroit. A lot of people couldn't handle it and left. I just thought it was an extension of Iran … I was well-suited to adapt." And finally, PC members possessed a hefty capital: language. Most taught English in Iran—and this American English was "Iran's language of 'development' and 'progress'" by the 1960s.[40] By way of contrast, before the 1940s US missionaries in Iran did not stress English teaching.[41] In sum, postcoup Americans and Iranians could not ignore the framing force of imperial power. To frame did not mean to determine, though. It

---

[38] Ibid.
[39] A useful set of reflections on Washington's embeddedness is the debate, in H-Diplo Roundtable XXI-42, of Daniel Bessner and Fredrik Logevall, "Recentering the United States in the Historiography of American Foreign Relations," *Texas National Security Review* 3, no. 2 (2020): 38–55. Available online: https://hdiplo.org/to/RT21-42 (accessed June 29, 2020). For a longer view, see Hoganson and Sexton, *Crossing Empires*.
[40] Quotes from this book on pp. 152, 157, 159, 163. Moscow sought to export Russian, too, in the Cold War. Rachel Applebaum, "The Rise of Russian in the Cold War: How Three Worlds Made a World Language," *Kritika* 21, no. 2 (2020): 347–70.
[41] Zirinsky, "Panacea," 127. The British sought to use English for their imperial ends, too, in Iran. "Sir Reader Bullard, Britain's ambassador to Tehran during the Second World War, wrote [a propos the British Council] that promoting English 'give[s] us contact with the younger generation and an opportunity to influence them in a pro-British direction.'" Robert Steele, *The Shah's Imperial*

meant that the inequality inherent in the postcoup US-Iranian relationship was always in the room when an American and an Iranian met. They could deal in myriad ways with it—but to honestly, fully, and lastingly ignore it was impossible. This dimension always advantaged the American, sooner or later, whether a man or a woman, white or non-white, old or young, rich or poor, heterosexual or not. It was the one non-variable in interpersonal US-Iranian dialogues.

Let me end with an argument. Perhaps more than other modern empires, the Cold War United States contained, or even unwittingly created, within itself and within the international milieu it helped shape, opportunities for popular protest and limited governmental emancipation in the Third World.[42] One reason for this is the heterogeneous demographic composition of the United States. This facilitated anti-racist and anti-imperialist alliances in the United States between often non-white US citizens and immigrants from the Third World, a development that peaked in the 1960s and 1970s. As Ida Yalzadeh illustrates, such alliances had not only general value. They mattered for concrete reasons like organizing protests, fundraising, and navigating the US legal system.[43] Furthermore, the acceptance, for economic and political *raison d'état*, of non-white worker and student migrants into the Cold War United States was a key precondition for such actors to be able to meet *at all* on US soil.[44] Rooted in the late Truman administration, this acceptance crystallized in the 1965 Immigration and Nationality Act. Despite limits, it abolished the 1924 Immigration Act and an official preference for white European migration that dated back to the republic's earliest days. Changes to US immigration law responded to sustained foreign and domestic pressures against such racism, and in effect energized African and Asian immigration.

A final aspect has to do with imperial Washington working with and through other nation-states, as already noted. This compromised such states' sovereignty, always *de facto* and often also formally, as when the Iranian Majles in 1964 granted US military personnel in Iran and their dependents full diplomatic immunity. Indeed, in Iran, Washington enjoyed its most far-reaching status-of-forces agreement worldwide. But it was easier for those nation-states to pursue *de facto* fuller sovereignty in word and/ or deed (while remaining allied with the United States) than it had been for European colonies to obtain *de jure* independence. The real powers and the trappings of power of the nation-states within the US imperial orbit really did matter. This was the case doubly because of the ever more global Cold War context of bilateral relations with

---

Celebrations of 1971: Nationalism, Culture, and Politics in Late Pahlavi Iran (London: I.B. Tauris, 2021), 101.

[42] This situation has European parallels. Various critics of empire demanded that political ideas and rights currents in Europe, especially democratic and/or liberal ones, cover them, too. See, e.g., Frederick Cooper, *Citizenship between Empire and Nation: Remaking France and French Africa, 1945–1960* (Princeton, NJ: Princeton University Press, 2016).

[43] See also Matthew K. Shannon, *Losing Hearts and Minds: American-Iranian Relations and International Education during the Cold War* (Ithaca, NY: Cornell University Press, 2017); Afshin Matin-Asgari, *Iranian Student Opposition to the Shah* (Costa Mesa, CA: Mazda, 2002).

[44] This held for other Western countries, too. Quinn Slobodian, *Foreign Front: Third World Politics in Sixties West Germany* (Durham, NC: Duke University Press, 2012).

Third World countries. While many countries and peoples depended on the United States, Washington also depended on them to protect US-defined security interests. Already in the late 1930s the threat posed by the rising Japanese and German empires made Washington broaden its national security conception beyond the American continent and the two oceans separating it from Eurafrasia. By the early Cold War that conception had become fully globalized as no point of the world was considered unimportant anymore to the United States' very own security.[45] This view gave Third World countries leverage vis-à-vis Washington and could help them to assert their sovereign elbowroom—as long as they remained within the US orbit, that is.[46] Here lay the very ambiguity of the US empire. To quote US Ambassador Armin Meyer, Washington had to "insure that after take-off Iran will still remain [a] member of our flying club."[47]

A good example of a US client state's own power appears in Garlitz's chapter. He shows that relatively low-level US state functionaries, here academic development agents, had little leverage over Iranian administrators. There were "limits of transferability" to US ideas and projects. Iranians took what they wanted—principally, the dollars underwriting US development projects—but often disregarded technical advice. Some "Americans ... promoted subjects that had previously enjoyed little or no standing within Iranian universities," and a good number of Iranian professionals felt that their social standing was being threatened. "Many American pedagogical reforms either met resistance from Iranian academic leaders or proved ephemeral." Even programs that were evaluated as having accomplished something, like USC's, ultimately had a "limited impact on the Iranian government," which it sought to help reform.[48]

Other examples involve highest-level decision makers. A case in point was the shah's pressure on Washington to accept his wish to buy more arms. He started to push hard in 1965, after the Kennedy administration, with which he had a rocky relationship, and once he started to become financially more secure. That financial security emerged a few years after the beginning of the oil-sales-related "subtle shift in the balance of power" that Brew diagnosed for the late 1950s, and especially following the 1963 White Revolution.[49] The shah was "tired of being treated like a schoolboy."[50] His pressure mounted as Washington got embroiled in Vietnam, and as it looked as if US military installations may have to move from Pakistan to Iran after Washington abandoned Islamabad in the 1965 war with New Delhi. In 1966 the shah

---

[45] David Ekbladh, "Present at the Creation: Edward Mead Earle and the Depression-Era Origins of Security Studies," *International Security* 36, no. 3 (2011–12): 107–41; Andrew Preston, "Monsters Everywhere: A Genealogy of National Security," *Diplomatic History* 38, no. 3 (2014): 477–500.
[46] Tony Smith, "New Bottles for New Wine: A Pericentric Framework for the Study of the Cold War," *Diplomatic History* 24, no. 4 (2000): 567–92.
[47] Quoted in Andrew Johns, "The Johnson Administration, the Shah of Iran, and the Changing Pattern of U.S.-Iranian Relations, 1965–1967," *Journal of Cold War Studies* 9, no. 2 (2007): 76.
[48] Quotes from this book on pp. 133, 141–2, 146–7.
[49] Quote from this book on p. 97.
[50] Johns, "The Johnson Administration," 83.

even threatened to buy Soviet arms, which he ultimately did.⁵¹ By 1967 Washington blinked. For the aforenoted Cold War considerations, it agreed to sell Tehran more arms, and at better payment conditions. This marked a turning point in US-Iranian relations, doubly because Washington phased out its development assistance the same year.⁵²

As this and myriad cases in this volume show, US-Iranian relations burst with fascinating developments and intriguing stories. Many remain untold. The authors of this volume prove they are worth telling and of genuine interest for specialists and other scholars alike.

---

⁵¹ Key documents for this story are accessible in *Foreign Relations of the United States, 1964–1968: Volume XXII, Iran*, documents 94–5, 98–100, 105, 108–11, 114, 124, 129, 136–46, 148–9, 151–4, 158, 160–1, 165–6, 168–76, 185, 191–2, 199, and 201. Available online: https://history.state.gov/historicaldocuments/frus1964-68v22 (accessed April 12, 2021). See also Johns, "The Johnson Administration"; Claudia Castiglioni, "No Longer a Client, Not yet a Partner: The US–Iranian Alliance in the Johnson Years," *Cold War History* 15, no. 4 (2015): 491–509. The Soviet arms purchase was minor, i.e., mainly political, and meant to signal to the world and Iranians that the shah was independent. The Johnson administration was angered but let the matter pass, as it did with a Soviet-Iranian economic project signed in 1966.

⁵² This trend was accentuated by the early 1970s. Roham Alvandi, *Nixon, Kissinger, and the Shah: The United States and Iran in the Cold War* (New York: Oxford University Press, 2014); Sepehr Zabih, "Iran's International Posture: De Facto Non-Alignment within a pro-Western Alliance," *Middle East Journal* 24, no. 3 (1970): 302–18, identifying détente as the underlying cause.

Bibliography

This bibliography includes a selection of sources used in the chapters and identified by the authors as significant to their approach to studying American-Iranian relations. This list of sources is by no means a comprehensive works-cited page for the volume. For a complete accounting of sources and full citations, consult the footnotes in each chapter. It is hoped that this list will serve as a bibliographic abstract that, in a few lines, provides a representative sample of our sources and methods.

Archives

Archives of the Ministry of Foreign Affairs, Tehran, Islamic Republic of Iran.
Brigham Young University, Provo, UT. L. Tom Perry Special Collections.
Briscoe Center for American History, Austin, TX. ExxonMobil Collection.
Church History Library, Salt Lake City, UT. Franklin Harris Diaries.
Library of Congress, Washington, DC. Manuscript Division, W. Morgan Shuster Papers: MMC323.
National Archives and Records Administration of the United States, College Park, MD.
    Record Group 59: General Records of the Department of State
    Record Group 286: Records of the Agency for International Development
    Record Group 306: Records of the United States Information Agency
    Record Group 350: Records of the Bureau of Insular Affairs
    Record Group 469: Records of US Foreign Assistance Agencies
    Record Group 490: Records of the Peace Corps
National Archives of the United Kingdom, Kew, United Kingdom.
National Library and Archives of Iran, Tehran, Islamic Republic of Iran.
New York Public Library, Manuscripts and Archives Division, New York City. Arthur Upham Pope Papers.
Parviz Shokat Personal Collection, Berkeley, CA. Accessed October 2019.
Presbyterian Historical Society, Philadelphia, PA.
    Record Group 91: PCUSA, Board of Foreign Missions, Secretaries' Files, Iran Mission, 1881–1968.
    Record Group 161: PCUSA/UPCUSA, Board of Foreign Missions / COEMAR, Secretaries' Files, Iran Mission, 1956–73.
Presidential Library of Harry Truman, Independence, MO. John Ohly Papers.
Presidential Library of Lyndon Johnson, Austin, TX. National Security File.
Princeton University Archives, Princeton, NJ.
    Alumni Records Collection
    Development and Resources Corporation Records
University of Arkansas Libraries Special Collections, Fayetteville, AR. Manuscript Collection 468: Bureau of Educational and Cultural Affairs Historical Collection.

University of California, Berkeley, Bancroft Library. Social Protest Collection: BANC MSS 86/157 c.
University of Michigan, Special Collections, Ann Arbor, MI. Labadie Collection.
University of Pennsylvania Museum of Archaeology and Anthropology Administrative Records, Philadelphia, PA.
    Horace H.F. Jayne Director's Office Records
    Tureng Tepe, Iran Expedition Records
    Unaccessioned Hasanlu Archive Correspondence Files
University of Warwick, Coventry, United Kingdom. British Petroleum Archive.
Utah State University, Logan, UT. Special Collections and Archives.

Digital Resources and Published Sources

Alexander, Yonah, and Allan Nanes, eds. *The United States and Iran: A Documentary History*. Frederick, MD: University Publications of America, 1980.
Amuzegar, Jahangir. *Technical Assistance in Theory and Practice: The Case of Iran*. New York: Praeger, 1967.
Bay Area Television Archive: https://diva.sfsu.edu/collections/sfbatv.
Ettelāʿāt
Foreign Relations of the United States (*FRUS*): http://history.state.gov/historicaldocuments
Foundation for Iranian Studies.
    Development Series: https://fis-iran.org/en/resources/development-series.
    Oral History Collection: https://fis-iran.org/en/oralhistory.
Klobe, Tom. *A Young American in Iran*. Oakland, CA: Peace Corps Writers, 2014.
Marks, Mary. *Walled In, Walled Out: A Young American Woman in Iran*. Oakland, CA: Peace Corps Writers, 2017.
Michigan Iranian-American Oral History Project: https://library.umd.umich.edu/miaohp/index.php.
Milani, Abbas, ed. *A Window into Modern Iran: The Ardeshir Zahedi Papers at the Hoover Institution Library and Archives*. Stanford, CA: Hoover Institution Press, 2019.
Peace Corps Iran Association: https://www.peacecorpsiran.org/cpages/home.
ProQuest Congressional.
ProQuest Historical Newspapers.
ProQuest History Vault.
Qatar Digital Library: https://www.qdl.qa/en.
Saleh, Ali Pasha, ed. *Cultural Ties between Iran and the United States*. Tehran: Her Imperial Majesty's National Committee for the American Revolution Bicentennial, 1976.
"Seven Years in Iran: The Final Report of a Technical Assistance Project in Public Administration under US Contract No. ICAC-1299." Los Angeles: University of Southern California School of Public Administration, June 1962.
Shuster, W. Morgan. *The Strangling of Persia: Story of the European Diplomacy and Oriental Intrigue That Resulted in the Denationalization of Twelve Million Mohammedans: A Personal Narrative*. New York: Century, 1912; Washington, DC: Mage, 1987.
Warne, William. *Mission for Peace: Point Four in Iran*. Bethesda, MD: Ibex, 1999.

Secondary Sources

Abrahamian, Ervand. *A History of Modern Iran*. Cambridge: Cambridge University Press, 2008.

Alvandi, Roham. *Nixon, Kissinger, and the Shah: The United States and Iran in the Cold War*. New York: Oxford University Press, 2014.

Alvandi, Roham, ed. *The Age of Aryamehr: Late Pahlavi Iran and its Global Entanglements*. London: Gingko, 2018.

Amanat, Abbas, and Farzin Vejdani, eds. *Iran Facing Others: Identity Boundaries in a Historical Perspective*. New York: Palgrave Macmillan, 2012.

Amin, Camron Michael. "Gender, Madness, Religion, and Iranian-American Identity: Observations on a 2006 Murder Trial in Williamsport, Pennsylvania." *Social Sciences* 6, no. 3 (2017): https://www.mdpi.com/2076-0760/6/3/85.

Ansari, Ali, ed. *Perceptions of Iran: History, Myths and Nationalism from Medieval Persia to the Islamic Republic*. New York: I.B. Tauris, 2014.

Bagot, David, and Margaux Whiskin, eds. *Iran and the West: Cultural Perceptions from the Sasanian Empire to the Islamic Republic*. New York: I.B. Tauris, 2018.

Bill, James. *The Eagle and the Lion: The Tragedy of American-Iranian Relations*. New Haven, CT: Yale University Press, 1988.

Brew, Gregory. "'What They Need Is Management:' American NGOs, the Second Seven Year Plan and Economic Development in Iran, 1954–1963." *International History Review* 41, no. 1 (2019): 1–22.

Chehabi, Houchang, and Vanessa Martin, eds. *Iran's Constitutional Revolution: Popular Politics, Cultural Transformation and Transnational Connections*. London: I.B. Taurus in Association with Iran Heritage Foundation, 2010.

Costigliola, Frank, and Michael Hogan, eds. *Explaining the History of American Foreign Relations*. 3rd ed. New York: Cambridge University Press, 2016.

Dabashi, Hamid. *Persophilia: Persian Culture on the Global Scene*. Cambridge, MA: Harvard University Press, 2015.

Dorman, William, and Mansour Farhang. *The U.S. Press and Iran: Foreign Policy and the Journalism of Deference*. Berkeley: University of California Press, 1987.

Garlitz, Richard. *A Mission for Development: Utah Universities and the Point Four Program in Iran*. Logan: Utah State University Press, 2018.

Gasiorowski, Mark. *U.S. Foreign Policy and the Shah: Building a Client State in Iran*. Ithaca, NY: Cornell University Press, 1991.

Ghazvinian, John. *America and Iran: A History, 1720 to the Present*. New York: Knopf, 2021.

Goode, James F. *The United States and Iran, 1946–1951: The Diplomacy of Neglect*. New York: St. Martin's Press, 1989.

Goode, James F. *The United States and Iran: In the Shadow of Musaddiq*. New York: St. Martin's Press, 1997.

Goode, James F. *Negotiating for the Past: Archaeology, Nationalism, and Diplomacy in the Middle East, 1919–1941*. Austin: University of Texas Press, 2007.

Green, Nile. "Fordist Connections: The Automotive Integration of the United States and Iran." *Comparative Studies in Society and History* 58, no. 2 (2016): 290–331.

Gutekunst, Miriam, Andreas Hackl, Sabina Leoncini, Julia Sophia Schwarz, and Irane Götz, eds. *Bounded Mobilities: Ethnographic Perspectives on Social Hierarchies and Global Inequalities*. Bielefeld: Transcript Verlag, 2016.

Heiss, Mary Ann. *Empire and Nationhood: The United States, Great Britain, and Iranian Oil, 1950–1954*. New York: Columbia University Press, 1997.

Kashani-Sabet, Firoozeh. "American Crosses, Persian Crescents: Religion and the Diplomacy of US-Iranian Relations, 1834–1911." *Iranian Studies* 44, no. 5 (2011): 607–25.

Katouzian, Homa. *The Political Economy of Modern Iran: Despotism and Pseudo-Modernism, 1926–1979*. New York: New York University Press, 1981.

Keddie, Nikki, and Rudi Matthee, eds. *Iran and the Surrounding World: Interactions in Culture and Cultural Politics*. Seattle: University of Washington Press, 2002.

Kramer, Paul. "Power and Connection: Imperial Histories of the United States in the World." *American Historical Review* 116, no. 5 (2011): 1348–91.

Maghbouleh, Neda. *The Limits of Whiteness: Iranian Americans and the Everyday Politics of Race*. Stanford, CA: Stanford University Press, 2018.

Matin-Asgari, Afshin. *Iranian Student Opposition to the Shah*. Costa Mesa, CA: Mazda, 2002.

McDaniel, Robert A. *The Shuster Mission and the Persian Constitutional Revolution*. Minneapolis, MN: Bibliotheca Islamica, 1974.

Menashri, David. *Education and the Making of Modern Iran*. Ithaca, NY: Cornell University Press, 1992.

Mobasher, Mohsen Mostafavi, ed. *The Iranian Diaspora: Challenges, Negotiations, and Transformations*. Austin: University of Texas Press, 2018.

Ninkovich, Frank, and Liping Bu, eds. *The Cultural Turn: Essays in the History of U.S. Foreign Relations*. Chicago, IL: Imprint, 2001.

Rosenberg, Emily S. *Financial Missionaries to the World: The Politics and Culture of Dollar Diplomacy, 1900–1930*. Durham, NC: Duke University Press, 2003.

Rostam-Kolayi, Jasamin. "The New Frontier Meets the White Revolution: The Peace Corps in Iran, 1962–76." *Iranian Studies* 51, no. 4 (2018): 587–612.

Schayegh, Cyrus. "Iran's Karaj Dam Affair: Emerging Mass Consumerism, the Politics of Promise, and the Cold War in the Third World." *Comparative Studies in Society and History* 54, no. 3 (2012): 612–43.

Schayegh, Cyrus, ed. *Globalizing the U.S. Presidency: Postcolonial Views of John F. Kennedy*. London: Bloomsbury, 2020.

Shannon, Kelly J. "Bernath Lecture: 'Approaching the Islamic World.'" *Diplomatic History* 44, no. 3 (2020): 387–408.

Shannon, Matthew K. *Losing Hearts and Mind: American-Iranian Relations and International Education during the Cold War*. Ithaca, NY: Cornell University Press, 2017.

Vejdani, Farzin. "The Iranians of AUB and Middle Class Formation in the Early Twentieth-Century Middle East." *British Journal of Middle Eastern Studies* 43, no. 4 (2016): 486–506.

Wang, Chih-ming. *Transpacific Articulations: Student Migration and the Remaking of Asian America*. Honolulu: University of Hawaii Press, 2013.

Yeselson, Abraham. *United States-Persian Diplomatic Relations, 1883–1921*. New Brunswick, NJ: Rutgers University Press, 1956.

Zeiler, Thomas. "The Diplomatic History Bandwagon: A State of the Field." *Journal of American History* 95, no. 4 (2009): 1053–73.

Zirinsky, Michael. "A Panacea for the Ills of the Country: American Presbyterian Education in Inter-War Iran." *Iranian Studies* 26, nos. 1–2 (1993): 119–37.

Zirinsky, Michael. "Render Therefore unto Caesar the Things Which Are Caesar's: American Presbyterian Educators and Reza Shah." *Iranian Studies* 26, nos. 3–4 (1993): 337–56.

Contributors

Camron Michael Amin is Professor of History at the University of Michigan-Dearborn. He is the author of *The Making of the Modern Iranian Woman: Gender, State Policy, and Popular Culture, 1865–1946* (2002) and coeditor (with Benjamin Fortna and Elizabeth Frierson) of *The Modern Middle East: A Sourcebook for History* (2007). Amin is the principal investigator for the Michigan Iranian-American Oral History Project and a former president of the Association of Iranian Studies.

Gregory Brew is a Kissinger Visiting Scholar at the Jackson Institute for Global Affairs at Yale University. In 2020 he served as Deputy Managing Editor at *Texas National Security Review* and from 2018 to 2020 was a Postdoctoral Fellow at the Center for Presidential History at Southern Methodist University. He has published articles in journals such as *International History Review, Iranian Studies,* and *Mediterranean Quarterly*. His forthcoming book is *Petroleum and Progress: Oil, Development, and the American Encounter with Iran, 1941–1965*.

Richard Garlitz is Associate Professor of History at the University of Tennessee at Martin. He is the author of *A Mission for Development: Utah Universities and the Point Four Program in Iran* (2018), and coeditor (with Lisa Jarvinen) of *Teaching America to the World and the World to America: Education and Foreign Relations since 1870* (2012).

John Ghazvinian is Executive Director of the Middle East Center at the University of Pennsylvania. He is the author of *America and Iran: A History, 1720 to the Present* (2021) and *Untapped: The Scramble for Africa's Oil* (2007). He coedited (with Arthur Mitchell Fraas) *American and Muslim Worlds before 1900* (2020) and has written in such publications as *Newsweek, The Nation,* and the *Sunday Times*.

Firoozeh Kashani-Sabet is Walter H. Annenberg Professor of History at the University of Pennsylvania. She is the author of *Conceiving Citizens: Women and the Politics of Motherhood in Iran* (2011) and *Frontier Fictions: Shaping the Iranian Nation, 1804–1946* (1999). Kashani-Sabet directed the Middle East Center at the University of Pennsylvania from 2006 to 2019 and was a fellow at the Institute for Advance Study's School of Social Science at Princeton in 2015–16. She is also the author of the novel *Martyrdom Street* (2010) and many articles and book chapters.

Kyle Olson is a postdoctoral fellow at Koç University's Research Center for Anatolian Civilizations (ANAMED), where he researches the connection between survey archaeology, dam-led regional development, and the history of Cold War geopolitics in Iran and Turkey. He has a Ph.D. from the Department of Anthropology at the

University of Pennsylvania where he was a member of the Penn Museum's Louis J. Kolb Society of Fellows. His dissertation is "Models of Trade and Polity Formation in Bronze Age Northeastern Iran, CA. 3200-1600 BCE." He is a translator and author of articles on Greater Iran who has participated in archaeological expeditions to Wisconsin, Illinois, Ohio, Hungary, Oman, Turkmenistan, and Azerbaijan.

Jasamin Rostam-Kolayi is Professor of History and Department Chair at California State University Fullerton. She is director of an oral history project on Peace Corps Iran and has interviewed many former volunteers. Her articles are published in *Iranian Studies, Journal of Middle East Women's Studies*, and *Middle East Critique*, and book chapters in *The Making of Modern Iran: State and Society under Riza Shah, Iran and the Surrounding World: Interactions in Culture and Cultural Politics*, and *The Routledge Handbook of the Global Sixties*.

Cyrus Schayegh is Professor of International History at the Graduate Institute of Geneva. He is the author of *The Middle East and the Making of the Modern World* (2017) and *Who Is Knowledgeable Is Strong: Science, Class, and the Formation of Modern Iranian Society, 1900–1950* (2009). He edited *Globalizing the U.S. Presidency: Postcolonial Views of John F. Kennedy* (2020) and coedited (with Andrew Arsan) *The Routledge Handbook of the History of the Middle East Mandates* (2015) and (with Liat Kozma and Avner Wishnitzer) *A Global Middle East: Mobility, Materiality and Culture in the Modern Age, 1880–1940* (2014).

Kelly J. Shannon is Associate Professor of History, the Chastain-Johnston Middle Eastern Studies Distinguished Professor in Peace Studies, and the Executive Director of the Peace, Justice, and Human Rights (PJHR) Initiative at Florida Atlantic University. She is the author of *U.S. Foreign Policy and Muslim Women's Human Rights* (2018) and of several book chapters and journal articles on US relations with the Islamic world and women's human rights. Dr. Shannon is also the winner of the Society for Historians of American Foreign Relations (SHAFR) 2019 Stuart L. Bernath Lecture Prize. She has written op-eds in venues such as *the Washington Post* and the *Berkley Forum* at Georgetown University, and she has given interviews for NPR and other media outlets. Dr. Shannon is currently writing a book on US-Iran relations from 1905 to 1953.

Matthew K. Shannon is Associate Professor of History at Emory & Henry College. He is the author of *Losing Hearts and Minds: American-Iranian Relations and International Education during the Cold War* (2017) and coeditor (with Mark Finney) of *9/11 and the Academy: Responses in the Liberal Arts and the 21st Century World* (2019). He has published articles in such journals as *Iranian Studies* and *Diplomatic History*, and his next book is titled *Mission Manifest*. It examines the Presbyterian missionaries within the context of the larger American-Iranian mission during the mid-twentieth century, and the book is forthcoming with Cornell University Press as part of the United States in the World series.

Ida Yalzadeh is Global American Studies Postdoctoral Fellow at Harvard University's Charles Warren Center for Studies in American History. Her book project is *Solidarities and Solitude: Tracing the Racial Boundaries of the Iranian Diaspora*. Prior to Harvard, she received her PhD in American Studies from Brown University in 2020 and, in 2020–1, was a Visiting Assistant Professor in the Asian American Studies Program at Northwestern University.

Index

Abadan 100, 105
ʿĀdel, Parviz 168, 173–4, 176
aggregated program quantity (APQ)
    system 102–3
AGIP-Mineria 106
agricultural projects 133–9, 146
  advancement in techniques 135
  emphasis on practical applications of
    knowledge 141–2
  extension service programs 136–7
  irrigation and mechanization
    engineering 137–8
  methods of demonstration 136–7
  operators and mechanics 137
  smaller horticultural equipment 138
  teaching Iranian extension agents 136
Ahmad, Jalal Al-e 151, 186
aid programs 11–12, 14, 102, 132, 140,
    146–7, *see also* agricultural projects;
    Institute (later College) of Business
    and Public Administration; Karaj
    Agricultural College; Teacher
    Training College
  acceptance of financial support and
    avoidance of American academic
    influence 143–4, 146, 147, 218
  and scientific progress 132–3
  US Agency for International
    Development (USAID) 154, 210
ʿAin al-Molk 80
Ajam 94
Alāʾ, Hossein 63
Alam, Asadollah 109–10
Alborz College of Tehran 10, 113–14, 121
Alborz Foundation 11, 115–20, 130
  cultural programming 117–18
  moved to property across from
    University of Tehran 118
  promotion of American culture 117
  student center 119–20
Alfonso, Juan Pablo Pérez 108
ʿAli-Akbar, Morteẓā 167
ʿAlikhāni, ʿAli-Naqi 103

ʿAli-Qoli Khān 21–2, 24, 28, 29, 44
  and Breed 21–2
  as Iran's *chargé d'affaires* 22
  and Sarkis Baba 30–1
  self-appointment as *chargé* 27
  and Topakian, conflict between 31
Alizadeh, Hasan 191–2, 193, 210–11
Alvandi, Roham 2
American Friends of the Middle East
    (AFME) 13, 14, 184, 189, 210
American Orientalism 7
American Peace Corps (*Sepāh-e Solh-e
    Āmrikā*), *see* Peace Corps
Amin, Mohammad 189–91, 193
Amin, Parvin 122
Amini, Ali 101, 105, 108
Amuzegar, Jahangir 139
Anderson, Bruce 137–8
Anglo-American diplomacy 73, 80–1
Anglo-Iranian Agreement
    (1919) 55, 78, 86
Anglo-Iranian Oil Company (AIOC; later
    British Petroleum) 9, 60, 90, 97, 99,
    101, 109, 212, 215
  concession 63
  growth and interference in Iranian
    politics 97
  nationalization of 98
Anglo-Persian Oil Company
    (APOC) 78, 79, 88
Anglo-Russian Convention (1907) 42
    n.30, 47, 75
Anglo-Turkish Agreement (1913) 74
Ansari, Ali 2
Ansari, Shapoor 192–4, 205
anti-imperialism 7, 41, 42, 50, 54, 177,
    179, 180, 217
anti-Orientalism 50, 54
Antiquities Law of 1930 8, 57–8, 61–4
  Article 11 (permits) 64–6
  Article 14 (*partage*) 66, 67–9
  oil and mineral exploration 71
anti-racism 217

antitrust legislation 99, 101, 210
anti-war movements 169, 178, 182
Arab/Arab world 73–4, 78, 82
    and Ajam 94
    dominance 90–2
    expansion of 77
    nationalism 73–4, 89, 90–1, 92
    and Persian Gulf 9, 81–2, 86
Arabian-American Oil Company (ARAMCO) 88, 103
Arabization 75, 77
Arab League 73, 89
Arab-Persian misunderstanding 92
Arab Student Association 179
Arasteh, Reza 147
archaeology/archaeological diplomacy 8, 57–8, 69–70, 210
    1962 law 72
    French monopoly, end of 59–60
    Iranian archaeology periodization 58
    permission and authorization 64–6, 69–70
    US archaeologists 71–2, 210
Armaghān Institute 116, 119–20
Armenians 26, 209
    merchants 211–12
    notables, as consuls 18
    settlement in Chicago 7
Aryanness 169, 170
Asian/Americans 182
Asian student organizations 179
Association for Iranian Studies 1
Assyrians 25, 215
    notables, as consuls 18
    passports renewal, for avoiding drafting into the US military 28, 30
    settlement in Chicago 7, 26, 28
automotive integration 8
Ayman, Iraj 145
Āzādegān, Akhtār 126

Baba, Sarkis 25–6, 28, 29
    and ʿAli-Qoli Khān 30–1
    and Mehdi Khān Qarāgozlu 30–1
Bagdasarian, Mihran 26
Bahāʾism 6, 18, 21–2, 28, 30, 44
Bahrain 74, 75, 80, 81, 91–2, 93
    America's oil interests in 87
    foreign prostitutes in 85–6, 94
    Iranians returning from 83
    nationality and immovable property law, 1937 82
    Persians in 82–6
    prohibition of Persian beggars in 85, 92, 94
    sovereignty disputes 81, 83
Bahraini, Haji Hamid Bin Haji Abud 85
Bahrainis and Iranians, cultural ties between 83
Bahrain Petroleum Company (BAPCO) 87, 93
Baladiyah of Manama 85
Ballard, J. Clark 142
Baskerville, Howard 36, 44, 70
Basrah 74, 76, 77, 79–80
Beatty, Gregory Alan 174
Belgrave, Charles 84–5
Bell, Gertrude 80
Benjamin, Samuel 211
Bennett, Henry 134
Berlin Crisis 108
Bill, James 70
Black Student Union 179, 180
Boyce, Annie 116
Boyce, Arthur 116
Breasted, James 66, 69
Breed, Florence 22
Bridgeman, Maurice 110
Brigham Young University (BYU) 11, 132, 133, 142–3, 146
Briskin, Dennis 157
Britain 206, 210
    and Arab complaints against Iran 84–5
    and Arabistan 77
    attention toward Arabian communities 93
    concessions 60
    control over Iran's oil production 78
    Great Game 3, 17, 34
    investment in Iraq 79
    and Iran's move to nationalize the oil industry 90
    and League of Nations maintenance 79
    master nationality rule 83
    Middle East dominance strategies of 78
    Persian Gulf policies of 74–5, 77, 89, 91
    and rights of Persian residents outside of Iran 82

supremacy in Iraq 78–9
underreporting of Iranian
  grievances 84–5
British Petroleum, *see* Anglo-Iranian Oil
  Company (AIOC; later British
  Petroleum)
Bunnell, Roy 135
bureaucratic inefficiency, of Iran 144
Bureau of American Affairs 6–7, 20
Burlington House exhibition 62
Busse, Barbara 118
Busse, Durwood 118
Byroade, Henry F. 99
BYU, *see* Brigham Young
  University (BYU)

Cairns, Frank S. 36
Carroll, William 142
Carter, Jimmy 151, 213
CENTO partners 207
Chicago
  Armenians in 7
  Assyrian Christians in 25
  Assyrian community in 28
  passport dispute 29
  World's Fair of 1893 6, 20, 23
Chicago, University of 68–9, 70
Chisholm, Archibald 92
CIA, and coup of 1953 against
  Mosaddeq 1, 10, 90, 98, 101, 132,
  151, 207, 210
citizenship and nationality law of 1925
  (Iran) 76
civilizing mission 40, 41
civil war (1900s) 24, 27
Clapp, Gordon 213
Cleveland, William 75
Clinton, Jerome 164
Cold War 1, 3, 4, 10, 77–8, 86,
  89–91, 93, 108, 115, 130–1, 183,
  212–13, 216–18
Collier, David 132
Commission on Ecumenical Mission and
  Relations (COEMAR) 119
Committee of Correspondence 127–8
communism 98, 144, 151–2
Community School 11, 115, 120–5,
  130, 210
  American population at 123

campus on American Mission Hospital
  site 123
educational nationalization,
  avoidance of 121
enrollments and popularity 122–3
at Iran Mission's Central
  Compound 121
and nationalism 122
Presbyterian guidance, under 124
response to educational demands 124
as school for English-speaking
  students 122
self-perception 124–5
Compagnie Française des Pétroles
  (CFP) 101, 103, 215
Confederation of Iranian Students
  National Union (CISNU) 168, 169,
  180, 182
Consortium Agreement (1954) 10, 97,
  99–100, 101–2, 111, 213
  aggregated program quantity (APQ)
    system 102–3
  and bidding 102–3
  and Iran's nationalization effort 103
  and NIOC 103–5
  popularity in Iran 105–6
  revenues 102
  and Ruhāni, negotiations 109
  shah's acceptance of 101
  Western companies' command of Iran's
    production 103
Constitutional Revolution 3–4, 7, 8,
  18, 24, 27, 33, 34–7, 54,
  55, 211
  Iranian women's contributions to 46
  and Progressivism 40, 45, 49
  and protests during 1905–6 34
  Russia's involvement in 39
  US noninvolvement in 35–6
  and US print media 43–6
Cossack Brigade 34, 35
Council of Ministers 60–1, 62, 63, 65
COVID-19 pandemic 149–50
Crane, Richard 25
Cravath, Paul Drennan 79–80
cultural diplomacy 71, 203
culture wars 77, 81, 93
Curtis, Jeffrey 156, 161
Curzon, Lord 76

Dabashi, Hamid 43
Daftari, Vidā 141
Damavand College, *see* Iran Bethel (later Damavand College)
D'Arcy, William Knox 97
D'Arcy concession 34, 63, 88, 97
Dawson, Thomas 157–8
Délégation scientifique en Perse 59
Detroit Free Press 186
Development and Resources (D&R) 213, 214
Devine, David 160
Dickey, Bruce G. 36
diplomatic histories 17–18
disciplinary powers, of the US 171–7
dollar diplomacy 47–8
Doolittle, Jane 115, 125–6, 128
Downey, Susan 163
Dreyfus, Grace 70
Dreyfus, Louis 70
Dubai 76, 80, 84
Dulles, John Foster 99

Eastern and General Syndicate, Limited 87
"East Is Red" (film) 179
Ebtehāj, Abol-Hassan 213
Ebtehāj-Samii, Nayereh 122, 128
education, in Iran, *see also* aid programs; Alborz Foundation; Community School; higher education
　acceptance of financial support and avoidance of American academic influence 143–4, 146, 147, 218
　female education 141, 143 (*see also* Iran Bethel School (later Damavand College))
　nationalization of 10, 125–6, 129
　networks 13
Educational Commission for Foreign Medical Graduates 184, 210
Edwards, Brian 6
Edwards, E. J. 48–9
Egypt 90, 207
Eisenhower, Dwight 90, 140
ʿElm, Mostafā 145
Embry, Bertis L. 137, 139
energy crisis (1960s) 110
energy markets 9–10, *see also* oil industries
Ente Nazionale Idrocarburi (ENI) 106
Entezām, Abdollah 101, 105, 106, 109
Ephraim Khān 53
Erikson, Bob 160
Exxon 95, 98, 99, 100, 101, 103, 109

Fallah, Reza 103, 110
Farāmarzi, Ahmad 83–4
Farkhān, Hushang 107
Farmanfarmaian, ʿAli-Naqi 145
Farzād, Nāhid 141
Fatemi, Ali 173 n.24
Faysal (King of Iraq) 80, 94
Ferrin, Augustin 81
Fifth Avenue art gallery 20
Fisher, Commodore B. 120, 121
Fisher, Franke Sheddan 120, 121–2
Fleming, Quentin 155
Ford Foundation 14
Foroughi, Mohammad Ali 63, 69
France 206
　archaeological monopoly, breaking of 59–60
　and Germany 205
Fraser, William J. 99, 100
Fuccaro, Nelida 94 n.110
Fung, Sherman 118

Gable, Richard 146
Garakani, Fakhri 214
Gass, Neville 100–1
Gay, Elizabeth 157
Geddes, David 143
Germany 89, 207
　and France 205
Gharb-zadegi (Westoxication) 5, 151
Ghazvinian, John 7, 215
Godard, André 60, 62, 63, 65, 67–8
Goode, James 69
Gottleib, Jeanette 157
Gray, Frances Mecca 128–9
Great Game 3, 17, 34
Gulf Oil 103

Habl al-Matin 74
Hajj Mirzā Mohammad-Ali Moʿin al-Saltaneh 205
Hamadan 120–1
Harden, Orville 99, 100
Hardy, Arthur 26

Harris, Franklin 133, 135
Hart, Charles C. 58, 68, 87
Hassani, Sarah 200–1, 202
Hearst, Phoebe 22
Hedayat, Mehdi Qoli 64, 65, 66
Hedayat, Sadeq 186
Hegland, Mary 159, 161
Hekmati, Amir Mirzā 201
Henderson, Loy 99
heritage diplomacy, *see* archaeology/
    archaeological diplomacy
Herzfeld, Ernst Emil 59, 60, 62, 66,
    67, 68, 69
  bill authored by 61, 63
  monuments register 60
High Council of Women's
    Organizations 127
higher education 140, *see also* education,
    in Iran
  American institutions of 14
  modernization and expansion of 140–4
  and nation's material prosperity 141
Hijaz 80
Hillman, Michael 151
Hills, Ralph W. 36 n.11
Hodgson, M. G. S. 187
Hollingsworth, Stanley 118–19
Holmes, Frank 87
Hornibrook, William 58
Hosseini, Farideh Freedom 200
Hostage Crisis of 1979–81 151, 164,
    172, 182
Hulac, Charles 116–17, 118, 130, 210, 213
human rights 5, 12
al-Husri, Sati 75

identity politics 9, 79, 84, 92
Immigration and Naturalization Service
    (INS) 171–2
imperialism 206, *see also* Pahlavi Iran;
    Qajar state
  European imperialism 206, 216
  and missionaries 4
  US imperial power 215–19
inequality 214, 215, 216–17
Institute (later College) of Business
    and Public Administration 11,
    132, 144–6
International Baccalaureate program 130

international students, and disciplinary
    powers of the US 13, 171–7
Iran-America Society *(Anjoman-e
    Irān-Āmrikā)* 117
Iran Bethel Alumnae Association 127, 128
Iran Bethel School (later Damavand
    College) 11, 115, 125–9, 129–
    30, 130
  curriculum and extracurriculum
    of 127, 129
  graduates from 127, 128–9
  and shah's White Revolution 127
  staff of 126
  students of 126–7
Iranian-American Christians 27
Iranian consulate (California), occupation
    by forty-one students 167–8, 181–2
  aftermath of 177–81
  as communist threats 173–4
  course of action by the US 171–7
  deportation threats to students 171–
    2, 175
  Iranian government and ʿĀdel's charges
    against students 176
  as a local issue 175
  model minorities, students as 169–70
  passports and student visas, issues of
    students 175, 181
  racial scripts 172
  reduced sentences for students 176
  support for students 177–81, 182 (*see
    also* Iranian Student Association in
    the United States (ISA))
  trial's transcript 174
  US media coverage of 172–3
Iranian consulates/diplomats 6, 17–25
  and citizenship 25–31
  establishment in Chicago 25
  honorary consul conferment of wealthy
    émigrés 32
  professionalization of 8
  staffing of 18, 19–20
Iranian diaspora 177–8, 185, 188, 197, 202
Iranian immigrants/migrants
  coming through Michigan for
    educational purposes 188
  increase in 215
  medical professionals 192–3
  permanent resident status 187

students 5, 12, 13, 187
  temporary visitors 187–8
Iranianness 4, 27
Iranian Revolution/Islamic Revolution of 1979 1, 3, 6, 150, 153, 164, 168
Iranian Student Association in the United States (ISA) 12, 168, 171–2
  cross-coalitional solidarity 177–81, 182
  demonstrations in support of the forty-one 180–1
  events to bring organizations together 179
  geographical branches, cohesion between 181
  non-Iranian support 179–80
  Northern California chapter 177, 179, 180, 181
  Southern California chapter 178
  ties with Leftist organizations 178–9
  US legal and media bias on 182
Iranian students, abroad
  and disciplinary powers of the US 13, 171–7
  privileges of 175–7
  socioeconomic factor for 195
Iranian Studies 113
Iran-Iraq War 153, 164, 191, 198
Iranzamin (a.k.a Tehran International School) 124, 130
Iraq 74, 75, 76, 77, 78–82, 86, 92, 94, 99, 103, 108, 123, 188
Iraq Petroleum Company (IPC) 87, 88
Iricon 103
Iriye, Akira 14
Irvine, J. Richard 120, 122–4
Irvine, Mary Ann 122
Ishāq Khān Mofakhkham al-Dowleh 19, 27 n.46, 209
  Iran's diplomatic corps under 19–20
  and Morteza Khān 20–1, 25
  professionalism and character of 21
Italy 206

Jablonski, Wanda 108
Jalāl, Ghaffār Khān 85
Jalāl incident 71
Jayne, Horace 8, 58, 60, 61, 62, 64
Jenkins-Madina, Marilyn 20 n.9
Johnson, Lyndon 111

Joint Comprehensive Plan of Action of 2015 201
Jordan, Samuel Martin 1, 4, 6, 10, 70, 116, 129

Kafoury, Stephen 163
Karaj Agricultural College 11, 132, 140–1, 146
  home economics and home extension programs at 137, 141
  research and demonstration farm 141–2
Karim, Persis 185
Kashani, Ayatollah Abol-Qasem 139
Kashani-Sabet, Firoozeh 37
Kelekian, Dikran 19–20, 23–4, 209–10
Kendall, Keith 162
Kennedy, John F. 11–12, 131 n.1, 150
Kennedy administration 156, 218
al-Khalifah family 81, 85
Khāneh-ye Irān-e Mishigān, see Persia House of Michigan
Khaz'al, Shaykh 77, 85
Khomeini, Ayatollah 3
Khuzestan 77, 78, 82, 97
Kirk, Odeal 138, 142
Klobe, Tom 149, 150, 160
Korean War 212
Krefter, Friedrich 68
Kuwait 74–5, 76, 80, 81, 82, 84, 87, 92, 99, 103, 108

Law for the Protection of National Vestiges, *see* Antiquities Law of 1930
Lawrence, Thomas Edward 80
League of Nations 78, 88
Leffler, Melvin 92 n.104
Lilienthal, David 213
Lorestān Bronzes 57
Lorimer, David Lockhart Robertson 77 n.23
Los Angeles 177–8, 178 n.44

Madsen, Louis 135
Maghbouleh, Neda 185, 186
Mahdavi, Mohammad Hassan 142
Majd, Mohammad Qoli 58
Majles 3, 34–5, 47, 53, 62, 63, 88–9, 134–5, 217
  dissolution of 39, 42, 48

royal interference 35, 45
support to Russia 39, 42, 49–50
Maktum, Shaykh Sa'id Bin 84
Martin, Vanessa 34
Mattei, Enrico 106
McCaskey, Charles I. 36
McGhee, George 156
McLeod, Kathleen 160
McNair, Thomas 117–18
Mehdi, Mirzā 84
"Met-Line" 106
Meyer, Armin 218
Michigan 185, 204–5
Michigan, Iranian-Americans in
  differences within 187
  documentation and institutionalization of their presence 186–7
  MIAOHP (see Michigan Iranian-American Oral History Project (MIAOHP))
  as micro-minority 185
  source of cultural and social history for 187
Michigan-Ann Arbor, University of 13, 188
Michigan Iranian-American Oral History Project (MIAOHP) 13, 184, 202
  characteristics and features of 185
  compared with Harvard Iranian Oral History Project 184
  focus on Iranian Diaspora experience 185
  political discussion aversion among interviewees 188
Michigan State University (MSU) 13, 188
middle-class Progressives 45
Millard, Hugh 58, 70, 210
Milligan, Cleve 137
Millspaugh, Arthur Chester 55, 212
Minā, Parviz 103, 107
minority groups
  disciplinary powers of US with regard to 13, 171–7
  ethno-religious minorities in Iran 32
  religious minorities, rights of 27
Mirzāyāntz, J. B. 62, 65
missionaries 206, 210, 211, 212, 216
  absence in US-Iran relations histories 114

activity in the postwar world 115
American missionary institutions 10–11
as carriers of US cultural influence 115
and imperial networks 4
Presbyterian missionaries 113, 115, 119
scholarship on 37–8
support for Constitutional Revolution 36, 44
Moallemian, Mahmoud Mark 194–6
model minorities 169 n.11, 175, 177, 182
modernization of Iran 131
  higher education 140–4
  impact of Western science on 132
  politics of material promise 132, 139, 146
  United States' portrayal of its efforts to 174
Molina, Natalia 172
Monroe Doctrine 43
Moore, Barkley 160
Mortezā Khān 20–1, 25, 27
  and Ishāq Khān 20–1, 25
  professionalism and character of 21
Mosaddeq, Mohammad 1, 9–10
  battle for economic independence and oil nationalization 77–8, 89
  coup of 1953 against 1, 10, 90, 95, 98, 132, 151, 157, 207, 210
  on US aid programs 139
Moshir al-Dowleh 19
Murko, John 176
Murray, Wallace 58, 69, 70–1
Museum of Archaeology, University of Pennsylvania 58, 65, 67, 210
Muslim Moro population, of Philippines 50–1

Nafisi, Fathallah 101
Nasr, Valiollah Khān 65
Nasser, Gamal Abdel 90, 207
National Iranian Oil Company (NIOC) 89, 98, 100, 103
  and Consortium 103–5
  explorations of non-Consortium areas 106
national security 30, 99, 101, 210, 213, 218
nation-states 2, 9, 35, 53, 182, 215, 217–18
Navāb, Hossein-Qoli Khān 53
New Deal 214

Newey, Paul 29
New York Times 43, 44, 45, 46, 49–50, 54
New York Times Sunday magazine 45, 48
Nivdun Khān 21, 46
Nixon, Richard 158
nongovernmental organizations (NGOs) 14
Northern California Iranians 180
Nurbakhsh School 125
Nuri, Hossein-Qoli Khān 6, 19, 20 n.9, 205

Occidentalism 186
oil
 discovery of 86–8
 global economy 99, 110
 government-sponsored price increases, protest against 149
oil industries 5, 9, 55, 78
 consortium (*see* Consortium Agreement (1954))
 dependence on revenue from 95–6, 99, 102, 106, 111
 discovery of oil 80, 92
 Iranian competence to manage 100
 local integration 96
 nationalization in Iran 9–10, 90, 97–8
 price and production, control of 96
Olson, Farrell 134, 138
Olson, Kyle 8
Ord, John 143
Organization of Arab Students 180
Organization of Petroleum Exporting Countries (OPEC) 95
 challenge (1960-4) 107–10
 divisions 108, 110
 oil price increase and profits sharing strategy 109
 shah's influence over policy within 108
Oriental Institute, University of Chicago 68–9, 70
Orientalism 52
Ottoman Empire 74, 206
Oveis, Mahin Shad 199–200

Page, Howard 101, 106–7, 109, 111
Pahlavi, Ashraf 127, 168, 174
Pahlavi, Farah 124, 129
Pahlavi, Mohammad Reza Shah 1–4, 78, 94, 95–6, 98, 115, 121, 125, 132, 151, 168, 175–6, 184, 204
 and arms purchases 218–19
 and Consortium 110, 111
 "Great Civilization" of 5–6
 income sources outside of Consortium control 106–7
 and Iranian Revolution of 1979 1
 and Jimmy Carter 151
 and Kermit Roosevelt 95
 Pan American agreement 106
 pressure on oil companies 97, 108
 prioritization of revenues increments from oil production 10
 revenue generating strategy of 111
 Soviet arms purchase 219
 Washington encouragement to sign contracts with Italian and Japanese oil companies 215
 and White Revolution 3, 5, 12, 110, 115, 127, 130, 157, 159, 168 n.7, 168–9, 218
Pahlavi Iran 1, 2, 4, 109, 111
 "alternative materialist vision" of 132
 focus on disruptive episodes 96
 Persian anti-Arab sentiment during 75
 and world order 77
Pahlavi, Reza Shah 4, 8, 10, 11, 58, 60, 70, 77, 88, 114, 121, 125, 126, 134, 140, 144
 military campaigns to unify Iran's provinces 77
 nationalization of foreign schools 114
 national program of authoritarian modernization 4
 prioritization of higher education 140
 reign of *see* Pahlavi Iran
Pahlavi University 144
Pakraduni, Haig Herant 20, 21, 24
Parkhurst, George 111
partage 66, 67–9
passports 28, 30
 Chicago passport dispute 28–9
 conflict related to passport stamps delivery 29–30
 and identities 76
 Iranian passports 18
 passport fees scandal 18, 28–9
 US passports 7, 26, 27
PATRIOT Act 172
Peace Corps 164–5, 192, 210, 213, 216

and CIA 158 n.33
as a Cold War program 151, 152, 155
cultural and language immersion during training 157
perspectives on 150–4
potential of 156
purpose, change in 155
Teaching English as a Foreign Language (TEFL) 159
and USAID 155
Peace Corps Agency 152
Peace Corps Iran Association (PCIA) 12, 153, 164
Peace Corps volunteers 5, 12, 113, 149
affinity toward Iranian language and culture 162–3
female volunteers 161
first contingent in Iran 154–5
individual narrator's emotions 162
in testimonies of positive interpretations 151
living conditions of 157
male volunteers 161–2
memories of 162–4
motivations to join 155–6
oral history narratives of 152–3
political consciousness development in Iran 157–8
reception of 158
social lives of 160–1
work in community development 159–60
Pejman, Firuz 172
Penn Museum *see* Museum of Archaeology, University of Pennsylvania
Pennsylvania, University of 58, 144, 210
Persepolis affair of 1934–5 68, 69, 70, 72
Persia House of Michigan *(Khāneh-ye Irān-e Mishigān)* 186–7, 188, 194, 195–6, 197, 198, 199, *see also* Michigan, Iranian-Americans in
Persian Antiquities Service 60
Persian Gulf 73
Anglo-American competition 75, 86, 92, 93–4
change of landscape 87–8
crude oil price cut 107–8
ethnic map of 80

identity politics 9
nationality issues 82–3
and territorial counterclaims 81–6
transformation, impact on urban and communal life 92–3
"Persian Palace" 6, 23
Persian rug/carpets trade 19–20, 23, 24, 211
Peterson, Melvin 136
Phillips, Sir Percival 79
PHoM Newsletter (Faslnāmeh) 187
Pittman, Don 133
Point Four Program 11, 113, 131, 131 n.1, 140, 154, 189, 207, 210, *see also* aid programs
budget constraints of 137
and Iranian Ministry of Agriculture 138
Iranian officials' expectations from 139
livestock improvement project 136
methodology of 134
purpose of 134
rural improvement initiative (*see* agricultural projects)
shortcomings of 132
and USU agricultural advisers 133
Pope, Arthur Upham 8, 58, 59–60, 61, 70
Portelli, Alessandro 153
power imbalances 72
Pratt, Henry Ruthven 20 n.9
Presbyterian Church of the United States of America (PCUSA) 113
alteration of mission 114
Board of Foreign Missions 119
and Evangelical Church of Iran 119
Presbyterian institutions 129–30
Presbyterianism 10–11
profit-sharing principle 10, 68, 88–9, 95–6, 97, 102, 106–7, 119
Progressive Labor Party 179
Progressivism 40, 45, 55
Purnell, D. C. 136

Qajar, Mohammad Ali Shah 33, 35, 45, 46
Qajar, Mozaffar al-Din Shah 6, 17, 32, 34, 97
Qajar, Naser al-Din Shah 3, 18, 19, 22
Qajar state 1, 3, 7, 18–19, 30, 34, 212
bureaucratic professionalism 18
collapse of 8, 19

dysfunction of 31–2
economic concessions of 34
and Iranian progress 19
and pro-Arab imperial policies 77
Qarāgozlu, Mehdi Khān 27, 28, 29
  and ʿAli-Qoli Khān, conflict
    between 29–31
  and Sarkis Baba, conflict
    between 29, 30–1
Qarāgozlu, Mirzā Yahyā Khān 60–1
Qom 106, 107
Qotbzadeh, Sadeq 173 n.24

racialization 13, 177, 186
racial scripts 182
Raein, Zohreh (Rāʾin) 198–9
Rahim, Abdol 84
Rahmanifar, Taraneh 196–8
Randolph, John 78
Reglement d'Application 60, 63, 64,
  65, 66
Reichert, Malno 141, 143
religious pluralism, in Iran 187
resource nationalism 107, 108, 111
al-Rezā, Haji Abd 86
Ricks, Tom 159
Roosevelt, Kermit 95, 108–9
Roskelley, Richard Welling 141, 142
Rostam-Kolayi, Jasamin 37, 185
Rowlee, Maud 120
Royal Dutch/Shell 98, 101, 103, 215
royalty expensing 109–10, 111
Ruhāni, Fuʾād 101, 108, 109
Russia 204
  Anglo-Russian Convention (1907) 42
    n.30, 47, 75
  Great Game 3, 17, 34
  invasion of Iran in 1911 35, 42
  involvement in Constitutional
    Revolution 39
  and Shuster's ouster 50
Rutis, Alfonso 20, 24

Sadat, Anwar 94
Sage College 125–6
Samiian, Effat 128
Samnar, Farhād 168 n.6
San Francisco Chronicle 173
Satia, Priya 76

Saudi Arabia 73, 81, 87, 88, 89, 91–2,
  93, 103
Schayegh, Cyrus 5–6, 132
Schmidt, Erich F. 65, 66, 67–8, 71
Segel, Kerry 162
Seitz, John 146
Seropian, Milton 20, 24
Seto, Paul 119–20
Seven Sisters (oil companies) 96–9
Seyāreh, Robābeh 85
Shannon, Kelly 7
Shariati, Ali 151
Shirts, Morris 143
Shoʿāʿ al-Saltaneh 42
Shokat, Parviz 175, 176–7
Shuster, W. Morgan 33, 36–7, 38, 42,
  210, 214
  about Iranians, Muslims and Islam
    51–2, 53
  American public's reception of 50–4
  anti-imperialist stance of 41
  criticism of Iranians 52
  as customs collector 40–1
  departure to Tehran 42
  description of Muslim Moro population
    of the Philippines 50–1
  early career 39–40
  economic mission of (*see* Shuster
    Mission)
  on Iranian women's participation in the
    revolution 52
  opposition to Britain and
    Russia 42, 48, 52
  and Progressivism 41
  Strangling of Persia, The (memoir) 38,
    50, 51–2, 54
  support to constitutionalists and
    nationalists 39, 42, 50, 51, 54–5
  and Taft 41, 41 n.29
  as treasurer-general 47–8
Shuster Mission 7, 8, 38, 39–42, 54, 55, 211
  dollar diplomacy 47, 48
  perceptions of Iran before 43–7
  perceptions of Iran during 47–50
  and Progressivism 40, 49
  public opinion on 54, 55
  studies on 38
Sinclair Oil Corporation 55
Smith, Myron Bement 70

Socialist Revolutionary Party 180
Society for Historians of American Foreign Relations 1
Society for National Heritage (SNH) 59–60
Socony-Mobil 103
Southern California, University of (USC) 11, 132, 133, 144–5, 146, 218
  International Public Administration Center 145
  participant program, view on 145
  social science research center, creation of 146
sovereignty 17–18, 33–4, 212, 215, 217
Soviet Union 207, 212
Spurlock, Jackie 149, 150, 163
Standard Oil 55
Standard Oil of California (Socal) 87, 103
Standard Oil of Indiana 106
Status of Forces Agreement (SOFA) 156 n.27
Stewart, George 133–4
Storm, William 146
structural inequalities 216
student activism, *see* Iranian consulate (California), occupation by forty-one students; Iranian Student Association in the United States (ISA)
Students for a Democratic Society 179
Suez Canal, nationalization of 90
Sulayman, ʿAbdullah ibn 87
Sunni Arab 9, 80
Susa 59
Sweden 206
Swensrud, Sidney A. 100
Syracuse University 136

Tabriz 26
Taft, William Howard 7, 39–40, 210, 211
Taft administration 47–8, 54
Takht-e Jamshid 1934–5 67, 68–9
Tariki, Abdullah 108
Tasbihi, Mohammad Hossein 162
Tavakoli-Targhi, Mohammad 186
Taylor, Jerimiah 171
Teacher Training College 11, 140, 141, 142–3, 146
teaching profession, attitude toward 143

Tehran, University of 11, 131, 140, 146
  American academics' pedagogical reforms, attempts at 133
  Karaj Agricultural College 11, 132, 137, 140–2, 146
  Teacher Training College 11, 140, 141, 142–3, 146
Tehran American School 123
Tepe Hissar 1931–2 67–8
territorial contraction, Iran's objections to 75, 81
Texaco 103
Teymourtash, Abdolhossein 62
third locations 214–15
third parties 203–4 n.3, 204–9
Third World 12, 152, 169, 177, 217, 218
Thomas, Tim 159–60, 214
Tobacco Revolt 3
Topakian, Haigazoun Hohannes 22–3
  and ʿAli-Qoli Khān, conflict between 28 n.49
  belly dancer scandal 23, 24
  carpet gift to Taft 24
  and Kelekian, rivalry between 23–4
  Persian carpet gift to Roosevelt 24
Trans-Iranian Railway 8, 62, 212
Truman, Harry 11, 131 n.1
Truman administration 89, 217
Trump, Donald 201–2
Tureng Tepe 1931 67
Turkish Petroleum Company 86
Turner, Frederick Jackson 6
Twin Pillar policy 81, 91, 93
Tyler, John 27

United Nations 14, 215
United Presbyterian Church 119
United States Information Agency 71
Upton, Joseph 70
Urmia 26, 28
US Agency for International Development (USAID) 154, 210
USC, *see* Southern California, University of (USC)
US citizenship
  of Assyrian migrants 26
  dual citizenship 27
  as a flag of convenience 26
  and Iranian Christians 26

naturalization 25–7, 28, 171–2, 187
US-educated Iranians, and shah's White Revolution 127
US immigration law 217
US imperial power 215–19
US (print) media 48, 174
  attention to Iran's revolution 55
  and Constitutional Revolution 43–6
  framings of Persia in 186
US oil companies 97–8, 111, *See also* Exxon; Gulf; Socony-Mobil; Standard Oil of California (Socal); Texaco
US state/nonstate actors 14, 209–15, 216
Utah State University (USU) 11, 131–2, 135–6, 142, 146

Vahābzādeh, ʿAli Asghar 145
Vaziri, Farāmarz 172
Venezuela 98
Voice of America 71

Walker, Rudger 135, 138
Walther, Karine 51
Wang, Chih-ming 182
Wangsness, Genna 154 n.21
Warne, William 139

Wayne State University 13, 188
White Revolution 3, 5, 12, 110, 115, 127, 130, 157, 159, 168 n.7, 168–9, 218
Wilkinson, Charles K. 70
Williamson, David 58, 61, 70
Wilson, Arnold 81
Wilson administration 55
Winsor, Luther 133
Women's Organization of Iran 127
Woodward, Frank 118
Woolf, Golden 143
World War, First 7, 18, 28, 35
World War, Second 9, 10, 89
Wulsin, Frederick R. 8, 58, 61–7, 70, 72, 210
Wulsin, Susanne E. 67, 70
Wysham, William 121

Yalzadeh, Ida 217
Yank, Ronald 176
Young, T. Cuyler 214

Zahedi, Ardeshir 6, 136, 207
Zahedi, Fazlollah 98
Zahedi, Mostafā 135
Zirinsky, Michael 37

www.ingramcontent.com/pod-product-compliance
Lightning Source LLC
Chambersburg PA
CBHW062138300426
44115CB00012BA/1969